THIS GREAT BEAST: PROGRESS AND THE MODERN STATE

You must understand, therefore, that there are two ways of fighting: the first using laws, the second force. The first belongs to man, the second to beasts. But the first is often not enough, one must have recourse to the second. It is therefore necessary for a prince to know how to make good use of the man and the beast. This precept was taught to princes by the ancients under the cover of allegory. They wrote how Achilles and many more of those ancient princes were entrusted to Chiron the centaur for their upbringing, so that they could be looked after under his tutelage. Having a half-man, half-beast as a teacher simply means that a prince needs to know how to use both natures, for the one without the other does not last.

Niccolò Machiavelli, *The Prince,* Chapter Eighteen

What piece of work is a man! How noble in reason! how infinite in faculty! in form, in moving, how express and admirable! in action how like an angel! in apprehension how like a god! the beauty of the world! the paragon of the animals!

Hamlet, II, ii

This Great Beast: Progress and the Modern State

BOB CATLEY
WAYNE CRISTAUDO

LONDON AND NEW YORK

First published 1997 by Ashgate Publishing

Reissued 2018 by Routledge
2 Park Square, Milton Park, Abingdon, Oxon, OX14 4RN
52 Vanderbilt Avenue, New York, NY 10017

Routledge is an imprint of the Taylor & Francis Group, an informa business

Copyright © R. Catley and W. Cristaudo 1997

All rights reserved. No part of this book may be reprinted or reproduced or utilised in any form or by any electronic, mechanical, or other means, now known or hereafter invented, including photocopying and recording, or in any information storage or retrieval system, without permission in writing from the publishers.

Notice:
Product or corporate names may be trademarks or registered trademarks, and are used only for identification and explanation without intent to infringe.

Publisher's Note
The publisher has gone to great lengths to ensure the quality of this reprint but points out that some imperfections in the original copies may be apparent.

Disclaimer
The publisher has made every effort to trace copyright holders and welcomes correspondence from those they have been unable to contact.

A Library of Congress record exists under LC control number: 97074439

ISBN 13: 978-1-138-36515-5 (hbk)
ISBN 13: 978-1-138-36516-2 (pbk)
ISBN 13: 978-0-429-43089-3 (ebk)

Contents

Preface		*vi*
Acknowledgements		*vii*
Introduction		1
1	Characteristics and Typology of the Modern State	10
2	Social Evolution and the Modern State	59
3	The Purpose of the State	88
4	Philosophy Dreaming: Idealist Approaches to the State	120
5	**The Seizure of State Power: Realist and Idealist Approaches**	155
6	The Preservation of Order: Leviathan and Behemoth	186
7	The Legitimate Representation of Interests: The People	220
8	Separating Powers or Willing **Unity**?: Montesquieu vs. Rousseau and Paine	245
9	The Extension of Representation	260
10	The Development of Social Rights and Social Democracy	283
11	The Mature Civilised State	310
12	The Behaviour of States in the International Arena	341
13	Globalisation and the State	376
14	The Future of the State	395
Index		421

Preface

Catley and Cristaudo defend Western Civilisation against all comers: against the rest of the world, especially the Third World, and against its own internal irritants: 'the scribblings of the intelligentsia' by idealist philosophers, feminists, greens, post-moderns, multiculturalists, Orientalist, anti-nationalists, socialists and Keynesians.

In quieter passages they acknowledge that realistic moderates in all those movements have contributed to the civilising process - their serious theme, echoing Edward Hallet Carr's in *The Twenty Years Crisis*, is that progress comes from a complicated mixture of realism and good intent, self interest and mutual concern.

But those calm passages are rarely the memorable one. As in *Paradise Lost*, the devil gets all the best tunes. The identification of civilisation's enemies is wildly, sometimes hilariously, politically incorrect.

Readers may not all be persuaded that social democracy is dead and gone and a good thing too, or that it is *right* for politicians to be habitual liars, but even the most hostile will find it hard not to enjoy the violence, fun and audacity of the argument.

Hugh Stretton, leading social democratic theorist and author of *The Political Sciences; Capitalism, Socialism and the Environment;* and *Ideas for Australian Cities.*

Acknowledgements

This book was mostly written during the Australian winter of 1996 when Catley had a virus and was unusually grumpy even for him. His wife, Pat, as always tolerated his bad humour and deserves great credit. Cristaudo **thanks Grumpy for getting him focused again;** his wife Jae for providing a creative home; and John West and Robert Mastripolito, fellow members of the band Making Monday, for the energy. Thanks to Stephen Wood and Chris White for much of the editorial tidying up. Leslye O'Shaughnessy put much effort into cleaning up a text which had mostly been typed by the authors. Chris Hill did the final polish and index.

Bob Catley
Wayne Cristaudo
Adelaide, July 1997

Introduction

> What is rational is actual and what is actual is rational.
>
> To comprehend what is, this is the task of philosophy, because what is, is reason...If someone's theory really goes beyond the world as it is and builds an ideal one as it ought to be, that world exists indeed, but only in his opinions, an unsubstantiated element where anything you please may in fancy be built.
>
> G.W. F. Hegel, *Philosophy of Right*

The development of states and societies in which people are free from political repression, in which almost all adult nationals have the franchise, in which people are sufficiently prosperous and socially unified that they do not resort to civil war to achieve their ends, and in which the overwhelming majority are free from material want is a recent phenomenon. None of these mature civilised states existed prior to the late nineteenth century, although their origins go back to seventeenth century England and the conditions which make them possible gain momentum in the latter part of the eighteenth century with the American and French revolutions. They are also scarce. No more than fifteen percent of the world's population, and probably closer to twelve percent, live in such communities.

In the mature civilised state, brute political power is not absent - - it stands at the ready against enemies, whether those enemies be criminals or invaders. But the flow of power in a civilised state is extraordinarily complex. And over a long time, some sections of humanity have had the good fortune to discover that brute force is often not the most effective way in which people can become prosperous and fulfilled, that power is not a zero-sum game. The human spirit has flung itself in a multiplicity of social directions as peoples have co-operated, conquered, surrendered, built, destroyed, argued, compromised, dreamed, hoped, erred, and sometimes understood what they have been doing. Violence and force have been the constant companions of social life as groups have plundered, killed, co-opted, and coerced others to do their will. Violence is intrinsic to the history of the sexes, races, nations, empires and tribes. Political power is first experienced as something brutal and terrifying, as something in which a power far greater than any single person is unleashed. The earliest law codes available to us from Mesopotamia and Assyria belie the ferocious brutality which is marshalled against those who dare to transgress what the law lays down. Torture, amputation, burning, violent death are not at the margins of social and political organisation -- they are the primordial modes of social and political organisation. In short, political power is first experienced as something bestial.

It is miraculous that some societies and some states have found a way to generate prosperity, social and political stability, a greater variety of life choices than under any other existing social forms, and political institutions which are responsive to the complicated, sometime contradictory alternatives that emerge in a free society. However, amongst contemporary Western academics in the human sciences a large number have been able to fashion careers for themselves by claiming to speak for the supposed victims of civilisation -- women, blacks, gays, trees -- by depicting mature civilised states as fundamentally oppressive.

In the historical development of the civilised and liberal-democratic states the acceptance of the legitimacy of the representation of different interests, and then the expansion of the interest groups whose rights were accepted as being legitimate has been accompanied by political struggle and philosophical disputation. The claimant groups have then typically divided into a realist and idealist wing. The realist faction argues in the main that the mobilisation of the members of the new interest group into a political organisation with political power will force the civilising state to accede to its demands for representation if its power is sufficient. While there is no *a priori* reason why the interests which presently control the state should concede to the claim there is also no *a priori* reason why it should not. The outcome will be determined by the process of political conflict and philosophical debate itself.

The idealist wing, on the other hand, tends to the view that it is in the nature of the state that it cannot accede to their political claim for representation. The claims of militant feminism, queer theory, post-colonialism, Green movement and post-modernism are the idealist wings of new claimants to the right to representation in the state. These claims by their realist counterparts have been already met. But the contemporary idealist claimants continue the radical democratic aspirations which have no grounding other than abstract ideas. The historical culmination of idealist radical democracy was Stalinism. That contemporary radical democrats fail to understand how the grim reality of the Gulag could have originated in the seemingly well intentioned egalitarian aspirations of nineteenth century socialists is indicative of the unsoundness of their intellectual methods and practices. Whereas the socialists found capitalism to be the blight upon the species, contemporary radical democratic idealists generally continue to blame capitalism as well as other causes to explain the oppression they believe characterises contemporary liberal democratic societies: viz., men, Euro-centric consciousness, or modernity itself. In effect, radical idealists continue the communist project of blaming the ills of the world upon the social relations which to a large extent have created political peace, freedom, and prosperity.

It is of no small significance that the first great idealist state theorist, Plato, was also the founder of the Academy. And it is no exaggeration to say that in this century, the most barbarous idealist states have found extremely strong support among the intelligentsia. Indeed, it has been the intelligentsia which has paved the way for and then legitimated the idealist dictatorships of this century. This is as true for fascist Italy, Nazi Germany, and the panoply of Marxist-Leninist regimes, as it is for Iran -- all of which are products of the idealist mind. The contemporary academic idealist tends no longer to recognise the Platonic affinity, partly because of an idealist construction of 'the people' which Plato never espoused, and partly because of an anti-objectivism that finds its anti-Platonist expressions in the philosophies of Friedrich Nietzsche and Martin Heidegger. The post-modernist fusion in a thinker like Michel Foucault of a communist and (non-) materialist (Marx), an aristocrat and voluntarist (Nietzsche), and a Nazi anti-materialist and anti-voluntarist and thinker of Being (Heidegger), makes complete sense only if one bears in mind what they all most hated: civilised society and its institutions. What unites political idealists is a desperate desire to substitute an ideal schema about how society should work upon the institutions which have an organic connection with civil society.

Unlike the idealists we base our study on the basis of real achievements. The method we adopt for analysing progress and the modern state is largely comparativist. The mature civilised state is contrasted with the three other kinds of states which we find today -- primitive, idealist and developmental states.

In so far as we draw upon a comparative method we follow in the tracks partly set down by Aristotle, and in modern times by Montesquieu and Tocqueville. Further, in so far as we observe and reach conclusions on the basis of actual struggles for power, we are also providing what may be called a political realist study and defence of the mature civilised state. This tradition can be traced back to Thucydides and in modern times is usually associated with Niccolò Machiavelli and Thomas Hobbes.

But we are also aware that there are strong idealist dimensions to the modern mature state. The American founding fathers and authors of the *Federalist Papers* display on every page their appreciation of classical political philosophy and the ideals which underpin the constitution. Likewise, the modern liberal democratic society is unimaginable without the political idealist philosophical writings of Jean Jacques Rousseau, Immanuel Kant or John Stuart Mill, or the ideals of social rights which were entrenched by decades of social democracy. Throughout this work we will trace the interplay between idealist and realist forces in the shaping of modern civilisation. Although we attack the excesses of idealism, we also recognise the value and necessity of idealism in the civilising process.

Politics should not be created by the Academy; but the Academy does have an indispensable role in social reproduction. Hence we defend idealism to the extent that it is integrated with, and thus compromised by real social powers which will not disappear without a great and bloody fight.

Our study, then, incorporates a comparativist, a realist and an idealist dimension - because we can only evaluate something by seeing it in its relationship to other real possibilities, on the basis of the real conditions under which it emerges, and by reflecting upon the ideals to which we aspire as a species. It is both a description and an evaluation of the forms of the modern state which take its benchmark from the highest state form that has hitherto been achieved by the species, the democratic and civilised state.

In making this claim, we are also inevitably drawn into a defence of the idea of progress. In the eighteenth century the Enlightenment philosophers wanted progress more than anything. They had had enough of outmoded institutions and miserable living conditions for the majority of people and believed that the freedoms they desired and the flourishing of modern science could create a new age. No doubt the term Enlightenment was a political ploy used by a group to invalidate social forces and practices which they opposed. Also their excessive idealism did lead to the reign of terror. But in insisting that there was a need for progress they bequeathed an invaluable legacy to modernity. Some social practices such as slavery and the denial of the franchise to law abiding adults are comprehensible in light of a particular historical mode of social organisation, but the practices and the orders which sustain them debilitate the energies and defile the dignity of those enslaved or denied their rights. To this extent, it was not difficult for a thinker like John Stuart Mill to be an advocate of both liberty and progress, and to see that the defence of the one will entail belief in the other. Likewise, when women received the vote progress had been made.

Yet, no word is more disparaged by contemporary political idealists today than 'progress'. The reason for this is that the academic idealist of the late twentieth century is so at war with the idea of civilisation (not the reality - for he or she desires its benefits), that no concession to its unique achievements can be made. Today, it is *de rigueur* to defend or agonise over clitoridectomy in Africa while attacking the disparity between men and women in high powered careers; or to attack any vestiges of Euro-centrism while ignoring the racism of non-Europeans; to attack the strategic interventions of the United States, while remaining silent on the internecine conflicts in India, Africa, and between Arabs in the Middle East. The Iraq-Iran War which cost over one million deaths excited merely a speck of the anguish of the Gulf War that may have caused twenty thousand.

This work, on the contrary, argues that such criteria as standards of living, career opportunities, freedom from arbitrary arrest, a free press, the guarantee of due legal process, a diverse array of cultural possibilities to choose from, highly developed technologies, and a panoply of service industries are the measure of a society's progress. Ultimately progress is not an idea that needs to be defended; its fruits are the reality toward which the overwhelming majority of people aspire. In saying this, however, two qualifications are in order.

First, progress, like freedom itself, is not inevitable. It must be guarded with vigilance. Rome is always in danger of being set ablaze or reverting to tyranny. It is important that there are enough people who love liberty, who don't spend all their time fiddling, and that they pay attention to what endangers it.

Secondly, the political and economic trajectory of progress is not necessarily reproduced, and certainly not at the same time, in all spheres of existence. Even if one rejects Rousseau's idealisation of the noble savage and his disparagement of civilisation, he has a point in distinguishing moral progress from scientific progress. Progress in a society does not necessarily translate into the aesthetic, the religious or spiritual or moral realms. Shakespeare and Sophocles have not been outmoded by *Days of Our Lives*, nor Bach by the Doors. The spirit is not more succoured by Protestant evangelists than by a Medieval church service, and Bill Clinton is not a better politician than Abraham Lincoln or Pericles. There are a range of attributes of the species that cannot be adequately discussed in terms of an historical evolutionary model - although it is an open question whether they may not entail their own (non-historical) qualitative scale. But in a mature civilised state, more people do have the possibility to choose if they want to read Shakespeare or Sophocles or watch *Days of Our Lives*, more people have the option of hearing Bach, because technology as well as its availability has improved. We can meaningfully talk about progress in the underlying material and institutional arrangements of life.

Mature civilised states first developed in the West. That is an historical fact. For many Western academics that alone discredits the value of the mature civilised state. There are a number of reasons for this. But a large part of the reason is the cultural legacy that was generated by Christendom, which includes: the idea of a universal spiritual commonwealth, which would bring peace, created historically over time (the mission of the church); the separation of the spiritual and secular spheres of existence, so that the state could never own the whole person; the evolution of a plural system of laws (made possible by a fusion of Aristotelianism and Roman Law, and feudal conflicts); the creation of modern science, brought about largely in defiance of the church and the scholastic philosophers but, nevertheless, relying upon a fusion of empiricism and the systemic method of scholasticism and a common European scholarly and scientific language bequeathed by the Church; the idea of representation first developed in the Middle Ages within the Church; the reworking of the idea of natural law which is the antecedent of the modern constitutional state and human rights; and the idea of the equality of souls.

Within this book we elaborate on most of these points and address others. For the moment it suffices to add that while the mature civilised state is a Western achievement which owes a great deal to its fusion of Christian, classical Greek and Roman roots, the West was never just the geographic West. Indeed, much of the potency of Western civilisation lies in the fact that it absorbed Asiatic and even Egyptian/African influences and it was more open to outside influences than the great civilisations of Asia. Conversely much of the early modern stagnation of China and Japan is attributable to their isolationism.

Because the modern state had its cultural, social and political origins in the West, it should be no surprise that the problems that were thrown up throughout the process of its creation were first dealt with by Western political philosophers. Thus we make no apology for our use of canonical thinkers to throw light upon the trajectory of the modern state. Regardless of what one thinks of the benefits of the modern world, there is a *modern world* because of the dynamism of Western values, technology, institutions and ideas.

In defending the mature civilised state, we wish to point out, however, that we are not merely defending the liberal democratic components of mature civilised states. As we shall see, the liberal democratic component of the mature civilised state is only one of its characteristics. The mature state is a complex of forces with different historical origins and functions. Most theorists of the state tend to isolate one or a few of the state's purposes and processes and mistake those parts for the whole. Liberal democratic theorists, for example, tend to focus upon the constitutional and representative components of the state. Marxists focus on the task of capital accumulation and the issues of the state become narrowed down to the ideological and repressive state apparatuses such as the police, prisons and the army: the representative system and its constitutional features count for almost nothing. Radical feminists tend to focus on abortion, pornography, issues around distribution patterns of career and child care. And many post-modernists have given up entirely on the idea of the state as a meaningful unitary concept, as they make a political act out of reading *Great Expectations*, or, if they are teaching Cultural Studies, watching *The Simpsons*, as if it were of equal political importance to a military engagement.

In this book we observe the origins and rationales behind the multi-faceted beast that is the state. We do not try and explain away its more brutal components by resorting to an idealist conception of justice, but we approach the subject from a recognition of its multiple tasks and purposes. As we show in this work, by the time of the American Federalist debates this view of the state best characterises what the modern state is: the maximisation of the coexistent forces needed for protecting civil society and providing people with security, as well as the opportunity to represent their interests. The liberal democratic state did not evolve out of thin air, when it came into existence it had to carry with it all the other interests and forces of the day.

Over time, social forces, interests and the abilities to articulate interests change. We thus do not talk about women's issues in the modern state prior to the end of the eighteenth century because there was no such political mobilisation prior to then and also no major articulation of women's interests as a political category. Likewise, we only address social justice as it emerges as an historical issue when working people became politically conscious of themselves and acted as a force with a political destiny. Partisans of every stripe invariably construct the state through the prism of their interests, but interests change. Thus we are now witnessing what appears to be the death of social democracy as the information revolution continues to impact through civilised societies.

The modern mature state is a multi-faceted creature whose powers are far from exhausted. What new limbs will evolve remain to be seen. But the mature civilised state is the most benign political force that has ever existed, and its benignness is due to the tasks it performs, the restraints placed upon it by civil society as a whole, and the personal interests of its members.

Like electricity, power may be benign or malignant depending upon the context of its unleashing. In the institutions of the mature civilised state a means has been found so that the wisest and the stupidest may pool their energies and interests into directing the future. The wisdom of these institutions is far greater than the capacities of those who hold office within them. Yet each office holder, even the most stupid one, is ultimately caught up in the push and pull of social energies which find outlets in the media, the ballot box, a protest, a lobby group, a university. Thus each one keeps the process going.

Those who hold power in a democracy may be little better in their hearts than those who were members of the National Socialist Party or the Communist Party, just as the idealists who claim to speak for all the victims of the earth are invariably no less greedy or self-serving than those they criticise. It was Kant who said that in a republican state a constitution had been found that could control even a race of devils. The magic of the mature civilised state is precisely that: it is built on an economy where private vices may create public prosperity and a political apparatus where liars, cheats and all manner of miscreants serve an ongoing public good.

1 Characteristics and Typology of the Modern State

> He who is unable to live in society, or who has no need because he is sufficient for himself, must be either a beast or a God: he is no part of a state
>
> Aristotle, *Politics,* 1, 14

The territory of the globe is divided into states with the exception of the southern polar region which has been forgone for the time being for lack of adequate technology. These two hundred or so states - the World Bank lists two hundred and nine economies but some do not fulfil the political criteria - differ in all manner of ways, but each has a government that attempts to control its territory. Although refugees deserve our sympathy, even if they number twenty or even fifty million they are the exceptions among a human population of nearly 5.8 billion. Almost everybody has a nationality and belongs to a state.

This system of sovereign states is a relatively recent development in the history of the human race. The first recorded interstate system was that developed by the ancient Greeks two and a half thousand years ago around the *polis* or city state. From that time we have our first records of social scientists: Herodotus the historian, Thucydides the analyst of international relations, Plato the political philosopher and Aristotle with his development of comparative politics. In no other part of the world did such a system develop although claims have been made for China's warring states period and sometimes for other periods on the Indian sub-continent.

The modern interstate system began to develop in twelfth century Europe out of the disputed medieval authority of feudal Christendom. It started to assume its modern form in the fifteenth century with the absolute monarchies of western Europe and the smaller principalities of renaissance Italy.[1] The modern state was given formal recognition at the Treaty of Westphalia in 1648, though at that time its definitive form had not been realised. As we shall see, the modern state has a number of different forms, though those different forms are shaped by different sets of problems. We argue that the form of a state is largely shaped by its social base -- though, as we shall also see, certain state forms often arise to enable a society to shift from one social base to another.

The modern state is constituted by a number of elements: a defined people, bounded territory, a culture, a sense of nation.

People

A state primarily comprises a number of settled people living together in usually contiguous territory.

The size of states varies enormously from the mass populations of contemporary China with 1.2 billion and India with over nine hundred million and growing more quickly, to the mini-states of the South Pacific like Nauru and Tuvulu who have populations of less than 10,000. This element of size provides a different dynamic to societies: for the very large, population control always assumes a greater significance, while for the very small the burden of maintaining the basic elements of a state apparatus produces severe resource allocation problems. But both can face the problem of overpopulation. Despite their small populations the Pacific island states may be more the endangered as their extremely fragile environments face simultaneously rapid population growth and territorial extinction with the possibility of rising sea levels.

The appropriate population for a given state is difficult to determine. But the *demographic transition* tends to follow a pattern. Low growth rate in poor societies is accompanied by high birth and death rates, whereas high growth is accompanied by high birth and low death rates, and this, in turn, gives way to low growth based on low birth and low death rates. Most of the Europe-derived populations - including the settler societies of North America and Australasia and the former communist states of the Soviet Union - are presently not reproducing themselves. In the longer run the populations of these states will decline without immigration. This is essentially because of the continuing fall in their birth rates which has followed on the introduction of easy methods of contraception and a major change in the social role of women, as a large number of women, for the first time in history, have economic independence. On the other hand, a number of poorer societies have been able to reduce their growth rates by a combination of rising incomes and government inducements including persuasion in Indonesia and savage penalties in China.

The problem of social reproduction for industrialised countries with declining populations is complicated by the fact that immigration easily leads to social strains. While cultural and social homogeneity do not guarantee political stability and economic prosperity, lack of social cohesion is a recipe for political instability.

Territory

The state has a clear location in physical space and has boundaries that are usually well defined by physical or other kinds of features. Exceptions here may include inhospitable terrain, but this did not stop the Chinese and Indian armies from fighting over an uninhabited piece of snow covered mountains on the roof of the world in 1959.

The characteristics of the territory itself and the kinds of production it encourages and methods of defence it demands may, in turn, influence the kind of people that inhabit it. The small and densely populated islands of Japan which were isolated for nearly a thousand years have produced a people of great uniformity, hierarchy and internal order. The rapid settlement of the wide territory of the USA by migrants from diverse sources has engendered a commitment to individualism. The wet rice farmers of Southeast Asia have generated very orderly societies from communal production and maintenance of water control systems.

The territory of the state is always jealously guarded and will be defended by force against other states. Indeed, *the* distinguishing feature of the state for many political scientists is its exclusive right to the legitimate use of force within its territory. The primary defence function of the state increases the resource allocation to the armed forces who may become significant in the state's political structure, at first perhaps to acquire and subdue new provinces, but later to supplement or overcome civilian authority. This is often described as the *security dilemma* - in preparing for self-defence the state provides itself with the capacity for offence which is often realised in offensive war.[2]

The physical location of the state can seriously effect the security function of the state in so far as the military arm of the state can be rendered more or less significant by geographic or other features. For example, the relative domestic insignificance of the British and US armed forces in their modern political constitutional history may be attributed in part to the security provided the one by its island character and the other by its distance from serious adversaries. On the other hand the important role played by the armed forces in Germany and Russia may be attributed to their both being denied natural boundaries and being surrounded by potential enemies whom they periodically fought. One could also argue that the origins of militarism in South America are to be found in the fact that the Spanish drew the colonial state boundaries around the military districts and these military organisations subsequently became the independent states.

Culture

The people within the territory usually begin with sharing, or soon acquire habits of living together which are called culture and include language, laws, religion, cuisine, architecture, clothing, entertainment, and an attachment to the environment that they collectively inhabit.

Language has always comprised a vital component of the modern nation state as it was developed in the sixteenth century in the West and then spread in the nineteenth century across Europe with its emphasis on linguistic nationalism. No doubt the French Revolution and its expansion on Napoleonic bayonets accelerated this process. After the First World War the victors redrew the political map of Europe along national frontiers. This linguistic principle was never entirely consistent since that principle had to coexist with others, including strategic and cultural considerations, and natural frontiers. Nonetheless it is indicative of the strength of the principle that even after the Cold War new demands for statehood emerged in

Europe based on the linguistic principle and were successfully achieved in Slovakia and may yet be in Belgium and the Basque lands of Spain. Languages almost always pre-date the state they cohere. The major exception to this has been Israel, the first Jewish state in two thousand years, that deliberately utilised Hebrew to reunite the *diaspora*. More commonly, states have been able to control language policy only at the margins, with Britain enforcing English on the Celtic fringes by use of the school system or China determining the official structure of modern Chinese.

Many Asian, Pacific and African states have had their boundaries determined during the colonial period by European map makers and administrators in the field. Consequently many languages and nationalities coexist in different configurations of power. A number of policies have been adopted to deal with such situations. In Indonesia, for example, a trading *lingua franca* native to the Sumatra/Malaya region was widely adopted in civil society even during the Dutch colonial period. After independence Indonesia made it the national language, as did neighbouring Malaysia. In South Africa a different resolution was attempted by the then dominant Afrikaan (Dutch derived) language speaking Whites who were imposing apartheid or racial segregation on the African population, and in the 1970s tried to also impose their language on the other communities.[3]

The system of laws is also vital to the creation of shared values as it provides a framework within which civil society may develop. The state generally provides and certainly enforces these laws, but if they are entirely imposed by it the risk of rebellion and disobedience arises. Successful legal regimes combine congruence between socially acceptable practices and mores, a professionally educated judiciary, a legal framework based on legal principles such as the presumption of innocence, the right to a fair trial, legal representation, and judicial impartiality. The soundness of the procedures, principles, professional behaviours is essential to a good legal system. Details between systems may vary. Some systems, such as those derived from England, are based in common law and the form of a trial may be adversarial in its nature, and may usually involve a jury. Others, such as continental legal traditions, may be grounded in a legal code, and the judge may play the role of an inquisitor, as he or she seeks to discover the truth of a case.

In a mature modern society, there is formal equality before the law. In some states discrete communities may be granted exemption from aspects of the law. In the more successful settler democracies the indigenous peoples are usually recognised as having traditions and claims that deserve special status at law. In some other countries immigrant populations may be granted similar dispensations. Such arrangements are sometimes warranted unless they become so widespread as to throw the entire system of equality before the law into question.

Religion is also an important component of culture. Religion in one form or another has, until very recently, been a universal feature of social organisation. In tribal societies, ancestral and animal spirits guide a people through the mysteries of life; in agrarian and imperial societies, priests studied the stars and peoples worshipped the heavenly spirits while imperial leaders were either gods or priests. Political authorities have invariably tried to link religious belief systems to their power for social and political compliance. Observing this, Marx termed religion the opium of the people. But such a view fails to grasp the psychological breadth and complexity of religious experiences and their (unintended) secular effects.

Peoples also often share a cuisine. At the first settlement of humans as agricultural people, their diets would have varied greatly and reflected the fauna and flora prevailing in the area and what could be domesticated in the climate. The habits of communal food production and distribution heavily influenced the social and political pattern of societies. Wet rice cultivation created dense populations in east Asia co-operating in the construction of the hydraulic infrastructure necessary for intensive cultivation. Hunter gatherer civilisations in Australia supported a sparse population of loosely associated communities trading with and warring on one another. Cattle rearing shepherds in the great Asian steppes enabled mobile state forms built around cavalry to dominate the Eurasian heartland for a millennium before effective artillery and infantry with firearms brought this dominance to an end.

The built environment is what a society does to its natural environment to make it more habitable for its culture and economy. Each society can be readily recognised by the style and form of this imposition on nature. The impact ranges from the Australian

Aboriginals who, while they did not leave a single building, so extensively fired the environment over a period of fifty thousand years, as to change its flora, fauna and climate. On the other hand the British so changed their islands by production and consumption as to have almost eliminated natural forests by the seventeenth century, thus forcing the development of coal power and with it an industrial revolution. The Dutch have been able to significantly extend the territory of their small country by their own distinctive architecture, the dyke system. The Chinese control of the water supply enabled their population of rice producers to be double that of the wheat producers in Europe by the early modern era. In order to achieve this they had to construct some of the most impressive water regulation systems ever devised, some of which are still in use two millennia later.

Before the age of the European creation of a world market, people were also identifiable by their local clothing styles. Some of these derived from the climate, like the Arab cloak designed to deal with the unusual circumstances of great heat in the day and cold at night. Others were to deal with primitive circumstances, like the 'naked savages' the Europeans observed in the South Pacific. Yet others again, like the Chinese, wore highly developed formalistic attire signifying facts about the wearer that ranged from occupation, wealth and rank. Interestingly, this time-honoured tradition survived even the excesses of the Cultural Revolution when the wearing of identical Chairman Mao suits was thought to be *de rigueur*, but in fact obscured subtle stylistic differences which marked exactly the same characteristics.

The national organic culture also includes distinctive characteristics of communal play. Every society has song, celebration, dance, mimicry, i.e. play woven into its fabric. Play is the moment in which a people express and observe their grief and their joy, their hopes and fears, their aesthetic sensibilities, their common appreciation and mastery of form. The sites and modalities of play vary from society to society and from age to age. In the poetically led culture of ancient Greece, tragedy and comedy were vehicles of social direction. In medieval Europe the fair, theatre and various martial practices were dominant among the masses, alongside religious activities organised by the Church. Today, civilised societies are entertainment societies. Even the dissemination of information is bound up with play and entertainment.

Alongside the arts, sport is another universal expression of the instinct of play. Like art, sport is an expression of energy and freedom which enthuses participants and spectators alike. The more proficiency one attains or aspires to attain, the greater the discipline and devotion it commands. Not only are the arts and sports great achievements of the species, their very existence points to the limitation of politics. Politics exists to preserve and, if necessary, to foster (but not dictate) the spheres and sites of play of the human spirit. Politics should be the handmaiden to the good life. Art and sport are our way of expressing that life is good, even in the face of hardship and tragedy. To be sure, for some people, nothing is quite like the adrenaline which accompanies the pursuit, attainment, and expression of political power. For them, politics is an end and not just a means. But the great flaw in the world view of those who want to create a radical democratic society is the false belief that everyone's life will be good if everyone is permanently engaged in political life.

Finally, mention must be made of the relationship people have to the particular environment they inhabit and claim to own. For some this attachment is deep and involves rituals that bond the people to the land. The Javanese cling to the religious and spiritual basis of their volcanic and fertile island. The Japanese have a tribal attachment to their home islands. Other peoples find their relationship to the physical environment more tenuous and have migrated in large numbers. The British have created entire other countries and migrate mostly to these 'Britains overseas', with their familiar civil societies. The other Europeans have also gone mostly to those destinations which they regard as a more advanced form of their homelands.

Nationalism

Nationalism takes various forms but usually incorporates the idea of shared collective history and identity, national character, often racism, and exclusivity as against non-members of the nation.[4] Historically, an overtly ideological component has also been important in formating national consciousness. All nations caricature themselves and other nations. These collective ideas have to have some basis in fact in order to survive, although their inaccuracy may increase with time, history, distance, or the prejudices and lack of ability in journalists. Despite the current popularity of Edward Said's idea of 'Orientalism' -- that 'the Orient' is a political creation of Western intellectuals for their own ends -- all societies have distorted and often unflattering perspectives of others to contrast with their own benign self-image. The clever English balance of power diplomacy becomes *Perfidious Albion*, the disciplined Japanese an unthinking automaton, the spiritual Indian a feckless pauper, free America the Great Satan.

One of the state's roles is the maintenance and reproduction of the nation's self-image. To a degree the state may try to use these myths as a method of social control. This is true not only of dictatorial regimes, like Burma (Myanmar) with its risible *New Light Of Myanmar*, but also of civilised societies like France with a long history of state owned broadcasting and more unusually its ineffectual efforts to regulate the French language and protect it from English or Franglaise. Rarely do efforts by the state to impose a nationalist ideology on an unwilling civil society work. Most spectacular in this respect was the Soviet effort which failed after three generations, and was in any case abandoned in its moment of greatest need, the Great Patriotic War against Hitler. In July 1941 Stalin switched his rhetoric from the 'workers and peasants state' to the 'motherland'. It is also the case that many of the methods of reproducing nationalism derive from civil society and its culture, as can be seen in the early modern period in the historical dramas of Shakespeare.

The idea of national character has little resonance among social scientists in the twentieth century, largely as a reaction to fascism and social Darwinism. It makes sense, though, to almost anyone who travels, and it was commonly used by philosophers in the eighteenth and nineteenth centuries.[5] The dismissal of the idea of national characteristics usually tends to go hand in hand with a belief in the complete malleability of human nature, which in turn fits neatly into the idealist dream of creating a perfect society. Although Marx plays no small part in the construction of this view of human beings, with his belief that class-consciousness was of much more importance than national consciousness, he thought that the lesser nations of Europe, including the Slavs, might have to be colonised by the more advanced, like the Germans, to get them going on the path of progress. Nevertheless, social circumstance and behaviours do differ geographically, and national character will differ according to the patterns of collective social formation.

In this way one might explain the bureaucratic nature of the Chinese, Russian and German nations by reference to their historical development in heavily populated imperial systems which in the latter cases had no natural frontiers. In Germany's case the formation of the nation was achieved under Prussian leadership, a state whose rise to great power status had been made possible by the barracks mentality of Frederick William and then accomplished by his militarist, though cultured son Frederick the Great. The Chinese who appear so docile in the face of the imperial mandarinate - communist or traditional - become some of the world's great capitalists when they migrate.

In the British imperial system Australia and Canada developed very high living standards and democratic states, while in South Africa the more diverse sources of migration have produced a fractured and violent society finding progress difficult to sustain. In Southeast Asia the nation states of Thailand and Vietnam find cohesion naturally easier to maintain as a result of the organic national linguistic community which forms the dominant component of their peoples. Indonesia will have to work much harder to achieve the same result in an archipelagian state of three hundred languages and thirteen thousand islands. Burma sits between these experiences with a majority nationality comprising over sixty percent of the people having to unite the others by force under SLORC's military rule.

One of the reasons for the development of the representative government/commercial society system in England was its early filling of the national territory by almost one linguistic group and the elimination thereby of serious external threats. It was then consolidated by conquest with the Welsh and the Act of Union with the Scots. This system was transplanted to America by grateful religious refugee communities who evicted the British state almost immediately after the only serious external threat to themselves - the French - had been defeated in the Seven Years War. This national character was dispersed through the lands settled under British law such that there may be a collective Anglo-Saxon character divided into various national sub-groups. Of course this does not have an ethnic basis and some thirty million of the US nation are of African ethnicity although they in turn form their own sub-category.

Typology of States

Peoples devise ways of organising themselves to produce and distribute commodities, create and develop their culture, and form and administer laws in ways that give some of the people power over others. The way in which these arrangements are managed is called politics.[6] Since Aristotle, observers have tried to organise the different ways in which these arrangements are made into intellectual categories. Thus states have been classified according to the system of government they utilise, and have divided monarchies from republics, or federal from unitary states, or two party from multi-party, or Congressional from parliamentary systems. Some critics regard attention to such details as inappropriate because such analysis may ignore the class composition, gender disposition, or the religious complexion. Equally ideological has been the contemporary inclination to divide states into those belonging to the First, Second and Third Worlds. This has been cemented by both usage and diplomatic practice at the United Nations and continues despite the end of the Cold War which brought the terms into existence. This is in the main a Marxist derived categorisation and anachronistic.

The First World, as described in the original French use of these terms in the 1960s, was the advanced and capitalist countries of Western Europe, North America, Australasia and Japan. This was identified by essentially the higher per capita income levels enjoyed in these countries. Although this condition did not entirely survive the 1970s, during which decade many oil rich OPEC states, of otherwise little economic development, surpassed the income levels of the OECD, and the 1980s, when some of the East Asian development states also passed the European per capita income levels, it is a testimony to the strength of politics as against science that the usage endures. Indeed, Singapore continued to press New Zealand to maintain its foreign aid donations after its own per capita income was greater than that of the donor! Most of these First World states are now defined as High Income by the World Bank in its annual reports and the two lists overlap almost perfectly.

The Second World comprised the Soviet bloc countries that had supposedly broken out of the world market and were forging an independent path to development. These communist states generally followed the model established by the Leninists after the Russian Revolution of 1917 as modified later by the Stalin regime in the 1930s. They were and are, where they survive as in North Korea, characterised by state ownership of the overwhelming majority of economic activity and oligarchic control of the state by one hierarchical political party. Since it was common, indeed typical for a one man dictatorship to emerge in these states as a 'cult of personality', this also needs to be added to characteristic features. In the absence of a civil society a state apparatus untrammelled by countervailing power probably has a strong tendency to move in the direction of dictatorship.

The Third World, in this lexicon, comprised the formerly colonial areas of Africa, Asia and Latin America, that had been extensively conquered and ruled by what had become in Cold War jargon the West and in the Marxist terminology, the imperialist states. An implied corollary was that the conditions of poverty enjoyed by the peoples of many states in this zone were created during the period of Western dominance.[7] This was a perspective not shared by the ideological creator of communism, Karl Marx, and in fact was contrary to the historical facts which had to be rewritten by Western trained dependency theorists to comply with its dictates.[8] It is the case, however, that the Soviets were quick to support the Group of Seventy Seven's demands for redress of this historic wrong and continuing economic exploitation, in the form of the program for a New International Economic Order at the United Nations in the 1970s. This was finally vetoed by the US Reagan administration in the early 1980s at the conference in Cancun, Mexico.

In the post-Cold War world this terminology is archaic and needs replacing. The Second World communist states have either dissolved or been changed beyond recognition with the sole exceptions of North Korea and Cuba. They are at different levels of development depending on their capacity to adjust to the world market and the study of them is now seen in terms of 'transitional' societies. The old Third World comprises diverse states some of which are richer than much of Europe and others that have descended into anarchy. The First World has been augmented in number and cannot be regarded as a fixed entity.

It is, therefore, difficult to arrive at a scientific characterisation of categories of state: ideology often overruns science in the academy. Nonetheless it is possible to use some relatively dispassionate criteria to place states into different life forms by reference to a combination of their physical/material and sociological/political characteristics and the degree to which these are changing. This delivers: twenty six wealthy democracies, living in domestic and external peace, or *mature civilised* states; about thirty middle income states with varying degrees of representative government and growing fairly quickly, or *developmental* states; about a score of countries controlled by an idealist elite which has imposed some form of dictatorship of the guardians, or *idealist* states; and about a hundred and twenty very poor states with various forms of ill-directed government which we may call *primitive* states.

Mature Civilised States

The more fortunate section of the human race inhabits a zone of states where, for the great majority of the population, life expectancy is long and exceeds seventy years; food supplies are diverse and reliable; accommodation in decent conditions with water, power and sanitation is assured; health services are provided; and civil peace can be assumed. There are less than thirty such states which may be called civilised and a little less than fifteen per cent of the human race live in them. They have both been established by and enabled the creation of civil societies in which power is shared largely by consent, human rights are protected and freedom coexists with order. In these societies per capita income exceeds $US 10,000 and literacy is almost universal. They are exclusively advanced capitalist democracies. These states include most of west and central Europe. In the region where the state was created these societies are eroding aspects of its borders and creating a European Union. The conditions of membership include of course the requirement that the state be a democracy and in fact civilised or advanced.

The states which fit this description in the mid-1990s included the USA and Canada in North America; Australia and New Zealand; and in Europe: Ireland, Spain, Britain, Finland, Italy, the Netherlands, Norway, Belgium, France, Austria, Germany, Sweden, Denmark, Luxembourg and Switzerland. Greece and Iceland are borderline cases which may be included as European Union members. In East Asia, Japan also complies with the category. The Bahamas is also a borderline case which may be included. Those borderline cases excluded here, comprise Singapore for not being a democracy, Taiwan for being in a civil war, Korea for being too low in per capita income but soon to join; and those included, Portugal which although being too poor for the time being is in the European Union. Members which might also make it in the longer term include the volatile Argentine, divided Cyprus, and the newly free Slovenia and Hungary.

This list of 26 mature civilised states out of a total of 209 states have a population of about 800 million people from a total global population of 5.8 billion. In other words only just over twelve per cent of the world's states may be termed civilised. This merely confirms a central point of this book: that civilisation is a difficult condition to cultivate, is rarely achieved and once hard won should be defended with resolve.

The political features that the developmentalist school of political science identifies as being peculiar to the civilised or advanced states may be listed as ten.[9] This is not to say that a state arrives suddenly at this condition and has all ten spring into existence. While this does sometimes occur - for example when a previously dictatorial regime is overthrown and a democracy comes back into existence, or when an occupying power creates a democracy out of a defeated fascist regime - usually a democratic state is cultivated by a civil society undergoing a profound transformation itself.[10] But what follow are features of the state apparatus, not the civil society, and as such are not necessarily the same as the conditions of a civilised community. The latter requires a developed civil society *and* a democratic state. For example former British colonies may maintain a democratic state but around a civil society that retains quite primitive characteristics like Papua New Guinea or

India. On the other hand an advanced civil society may coexist with an autocratic state, like Singapore, but probably not for very long.

The first feature is that the system of law making is codified and systematised into a constitution, which is usually written and may therefore be examined by citizens and others. The British, of course, appear to constitute a major exception here in so far as their constitution is not written in one place but comprises historical practice as organically evolved since the *Magna Carta* of 1215. Most other civilised states have a written constitution which may be of long standing, like the American, or more recent, like the French (although it is based on the 1789 Bill of Rights), and subject to periodic amendment. In the case of Australia, the constitution is actually an Act of the British Parliament passed to enable the voluntary creation of the state of Australia from six British colonies in 1901. This followed an extensive debate throughout the continent about the formation of the nation, not unlike the Federalist debates in the USA a century earlier, but reflecting the more statist ideas of the time and including consideration of the female franchise (although no women were directly involved in these debates), the absence of slavery, but the exclusion of the native people. Such a constitution essentially sets out how a law may be created, by whom and how they get to that position.

The second feature involves the incorporation of the separation of powers into the system of government. This is the principle that those who make the laws should not enforce them nor interpret them. The enunciation of this doctrine is usually attributed to Montesquieu. These three functions of government are called the legislature, which makes the laws, the executive which enforces them and the judiciary which interprets them. Civilised states share the habit of separating these powers. The most formal expression of this principle is to be found in the US constitution where it was debated by the Federalists and then enshrined by the Founding Fathers. The President may formulate the national budget or declare war or sign treaties but the Congress must ratify these procedures. In the case of the League of Nations, for example, President Woodrow Wilson, himself an idealist and former political scientist from Princeton University, initiated and signed the Treaty that created it, but the US Senate, where isolationist sentiment was still strong, refused to ratify it and the US was never a member of the League that it created. Usually authorities call the British method of separating the powers the Westminster system and the American method the Congressional system. It is believed by most that the US system gives less power to the executive or government by placing more controls on it from the Congress and Supreme Court than does the British system. But all manner of hybrids are to be found, including France with a strong President and Italy with a diminished government but formidable state economic sector.

The third procedure concerns elections. In general, civilised states elect the legislature and the executive but appoint the judiciary from qualified jurists. This is not always the case and in the USA most such officials are elected, in conformity with the thinking of late eighteenth century democrats, although the Supreme Court judges are nominated by the President and ratified by Congress. In Europe, where the Napoleonic Code is still influential two centuries after the little dictator, magistrates also often undertake investigations which would in the common law countries of the old British colonies be pursued by police. The critical elections, however, are those which determine the executive government. In the Westminster system the people elect the legislature or Parliament, and then it elects the government or Ministry. In the Congressional system the people directly elect the President who then appoints the Cabinet - or group of Ministers - who run different parts of the government bureaucracy. In France, still concerned about the instability of the post-war republics, the President is elected every seven years in run off ballots that continue until one candidate gets 50% of the votes cast and is very powerful. In Germany, the Chancellor comes from the Bundestag's majority party or governing coalition where, to avoid the experience of the weak and vulnerable Weimar republic of the 1920s, minor parties have to get 5% of the vote to be represented.[11]

The election procedures themselves follow a wide diversity of practices. In Britain, the first past the post, single member, geographic constituency is the system which has evolved over a thousand years, although it was not always so dominant and in living memory the two ancient Universities, Oxford and Cambridge, elected members to the House of Commons. In other countries various modifications to this system have been adopted, including proportional representation, which is common in Europe but often criticised for giving too much power to minority parties and compromising the ability of the system to protect itself. In others again, like Australia, voting has been made compulsory after the voter turnout dropped below thirty per cent in the 1920s. It is also often the case that a different system is used for electing people to the different Houses of Parliament or Congress if more than one exists. The Upper House may indeed seek to represent a different feature of civil society. Hence in the federal systems of the USA, Australia and Germany, the Upper House, often called the Senate, is elected to represent the states who came together to form the sovereign state concerned. In the UK the House of Lords represents the privileged and is a mixture of hereditary and appointed members with its limited power reflecting its undemocratic nature. In New Zealand a unicameral unitary system of democracy prevails producing an extremely powerful executive government between elections, recently reduced by the introduction of a part proportional system. Notwithstanding these variations the legislatures in these civilised countries are democratically elected and make the law under an established constitution.

Fourthly, it is also important that the government actually *be* periodically changed. One of the important features of a democratic and civilised state is that the executive can be changed without any serious disruption to the civil society that it is there to serve. Some states, that in so many other respects appear civilised, do not in fact make the grade because an executive has found methods within the formal democratic processes for perpetuating its own rule. For example, Singapore, which inherited a formal democratic system from the British in 1963 and then retained it in 1965 when it broke from the Federation of Malaysia, has never had a change of government. Through a variety of procedures including special powers also delivered by the British from the period when they were fighting the Communist insurrection in the 1950s, the government dominated by Lee Kuan Yew and his Peoples Action Party (PAP) has eliminated electoral threats to it during the last three decades. These methods have included imprisonment, harassment by the legal system it controls, censorship and bankruptcy by civil court action heard by judges it appoints. Indeed, Lee was installed in control of the PAP by the British arresting his majority opponents on the governing council in the late 1950s and doing the same sort of favour in operation Cold

Storage in 1963. The Japanese electoral system was similarly corrupted by the Liberal Democratic Party until its defeat in 1993. During four decades of rule the LDP maintained a rural gerrymander, franchised its safe seats by selling them, had carefully drawn multi member constituencies and suborned the state apparatus and big business sector. When the economy faltered in the early 1990s the political system collapsed and the LDP went into temporary opposition.[12]

The continuity of the system of government in these civilised states is provided by a public service or bureaucracy. Most commonly this bureaucracy is believed to be politically neutral in so far as the conflicts between the political parties competing for control of the state are concerned, although it is fiercely protective of the system itself. This function of protecting democracy is overtly conducted by the police with provision commonly made for emergency powers, in the event of the state coming under serious threat, and the intervention of the armed forces. Such powers are rarely needed in civilised states but are more often used than is commonly believed. The British have been running Northern Ireland under such provisions since the outbreak of the most recent bout of 'Troubles' in 1969. Effectively, civil society has broken down and two communities are engaged in a civil war with one another which the semi-colonial British state is reluctantly arbitrating. Emergency powers have also been invoked in Australia, during the South African rugby tour of Queensland in 1971, the USA during the equal rights demonstrations in the 1960s and Vietnam War periods, by France during the Algerian War of Independence, and again in Britain in the early 1970s coal strike conflict. All civilised states also have covert agencies for protecting the state against its external and internal enemies. These are sometimes difficult to control but provide a vital function, the absence of which was partly responsible for the accession to power of the Nazis during the Weimar Republic.

The political independence of the bureaucracy is, of course, something of a myth, but one that is important to the functioning of these states. In fact bureaucrats often benefit from having party allegiances and get preferment when their political allies are in power. In the USA this is formally recognised and many office holders that in other civilised states would be continuous are changed with a new administration. In the Westminster system political neutrality is assumed but in fact senior bureaucrats are often replaced with a change in government. Further, defeated or retiring politicians of a regime may be rewarded with a political appointment in the bureaucracy, particularly in the foreign service and as Ambassador.[13]

Fifthly, the civilised state does and must keep out of civil society as far as possible and permit the pursuit of those various activities which characterise a free citizenry. In this category are included the right to assemble, combine, protest, express opinions and publish them, and own property under legal title. The right to assemble is hard won and still usually controlled by the Riot Act or its equivalent. In Britain this was used viciously at Peterloo in 1819 and forms part of the core of liberty acquired by the British against the Leviathan they had constructed to preserve order.[14] The anti-combination Acts were repealed in the nineteenth century and permitted the formation of trade unions which, while now an anachronism for many workers are still an entitlement. Protest against particular laws is an inherent right in a civilised state and organised protest against the Poll Tax led to the destruction of the Conservative Prime Minister Margaret Thatcher that had otherwise done so much in the cause of liberty in trimming the expenditure of state, its control over sectors of economic activity and the closed shop version of British unionism (despite her fatuous remark that there is no such thing as society and her personal aggrandisement). The expression of opinion is vital to the cause of a free civil society and the pursuit of censorship by the politically correct movement in the 1990s was too close to the Platonic idea of the Guardians to deserve any support whether it came from the feminist, Multicultural or gay totalitarian idealists. The imposition of censorship in any cause other than the preservation of the state itself - that is military secrets - is the hallmark of creeping primitiveness.

The sixth feature of a civilised state is the protection of the minority from totalitarian or arbitrary rule by the majority. Many states have deployed legal sanctions to ensure that minority groups formed by various social categories - religion, race, culture, language or sexual preference, for example - are not discriminated against. This is understandable and even, in some cases, involving indigenous peoples in settler states or migrant communities actively recruited, laudable.

But the greater cause is that of freedom and if there is not the support for such action in civil society such actions invite a hostile backlash from the majority community, and if there is such support it is not required. In the case of Northern Ireland it may be observed that the immediate cause of the existing, post-1969 'Troubles' was the domination of the majority Protestant community of the state to the detriment of the minority Catholic community. In this case the British constitutional system, which was devised for quite different conditions, had failed to provide an adequate power sharing arrangement and idealist terrorists stepped into the void.[15]

The seventh feature closely resembles the sixth and concerns protection for citizens from arbitrary treatment on the basis of specific and irrelevant characteristics like gender, race or religion. This form of policy was actively pursued by special and generous state funding for Aboriginals in the later years of the Australian Keating government and so energetically that it elicited a substantial backlash from the dominant community which contributed to its record defeat. Even a generous civil society may not welcome the enforced and expensive dissolution of its traditional prejudices. But clearly if they are not constrained by law racist social practices will be extremely detrimental to the evolution of a civil order.

The eighth characteristic of the civilised state is the one that has received most attention recently and involves the opening of the state's processes to public scrutiny. On the one hand this has resulted from the continuing pressure from citizens for more access to the decisions which affect their lives and the consequential establishment of Ombudsman's offices and similar avenues of appeal against the activities of the state. Alongside this has been the passage of Freedom of Information legislation throughout the civilised world giving citizens the entitlement to open the previously secret files of the state. And on the other hand there has been an enormous growth of the media apparatus trying to expose state secrets, a function hugely accelerated by the American opposition to the Vietnam War and the Watergate affair which has made every journalist since Woodward and Bernstein want to destroy at least one political career.[16] The effect of these two parallel developments has been that there are no state secrets in the civilised state outside the military sphere, and precious few within it.

Liberal access to citizenship is the ninth characteristic of the civilised state. This is not to say that any person may join it at will. Any sovereign state has the right to exclude non-citizens from its borders and only in exceptional circumstances may this right be abrogated. In the 1950s the British state allowed the right of migration to Empire subjects with the effect that the resulting large number of migrants placed a considerable strain on the tolerance of the civil society of the indigenous community. The migration levels were subsequently curtailed but not before deep fissures had been created within the community thereby contributing to the widespread urban riots of the 1980s. In Germany the Law of Return was designed to provide refuge for Germans caught in the communist part of the country after the Soviets occupied it. It was then used by persons of other nationalities seeking to enter Germany for its higher wage rates and also had to be abandoned. Similarly, while the civilised states all accept some obligation to alleviate the suffering of political refugees, this need not be met by offering them migration entitlement, as is Australian policy. An effective civil aid program would serve as well, as is the Japanese and Scandinavian practice. But for people who are members of civil society they are entitled to be and are active citizens in the civilised states. As such, a civilised state must make some provision for their better integration.

Finally, the civilised states have accepted responsibility for the provision of some of the social services that might have been provided by civil society in the past. These include educational, health, infirm care and various other social welfare services, and regulatory processes, such as minimum wage and occupational safety standards, that vary from time to time depending on the outcome of the political conflicts taking place in that state. In general, these are fairly standard across the civilised world and have resulted from the ascendancy of the social democratic project and the adoption of its core demands during the twentieth century. Their implementation has meant, however, that many of the reasons for the existence of social democratic institutions have gone since the state is administering their program, and everywhere union membership and political support for social democratic parties is in decline. This is a healthy corrective to the tendency for state power to expand, a process which if it continued would have led to the continuing erosion of civil society, the base on which civilisation rests.

Developmental States

Another twenty five states are successfully seeking to replicate the trajectory of progress already achieved by the civilised zone and may be called developmental states. These states have been able to mobilise their societies and physical resources in such a way that they are achieving progress towards a civilised condition. While these states may have serious areas of poverty, poor conditions of living and low average per capita income rates, what distinguishes them is the way in which their economic and social indicators are changing rapidly and displaying the promise of imminent civilisation. Many of the states of East Asia are pursuing this course and are at different stages of this developmental route. In addition, some of the South American countries including Chile and Mexico, and also perhaps Brazil and Argentina are in this category.

It is in East Asia, however, that the liberal view of economic, social and political progress is most clearly being achieved. This is not to say that this will occur in all regions settled by the human race. It is also not to say that it will occur in all states of the East Asian region. And it is finally most certainly not to say that once achieved a civilised condition will be maintained permanently and without careful cultivation. On the contrary, the establishment of the civilised state and civil society is a rare enough achievement historically and enjoyed by only a small minority even as the millennia turn.

East Asia rivalled Europe in progress even as the Enlightenment project was launched. China had been in the forefront of technological and industrial progress into the sixteenth century. It then experienced arrested development and largely stagnated until confronted with superior European power in the nineteenth century. Two major explanations may be offered for this phenomenon. On the one hand, for internal political reasons, perhaps to do with a high level of self sufficiency, the Celestial Empire closed itself from the outside world and no longer joined the progress experienced elsewhere as ossification set in. On the other hand, unlike the states of Europe, it did not face continuous competition and could afford to ignore progress elsewhere as unlikely to effect its interests based on previous experience. It was wrong and paid the price.

This is not to say that China had generated any extensive discussion of the virtues of democracy and progress. Indeed, it was self satisfied and dictatorial until humiliated after the Opium War of 1840. It then underwent a profound internal conflict about its future following the collapse of the ruling (Manchu) dynasty in 1911 as had happened so commonly in the past. As a result, the hegemonic state that had directed the East Asia state system for so long by virtue of its superior power was in decline as the Europeans arrived. They established direct or informal rule over the entire region, created spheres of influence in China and seized territory from it. Consequently, the beginnings of resistance to European power were to be found not in China but Japan.[17]

At the time of its enforced opening to world commerce Japan was an isolated, feudalistic and military society with some advanced manufacturing techniques and a good craft base.[18] Its ruling elite quickly mobilised the state via the Meiji Restoration of the centralised monarchy to emulate the European passage to progress. To this end they copied many Western methods of organisation, production and battle, but not Western civil society or political philosophy, except ironically Marxism. This quickly gave Japan a powerful state apparatus which dominated East Asia, fighting a series of successful expansionary wars until defeated in 1945. It had done this under a system of government that contained elements of emperor worship, racist fascism and militarist rule.

The Japanese had started the rapid economic development pattern of East Asia and, incidentally in the process disproved dependency theory. They showed that societies could adapt Western production techniques and replicate the power and wealth provided by an industrial revolution. What Japan had not done was develop a civilised state. The Western institutional forms of democracy had not been accompanied by its Enlightenment ideals of equality and progress, and had been devoured by an imperial and militarist state. This was only reversed when it was occupied by the leading civilised powers of the day (including the British represented by Australia) under the leadership of the USA, after 1945. They created the civilised Japanese state.[19]

During the first two or three years of the Occupation the Americans seriously pursued liberal policies of dismantling those elements of the Japanese state which had made it militaristic - the divine imperial throne, the armed forces and the oligopolistic corporations or *zaibatsu* - and creating a republican constitution. They also determined to establish a liberal international trade regime which would dismantle the restrictions on trade which had given Japan the reason to go to war in the 1930s. That the Americans then changed their minds and tried to make Japan a bulwark of capitalism against the expanding communist bloc did not matter. The pacifistic elements of civil society that had been created by Japanese development and then unleashed by defeat and the US Occupation could not be dissuaded. Japan adopted a 'Peace Constitution' in 1951 which severely limited its armed forces and became thereafter, arguably, the first model *trading state*.

During the next four decades Japan was one of the fastest growing economies in the world. Throughout this period it used a system of state intervention in a still rather oligopolistic economy to assist capital formation and economic progress.[20] Such *dirigisme* has not been unusual among late developing states in Europe or for that matter the English speaking world like Australia and the US itself. But the roots of Japan's success were to be found elsewhere: a continuing American commitment to and enforcement of an increasingly liberal trade regime in which the productive Japanese economy had access to the markets and raw materials that formed the basis for its export-oriented industrial growth strategy. Japan was able to pursue an external policy with no significant capacity to project power, despite its far flung economic and strategic interests, under American auspices formally enshrined in the Security Treaty between the two states.

Japan's growth was critical in establishing the basis for the creation of development states in East Asia. It provided a policy and social model which could be emulated. It was a large and growing market in the region for industrial product from other East Asian economies. And it was a source of investment capital, particularly as its own labour got very expensive and its environmental concerns too strong and its capitalists looked for cheaper foreign production platforms.[21] Japan was a remarkable success story of the transmission of a set of European Enlightenment ideals and structures to a non-European environment. But until the 1990s it lacked a liberal civil society.[22] During the early 1990s Japan experienced a series of setbacks including an economic recession, a humiliating bill for the war the US fought in the Gulf to protect its access to oil and a large financial calamity in the form of the securities scandal. As a result the Liberal Democratic Party, that had run the country as a near corporate state since the mid-1950s, lost the watershed 1993 election and Japan entered the civilised world of real political life of accommodating competing political interests.

During the 1960s the Republic of Korea, and Taiwan, started to emulate many of the features of the Japanese economic system of state intervention, only under military regimes. As former Japanese colonies they were well connected to its economy. After they had developed their economies with per capita incomes at levels similar to those prevailing in the poorer countries of Europe, that is about $US 8,000-$9,000 annually, both undertook political transformations which made them fully democratic by the mid-1990s. Although some suspicions have been registered particularly about Taiwan, no-one doubts their elections were free and open.

Two former British colonies made their growth rates less dependent on state management. Singapore resumed its position as the centre of the commercial world of Southeast Asia and became its trading, planning, tourist and financial centre. Hong Kong did much the same in southern China and also created high per capita incomes. But for strategic reasons Britain handed the Crown Colony back to semi-idealist and dictatorial China in 1997.[23]

This pattern of rapid economic growth is now being emulated in the six other member states of the Association of Southeast Asian Nations (ASEAN) although from different bases. Malaysia and Thailand are now described as middle income industrialising states, new NICs, with fairly democratic political structures, although with blemishes that the Malaysian Prime Minister sensitively describes as the 'Asian Way'. Indonesia and the Philippines have lower income levels at just under $1,000 annually but rapid growth rates that are moving them up the ranks of low middle incomes as defined by the World Bank. There are also some small signs of political liberalisation of the military backed regime in Jakarta, and Manila remains democratic after the Peoples Power revolution of the mid-1980s. The Sultanate of Brunei sustains high income levels by floating on oil. Vietnam as a former communist state trying to be in transition is more problematic and, while its growth rates have recently been high, they would want to remain there for much longer before it could be referred to with optimism. It remains more primitive than transitional or developmental.

These high growth rates have been achieved in the developmental states by accessing the world market in goods, capital and technology which the civilised states have created and sustained. This has clearly not been lost on the other regional regimes, many more of which are also trying to liberalise their economies with a view to joining the economic boom. The new military regime in Burma since 1988, the State Law and Order Restoration Council (SLORC), is combining severe political repression with slow economic reform. The Laotian communists are slowly opening up. And Cambodia is trying with limited success to recover from arguably the most idealistic regime of the twentieth century - that of Pol Pot - which may have killed one third of the population in pursuit of its ideal, of a pre-colonial Kampuchea learned at the Sorbonne.[24] Perhaps most significantly, and notwithstanding its strategic antagonisms with the island regime, Beijing effectively launched an emulate Taiwan campaign in 1992 following the southern tour of the ageing Deng Xiaopeng. Seeing the improved economic conditions in the southern provinces and aware of internal Communist Party debates about the Taiwan model and its impact on south China since the start of liberalisation since 1978, Deng called for more economic reform.[25] The signs of this producing significant political change in the communist dictatorship are still limited, however, and only the most optimistic would claim there has been any more then a movement from a totalitarian to an authoritarian system of rule. The combination of an ancient and dictatorial political heritage and an idealistic Maoist disaster will take some generations to rectify. Meanwhile China was in transition from an idealist to a development state, and from dictatorial to authoritarian rule. Its people could be grateful for such small mercies.

Idealist States

In another twenty states, zealots of one or another variety have seized power and taken states into a blind alley where the pre-conditions for progress have not been nurtured. They are states where the Platonic philosopher in one form or another has become king and sought to refashion a social organism which has taken hundreds of years to create into the image of their ideal type, in which the politics of competing interests are to be eliminated. These are states which have not joined the generalised trajectory of progress and include all the communist states; those former communist states which have not been able to reform; those states run as theocracies in the Middle East like Iran, Saudi Arabia, Iraq and recently Afghanistan; idealistic dictatorships like Libya; and to a large extent communist China.

In this century the communist states have been the most enduring idealist states, though the political 'success' of the communist parties invariably arose from other causes, including sheer military might, overwhelming support for land reform, and nationalist sentiments. The more industrially developed a country was, the less prone were people to communist idealism. In the USA, for example, communists were supported by the joint subsidies of the Soviet Government and the Federal Bureau of Investigation, needless to say for completely opposite reasons.[26] In China and Vietnam the communists achieved mass support on the twin planks of nationalism and land reform, neither of which were Marxist political objectives. In eastern Europe communism achieved power through the military might of the Red Army and with a leadership of intellectuals, many of whom had spent the War in Moscow. In other Western countries the communist party achieved its strongest proportionate influence among that sector of the population where idealism is strongest - in the academy. The role of Marxism in forging national history schools has been notably strong. Nonetheless after 1945 the Soviet Union was militarily the second strongest state in the world and able to deploy considerable resources to recreating its state form elsewhere, if for no other reason than strategic advantage.

The Soviet style idealist state suffered from three fatal deficiencies. In the economic sphere it could not grow beyond the structure of primitive industrialism because its system deliberately prevented individual initiative and so it came to stagnation. In the political sphere it could not achieve legitimacy because its functioning rested on a lie about representation that everyone came to realise. In the social sphere it forbade civil society and sought to replace its private morality by the state. Since the state had no such morality none existed, and when the repressive state apparatus was finally removed in 1991 the old former Soviet society faced great problems in constructing a private economy and society. Where the Soviet style state had been more short lived, like Poland, Hungary or Slovenia, the task proved easier.[27] In fact most of the former Soviet style states were best described as transitional states trying to become one of the advanced capitalist democracies they had once taught their population to despise.

The other idealist states are more difficult to deal with but two examples may suffice. Libya had been an Italian colony and achieved independence after the defeat of Mussolini. At first it was run by a benign old monarch, King Idris. He was overthrown by an ambitious colonel, Gaddafi, in 1969. Gaddafi then led the nationalist charge to throw out Western military installations and then nationalised the American oil companies. This proved to be a wise move. He was then able to press the OPEC states to increase the price of oil and increase their revenues with no apparent disadvantage. In 1973, with the West mostly supporting Israel against the Arab states in the Yom Kippur War, OPEC increased the price of oil by 400% and imposed some embargoes, including on the US military. OPEC states revenues increased rapidly and to substantial levels.

At that point Libya was well in front. Gaddafi then embarked on an adventurous policy of expanding his state of four million people into a major regional power, challenging the Western presence in the region and creating an entire idealist political philosophy he intended to enforce, at least in Libya, by state terror. This was a disaster. He funded a variety of revolutionary groups from Europe, South America and Asia; bankrolled the most extreme PLO factions; and established a bizarre personal dictatorship based on the Third Universal Way. This was all well and good until his support for terrorism against US personnel in Europe led to American retaliatory air strikes in 1986 and the imposition of trade restrictions. Gaddafi retreated into his small idealist state and avoided provocation of his numerous enemies.[28]

The Islamic Republic of Iran presents a different case. During the First World War Iran was the site of intense rivalry between the British, Germans and Russians, a rivalry which was only heightened by the development of its huge oil resources. In 1921 a Cossack commander Colonel Reza Khan staged a coup against the Qajar dynasty and five years later was crowned Reza Shah Pahlavi. During the 1930s he got into conflict with the Muslim clergy and drifted into the German camp. An Anglo-Russian occupation put an end to this during the war and replaced Reza with his son. In the 1960s Iran was introduced to various forms of modernising politics with the Shah proving ascendant with his White Revolution.

The White Revolution was a program of social and industrial modernisation that was opposed by the communists - the Tudeh party - and the Islamic clergy for different idealist reasons. The Shah set up a repressive state apparatus to deal with the communists but by the late 1970s it was the clergy causing him most trouble. In the midst of the increasing repression which followed, the US, then under Jimmy Carter, the Shah's major patron, urged him to leave the country. The intention was to create a more democratic Iran.

In the complex political struggle which followed the Shah's departure and the mob violence which enveloped the country the modernising republicans faced the Islamic clergy. In the only free election to be held the leading democrat republican, Bani-Sadr, scored a resounding victory in 1980. He was then outmanoeuvred by the clergy who set up a Council of Guardians to ensure that Islamic law was maintained. Certainly the emergency created by the Iraqi attack later in 1980 did not help the modernisers' cause and they were defeated. The Islamic republic then set about creating an idealist Islamic state, reducing living standards by about a half in the 1980s, and supporting a wide range of terrorist groups throughout the Middle East.

By the 1990s there were signs of growing opposition to the clergy's rule with a reduced voting support at the 1993 elections and riots in response to increased poverty, unemployment and economic disruption. It might be that Iran would revert to the status of the development state that it had once been. It was indeed clear that there were deep divisions among the Iranian population concerning the proper purpose of their state. This was a debate not confined to Iran.[29]

Primitive States

Primitive states have poorly developed civil societies in which the per capita income is below $US 1,000; life expectancy is often much lower than sixty years; for many accommodation is primitive; water power and sanitation are uncertain; food is sometimes scarce; civil peace periodically breaks down; and illiteracy is widespread. These societies have often been colonised and so are not identical to a pre-progress civilised state because they usually contain a sector of the population and economy which is aware of progress and is often related to the wider civilised world. Colonialism has often created this enclave. What principally characterises these states is an inability to generate the process of progress on a society wide basis. These states are to be found in sub-Saharan Africa, central America and most of South, Central and continental East Asia.

Most of sub-Sahara Africa is in this condition although the status of the Republic of South Africa is yet to be finally resolved. The Europeans penetrated Africa in the sixteenth century and used it as source of slaves for transportation to the Americas particularly for the plantation economies they were creating in the Caribbean, the southern states of the USA and in Brazil and the Spanish colonies. Most of these slaves were bought from other Africans who had practised this evil trade for some time previously, and extensively with the Arab civilisation to the north, where it is still practised in some states including Sudan.

In the late nineteenth century the European states began the colonisation of Africa in a serious and competitive manner. This conquest was undertaken at almost exactly the same time and in a similar fashion to the European conquest of Southeast Asia - that is during the 1870s and by expansion from the already established coastal trading stations. In the case of Africa the resulting colonial division was formally recognised at the Treaty of Berlin in 1884-5, when the neat divisions between colonial territories which presently survive as state boundaries were drawn by European map makers more eager to avoid inter-imperial conflict than to create national entities.

The European colonisers established colonial regimes all over Africa, Italy seizing the final territory, Ethiopia, in 1936. These colonial states were created mostly for the profit of the metropolitan countries and it is not surprising that they assumed a similar form. The tribal boundaries which had previously if loosely defined political authorities on the continent were subordinated to the lines drawn by Colonial Office Bureaucrats five thousand miles away. They then set up local armed forces, with local personnel drawn from particular and often alienated minorities, police forces utilising existing local traditional authorities, where possible, and a tax collecting regime to create the revenue for the provision of infrastructure. They also encouraged private investment, mostly in the primary production sector for profitable commerce.

Not much technology transfer took place into the industrial sector which barely existed. When Africa was emancipated from European rule mostly during the 1960s and 1970s, the major legacy was the state apparatus itself. The strongest component of this political device proved to be the military and a major and recurring feature of independent African states has been the army's seizure of power. This has often been resisted or sponsored by tribal based political organisations which have not been superseded by state based or national organisations. The result has been endemic civil unrest, rebellion, civil war and military despotism throughout the continent.[30]

The major exception to this process has been in the Republic of South Africa where a serious industrialisation program was undertaken. This was made possible by the existence of a settler community, who used state intervention and tariff protection to redeploy the wealth won from rich mineral deposits to create an industrial society and state. This segmented and racist regime, however, could not survive global emancipation and progress. But the multi-racial democracy which followed the successful African revolt, led by Nelson Mandela, inherited considerable internal disorder and it was not clear whether it would survive as a non-primitive state in an otherwise primitive continent.[31]

Most of South Asia can also be placed in this primitive category. If the problem in Africa has been essentially the inability of the continent to create state structures capable of producing the civil order which is an essential pre-condition for progress, in South Asia it has been population growth which has eroded the hard won economic gains. India is the second most populous state in the world after China, and despite the hierarchical social structure which the British inherited from the Mogul empire when they colonised the country during the nineteenth century, the independent Indian state assumed a democratic form in 1947. Except for a three year period of emergency rule in the 1970s it has remained democratic. Indeed, its federal character, written constitution and lively and competitive political party structure, honour the forms of political democracy. But it has poverty on a scale so widespread that its social conditions overwhelm its political achievements.[32]

Dependency theorists have been quick to attribute this condition to the legacy of British rule, where the reverse is clearly the case. The British built an infrastructure and political regime that laid the framework for an Indian economic miracle. It never occurred. In part this was because of the Indian alignment with the Soviet Union and its commitment to many forms of the planned socialist economy which produced advanced, although inefficient, heavy industry sectors alongside traditional peasant agriculture. But in greater measure it has been the inability of Indian regimes to deal with a population growth rate which places permanent and unending pressure on its infrastructure. The one serious attempt to deal with this problem was taken in the 1970s by Indira Ghandi who lost the subsequent election because of it (and was later assassinated for trying to deal with internal ethnic based insurrection). This attempt was never to be repeated.

The other states of the sub-continent have faired little better. Pakistan was created by the Muslim minority who refused to join the secular Indian state and created an independent Islamic republic after extensive religious conflict during which millions of people were killed during the late 1940s. Many more fled to Pakistan as religious refugees. In 1972 following the successful Indian backed insurrection in the eastern part which became Bangla Desh, the state was divided in two. The two successor states have been plagued by excessive population growth, widespread poverty, civil insurrection and periodic military intervention.

The island state of Sri Lanka, then Ceylon, achieved independence as one of the most prosperous countries in Asia with a well developed welfare and educational system, which also provided a surplus of well-educated Trotskyites. It, too, succumbed to the principal problems of the primitive states elsewhere - population growth and civil disorder. Population growth has placed unbearable strains on the country's infrastructure and living standards have declined pretty steadily. In addition, since the early 1970s the Tamil minority in the north of the country has been in a state of permanent insurrection, from time to time supported by India. This has served to ensure that foreign investment has effectively boycotted the country and deprived it of the benefits of economic progress.[33]

The central American states have been plagued with the problem of militarism inherited from the military system of rule imposed by force on the region by Spanish rule. Spain has itself had difficulty in shrugging off this legacy, even with the proximity of democratic Europe to help it. This has compounded the problems involved in creating a viable civil society on a hugely inegalitarian base and a population culturally divided between impoverished Indians and better off immigrant derived communities. In all the Caribbean countries these problems are compounded by the legacy of the slave based economies and societies. As the need for plantation based production of tropical commodities declined and other areas produced them more cheaply, so the worth of the West Indian islands declined and the prosperity of their inhabitants fell. In some, tourism provided alternative employment; in others, financial manipulation and tax havens gave some industry; in others again, like Cuba and more briefly the Dominican Republic and Grenada, a lurch to socialism provided some possible respite with the promise of Soviet subsidies. But in general, poverty was the order of the day, compounded in Haiti by the political legacy of the Tousaint L'Ouverture successful slave revolt of the Napoleonic era.[34]

South America has provided instances of most categories of state all tainted with the intervention of overdeveloped military apparatuses. With the assistance of oil revenue the already advanced state of Venezuela was able during the 1980s to head successfully towards civilised status. Argentina was among the very front rank of societies in the early twentieth century when its mostly Spanish and Italian settlers were able to develop high income levels. This was based on a cattle grazing industry utilising the very fertile alluvial soils deposited by the River Plate. Buenos Aires was one of the largest and richest cities in the world. This laudable social experiment, like so many others on the continent, fell victim to the military when a popular Colonel Perón took state power and allowed consumption by the masses who supported him to exceed the economy's capacity to produce. The country was reduced to ruin and shortly thereafter to a vicious military dictatorship which set about murdering up to 40,000 of its young before overreaching itself and starting a war with Britain. Its defeat in the Falklands War restored democracy to the country which then regained the opportunity to join the civilised world if it could recover its economic dynamism.[35]

Military rule lasted twenty years in the continent's largest state, Brazil, after a coup against an honest and potentially progressive government in 1964. The generals again left their barracks in Peru in 1972 and they made some progressive noises about economic development and land redistribution, but, in the long run, soldiers in power invariably become the enemies of civilisation. In 1973 the Chilean army overthrew the socialist regime of Salvador Allende and instituted a regime of terror supported by the USA until the ending of the Cold War in the late 1980s saw a return to civilian rule and effectively the creation of a development state. In other states of the continent the military also has been regularly in power, including Paraguay, Colombia - where the drug barons have often been richer then the state - and Ecuador. Military intervention in the political process is endemic in poorer countries where the balance of political forces is more heavily weighted to their advantage. In South America, however, the practice has been particularly virulent in societies whose income levels might have eradicated the pattern were it not for the Spanish legacy of a political armed force.

Many of the island states of the Pacific also belong here among the primitive states. While some of the Melanesian states of the region may have sufficient territorial base to establish a proper state apparatus, most of the Polynesian South Pacific Forum member states and their Micronesian neighbours are too small to afford a functioning progressive state. The larger Melanesian territories of Papua New Guinea, Vanuatu and the Solomon Islands have the timber resources and to a degree, mineral deposits to lay the basis for orderly development. They have all been badly managed after periods of colonial rule that ill prepared them for what now appears to have been premature independence. Despite, and indeed perhaps, because of their indigenous democratic traditions, none of them have been able to launch convincing growth patterns. The largest of them, Papua New Guinea, almost continually faces the threat of bankruptcy, a condition only staved off by large amounts of Australian aid. Its most promising sector is mineral extraction and that is resisted by traditional landowners often committed to cargo cults and encouraged by legal firms from the civilised states suing companies for environmental despoliation and legal fees. The Solomon Islands faces bankruptcy also after extensive government corruption.[36]

The smaller countries of Polynesia are dependent on remittances, aid and tourism. The young people in particular of Tonga, the Cook Islands, Tuvalu and Samoa leave these beautiful but nearly barren, volcanic outcrops for employment elsewhere, particularly in New Zealand, Australia and the USA. Their remitted earnings contribute heavily to the national economies. Aid programs from the same three civilised states supplement this income. And more recently they have developed tourist sectors of some significance, although getting an infrastructure built is often difficult. At the centre of Polynesia, Fiji, a further problem survives in the form of a large Indian community introduced as indentured labour for the sugar industry and now comprising over forty per cent of the population. When they acquired political office in 1985 through the ballot box they were overthrown by an exclusively Polynesian Army that then changed the constitution to guarantee Fijian rule. Multicultural theory notwithstanding, civilised states rarely flourish with a seriously pluralistic population. After ten years of emigration by the Indians and higher population growth by the indigenous Fijians formal democracy seemed possible to restore by the late 1990s.

For the foreseeable future the development of the small and micro states of the South Pacific will depend on the good offices of their larger neighbours.[37] They will no doubt be relied on for markets, labour, aid, and tourists. They will also be criticised for their provision and blamed for the condition of these micro societies in one way or another. Such is the nature of supplicant states.

Colonisation and the Creation of States

The state form itself was spread from Europe throughout the world principally by the process of colonisation. Societies which were brought under European control were organised into colonial states, which later became independent and sovereign states. The Europeans had various motives, mostly exploitative, for this process of expansion and conquest, but the effect was to bring the most developed political structure - the state - to regions which had civil societies that had not evolved to an equivalent level. The effect was to leave the administrative shell of the state which was treated for purposes of analysis and by international society as if it were the same kind of state that had evolved in the civilised zone. In fact the primitive state had some quite different characteristics which sprang from its distinct historical origins.

The process of colonisation occurred in four phases. The first phase was dominated by the Spanish and the Portuguese. This started in 1492 and continued into the late seventeenth century. It made the Habsburg dynasty the first serious world power with territories extending from present day California to Tierra del Fuego in the Americas, to the Philippines in East Asia, making the Pacific effectively a Spanish lake for three hundred years, and across the Spanish and Austrian lands of Europe. They ruled this with the best infantry in the world and looted it with the most advanced piece of technology then existing, the Spanish galleon. This device was designed to carry booty and was therefore difficult to manoeuvre, a characteristic which was later to make it vulnerable to British sea power. The Spanish had to share global mastery with the Portuguese under a deal brokered by the Pope in 1494 which gave the Portuguese Brazil (although that boundary was to get very confused) and the African route to Asia. As a small state the Portuguese had only the resources at first to take trading outposts but it ran these through Africa, Goa in India, Timor in the Indies, Malacca in Malaya, Macao in China and as far as Japan. This untidy collection was to be a hard one to unite. Both these early colonial states left their imprint on their colonies, replicating their own government's features of despotism and militarism. Just as the Iberian metropoles themselves were later to be vulnerable to fascism, so their emancipated colonies were to later continually fall under the control of dictatorial rule, at first militarist, then Fascist and in some cases communist.

In the second phase, and during the early industrial revolution which was then starting in eighteenth century Britain, the new commercial powers of Western Europe waged a series of what amounted to world wars to extend Europe's dominion and to carve up the declining Iberian empires. The Iberians were challenged by the British, French and Dutch, who also warred among themselves. Battles were fought on all continents and oceans and reached their apogee during the Napoleonic Wars. The result went to Britain, newly industrialised and not fully committed on the European continent where it pursued balance of power diplomacy. In the process, however, the British had lost much of their North American empire to a newly independent state, the United States of America, although it retained the Canadian colonies including Quebec which it had won from France in the Seven Years War.

The third phase of European colonialism occurred during the nineteenth century when Britain was the effective hegemon in the world market. Its dominance rested on the power of the British navy and the strength of the British economy, reflected in London being the financial capital of the world. During this period and no doubt largely for their own advantage, the British made the first attempt to organise a global order of free trade. From 1815 to the early 1870s London set about opening up the world market to international and particularly British commerce. The basis for a global economy, capital market, and transport and communication system was laid at that time. Its language was English, brought from Denmark by invaders, the *lingua franca* invented in the market places of medieval England, and continually adapted by a creative people to whatever task civil society demanded of it.[38]

The fourth phase was dominated by a number of competing industrial and imperial states challenging the pre-eminence of Britain and carving the world into economic spheres of influence and colonial control. At first the British worried about the rising power of Germany that was united in 1871 under a militaristic regime using its superb army to defeat successively the Danes, Austrians and French. The mark of these Junkers on Germany was to take seventy years and two large wars to drive from Europe, and it was only civilised by two defeats and occupations. The USA also caused concern after it emerged from its Civil War with the world's most powerful military machine, soon to be dismantled but a sign of things to come. At the turn of the century the British capitulated to American power in a series of minor disputes and set the pattern in Anglo-American relations for the foreseeable future.[39]

A strong and centralised Japanese state also emerged after the Meiji restoration in 1868. The Japanese case made it clear that non-European powers could utilise the state to achieve development and progress where the will and social cohesion existed - a fact conveniently ignored by the later supplicant states and their post-colonial apologists. This required the British to shore up some military positions to defend a profitable imperial structure based on India, Australia and Malaya. Singapore was to become its unsuccessful strategic centre. Japan, like Germany was only to be civilised by a major defeat and occupation during which it was socially restructured. After two enormously destructive wars, partly over possession of the world market, the Americans emerged as dominant with a determination to eradicate colonialism and its demise was thereby accelerated.

The colonial states which the European and other imperialists created were replicas of those developed in Europe, without the quality of sovereignty which was added with independence. Local people were organised into territories with bureaucracies, armed forces and police. In other regions, particularly where the local people were not sufficiently developed to provide a profitable work force, the land was cleared and settlers introduced either from the metropolitan country or elsewhere. In Singapore, for example, an almost uninhabited island was settled after 1818 by Chinese migrants who formed an entrepot that was to become the political and military centre for British colonial power in Southeast Asia for one and a half centuries. Some societies which could not organise any means of resistance were eliminated by the ferociously competitive inter-state system.

In Australia the primitive civilisation of the aboriginal people did not enable them to organise effective military resistance and, although some guerrilla wars were fought against the invading British settlers, for the most part the existing civilisation was destroyed.[40] In some areas this was caused by the introduction of disease; in others by the destruction of the physical environment on which Aboriginal culture depended; and in others again by their deliberate destruction by the settlers whose livelihood was threatened by the customs of the indigenous people. In much of South and Central America slave labour was introduced from Africa. In parts of Africa and the Pacific Asian indentured labour was brought in. The precise formula varied from place to place.

Decolonisation and the Creation of Primitive States

These colonial regimes then became independent and sovereign states over a period which spanned nearly two hundred years, in six phases.

The first area to achieve independence after the restructuring imposed during the period of colonisation was the Americas, mostly during the late eighteenth and early nineteenth centuries. The new states were to bear the marks of their colonial rulers. The USA developed an oligarchic democracy with dispersed state power reflecting its origins as religious refugee settlements, ruled by a commercial empire. The new state with its dispersed and separated authorities then united under federal powers and undertook a period of territorial expansion to its manifest destiny of borders on the Pacific Ocean and acquired settled land from the Spanish and French in the South and the Russians in Alaska. During this process of expansion it had to fight another war with the British and British Canada in 1812 and another with Mexico in 1836 to acquire Texas.

Most importantly it had to resolve the issue of slavery. Slavery was incompatible with the new British imperial free trade system and if that were to be successfully transplanted to America, slavery had to be abolished. This in turn required a settlement of the division of power between the central and federated state authorities. President Lincoln waged a determined war, 1860-65, to unite a major commercial civilisation. It was not a war between two democracies, since the Confederacy gave no votes to slaves or women or unpropertied men. The abomination of slavery was also something that united almost all modern philosophers in their hostility. The southern Confederation could lay no claim to being deserving of freedom as a community while it defended slavery. The North may have had purely pragmatic reasons for emancipating slaves, but had to win in order to destroy barbarism and to create a civilised state. It then went about this process by accelerated industrialisation behind the tariff and a massive immigration program.[41]

Shortly after the thirteen colonies had liberated themselves from the British, many of the Spanish American colonies achieved independence. This was during the Napoleonic Wars when Madrid was under French control and at war with the British. The independence movements were often sponsored by the British in pursuit of free trade and led by local military personnel, Simon Bolivar being the most famous. One result has been a powerful role for the local armed forces in the political process, the stunting of commercial civil society and a retarding of the new states' development. Few of them, in fact, have developed to be above the rank of low medium level income today. They rarely created commercial structures with strong civil societies. Argentina was the major exception, populated by Spanish and Italian migrants with a weak Indian and African component, until it too fell victim to the man on horseback, Juan Peron, in the 1940s.

The second phase of colonial emancipation occurred after the First World War and the simultaneous defeat of four major imperial systems: the Hohenzollern/German, Habsburg/Austrian, the Tsarist/Russian and the Ottoman empires. The collapse of the first three at almost the same time in 1917-18 enabled the redrawing of the map of Europe, mostly under the direction of the leading civilised states of the world at the time, the British, French and American, operating through the League of Nations. Liberal theories dominated the thinking of the victorious powers. The result was a redrafting of the map of central Europe along largely national community lines and the creation of a number of newly sovereign states that were national, liberal and democratic. Almost all of them were to fall victim to the subsequent geopolitical conflicts with fascism and communism and not renew their trajectory towards civilised status until the end of the Cold War in 1991. It was a long dark night.[42]

The successor states to the Ottoman Empire fared differently. The objects of various geopolitical deals, done often in secret by the Great Powers with the aims of winning the war and then pursuing interests in the peace, the people of the Middle East mostly achieved the ingenious Mandate, or temporary colony, status under the League.[43] As was the case in much of Africa, the state frontiers of the region were then drawn by the straight edge rulers of European map makers. New dynasties edged into power at Great Power behest, and a new Jewish homeland was initiated. The result was a dozen or so new states achieving independence over the next three decades with authoritarian rule, highly susceptible to the intervention of foreign powers, and also vulnerable to anti-Western religious Islamic revivalism. As oil displaced coal as the world's major source of traded energy and the region emerged as the world's major cheap source of that commodity, Great Power contention in the area became a major source of state structures, and authoritarian client regimes became common.[44]

The third phase of decolonisation occurred in Asia after the independence of British India in 1947 and continued through the 1950s. After the anti-imperial British post-War Labour government, under American pressure, determined to quit a Raj that was increasingly restive and less profitable, the British imperial structure in Asia was progressively dismantled. Everywhere the British deliberately left democratic state structures in place.[45] Much of this democratic structure survived. India remained the world's largest democracy, denied civilised status by its rampant poverty, poverty which anteceded colonialism and which the British could not resolve. Pakistan, a state deliberately created for a religion, was beset by militarism and later partitioned into two unstable, poor and violent societies. Sri Lanka was unable to resolve an ethnic conflict between the Singhalese majority and Tamil minority which produced a civil war and 50,000 deaths. Burma enjoyed a decade of quasi democracy before going down in 1962 to a military dictator, Ne Win, of the kind that had traditionally ruled the country. In Southeast Asia the British were to leave two largely democratic states - Malaysia and Singapore - with overdeveloped security apparatuses that were designed to cope with the 1950s communist revolt. Both showed some promise of joining the civilised world with exceptionally high economic growth rates and tolerable inter-communal relations.[46]

The French and Dutch empires in Asia did not bow out so gracefully. The French fought for their Indo-Chinese empire well beyond the range of both decency and profit. When they faced defeat by communist led insurgents, they handed over to the Americans who most unwisely accepted the challenge. As a result Indo-China has been the location of some of the late twentieth century's most bitter conflicts and primitive idealist regimes.[47] This was then further complicated by the Chinese support of Pol Pot's Cambodia and the Russian support in Vietnam. It will take generations to recover. The Dutch, because smaller and less competent, completely failed to regain the Netherlands East Indies in 1945, after the Japanese had evicted them in 1942. The successor Indonesia regime started as a constitutional democracy but descended into a near bankrupt run by the demagogue Sukarno.[48] As a result Indonesia only later had the possibility of creating a development regime, which it eventually did after the blood bath of 1966. Thus, two otherwise civilised European states behaved contrary to both their interests and progress, a record repeated by others in Africa.

The fourth phase of the transition to independence was centred on Africa and began with Ghana in 1957 and continued until Namibia achieved sovereignty in 1990. The boundaries that had been drawn between the states were mostly European devised - many at the Congress of Berlin in 1884-5 - and often did not reflect any geographic or social features. The European colonialists often departed quickly and left little state infrastructure, like the Belgians from the Congo who nonetheless returned to protect their mining ventures. Much of the colonial economy of Africa had been built on resource extraction and had rarely laid the basis for modern economic development.

The state forms after independence often started democratic but quickly succumbed to local tribal divisions and conflicts or the superior power of the armed forces, the most developed component of the colonial and post-colonial state apparatuses. In some of the states bitter anti-colonial wars were fought resulting in near ruinous destruction, notably against the stubbornly imperial Portuguese in Angola, Mozambique and Guinea-Bissau. Almost everywhere the maintenance of civil society against corrupt and dictatorial regimes, some as in Zambia, Tanzania and Ethiopia, established in the name of African Socialism, and internal war, became a major problem. In much of Africa the functioning of the state outside its repressive apparatus often proved inadequate.[49]

The combined result of these afflictions was a negative economic growth rate and widespread poverty and barbarism throughout the continent. The only economies with a substantial productive base were in Zimbabwe and South Africa where race relations made progress problematic. In South Africa the White population adopted the classical policy of industrialisation, tariffs and state direction, variants of which had been successfully used in Germany, the US and Australia. They had, however, done so by taking advantage of African cheap labour and then trying to create a state which accommodated the fascist and racist inclinations of the Whites and the demands for self-determination by the African masses.[50] The task proved beyond them and in 1995 the state moved to majoritarian rule in a circumstance where civil society was fractured, incoherent and extremely violent. The outcome was not possible to foresee.

Equally, Kenya under African rule struggled to ensure that the agricultural base established with European capital survived African political power. The Portuguese settlers left Mozambique and Angola to their murderous civil wars in the mid-1970s. West Africa experienced civil wars, coups and tribal based conflicts with a regularity that eventually took them off the front pages. The central African states of Rwanda, Burundi and Zaire imploded into anarchy and genocide in the mid-1990s. For this primitive circumstance various explanations have been offered: the backwardness of traditional African society; the rapacity of European colonial rule; exploitation by international investors; the triumph of tribalism and the military over a national civil society; and the incompetence of Africa's politicians. All have no doubt played their part.

In the fifth phase of decolonisation the smaller states of particularly the South Pacific became independent. The process started in the 1960s and largely came to a conclusion in the mid 1990s, although some colonial territories of France (New Caledonia, Tahiti), New Zealand (Cook Islands), and the US (Samoa) remained. These states were sparsely populated and poorly resourced and would have trouble creating complete state apparatuses, leave alone a developed civil society. At the same time Britain handed Hong Kong back to China (1997) as would Portugal with Macao (1999). This left France with small colonial possessions which it heavily subsidised financially, principally in order to retain a site in French Polynesia for testing its nuclear weapons and retain the facade of being a world power.[51]

In these former colonial territories the political and intellectual elites debated the forms their states should take during and after the transition to independence. These debates and the social environment in which they were undertaken were wholly different from those experienced by the civilised states of Europe and any examination of them must start with that consideration. They were influenced by a combination of local traditions that survived colonisation, Western ideas and institutions that were imported during colonisation, ideologies which emphasised the exploitative nature of their relationship with the West and the major idealist thought system of the day, communism.

The last great European centred colonial empire was also the most idealist, that of the Soviet Union. By the 1980s and as a result of almost six decades of remorseless expansion the Soviet empire comprised three layers. The outer layer was those states it had brought under its informal influence in the regions outside Europe, which emulated much of its rhetoric and internal structure and which it heavily subsidised. These included Cuba; the three states of Indo-China under Vietnamese dominance; some African states like Angola, Mozambique, and Ethiopia; some states in the Middle East like Syria and Yemen; and a number of other countries less closely aligned with Moscow like India. The second layer was the People's Democracies of eastern Europe that had puppet regimes imposed on them by Moscow in the 1940s and were as a result of geographic contiguity under effective Russian control. The third layer consisted of those nations which had been annexed to the Soviet state either by its Tsarist predecessors or by the Soviets themselves and included the three Baltic peoples, the countries of the Caucasus, like Georgia, and the mostly Muslim states of central Asia, like Tajikstan, Kazakhstan and Uzbekistan.

In the mid-1980s the new Soviet leadership of Mikhail Gorbachev started to discard these possessions as a result of the cost of its imperial overextention. During a process which lasted six years the Soviet imperium was dissolved, leaving nearly twenty successor states having to cope with readjustment from membership of an idealist and repressive imperial structure to membership of the wider global community.[52] Communism had posed the most serious challenge to progress in the modern era and, unlike fascism which was defeated by war, was destroyed by its own inability to function as a real social system.

Primitive states cannot be analysed nor judged by the same criteria as civilised states. They are mostly the products of the imposition of an advanced political form, the sovereign state, on poorly developed civil societies. Their complaints that the standards created by the Western canon of intellectual thought is imposed on their behaviour unfairly is often well made. They are more primitive organisms for whom lesser and more primitive standards may well be more appropriate.

Notes

1. Mark Greengrass, ed., *Conquest and Coalescence: the Shaping of the State in Early Modern Europe*, London, E. Arnold, 1991; and Richard Bonney, *The Early Dynastic States, 1494-1660*, Oxford, Oxford University Press, 1991.
2. David Downing, *An Atlas of Territorial and Border Disputes*, London, New English Library, 1980; Naomi Chazan, ed., *Irredentism and International Politics*, Boulder, Lynne Riemer Publishers, 1991.
3. Jung Min Choi, Karen A. Callaghan and John W. Murphy, *The Politics of Culture: Race, Violence and Democracy*, Westport, Praeger, 1995.
4. Ernst Gellner, *Nations and Nationalism*, Oxford, Blackwell, 1983.
5. See David Hume, 'Of National Characters' in *Essays: Moral, Political and Literary*, Indianapolis, Liberty, 1985; Immanuel Kant *Toward an Anthropology from a Pragmatic Point of View*; G.W. F. Hegel *Philosophy of Spirit*, part 3 of the *Encyclopaedia of the Philosophical Sciences*.

6. Harold Lasswell, *Politics: Who Gets What, When, How*, New York, Meridian, 1958.
7. Pierre Jalle, *The Pillage of the Third World*, trans. Mary Klopper, New York, Monthly Review Press, 1968.
8. L.S. Stavrianos, *Global Rift: The Third World Comes of Age*, New York, Morrow, 1981.
9. Bob Catley, "Economic Development and Political Democracy: the Case of Southeast Asia", *Current Affairs Bulletin*, Sydney, Feb-March 1996.
10. B. M. Siegan, *Drafting a Constitution for a Nation or Republic Emerging into Freedom*, Fairfax, George Mason University Press, 1994.
11. David P. Conract, et al, eds., *Germany's New Politics: Parties and Issues in the 1990s*, Providence, Berghahn Books, 1995.
12. Junichiro Wada, *The Japanese Election System: Three Analytical Perspectives*, New York, Routledge, 1996; and Purnendra Jain, "The 1996 Japanese elections", *Current Affairs Bulletin*, Dec 1996-Jan 1997.
13. Eva Etzioni-Halevy, *Bureaucracy and Democracy: A Political Dilemma*, London, Routledge, 1983; and David Beetham, *Bureaucracy*, Milton Keynes, Open University Press, 1987.
14. Joyce Marlow, *The Peterloo Massacre*, London, Rapp and Whiting, 1969.
15. Paul Arthur and Keith Jeffery, *Northern Ireland Since 1968*, 2nd ed, Cambridge, Blackwell, 1996.
16. Bob Woodward and Carl Bernstein, *All the President's Men*, [1974] New York, Simon and Schuster, 1994.
17. J. A. G. Roberts, *A History of China*, Gloucester, Alan Sutton, 1996; and George Nye Steiger, *China and the Occident: the Origin and Development of the Boxer Movement*, New York, Russell and Russell, 1966.
18. Jon Halliday, *A Political History of Japanese Capitalism*, New York, Pantheon Books, 1975.
19. Sydney Giffard, *Japan Among the Great Powers*, New Haven, Yale University Press, 1994.
20. Chalmers Johnson, *MITI and the Japanese Economic Miracle: the*

Growth of Industrial Policy, 1925-1975, Stanford, Stanford University Press, 1982, provides a strong argument for this case.
21. Miyohei Shinohara, *Industrial Growth, Trade and Dynamic Patterns in the Japanese Economy*, Tokyo, University of Tokyo Press, 1982; and Walter Hatch and Kozo Yamamura, *Asia in Japan's Embrace: Building A Regional Production Alliance*, Cambridge, Cambridge University Press, 1996.
22. For an illuminating report on the Japanese prison system see 'Hard Time', *Time Magazine*, 28 Oct 1996.
23. Mark Roberts, *The Fall of Hong Kong: China's Triumph and Britain's Betrayal*, New York, Wiley, 1994.
24. David Chandler, *Brother Number One: A Political Biography of Pol Pot*, St Leonards, Allen and Unwin, 1993.
25. Stuart Harris and Gary Klintworth, eds., *China As A Great Power, Myths Realities and Challenges in the Asia-Pacific Region*, Melbourne, Longman, 1995.
26. Harvey Klerhs, et al, *The Secret World of American Communism*, New Haven, Yale University Press, 1995.
27. John R. Robbins, ed., *Slovenia*, publication forthcoming, especially the introduction; and John R. Robbins, 'The Formation of New States: The Case of Slovenia', *Current Affairs Bulletin*, Aug/Sept 1996.
28. Brian L. Davis, *Qaddafi, Terrorism and the Origins of the US Attack on Libya*, New York, Praeger, 1990.
29. Ahmed Hashim, *The Crisis of the Iranian State: Domestic, Foriein and Security Policies in Post-Khomeini Iran*, Adelphi Paper, 296, Oxford, IISS/OUP 1995.
30. Rudolph von Albertini, *European Colonial Rule, 1880-1940: the Impact of the West in India, Southeast Asia and Africa*, trans John Williamson, Oxford, Clio Press, 1982; Walter Rodney, *How Europe Underdeveloped Africa*; and Julius Ihonvbere, 'Democratic Transitions in Africa', *Current Affairs Bulletin*, Oct-Nov 1996.
31. Allister Sparks, *Tomorrow is Another Country: The Inside Story of South Africa's Negotiated Revolution*, London, Mandarin Press, 1995.
32. Dietmar Rothermund, *The Indian Economy Under British Rule and*

Other Essays, New Delhi, Mahanbar, 1983.
33. Douglas Allen, ed., *Religion and Political Conflict in South Asia: India, Pakistan and Sri Lanka*, Westport, Greenwood, 1992; and Mushiral Hazan, ed., *India's Partition: Process, Strategy and Mobilisation*, New Delhi, Oxford University Press, 1993.
34. C. L. R. James, *The Black Jacobins: Toussaint L'Ouverture and the San Domingo Revolution*, 2nd ed, New York, Vintage Books, 1963.
35. David Rocke, ed., *Argentine in the Twentieth Century*, London, Duckworth, 1975; and Lawrence Freedman, *Signals of War: the Falklands Conflict of 1982*, Princeton, Princeton University Press, 1991.
36. Robert F. McKillop, *New Directions in Australian Aid: the South Pacific Perspective*, Canberra, ANU, 1992.
37. Jeremy Carew-Reid, *Environment, Aid and Regionalism in the South Pacific*, Canberra, ANU, 1989.
38. Albert Imlah, *Economic Elements in the Pax Britannica: Studies in British Foreign Trade in the Late Nineteenth Century*, 2nd ed., New York, Russell and Russell, 1969.
39. Alexander E. Campbell, *Great Britain and the United States, 1895-1903*, London, Longmans, 1960.
40. Charles D. Rowley, *The Destruction of Aboriginal Society*, Ringwood, Vic., Penguin, 1972; and Robert Murray, 'What Really Happened to the Kooris?', *Quadrant*, November 1996.
41. Elbert B. Smith, *The Death of Slavery: The United States 1837-65*, Chicago, University of Chicago Press, 1967.
42. Ivan T. Berend, *Central and Eastern Europe, 1944-1993: Detour From the Periphery to the Periphery*, Cambridge, Cambridge University Press, 1995.
43. Francis P. Walters, *A History of the League of Nations.*, London, Oxford University Press, 1952, 2 Vols.
44. Fred Halliday, *Arabia Without Sultans*, Penguin, 1979 and, Elie Kedourie, *Arabic Political Memoirs and Other Essays*, London, Cass, 1974.
45. Seymour M. Lipset and Reinhard Bendix, eds., *Class, Status and Power: social stratification in comparative perspective*, New York, Free Press, 1966.

46. Lennox Mills, *British Rule in East Asia: A Study of contemporary government and economic Development in British Malaya and Hong Kong*, New York, Russell and Russell, 1970; Harold Crouch, *Govenment and Society in Malaysia*, St. Leonards, N.S.W., Allen & Unwin, 1996.
47. Philip B. Davidson, *Vietnam at War: The History, 1946-75*, Navato, Presidio Press, 1988; Gabriel Kolko, *Anatomy of A War: Vietnam, the United States, and the modern historical experience*, New York, Pantheon Books, 1985; and 'Winning the War and Losing the Peace', *Journal of Contemporary Asia*, 1994; and Chandler, *Brother Number One, op. cit.*
48. Colin Brown and Robert B. Cribb, *Modern Indonesia: a history since 1945*, London, Longman, 1995.
49. William H. Friedland and Carl G. Rosberg, eds., *African Socialism*, Stanford, Calif., Stanford University Press for Hoover Institution on War, Revolution, and Peace, 1964; Henry Bernstein and Bonnick Campbell, eds., *Contradictions in Accumulation in Africa*, Beverly Hills, Sage, 1985.
50. Bernard Makhosezwe Magubane, *The Political Economy of Race and Class in South Africa*, New York, Monthly Review Press, 1979.
51. Ramesh Thakur, *The Last Bang Before A Total Ban, French Nuclear Testing In the Pacific*, Canberra, Peace Research Centre, 1995.
52. Adam Zwass, *From Failed Communism to Underdeveloped Capitalism: The Transformation of Eastern Europe, The Post-Soviet Union and China*, Armonk, M. E. Sharpe, 1995.

2 Social Evolution and the Modern State

> A righteous man regardeth the life of his beast
>
> *Proverbs*, 12, 10

In the last chapter we looked at the kinds of states which confront us today. People who participate in rulership work with a combination of ideas, whether traditional or radical, realist or idealist, good (i.e. ideas which, in the long term, are beneficial to the majority of a society) or bad. States are also enmeshed within the social conditions of their time and the problems those conditions create. The pressures created by the mode of social organisation do not vanish simply because those holding state power want to view the world a certain way. Moreover, as the examples of communism and fascism demonstrated, what on the surface appear to be ideologically disparate orders may be essentially similar responses to social crises. In this work we have provided a simple, yet useful, bi-polar model -- realist and idealist -- to designate (a) those responses to reality which factor in the, often, grim, but enduring obstacles to social harmony (i.e. realist responses) and (b) appeals (whether tacit or overt) to moral character or principles in order to improve social conditions (i.e. idealist responses).

Later we shall observe idealist and realist responses to the social events which have informed key theoretical understandings of the evolution of the state. Here we shall focus upon the major kinds of societies which underpin states: they are agricultural, industrial, service-based and information-based societies. Moreover, the analysis that follows is based upon the fact that these modes of social organisation and reproduction have emerged sequentially, that is to say, these modes of social organisation are indicative of the evolution of social organisation. Further, we then consider the relationship between political organisation and social organisation.

The social base of a society is the recurrent raw reality which rebounds upon our understandings when it is misconstrued. To be sure, our ideas are etched into every action we undertake, but because there is a hiatus between what we want and what there is, or what we think there is and what makes us rethink our reality, it is methodologically valuable to distinguish between the social base and the ideas which people deploy to grapple with the problems it throws up. We do not thereby wish to make dogmatic metaphysical pronouncements, as Marx and Engels were prone to do when they transformed a valuable historico-sociological technique into a dogmatic attack upon political economists, but simply to note the correlations between social bases and political forms.

Agriculture

In agricultural societies the city politically dominates the country to the exclusion of a generalised civilisation. This was common in sixteenth century Europe, contemporary Africa and parts of Asia including, for example, Burma and China. In these societies the majority of the population live in the countryside, agriculture is the principal occupation, communications and transportation are localised. In agricultural societies the power of the state tends to be the preserve of a land owning elite which uses the armed force of the state for internal control and, where possible, external expansion. It uses a hierarchical ideology, often religious and submissive to authority in character, to enforce this order. A despotic and individual sovereign authority is a common feature of such states as benevolent despot, oriental despot or cult of personality.

A common feature of such societies is the attempt to reinforce state and elite authority by use of religious doctrine. In South Asia this often took the form of Buddhism with its emphasis on spiritual virtues, poverty and the process of reincarnation. In China the dominant code was Confucianism although this did not wholly prevent the outbreak of peasant insurrections which were a regular feature of imperial Chinese history. In the Kampuchea of the Khmer Rouge and Maoist China communism was used in effect for the same purpose of disciplining the peasantry. The medieval church did its best to construct such a system of social control based on the local church, land ownership, the confession and the political passivity of Christ. But the Church also had other facets to its faith which proved to be more dangerous, including concepts of spiritual equality, redemption and a philosophy of activism where God's commands were superior to political commands.

At the onset of the modern age in Europe almost all the major states were agricultural, except for some of the remaining city states of Italy, notably Venice which may lay claim to being the first capitalist society. Perhaps not surprisingly the early theorists of the state, including Niccolò Machiavelli, were from the peninsula. These city states provided early examples of the behaviour of their larger nation state successors in the form of what we now know as Realpolitik, *raison d'état* or determined pursuit of self interest. Their larger successors including Spain, Portugal, England, France, Austria, the Netherlands and, later again, Prussia and Russia, were not just trading cities but extensive agricultural based civilisations. They developed a more extensive system of bureaucracy, tax collection and technological innovation.[1]

What principally distinguished them from the contemporary agricultural state was that they were among the more advanced societies in the world at the time, with the partial exception of China until the late eighteenth century. As a result, the internal changes that began at the end of the Middle Ages to create the idea and social fact of social progress took people into uncharted waters. The internal changes were mostly generated by civil society; in agricultural production including rotation farming and the use of root crops; improvements in transportation systems by land and particularly sea; and the adoption of new military technologies starting with the crossbow and continuing into gunpowder, which made the feudal order less readily enforceable. The baronial fortress could no longer withstand the monarch's gun train. With these changes local fortifications and political power centres gave way to central state authority, wider national economies replaced regional ones and production diversified.

This is sometimes called the transition to the absolutist state. What is meant here is that the feudal hierarchy of Christendom, which had never in any case been as centrally authoritarian as either the Roman or the Chinese imperial systems, progressively broke up into nation states. In turn each of these states established a centralised authority which prevailed over the lesser authorities of both the secular and spiritual world. This first started in western Europe where a number of fortuitous circumstances including geography allowed England to defy imperial and papal authority. Henry VIII defied the Pope, seized church lands and distributed them to his own loyalists, and created a national faith or ideology in the form of the Anglican Church. This rebellion then spread throughout Europe where Martin Luther had already given it a life of its own. In that process new political alliances and allegiances could be and were formed and philosophers started to speculate more clearly about the possibilities of free societies because they could see them coming into existence as they wrote.

During the sixteenth and seventeenth centuries western Europe urbanised and the cities became centres of handicraft production, trade and commercial capital. These commercial capitalists were to provide much of the finance for what were then termed the 'voyages of discovery'. Although Italian explorers were often at the fore after the remarkable voyage of Marco Polo to China, they were invariably financed by the wealthy monarchs of the West as was the case with Christopher Columbus and Cabot. The result was the creation of an embryonic Europe wide system of trade and production. The political authority which emerged from it was the sovereign state.

The first assertions of sovereignty were made by monarchs claiming the divine right of kings, although some of these were of course like England's Elizabeth I, queens. As they acquired the physical and military means to assert their authority against the dictates of a centralised Christendom - and Richelieu invoked *raison d'état* to justify his alliance with the Turkish heathen - so they asserted their sovereign political and religious power, if necessary by the creation of national churches as in England and Sweden and later even Catholic France. The internal structure of these societies became in the process *more* centralised. Their external behaviour became even less constrained. The principal thesis of Machiavelli was that *The Prince*, the state, should pursue its own sovereign interest. If it did not the implication was always that he was doing too little for the interests of his state and subjects. The major assertion of contemporary political philosophy was the divine right of the sovereign monarch who derived authority from God.

This situation did not long survive. In the first place people began to challenge what amounted to a claim for absolute political power by the monarchs and this first occurred in a serious way in England. While the opposing forces that fought the English civil war were too complex to be readily grouped into easy social categories the point may be made that as England urbanised so the people that gathered into these new towns were not so easily won to the idea of absolute monarchy. The ideas and debates generated by this novel intellectual phenomenon spread quickly to the other urbanising countries of Europe and helped produce during the eighteenth century what we now know as the Enlightenment. Today it is fashionable in the Western academy to describe the ideals of the Enlightenment as discredited because they did not, for example, deal with the colonial condition, gender inequality or gay rights. This is anachronism taken to the level of depicting Shakespeare as a dead white male and minor television script writer.

The Enlightenment thinkers were trying to deal with two of the major political issues of the day which concerned the rising urban intelligentsia: How to establish a just but orderly society as against that of the *ancien régime*? And how to establish peace between continually warring sovereign states without destroying their liberty? These questions are as important today as are indeed some of the answers they provided. These answers were to contribute to the next cataclysm for the *ancien régime* as Paris, the capital of Europe's *salons*, fell to the enemies of absolute monarchy in 1789. They then under the Napoleonic dictatorship spread the destruction of divine right throughout the continent. This process was to involve widespread warfare and death. These were both mightily assisted by the industrial revolution then underway in Britain and spreading into Europe.

During the seventeenth century England created a commercial civil society in form like that of Venice but on a far greater scale and with a greater impact in the affairs of Europe through the New Model Army of Cromwell and the balance of power strategy of William of Orange. In the eighteenth century the United Kingdom commenced the process of industrialisation for the first time in human history. The dominant current of interpretation of this profound social and economic transformation in recent times has been from the Left, and as a result many of its consequences have been decried. But this progress laid the basis for a modern state with a system of representative government encompassing a broad franchise and made England the most powerful country in the world with one of its highest living standards. That is why, as we will see, Montesquieu used England as his model for what France should be.

The agricultural societies outside Europe derived both disadvantages and benefits from this process in Europe. On the one hand it is true that the centralised agricultural states of Europe did engage in external conquests and that while their technological level was little different to that of China it was greatly superior to that of the societies of the Atlantic littoral which they first encountered in the sixteenth century. The result was a wave of invasion, conquest, plunder, violent deaths and, in some cases of the Caribbean islands, genocide. On the other hand the societies of Europe were creating an advanced civilisation from which these societies could aspire to benefit.[2]

Contemporary agricultural states are not like those of Western Europe which largely ceased to exist in the nineteenth century when they transformed into industrial states. While a simple reading of the social, economic and demographic figures for Burma, to take an example, might give the impression that it resembles Britain in the late eighteenth century, this would be an entirely unwarranted conclusion to draw in the political and developmental sense. On the one hand the effects of the civilised world have spread to Burma as a concrete reality, whereas in the British case they could only exist in the eye of an Enlightenment philosopher. This has mobilised the people of

Burma behind a liberal organisation, the National League for Democracy, and the demand for a civilised state. On the other hand, the military dictatorship, SLORC, has available all the power of a modern state, military, political and ideological, to control a dispersed population of mostly rice farmers. True, there is now more pressure from the international community, particularly the USA, to comply with the norms of contemporary civilisation, but there remain many primitive states, like China, ready to assist in their avoidance.[3]

If the evolutionary process of Europe is to be taken seriously as a model for contemporary primitive and development states, and there are sound, though not overwhelming arguments for so doing, then it should be clearly stated. The civilised European states went through a long and often painful development trajectory which involved national unification under absolutism (dictatorship), civil war, military rule, intense and violent political struggle and a series of inter-state wars before arriving at the modern state form. During that time they also went through an intense social upheaval which laid the basis for the industrial revolution. To expect the contemporary agricultural and primitive states to make this transition quickly may be unreasonable. To expect them to do so painlessly is probably beyond the question. That some of them are actually doing so at all is a miracle.

Industry

The sources of the political processes which were to destroy the absolutist state were to be found in the profound social transformation then occurring in the most civilised states of Europe, particularly Britain but later France and the Netherlands. During the eighteenth century these changes accelerated. Agriculture became more productive and people left for the towns. In the urban areas the commercial financiers facilitated the creation of more concentrated factory industry and more widespread division of labour. Technological innovations made industry more productive and the country more prosperous. The application of new energy sources like the steam engine accelerated these developments by the end of the century and the new textile and steel industries mushroomed in the northern parts of the United Kingdom. Improvements in health technology led to rapid population growth and a larger market, which in turn encouraged the division of labour and mass production. It is true that the state often assisted these processes by, for example, delivering the Enclosure Acts to drive people off the land. But the changes were initiated and driven by civil society.[4]

As people left the traditional economy and life forms of the countryside for the new urban centres and occupations, so their energies were mobilised. They gathered together more often and read the new media and ideas. Novels and embryonic newspapers began to appear with Fielding, Richardson and the *Spectator*. These new urban classes demanded more say in the running of the state just as they acquired more power in the running of the economy and civil society. In France, which had become the most centralised and richest of the European states, the upheaval concentrated, like all of France, in Paris. In Britain, lacking a standing army, power was more diffused throughout the country and the political transformation took place in a more measured fashion. But the consequences in both countries, and eventually elsewhere throughout Western Europe and many of the West European settlements outside Europe, was the creation of representative and then democratic states.

For every country that undertook an industrial revolution under the direction of a democratic state, and these are mostly English speaking, there are many more that did so under dictatorial rule. During the height of the social upheaval of the industrial revolution no more then five per cent of the British population had the franchise. The US state was inundated with powerless immigrant workers and newly emancipated slaves during the equivalent period in the late nineteenth century. The slightly more democratic French lurched from regime to regime in 1815, 1830, 1848, and 1871. The only industrial revolution in Africa was successfully supervised by a near fascist Afrikaner racist regime after 1948. Perhaps only the Antipodean and Canadian British colonies and Israel (also a former British colony) can claim an historical congruence of industrialisation and democracy.

The more common experience of industrialising societies is the creation of a modern repressive state apparatus in a military, fascist or communist form. This may reflect the homogenisation of the urban work force and population that early industrialisation and the creation of proletarian suburbs brings. It may also reflect the need for the imposition of greater social and industrial discipline required by the age of the domination of the machine. It could also be a reflection of the greater likelihood of social disharmony and revolt as people are pushed off the land and into industrial cities in which their living conditions may be, at first anyway, substantially worsened. The same process is now being attempted in China where it is estimated that a hundred million peasants are on the move from a newly privatised agriculture to cities just undertaking industrialisation.[5]

In much of Europe the later industrialising countries did so under military regimes. Germany was united by force of arms under Prussia's Bismarck with three wars against Denmark, Austria and France, and industrialisation continued under a state run by a military caste of Junkers from the less developed east. Some of the success of German industry at the time was attributed to its military style discipline and the close connection between the often aristocratic family owned heavy industries and their equivalents in the state machine who used tariff protection, government contracts and training programs to assist industrial development. The state was also used to oppose the organisation of labour against capital and more particularly to fight the popular German Social Democratic Party, then the most powerful in Europe. This contrasted with the more *laissez faire* British and US practices, although they were of course no strangers to union busting. The Habsburg's Austro-Hungarian Empire was similarly militarist until its destruction.[6]

Following the defeat of the Central Powers in 1918 and the brief post-war period of democracy, almost the whole of central Europe, an industrialising zone, became fascist. Italy started the process in 1922 and excused itself for making the trains run on time, an industrial boast if ever there was one. The German people voted the Nazis into power in 1933 and as the main beneficiaries of Hitler's New Order in Europe continued to support them until the war was clearly lost. Even their genocidal policies were pursued with industrial efficiency and organisation. The smaller powers of central Europe joined this sociological phenomenon under a band of unlikely people's leaders (or Führers) that included Admirals, Princes, Cavalry officers and socialist politicians. These states had in common the desire for, although not necessarily the achievement of industrial and national efficiency. The habit spread to the retarded developers on the Iberian peninsula in the 1930s - and to some of their former colonies notably Argentina - but they had the uncommon good sense not to join the war, except against the Soviet Union. Hence Franco's regime lasted until the death of *Hitler's Child* in the early 1970s

The Soviet regime resembled that of the fascists in many important respects, and indeed both Mussolini and the Chinese nationalists, the Kuo Ming Tan (KMT) utilised Leninist party organisation methods. The Soviets used the state to construct a heavy industrial base in emulation of what they thought were capitalist methods of mobilising labour into the industrialising cities.[7] They also set up state farms which they believed, quite wrongly, would be more efficient than the private but large farms beginning to dominate capitalist agriculture. And the methods of social control utilised during this extremely disruptive process were the same as elsewhere in the one party state: bring unions under state control; punish disruptive and unproductive workers; collectivise the life forms of the proletariat; exploit it mightily; and propagate the ideology and propaganda of conformism, or 'socialist realism'. The similarity between the art forms of the Stalin and Hitler regimes is quite striking and reflects the same purpose; the attempt to subordinate civil society to the state. The Soviets were somewhat more successful. Their intellectual position that all art is political and serves a particular ideology coincides of course with the anti-aesthetic position of the later post-modernists.

Most of the industrialising countries of the development states have used similar repressive or collectivist regimes during the early phases of industrialisation. As in the case of the civilised states who have industrialised before them the development states use authoritarian regimes for much the same purposes, often untroubled at first by enlightened mores. Nonetheless as development proceeds the same political issues are often generated. The types of regimes experienced are often the same as in Europe although they have also tapped into local traditions.

The most common regime type for industrialising states remains military control. During the early part of the twentieth century the Japanese military attained substantial political power and retained it, together with the frequent veto of assassinating politicians, until 1945. This despite the fact that Japan was formally a constitutional imperial system like Britain. The South Korean state was effectively a military dictatorship under Syngman Rhee, General Park and General Chun throughout almost the entire industrialisation process from 1953 until the late 1980s. During that time labour repression was particularly severe as the state tried successfully to attract foreign capital from civilised states with its offers of cheap labour and low taxes. The Republic of China on Taiwan adopted a similar strategy under the control of the KMT, which was after all a Leninist organisation and ruled without the need for elections since many of its constituents on the mainland were under the control of the 'communist bandits'. In both these cases the state was also able to use the successful propaganda ploy that industrial and political discipline was necessary in the face of communist threats from vile regimes that claimed their territory - both true enough claims.

Other states in East Asia have also been able to use the military form of government to good development effect. In the case of Indonesia the early years of independence were marked by a chaotic and increasingly radical form of democratic government that presided over the decline of the economy. During the early 1960s this was replaced by an even more rhetorically radical government under President Sukarno that did even more damage to economic progress. Following an abortive coup in September 1965, a civil conflict broke out in 1965-6 that was won by the military after about a million communists and their sympathisers had been killed. For the next thirty years the country was run by the New Order regime under President (General) Suharto. This produced a compound growth rate over six per cent annually, a stabilised and controlled electoral system, the army and its political wing GOLKAR at the core of the state, and a successful nation building policy that kept a nation of 13,000 islands and 300 languages together quite effectively. By the mid-1990s the country had joined the low-medium income countries at about $US1,000 per capita annually.[8]

Other development states have also taken the military option with some success. Thailand has had an influential military apparatus since the revolution of 1933, although it retained the monarchy. The King who assumed the throne in 1946 retained it for nearly fifty years and through his personal popularity gave a regime dominated by generals some legitimization. By clever diplomacy with the British and French and then shifting sides during the Pacific War Thailand avoided both colonisation and defeat. It then went with the US in the Cold War and has made some accommodation with the rising power of China since. After the economic stimulation of the Vietnam War ended, the Thais started industrialisation and since the 1980s have been growing at around eight per cent annually while slowing population growth to almost replacement rates. It is now a clear middle income country on around $3,000 per capita annually. In 1992 the military was removed from power following mass demonstrations and the personal intervention of the King.[9]

The capacity of the military to play a role in the long process of national development towards a civilised state has already been described in Europe, notably in the case of Britain (Cromwell), France (Napoleon) and Germany (Bismarck), although the importance of the domestic social control regimes established during these periods are often overlooked. These men are now national heroes. The SLORC regime in Burma has used the years since its assumption of power in 1988 to establish national order by repressing the popular civilian opposition, the NLD led by Nobel Prize winner Aung San Suu Kyi, defeating the twenty or so regional insurgencies, and trying to set up an Indonesian-style political system which it can dominate and use to achieve similar international acceptance. It is simultaneously trying to get the stagnant economy to grow by opening it to the international economy and deregulating it internally, in the hope of generating thereby some popular support. So far it is having less success in these spheres than in establishing national unity. It is an aspiring military development state, but presently primitive.[10]

Fascist regimes have been unusual outside Europe. The only ones that might be truly placed in that category were the Peronist regime in Argentina in the late 1940s and the Paraguayan Stroessner regime. In fact, however, Peronism had a populist character that was so strong among the poor that by ignoring industrial development it actually contributed to the ruination of the economy. The KMT was often accused of this practice but is more properly seen as a militarist regime. The Marcos regime in the Philippines had some of the features of fascism but did not get its party machine for mass mobilisation to any thing like the levels of the European fascists and, in any case, it looted the economy rather than vitalised it. The fascist regime probably belongs to a particular conjuncture of international and economic circumstances in 1930s Europe, when states wanted to mobilise the masses for war and contain them away from the communists. As a style of state its success was severely constrained by its total defeat by the civilised/communist coalition.[11]

Communism has been much more popular as a state form in industrialising regimes in East Asia, and elsewhere for that matter. The most important examples of communist regimes outside the Soviet Union and its immediate European satellites have been North Korea, Vietnam, Cuba and China. The case of Cambodia, where industrialisation was not the issue, is best considered as separate form of an idealist state. The African states like Ethiopia, Mozambique, Angola and Congo (Brazzaville) have only been communist in name, and the Sandinistas in Nicaragua were a temporary aberration. As a result of its alignment with the Soviet Union India had some of the features of a communist economy but its poverty so overwhelms its other features as to make consideration of its primitive nature the dominant issue.

The small communist states pursuing industrialisation have all been considerable failures that might best be considered alongside the African experience were there not such important strategic issues to consider. Never discount the importance of luck in the political process. The founding dictator of North Korea, Kim Il Sung, certainly possessed it in abundance.[12] Having been installed by the Soviet pack train in 1945 and then being armed by them, he first killed all his rivals to power. He then attacked the state of South Korea in 1950 and survived despite massive destruction thanks to the intervention of the Chinese army which suffered two million dead in the process. He was then revived after the 1953 truce by Chinese and Soviet aid. When the two communist giants split he declared his neutrality and got substantial aid from neither. By the 1970s the state was a repressive basket case whose diplomats turned to drug running to raise funds and whose agents blew up a South Korean ministerial delegation while visiting Burma. By the time of his death in 1994, and the cautious succession of his son, Kim's fiefdom was poor and starving. It was then revived by a huge US bribe not to produce nuclear weapons. It remained one of the poorest and most isolated states in the world.

The Cuban communist state has been similarly dominated by one family, Fidel Castro, and his brother Raoul who runs the security services. Following the 'popular revolution' in 1959 Castro pursued a socialist state against the private interests of the US corporations, which dominated the economy, and the strategic interests of the US state that did not want a Soviet ally 90 miles from Florida. The US imposed an economic blockade on Cuba in the early 1960s which effectively forced Cuba into the Soviet bloc, a not unwelcome development for Castro. Due to Cuba's inability to diversify its economy away from sugar production, the island became increasingly a Soviet dependency maintained for strategic purposes with annual subsidies of up to five billion dollars by the mid-1980s. When the Gorbachev leadership began to dismantle the Soviet system Havana was told the subsidy would be withdrawn. Like North Korea, Cuba entered the economic basket case syndrome which it tried to alleviate with foreign investment from sources other than the US with very limited success.[13]

Vietnam had a little more fortune. The communist party seized control of its nationalist movement in the 1940s by clever policy and assassinations. It then mobilised support on a nationalist and land redistribution program and fought the French to a standstill with Chinese aid by 1954. The country was then divided at the Geneva conference. The US supported the non-communist southern state and war broke out with the north seeking to enforce reunification. Hanoi evicted the US in 1975 and set about uniting the country under a socialist system. It was a disaster. The economy had been wrecked by a long series of wars. The English-speaking middle class fled the country. The Chinese became very hostile when the Vietnamese decided to align with Moscow and backed the Pol Pot Cambodian regime in its attacks on Vietnam. In 1978 Hanoi decided to invade and occupy Cambodia as the easier option. The result was economic sanctions from the West and a war with the invading Chinese. Hanoi became even more dependent on Soviet subsidies of about four billion dollars a year. In 1985 Gorbachev, who was by then trying to lessen the imperial burden on the Soviet economy, told them these were being ended. Vietnam then began a process of economic reform called *Doi Moi* designed to liberalise and make it more efficient and attractive to foreign investors. It tried to do this without the Communist party sharing power. The results of the process remain uncertain as the Vietnamese regime oscillates between periods of liberalisation and repression depending on the strategic assessment of whatever faction happens to hold sway at the tie.[14]

These three states had the misfortune to tie their fortunes to the declining Soviet imperium, partly as a result of being in conflict with the major Western powers and seeking allies. Strategy has always been a component of progress and the wrong choice in a war or struggle between great powers can be very costly. The defeated may then complain at the unfairness of an historical process which delivers Czechoslovakia to the Soviet Union, Ireland to the British or Taiwan to the Chinese.

The Chinese communist regime because of its bulk would always have more options after its gaining power in October 1949 following the long multi-sided struggle to succeed the Manchu dynasty. After some initial hesitation it decided to join the Soviet bloc after Mao visited Moscow and signed a treaty with the Soviets in February 1950. The Soviets rewarded the Chinese with one of the largest transfers of capital and technology ever made by one state to another. This served to ensure that the Chinese emulated the now established Soviet model of state owned industry and trade; that it redistributed land; and that it established a one party dictatorship which extended to revolutionary street committees to control popular behaviour. Again a result, if not a stated purpose would be to destroy civil society, a fairly weak reed in traditional Chinese imperial society in any case. A peasantry controlled by the combination of the landlords, police and the mandarinate had not exactly enjoyed a vigorous debate about the principles of the European Enlightenment. To criticise the Europeans for not exporting these principles to such inhospitable soil is to be naive in the extreme about the political process.

This pro-Soviet period came to an end in the late 1950s when Mao Zedong launched the Great Leap Forward. Mao launched the Great Leap as an act of premeditated idealism that could not be accomplished, as he was correctly warned at the time by his ultimate successor Deng Xiaopeng. To meet the large output targets set for country iron furnaces, for example, peasants melted good cooking pots into useless lumps of metal, used their furniture and doors to fuel the fires, and threw in the now unattached door handles, before confronting the fact that they had been too busy to plant the next rice harvest. In the famine which followed many of them died, although this fact was largely unknown outside China until the 1990s. Even the sympathetic Marxist historian Eric Hobsbawm calculates that over 30 million people died.[15] That is, the economic policies of Mao Zedong killed more Chinese in a shorter period than Hitler killed Russians during his forces' invasion of the Soviet Union.

One result of this behaviour was that even the Soviets broke with Mao's regime and unilaterally withdrew their aid program. For the next decade or so the Maoist leadership then drove China into another bizarre and deadly idealist experiment called the Great Proletarian Cultural Revolution. In this projection of near anarchy, from which only Mao himself and the Chinese strategic nuclear weapons acquisition program were excepted, juvenile Red Guards terrorised what there was of civil society and reduced sections of the country to chaos and cannibalism.[16] This only came to an end when the Chinese communists, in fear of invasion from the Soviet communists forged an effective alliance with the USA in 1971 following Kissinger's shuttle diplomacy. This alliance between the most idealist and dictatorial regime in the world and what it described as the leading capitalist power survived until Mao died in 1976. After two years the man that Mao had often called 'China's leading capitalist roader', Deng Xiaopeng, assumed power.

After 1978 the new leadership tried to turn China into a development state under communist authoritarian political control. At first it implemented the 'Four Modernisations' of agriculture, industry, science and technology, and the military forces. These in fact meant the abolition of the communes and the re-privatisation of land ownership in agriculture, the introduction of the market and some private relations in secondary industry, the abandoning of the Maoist dream of replacing technological change (progress) with mass mobilisation (politics), and the pursuit of serious great power status. In the 1990s these reforms were intensified and China became the world's largest recipient of (capitalist) foreign investment and its fastest growing substantial economy. Yet it remained somewhere between a primitive state and a developmental state with fast-growing coastal southern provinces hosting many millionaires coexisting alongside rural internal provinces and northern areas dominated by large industrial conglomerations established during the Soviet period where workers enjoyed the 'Iron Rice Bowl'. Deng's daughter became the leading real estate agent in the southern city of Zhenzen and Rupert Murdoch's global media giant, News Limited, published his biography and got the pay TV rights for southern China.[17]

In the main the period of industrialisation is not one when democratic states are the typical political model. But the very success of industrialisation does produce the social forms and classes which generate pressures for democratisation. As industry develops so does the urban population and with them trade unions for workers and intellectual bodies including student unionism for the middle classes. These become the centres of not only the new industrial economy but also the demand for widening control over the state's decision making procedures. As the industrialisation period comes to a successful conclusion so the state tends to give way to these demands since the next phase of progress is not fully attainable under a dictatorial regime. The landscape of mature industrial society is an urban one dominated by a proletarian suburb, privately owned power utilities, mass transport systems and the modern factory. These are all replaced in the post-industrial phase.[18]

Services

As secondary industry becomes more productive and the service sector replaces both agriculture and industry as the principal form of occupation, so people must devolve the economic and social command structure and the state takes on a liberal and democratic, but often still interventionist form. In these societies as the economic and social organisation requires dispersal of authority so a similar diffusion of political power is required to enable efficient functioning. The corporatist state is unable to manage such a process and dissolves in all its forms, as has happened in the Soviet Communist bloc, to fascist states and to some of the military regimes of East Asia and South America where they have generated progress. The only states that have entered this next phase of development have been advanced capitalist democratic states.

In the transition to this stage many states retain features of the corporate and industrial period displayed in the political ideology of labourism or social democratic political parties, and in the semi-collectivist economic doctrines of state interventionism often called Keynesianism or even *dirigisme*. The political form is a democratic conflict between the forces of Right and Left representing class formations created in the industrial period but now in the process of dissolution. As this occurs the trade unions decline, Labour and Social Democratic parties metamorphosise, if they survive at all, and the Keynesian management of the economy is progressively abandoned.

The first state to enter the service state period was the United States after the Second World War. The first indication of this transition is the achievement of such productivity in the secondary industry sector that the proportion of the work force engaged there declines to about a fifth of the total work force. This is the equivalent of the earlier transition to an industry phase when the agricultural work force experienced a similar decline. Typically, the agricultural work force now moves to less than five per cent. Secondary industry achieves this by developing very high productivity levels, at first associated with the assembly line developed in the automobile industry by Henry Ford which then spread throughout the sector to other consumer durable products and even some capital stock production. This was then extended further by the application of automation to the assembly line itself and, starting in the 1970s, the introduction of robotics and computers to production. In some industries, including automobiles some further efforts were then also made to intensify the division of labour by internationalising the production of components.[19]

The USA was not at the forefront of all these innovations and indeed other European and East Asian countries were to surpass US productivity levels in many sectors of industry by the 1980s. But the first state with such a broad based, high productivity industry base was the USA. The effect was to shift the focus of civil society to distributing and selling products which it could now actually make very cheaply. This characteristic was heralded by efforts to build in obsolescence and fashion components to keep consumers buying new product. The new industries which came into existence then were devoted to making commodities cheaper or more attractive at the point of sale. They included transportation and distribution; finance, banking and insurance; and advertising, sales and promotion. These industries in the first instance were themselves mass production industries that could be organised in similar manner to the assembly line. The characteristic workplace of this stage which replaced the large production plant became the office block; the mass transit system was replaced by the automobile; and the shopping mall dispersed the population away from the residential suburb which was already being dismantled by the automobile. Mass undifferentiated population was being replaced by increasingly individualised households.

The effect of this stage of progress on the state was to reduce the ideological component of its political processes and at first to increase demands on it for the delivery of mass services which had until that time been the province of the civil society. American politics had always been less divided by ideology than European politics. In the post-1945 period American domestic politics as noted by Daniel Bell, became even less ideological, a process somewhat masked by its external ideological rhetoric demanded by the Cold War.[20] The difference on domestic policy between Nixon and Muskie by the 1970s was minimal. At the same time the American state, in a fairly bi-partisan way, got involved in the delivery of a range of services that were common in Europe but earlier eschewed in the US: anti-poverty programs, some health services, minimum wage enforcement, compulsory education, urban renewal, anti-discrimination policies, and even a commitment to job creation essentially by social democratic deficit budget financing. American political conflicts became increasingly personality conflicts with some coalition building on particular social issues like abortion, rather than Right/Left ideological contests. Clinton was to win a second term in 1996 on a centrist platform.

The same process was to take place in Europe as the old industrial class formations that had produced the historical Right/Left conflict across the continent for the previous century were eroded by social and economic change in the civil society. Centrist parties pursued pragmatic policies. The strong electoral appeal of social democracy in an era of mass and fairly undifferentiated labour, which characterised the industrial and early services period of the state, declined. The doctrines of Keynes sprang from the 1930s depression and were created to resolve the problem of lack of demand for industrial output within a closed national or imperial economic structure.[21] The marriage of these two idealist systems enabled the gradual expansion of the state sector at the expense of civil society throughout Europe until the 1980s.[22] It then became clear that this process was eroding the competitiveness of European industry as against that of Asia and North America, that the protectionist policies of the European Union were only compounding this problem, and that the add-on costs of European labour were creating economic rigidities and worsening the unemployment rate, which already stood at two or three times that elsewhere. The result was a political counter attack on social democracy in Europe.

The first premeditated and considered assault on the welfare state system which social democracy had created in Europe was that of Margaret Thatcher's Conservative Government in Britain, 1979-91. This was repeated by the Socialists under President François Mitterand after the economic crisis of 1981-2 when it became clear that the stimulation of the French economy had only resulted in spiralling national debt. In Germany the Christian Democrat Government of Helmut Kohl after 1983 tried to move in the same direction and cut state expenditure but was encumbered with the former East German bread basket case from 1990. The Swedish Social Democrats had their worse election result since 1928 at the 1991 election. Similar events occurred in Italy, Spain and Portugal. In 1992 the European Union tried to formalise this process of arresting the growth of the state sector by means of the Treaty of Maastricht enforcing financial discipline on member states. If they wished to gain advantage from joining the European monetary union they had to meet financial targets which meant controlling state expenditure.[23]

This defeat of the social democratic project was caused by two processes occurring in civil society. On the one hand, as the old industrial patterns of work and habitation were eroded by transition to a services (and then an information) society, so the rhetoric of egalitarianism became less attractive to electorates than one referring to liberty and choice. On the other hand, the creation of a global market particularly in finance from the early 1980s made the pursuit of purely national economic demand stimulation not only difficult but ruinous. In the early 1980s Mitterrand's France was the first civilised state to discover this. The Australian Labor Government experienced the same problem in 1986 when it went through the 'banana republic' crisis.[24] On gaining office Bill Clinton discovered in 1993 that the bond market placed limits on even his weak social democratic election platform, and he abandoned it.[25]

In the 1990s the old electoral political structures in the civilised states were radically changed and social democracy defeated. In Europe almost no social democratic government survived to 1996 and in opposition, like the British Labour Party, they abandoned its principles. Only France in June 1997 elected a serious socialist, public sector oriented government to confront the market. The US Democrats had only been tepid social democrats and they entered the 1996 Presidential elections as a business party and one that had withdrawn Americans' entitlement to welfare benefits. The Australian Labor Party having, after electing Paul Keating Prime Minister in 1991, decided to abandon liberal economic reform and return to some of its social democrat roots, was nonetheless decimated in 1996. In Japan the defeated LDP government was replaced by a shifting coalition of very diverse parties unable to cohere a joint long term program, and the LDP returned to power in 1996. The New Zealand Labour Party, having introduced the most right wing economic policy in the country's history in the 1980s returned its worst popular result in decades in 1996.[26]

The social democratic project survived the transition to a services sector but not the maturation of that form of civil society. The backbone of the social democratic political bloc was in the end the industrial work force and its demands for collective and democratic equality. As this sector of labour became an ever smaller part of a work force now dominated by the service sectors so support for social democracy weakened. In the new industries it was very weak indeed.

Information

> "Riding the Fifth Wave: Is the world entering a new phase of economy development fuelled by information technology?" *The Economist*, October 1996.

In the latest order, society treasures information products in its educational, news, culture, sport, entertainment and business forms. It draws fewer boundaries between these forms of information in large part because they are generated by the same technologies and disseminated by the same media. The state plays a small part in these activities and it is difficult to envisage a mass movement demanding that it increases its role. A larger sector of the work force is deployed to these activities. In the main, they are not industries where the workforce is employed in conditions of a large undifferentiated labour force and their extreme segmentation renders them less susceptible to appeals of mass mobilisation. In any case the economy as a whole is less available for state management, partly because these industries are themselves not as amenable to state direction and regulation as the industrial and service sectors, and partly because globalisation makes national economies more interdependent. And as a fortress of and between the societies in the civilised zone the state becomes less significant. Nonetheless it does continue to protect its societies from the primitive zone, whose states must make the transition to progress to be admitted to civilisation. Until they do they may present various problems for the civilised international community, including a refugee exodus, threatening trade routes, dispersing life threatening diseases and degrading the environment.

In this form the politics of the state moves closer to rational administration with the political class's primary role becoming the explanation of the tasks and options of government to the people who choose the appropriate outcome, just as they do in their activities of managing the information based economy. The political class also has to legitimise the state to those sectors of the population still outside the modern civil society and displaying supplicant attitudes. As the civilised states complete their demographic transition and population stabilises where it does not decline, and as the productivity and price of labour rises and with it income levels, so the demand pattern of consumers change. A smaller percentage is spent on the now much cheaper necessities of the industrial era - food, accommodation, public transport and basic education - and a larger proportion on the new information based industries. These include computers, further education, news, leisure and sport, tourism, advertising, entertainment, culture, the environment, politics and administration, the media and electronic information.

The computer revolution is at the heart of much that is changing in civil society. It has certainly made every sector of the economy more efficient. It has enabled programmed irrigation automation in agriculture, the application of just-in-time production techniques on assembly lines, the provision of near instant and selective data in finance sector offices, and base inventory levels in retail distribution to take a few examples. It has also enabled the individual as a worker and consumer - in many instances the difference is becoming less clear - to access incrementally greater sources of information through narrowband television, the fax and then the world wide web of the InterNet and E-mail. The net is accessed by over 40 million people concentrated in the civilised states' information sectors and forming a discrete and advantaged information strata. While much of the hard ware for this information system is built in low wage primitive and development states, its usage is in the civilised states where much of the software program and information content is developed.[27]

The use of these systems is also concentrated in the post-compulsory education systems of the civilised states. Although the technology of the Net itself was developed by the US armed forces - in a rare example of the state initiating progress, a happenstance usually involving the military function - its application has been taken up by civil society. These education systems themselves have all been radically restructured in the past decade. In recognition of the fact that skills for working people now have to be changed more quickly to correspond to the acceleration of technological change so education systems have been made more flexible, more diverse, more accessible, more competitive and more internationalised. In all civilised states the university systems have been extended but their provision made more like a commodity than a right in recognition of the higher earning power their products deliver to their consumer. More people access post-compulsory education more often, more people work in it and it is more private and market driven.[28]

The generation and dissemination of news has also expanded greatly as an industry and is no longer confined to the distribution of morning broadsheets owned by press barons, although they certainly still exist. News is now gathered by a diverse system of reporters who range from the most illustrious and well respected foreign correspondent to the local scribe dealing with elections to the local council. It is disseminated by a wide range of outlets from the throwaway paper on the front lawn, through the still surviving broadsheets, very few of them now evening, to regular radio reports on dozens of stations, to the TV news on broadband, narrowband and news only pay and free to air TV initiated by Ted Turner and CNN. If that is not enough there are reports on the Net. The combination of this system with the extension of the education system means there are *no non-military secrets* in the civilised states which cannot be uncovered and understood by the people. In order to ensure this is the case these states have all enacted Freedom of Information legislation which entitles the electorate to what had been the state's secrets.

This news is now so closely entwined with the leisure and sports industries as to make them often inseparable and a branch of show business. Since the results of their activities is delivered through the same media in the same bulletins, and since leisure and sports news are as of much interest and arguably importance in the lives of the people as the other news, and since sports and leisure are now major industries in their own right, it is unsurprising that sports stars are often more well known and often more well paid than the wielders of state power. It is certainly the case that the experts, the advertising industry, believes that they have more power over peoples' opinions and uses them more often to try to sell commodities. The true measure that the information society places on different components of information may be judged from the time allocation of a prime time TV news bulletin: five minutes for disaster and local news; five minutes for national news; five minutes for world news; seven minutes for sport; three minutes for weather forecast; and five minutes for advertising.

The state then has to use the same techniques to promote its (political) products as do other industries which are in the same line of business, that is, the producers of information and services.[29] Politicians require the same attributes that other promoters of goods require, and try to assume the same characteristics on the relevant media. In this case it is usually and pre-eminently the Television from which an ever rising proportion of the people get their news. This has been intensified recently by the opening of Parliamentary and more Congressional proceedings to radio and TV broadcasts. One result is a further degradation of the ideological and idealist component of political behaviour as politicians become media performers or in the case of Ronald Reagan the other way around.

The new industries are also becoming more specialised or boutique in their delivery of information and services as the computer revolution permits the narrow market segmentation of delivery. Tourism packages are now available in enormous diversity, and while they still use cheap and mass delivery services like the wide bodied jet, the industry is able to combine them in an infinite variety of combinations. Advertising is also segmented into specialised markets as the mass circulation tabloids and broadband radio and TV lose their control over the market and a typical civilised state citizen accesses multiple media outlets each day and an age or occupation or interest group can be identified and targeted. Culture becomes similarly concentrated into market segments and arguably the national culture now embraces advertising which usually averages around ten per cent of TV casting which is for many citizens still their major cultural source. Indeed, in these circumstances it is not surprising that the environment has emerged as one of the major political issues of the contemporary civilised states since it one major issue that these segmented markets all share.

The effect on the political processes of the civilised states of these new activities is considerable. In the first place they provide the citizen with more complete information about the political system and the behaviour of politicians. Policies have to be argued through in something like the way that people are persuaded to buy commodities and entertainment events. But since they have all been better educated in scientific method and the pursuit of interest, the political process must contain a rational and interest coalition-building component. Since the new industries, and now many of the older ones, don't employ undifferentiated labour, the appeal of trade unions and their social democratic ideology is in sharp decline. Appeal to voters can no longer be framed largely or even solely in social class terms, since for most people such categories don't exist. And even if they did they do not nor want to belong to them.

These civilised states are becoming more like one another politically with their highly developed system of political representation and transparent state apparatuses, not only because their civil societies are producing the same changes in economic and social organisations but also because they are co-ordinating their policies. There are a wide range of bodies which convene conferences, recommend policies and research political options for the civilised states, whose ministers and officials are in any case in regular bilateral communication with one another. These multinational forums include the Organisation for Economic Co-operation and Development (OECD), the World Bank and Group of Seven at a peak level, and numerous bilateral, functional and regional organisations including the WHO, ILO, APEC, the EU and NAFTA, Closer Economic Relations (Australia and New Zealand). It is hardly surprising, if only for this reason, that their state policies often coincide on a wide range of issues. But they are also dealing with the wider process of globalisation, of which more will be said later. [30]

Notes

1. Richard Mackenny, *The City State 1500-1700: Republican Liberty in an Age of Princely Power*, Basingstoke, Macmillan, 1989.
2. James Long, *Conquest and Commerce: Spain and England in the Americas*, New York, Academic Press, 1975.
3. Christopher Ogden, 'Tightening the Screws on Burma', *Time Magazine*, 28 Oct. 1996; Bob Catley, 'Burma: The Last Frontier?', *Quadrant*, 1996.
4. T. E. Ashton, *An Economic History of England: the Eighteenth Century*, London, Methuen, 1961; and E.P. Thompson, *The Making of the English Working Class*, Harmondsworth, Penguin, 1968.
5. Greg O' Leary, 'China's Economic Road', *Current Affairs Bulletin*, June/July 1996.
6. Clive Trebilcock, *The Industrialization of the Continental Powers, 1780-1914*, London, Longman, 1981.
7. Hiroaki Kuromiya, *Stalin's Industrial Revolution: Politics and Workers, 1928-1932*, Cambridge, Cambridge University Press, 1988.
8. Hal Hill, *The Indonesian Economy Since 1966: Southeast Asia's Emerging Giant*, Cambridge, Cambridge University Press, 1996.
9. Clark D. Neher, *Democracy and Development in Southeast Asia: the Winds of Change*, Boulder, Westview, 1995; and E. Laothamatas, ed., *Democratization in Southeast Asia*, Singapore, ISEAS, 1996.
10. Andrew Selth, *Transforming the Tatmadow: the Burmese Armed Forces Since 1988*, Canberra, ANU, 1996.
11. Stanley G. Payne, *Fascism: Comparison and Definition*, Madison, University of Wisconsin Press, 1980.
12. Dae-Sook Suh, *Kim Il Sung: The North Korean Leader*, New York, Colombia University Press, 1988.
13. Jean Stubbs, *Cuba: The Test of Time*, London, Latin American Bureau, 1989; Rhonda Pearl Rabkin, *Cuban Politics: The Revolutionary Experiment*, New York, Prager, 1991.
14. George Irvin, *Vietnam: Some Macroeconomic Dimensions of Doi Moi*, The Hague, The Institute of Socialist Studies, 1994, Working Paper No. 174; Vu Tuan Anh, *Development in Vietnam: Policy*

Reforms, and Economic Growth, Singapore, Institute for Southeast Asian Studies, 1994.
15. Eric Hobsbawm, *The Age of Extremes: the Short Twentieth Century, 1914-1991*, London, Michael Joseph, 1994.
16. Ross Terrill, *Mao: A Biography*, Sydney, Hale and Iremoger, 1995.
17. I. Keun Lee, *New East Asian Economic Development: Interacting Capitalism and Socialism*, Acmonk, M. E. Sharpe, 1993.
18. David Clark, *Post-Industrial America: A Geographic Perspective*, New York, Methuen, 1985; and H.V. Savitch, *Post-Industrial Cities: Politics and Planning in New York, Paris and London*, Princeton, Princeton University Press, 1988.
19. John Matthews, *Age of Democracy: The Politics of Post-Fordism*, Melbourne, Oxford University Press, 1989; Ash Amin, ed., *Post-Fordism: A Reader*, Oxford, Blackwell, 1994.
20. Daniel Bell, *The End of Ideology: On the Exhaustion of Political Ideas in the Fifties*, revised., Cambridge Mass., Harvard University Press, 1988.
21. J. M. Keynes, *The General Theory of employment, interest and money*, New York, Harcourt, Brace & World, 1935.
22. Doug McEachern, *The Expanding State, Class and Economy in Europe*, New York, St Martins Press, 1990.
23. Jonathon Story, ed., *The New Europe: Politics, Government and Economy Since 1945*, Oxford, Blackwell, 1993; Christopher Anderson, *Blaming the Government: Citizens and the Economy in Five European Democracies*, Armonk, M.E. Shape, 1995; Andrew Duff, John Pinder and Ray Price, eds., *Maastricht and Beyond: Building the European Union*, London, Routledge, 1994; Lorenzo Bini Smaghi, *et al*, *The Transition to EMU in the Maastricht Treaty*, Princeton, Princeton University Press, 1994.
24. Bob Catley, *Globalising Australian Capitalism*, Melbourne, Cambridge University Press, 1996.
25. Bob Woodward, *The Agenda; Inside Bill Clinton's White House*, New York, Simon and Schuster, 1994.
26. Jack Vowells, 'The New Zealand Election', *Current Affairs Bulletin*, Oct./Nov. 1996.
27. Christine H. Boyer, *Cybercities: Visual Perception in the Age of*

	Electronic Communication, New York, Princeton Architectural Press; and Susan Leigh Star, ed., *The Culture of Computing*, Oxford, Blackwell, 1995.
28.	Geoffrey A. Hamer, *The Use of Technology to Deliver Education in the Workplace*, Canberra, AGPS, 1993.
29.	William Atkins, *Satellite Television and State Power in Southeast Asia*, Mount Lawley, Edith Cowan University, 1995.
30.	Hamish McRae, *The World in 2020: Power, Culture and Prosperity*, Boston, Harvard Business School Press, 1995.

3 The Purpose of the State

> Betray the trust:
> Keep nothing sacred:
> 'tis but just
> The many-headed
> beast should know.
>
> Lord Tennyson, To -, after reading a life and letters

From its inception the state has had numerous purposes including ensuring territorial security, preserving order, expanding territory, regulating and administering the reproduction of the society as a whole and the various social strata that are contained within the community and which fall within its zone, mediating between disputing parties, representing real social interests, setting down the rules of punishment and permissible interaction between respective groups and individuals within groups, punishing wrongdoers, and providing some of the conditions for cultural development and economic growth. The state has always been involved in acts of creation, maintenance, continuity and change. Further, while the state contains a composite of purposes, a particular purpose of those holding state power at any given time may give that particular state much of its character, as is most obvious when a state is conceived by idealists primarily as an ideological instrument.

Because different people with different ideologies may attempt to do different things with the state it may seem as if the purpose of the state is whatever people want to do with it. But this way of looking at things fails to appreciate that the state is not simply the expression of will. Like any other social organisation a state may fall into the hands of those who try to use it for purposes which are contrary to its nature. Insofar as the state is by necessity a complex system for the organisation, direction and command of power, a state will always fulfil some of its purposes even when it is in the hands of maniacs. But a state cannot be made to do everything which its temporary controllers instruct it to.

A state cannot be made, for example, to defy economic laws. It may try to avoid them but the abandoning of economic calculations will produce disastrous consequences. Nor can it easily abolish the different political interests which are the expressions of entrenched social patterns. Although states may vary in form, according to the political purposes which require state organisation, the very existence of the state *qua* state rests upon objective circumstances involving a certain scale and complexity of social organisation. Thus, while we may try to pursue different ends as a species, the role of the state in assisting us to reach them will require that they are commensurate with the nature of the state: it would be stretching meaning, for example, to argue that the state is consistent with a hunter/gatherer civilisation. To talk, then, of the purpose of the state is to talk about what it does best. The state has evolved as a multi-faceted political organism, capable of deploying different parts of its composition at different times as the occasion demands. But the multiple purposes of the state has often been overlooked by state theorists.

Marxist theorists sought for generations to discover *the* purpose of the state. Or, more accurately, since they already knew that the purpose of the state in capitalist society was to assist in the extraction of surplus value from the working class, their intellectual labours were oriented towards discovering precisely the role which the state played in this imagined process. Their theories ran through different parties of the bourgeoisie conspiring with capital, to imperialist states buying off the workers with the fruits of colonial exploitation, to the social democratic ideological deception and back to the political parties conspiring with capital running the 140 year stretch from *The Eighteenth Brumaire of Louis Napoleon* to *Socialist Register*. The only interesting interlude in the entire panoply proved to be Gramsci's idea of cultural hegemony to which the now post-Marxist post-modernists have clung like a shroud. People behave in the unsocialist fashion that they do because of the imposition of the dominant or hegemonic culture on them. 'The ideas of any society, including common sense, are the ideas of its ruling class.' Meanwhile the capitalist societies under investigation have transformed into mature civilised states and the creations of the Marxist school have come and gone like some medieval Christian heresy.

A similar observation can be made of radical feminist critics of the mature state who examine the state through the single and apparently unproblematic variable of the category women, who, in turn, are invariably treated under the dominant variable of victimhood. Catherine MacKinnon's work is a classic example of this. She believes that 'All women [excepting herself?] are controlled by definition by men. Gender socialisation is the process through which women come to identify themselves as sexual beings, as beings that exist for men'.[1] The state is presented as a masculinist instrument invented for the purpose of torturing women. MacKinnon's arrogance toward women who think differently from her, which is the overwhelming majority, is only matched by her sheer indifference to/ignorance of history and culture. The civilised states have a variety of policies towards women including discriminating in their favour at work since the Factory Acts of the nineteenth century, in many pension and welfare arrangements and in the provision of encouchment leave. Where they have been shown to have discriminated against women, for example in recruitment and promotion in the bureaucracy, they have acted to stop such practises.

The most common post-Marxist reading of the state is to work with an alignment of four major variables: class, race, gender, ethnicity. People who deploy these variables to tell their story about the state and society think they are engaging in a richer presentation of social reality. However, the deployment of these four variables does not lead to a more multi-dimensional, and hence truer picture of reality, because the four variables, which are simply sub-species of the genus domination, merely conspire to tell the mono-dimensional story of society and the state as systems of domination. The problem is not the usage of the concept of domination when discussing the state. For states have always been in the business of domination -- they must dominate enemies, whether they be foreign aggressors or criminal. In other words, domination is part of their existence. But they also do many other things.

Hence these radical schools attempt to describe a complex organism like the modern state in cartoon forms that are best known as class theory, Orientalism, women's studies, and multiculturalism. If they are taken as narrow criticisms of the policy of a particular government towards particular groups of citizens there may be nothing objectionable with these perspectives. Indeed, it is from such schools that the very tensions which have been so important to the generation of progress have often arisen. It is when these perspectives demand that the entire state and political process be viewed merely from that viewpoint that bigotry and ideology sets in. Class does not dictate strategic calculations; race does not dictate policy in the sphere of science and technology; Orientalism has little significance for road planning; and discrimination against women is not evident in health policy when women get eight more life years than men or in incarceration rates where men are overwhelmingly overrepresented.

Defending the Realm

The modern state must always retain the core function of the state, which is the defence of its civil society.

From its inception defence of the state has been critical to the preservation of a particular mode of social reproduction. Historically, the three earliest forms of conflict which may be said to be political involve either pre-national political entities, whether tribal or nomadic in character, or the imperial state forms which grew to preserve the agrarian societies which arose around the great silt plains of the great rivers -- the Nile, the Euphrates, the Ganges, and the river systems of China. The tribes which usually consisted of a number of families could not generally compete with the more numerous and technologically advanced agricultural states and were either conquered or incorporated. Where great distance had allowed a tribal society to survive until encountering an industrial state, as in Australia and the American plains, then destruction was universally almost total.

Consequently equestrian nomads from the central Asian steppe provided a formidable adversary against the imperial states for a while. They conquered China, India, ancient Rome and Asia Minor. But they were no match for military technology. The invention of gun powder overcame the effect of mass cavalry in the late Middle Ages. After the collapse of the Roman empire had left discrete agricultural societies all over Europe obstructing the revival of a continental economy, the innovation of gunpowder also rendered local fortresses vulnerable to the monarch's artillery train and enabled the creation of unified and larger national economies and tax collecting systems. States were more able to protect themselves against external foes and subjugate internal insurrections.

Externally, the defensive requirements of the European states, which became increasingly shaped by their military competition between one another drove the technological progress which was to make Europe, led at first by the imperial Habsburgs, the most powerful region in the world. Internally, the requirements of domestic order strengthened the policing mechanism of the state against potential traitors. This spurred the creation of state bureaucracies, standing armies, and other police functions that first achieved a sophisticated and recognisably modern form in Richelieu's France.

While it is obvious that a state which is unable to protect itself from external enemies will be swallowed up by such an enemy, it is equally important for a state to protect itself from internal enemies, especially in times of war or crisis when the stability of the state is under threat. States which have been unable to achieve order have rarely achieved progress. In the modern world, the region which has the least progress is also the region which is most lacking in political order -- sub-Saharan Africa. But order in itself does not guarantee progress. The most orderly state on this continent, South Africa, imposed order so successfully after the Nationalists took power in 1948 that it took the country in a direction that gradually ground it to a halt and then to a condition of civil war before a thorough transformation was imposed.

The state must also pay attention to the defence of its core culture within the civil society and maintain state policies within the parameters it dictates. This can cut both ways. All the great tyrants of the twentieth century have used the cultures of their subjects to assist their domination. Hitler's utilisation of Germanic myths and legends facilitated his domination of Europe and genocidal policies towards the Jews, both of which received mass support until he faced military defeat. The German state should have generated stronger restraining influences, but the Weimar Republic was not up to the task. Stalin used Russian history to justify his purges in the 1930s. The Leninist doctrine itself on which the Soviet state was based had no opposition to restrain Stalin or a patriotic component to rally mass support against Hitler. Mao behaved like a Chinese Emperor, living in the same Palace, reading the same dynastic chronicles and behaving in the same murderous way towards the peasants he always claimed to represent. Deng Xiaopeng was later to be forced back onto the impulses of Chinese nationalism to defend a regime by then roundly despised. These states were in the event of crises to depend on the core values they claimed to have abolished.

De Gaulle proved more constructive for France. He started his *Memoirs* with the thought that all his life he had had a special idea of France and its glory.[2] He played the patriot throughout, even if his resistance fighters had little impact on the German occupation of France which was evicted with Anglo-American force. During the later Algerian War, however, De Gaulle was able to make a political rebirth and a substantial contribution to the rebuilding of France as a European power. Elected by the Right he abandoned Algeria and rebuilt the social fabric of metropolitan France. The subsequent development of that country cannot be understood without reference to its earlier history as the most powerful and revolutionary country in Europe, demoted by Germany to the second rank during the twentieth century, and trying to offset that humiliation by whatever tool came to hand - a global empire of microstates, a UN Security Council seat or some nuclear weapons. Nonetheless, and with the assistance of the rapprochement with Germany, as later expressed in the European Union, De Gaulle was able to lay the basis for a powerful and prosperous France, true to its own mythology.

To the south almost exactly the opposite occurred when both Spain and Portugal receded to the hinterland of developing modern Europe when seized by dictators. In the Spanish instance General Franco took advantage of the political turmoil of the Spanish Republic in the 1930s to invade the metropolis with its own North African armies and commence the civil war that lasted until 1939. Franco stood for traditional Spanish values of obedience, monarchy (ironically) and military rule. He was assisted in his quest by Fascist military aid from Germany and Italy and the small scale assistance and consequent faction fighting that came from the pacifist democracies of the West and the Stalin dictatorship. The idealists of the Republic destroyed themselves and the man on horseback triumphed.[3] Franco's Spain with its *dirigiste* and part clerical state remained outside the prosperity of post-War Europe and only joined that condition when Fascism was ended. Democratic Spain after the 1970s became one of southern Europe's showcases.

On the other hand the intervention of the Islamic Mullahs in Iran to defend what they perceived as the traditional culture of that country has had more difficult repercussions. They seized control of the state from the elected democratic republicans in 1980 and were able to take the country away from its progressive path and back towards an idealist mediaeval theocracy. They also thereby invited invasion by the neighbouring military dictatorship in Iraq always eager for more territory and resources. In this case the enthusiastic maintenance of tradition by the state actually arrested the potential for progress which had been initiated by the Shah.

The maintenance of a nation's culture is therefore not a hard and fast rule but one requiring an assessment of the times. The US opened itself to the mass immigration of the late nineteenth century and thereby created the most powerful state in the world on the basis of the newly invented melting pot theory of cultures. In fact, however, most of these cultures integrated into and substantially changed the American culture already established - a variant of the English speaking Anglo-Saxon culture of Britain. The two major exceptions to this were in fact already in existence in North America before that wave of mass immigration started - the African American community and the French speaking Canadians. They were to prove difficult to accommodate. Australia was also to open its doors to large scale migration after 1945 and such migrations also largely integrated into the dominant Anglo-Celtic culture, although later under the rather deceptive rubric of multiculturalism.

Clinging grimly to the cultural traditions of the past can be as damaging as not trying to defend them. It may be most fairly said that a tolerant community and civilised state is hard won by generations of actual political conflict and polemical ideological struggle and should not be lightly passed over to the intellectual fad of the day - be it communism, multiculturalism or post-colonialism. Nonetheless slavish adherence to the practises of the past is rarely a sound path towards an advanced civilised state. The point about the mature state is that its diverse, tolerant and democratic structure is designed to hear all viewpoints and to resolve them by reference to the legitimate representation of interests. It is the state form most likely to come up with the right decision.

Justice and Law

Along with the role of protection of a people and its form of life, the earliest rationalisation for the state has been the provision of justice to its inhabitants so that they can continue their mode of life in the way that they are accustomed to. Justice, law and the state form an interpenetrating triad. Each donates a range of problems which cannot simply be subsumed under one of the others. Further, the terms may be turned against each other - a law may be said to be unjust, a state may be said to be acting unlawfully, a state will make decisions that may be impossible to justify by reference to any standard of justice that will satisfy a moral philosopher, but the circumstances may be considered to be of greater importance than justice - strategic interests are the most obvious case in point. But just as each point of the triad is constituted by its own field of relationships, each point ultimately seeks the other for its own stability. Those who seek justice invariably want the outcomes they support to be consistent with the law, even if that means changing the law. The law is the visible sign of justice. Those who claim that the state is acting illegally, whether by reference to a constitutional principle, a principle of international law, or, more contentiously, a principle of natural law, still want to rein in the powers unleashed by the state in accordance with general rules.

States, on the other hand, invariably plead the justice of their actions, even when their actions are barbaric. The Soviet Union, although denying that there was any universal concept of justice, relied upon Western intellectuals to justify the show trials and the gulags. Also, states cannot always comply with laws: areas of intelligence and covert operations take part in the shadow of the law. In liberal democratic states, the state goes to some length to legitimise and shroud the assassinations and intrigues in which the beast engages so that the majority of people can sleep soundly. In dictatorships, where the balance of powers is not so delicately poised, where enmity is more engraved into the day to day textures of peoples lives, the beast is more visible. Indeed, visible terror may be precisely what the ruling class want, even need to display to preserve their power. Much state power, then, reveals itself as what it always must be in the moment of crisis: raw, terrifying force. A state which lacks this force will never be able to maintain the civility of lawlike behaviour or its ideals of justice.

Of the three forces, law is already found in tribal social systems. The idea of justice is latent in the concept of law, but justice is only formulated with clarity in its own right once the state already exists. Prior to a highly sophisticated culture, justice and law are equivalents inscribed in the tribal rules which enforce strict codes of identity and acceptable behaviour. There is only room for a collision between these forces once there is the possibility of alternative laws. It is significant that the first detailed depiction of the doctrine of natural law - the doctrine that there are laws inscribed in the nature of things which are superior, more divine than human laws - occurs in the context of a decision that must be made where civil war has taken place. Antigone's wish to bury her dead brother Polynices, who has led a rebellion against Creon, is presented as a collision between obedience to a higher, universal law and the authorial command of a king who has defeated his enemy and wants to preserve order.[4] Justice, then, becomes one of the first problems that presents itself to the conceptual cast of mind; for the philosopher is able to create the conceptual cleavage between law and justice and ask after the essence of each, as Plato does in the *Minos* and *Republic* respectively. That is to say, the tragic poet first depicts the problem; the philosopher then tries to resolve it.

The field of justice, law and the state is constantly expanded via the fissions and fusions of this triadic cluster. The state cannot escape justice and the law. Justice and law remain an intrinsic part of the state's purpose, regardless of how unjust or how illegal particular states are. Thus, for example, the Nazi state was a legal monstrosity in all manner of ways: its judges had sworn an oath to Hitler and they wore swastikas in the court room, thus openly demonstrating their party affiliation; they had the task of guessing the Führer's will in any given case; they were working under a system which had not repealed laws from a code that in some respects, necessarily contradicted Nazi commands; their sentences were harsh and brutal and violated any natural sense of parity between crime and punishment. Yet in spite of all this, as Lon Fuller has correctly pointed out in a famous debate with the British legal positivist H. L. A Hart, a vast range of laws concerning the reproduction of daily life, laws such as contract, marriage, torts, continued.[5] Likewise, in the Soviet system, there were huge caverns in the legal relationships within the society which has played a large part in contributing to the chaos in the former Soviet Union, but here too there were a range of laws necessary for the administration of daily life.[6]

Again, the same kind of argument can be made about justice. As lacking in justice as both these totalitarian systems were, each new outrage was legitimated by an appeal to justice. Justice is the inevitable rhetorical currency for the deployment of power, when weapons are not used, and it is invariably invoked even when they are used.

The further a state strays from a coherent system of law and a coherent conception of justice, the more internal danger it falls into. The reason for this is that a lack of coherence helps foster a culture of lawlessness and violence, so the state increasingly resembles a prison camp if the ruling class is sufficiently equipped, or like a war zone, when its power is more precariously balanced. Again if we take the examples of Nazi and Soviet legal culture, both legal cultures were extremely weak and thus there was little restraint upon state apparachiks feathering their own nests to almost unlimited degrees while the rest of the population lived in misery. While the conquest and looting of Europe improved the lot of many Germans only intensification of spying and fear kept the populations in check in the Soviet Union and its satellites.[7] East Germany, which had the double experience of Nazis and communists fostered a culture in which husbands and wives and children each spied on each other. Once the ruling class becomes thoroughly sick of itself and tired of its gangster like methods, a factor accelerated by a moribund mode of economic organisation, the state must change direction[8] A state cannot survive if the forces which vitalise it -- such as its economy and legal system -- are imploding under inefficiency and/ or corruption.

98 This Great Beast: Progress and the Modern State

Voluntarist theories of the state, which include post-modern accounts, invariably miss this simple point because they think that a state can do anything, because 'there is no truth.' The truth is, though, that human responses to similar circumstances are rather similar. Thus it was that law evolved in tribes all over the world amongst groups that had no contact with each other; political authorities evolved in settler societies on different parts of the earth because of common problems of crop protection and distributions of tasks and administrative functions; writing evolved when administrative records were required to keep track of costs and to send messages; and private property developed everywhere as a means of protecting the fruits of labour. Thus it should not be a surprise to anyone that when societies want to modernise and to reproduce themselves so that their populations have access to a range of consumer goods, they will, in spite of cultural dissimilarities, tend to adopt similar political and economic mechanisms, similar legal frameworks and similar conceptions of justice. The one area where Marx has been least followed today is in the one area where he got it fairly right: that the technical conditions of social reproduction impact on aspects of existence, though, as Max Weber cleared up, other spheres of life such as religion, social structure and geopolitics may also impede or accelerate economic life, and thus the technologies of a society.

While madcap economic practices impress themselves with inescapable grimness upon a nation, the cracks in seemingly more abstract concepts of social reproduction are much harder to detect. The concept of justice, for example, is a part of the fabric of every society. While there is no universal consensus about exactly how it can be defined, if a false conception of justice gains widespread acceptance in a community which creates impossible demands and expectations it can have very serious consequences. This problem was picked up by one of the most insightful social scientists of this century, Friedrich von Hayek. Along with his mentor Ludwig von Mises, Hayek predicted why a planned economy could not deliver high standards of living.[9] He also predicted that Keynesianism would come unstuck. Hayek's other main contribution to social science was the warning he made against a major shift that had taken place in the conception of justice. Social justice, he warned was a chimerical concept, the widespread deployment of which would have very deleterious consequences for society. His most elaborate defence of this argument was made shortly after the appearance of John Rawls' *Theory of Justice*, which in turn was the definitive philosophical expression of the social democratic conception of social justice in the late twentieth century.[10]

Rawls argues that it is the responsibility of a society to distribute some basic goods, such as rights, liberties and wealth fairly. Wealth is seen as a social creation and hence the merit principle should not be applied for its just distribution. In order to come up with a principle that Rawls believes will settle once and for all the overarching principle of justice for a liberal democratic society, he sets up what he considers to be a just procedure. One is invited to drop all knowledge of one's own situation and interests - one's given generation, race and gender (although he was picked up by Susan Moller Okin for neglecting to mention this one)[11] and chosen lifestyle, bank balance, religion, hobbies, class, and sexual preference. Standing behind the veil of ignorance in this 'original position', Rawls claims that anyone who did not know how they would fare once they stepped from behind the veil and into a life would choose a principle of justice which would give everyone equal rights and liberties. From this he argued that social and economic inequalities had to satisfy two conditions open to all: 'first, they must be attached to offices and positions open to all under conditions of fair and equal opportunity; and second, they must be to the greatest benefit of the least advantaged member.'

Just as Marx had only ever truly considered the economy from the perspective of the labourer without initiative, Rawls considers redistributive social justice in terms only of its beneficiary. He does not ask how wealth is generated, hence he ignores the important economic question that was to be so significant in the failure of communist economies: the psychology of and incentives required for wealth creation. He pleads neutral on the problem of the productive superiority of communism and capitalism, but he does not examine how distribution impacts upon production. Rawls's definition of fairness, then, conflicts with the *modus operandi* behind the economic prosperity of market economies, self-interest. People will put up with paying taxes if they can't find any way to get around it, if they don't consider them excessive, and if everyone else has to do the same. But if whatever work they do must only be to benefit the 'least advantaged member of society', many will not do it. One obvious reason for this is that the idea of the least advantaged member makes no sense. Nature, as the novelist Josephine Hart has one of her characters say in the novel *Sin*, is never bountiful in all respects.[12] Rawls forgets this simple truth, and, like so many social democrats, reduces life to bundles of already existing opportunities and wealth, which should be more equally shared. Which is precisely how the tenured academic encounters society.

But opportunities and wealth are means for unlocking all manner of things. To someone who thinks in terms of a singularly favoured group of people who have it all - white middle class males - and the social victim, the least advantaged person would be, as numerous jokes deriding political correctness conclude, the working class, black, lame, lesbian. But the simple-mindedness of just assuming that working class, or black, or gay people are victims is obvious if one thinks just a little more about how life creates choices. If one were behind the veil of ignorance and could choose to be white, male, wealthy, but have an incurable skin disease where the flesh rotted off, have a temperament which alienated people and experience bouts of chronic depression, or be a working class, black, lame lesbian, with a great sex life, good friends, and a happy demeanour, few would consider the black woman as more disadvantaged than the white man. However, if the white male in the above condition knew that he would have a remarkable talent which would enable him to create a work of literary genius he may not swap places regardless of how bad his health, his depression, or loneliness was. He may not even consider himself disadvantaged. In real life, the concept of the 'least advantaged member' as deployed by Rawls is meaningless. Indeed, the more existentially disadvantaged one is, often the less useful is any action by the state. The problem with Rawls's idea of the 'least advantaged member' is not only that it is meaningless, but the definition of justice he sets up sends out a signal to people to construct themselves as victims in order to reap advantages from the social system.

Rawls' concept of social justice as 'fairness', was constructed around a social process already largely in existence in Western Europe and then taking place in the United States. It was a highly elaborate way of legitimating programs such as gender and ethnic based affirmative action, the purpose of which was to change social patterns to conform to standards of parity in keeping with what some people claimed was fair. Social justice was meant to equalise benefits, but there was less attention given to equalising burdens, because, it was implied, just being a certain kind of person was burdensome.

This way of thinking which still has widespread support is ostensibly idealist but actually realist, since for all its claims about unfair groups and systemic discrimination, it is simply a way for some people to get access to resources which they would find it harder to get on meritocratic principles and without the policy and the rhetorical ploy. The system does not eliminate losers, it just attempts to alter the categories of the winners and losers. It is no accident that this policy is, as is often pointed out, not resorted to in fields where the immediate stakes are extremely high such as surgery, dentistry, or flying jet aeroplanes, but it is of extreme importance in areas such as the public service, university appointments in the arts and social sciences and representative functions of the state.

The argument of affirmative action also rests on a failure to explore why the occupations of different groups are patterned in different ways.[13] Having said that the society is unjust, that it reproduces itself through discrimination and that positions in it are filled by ideological criteria, there is no need to find out why society is patterned in a particular way. The words capitalism, partriarchy and racism relieve intellectual idealists of doing real intellectual work. All they need do is selectively look for inequalities. The long term effects of demeaning social organisations by reducing the merit component of recruitment of their personnel is in any case rarely considered and will afflict another generation.

In contrast to Rawls, Hayek saw that the concept of social justice would have to lead to an erosion of respect for the law, that it would encourage the proliferation of claimants for resources *as* social justice, that this in turn would encourage politicians to use the state as a money bin to buy off groups, that it would further encourage legislators to use the law instrumentally to advantage whatever group at that moment had political clout. Further, it would lead to an increasing emphasis upon planning based on political and not efficiency or productive criteria. In fact, as he points out, a consistent policy of social justice could only be pursued through a planned economy - a system of economic activity which cannot function for other reasons. Hayek believed it was the height of immaturity for people to place their faith in a group of people who think that they will be able to generate the prosperity to aid all their designated victims. What is inevitable, says Hayek, is that a culture is being fostered where no one will want to work, no one will respect the law, and where planners will have excessive control.

For Hayek, the rhetoric of social justice is a dangerous mirage because it seems so plausible, yet its consequences are so socially devastating. Its plausibility rapidly disappears though, according to Hayek, if one sees that justice is not so much a directive tool for society as a whole, but a rule of redress that can only be applied to particular persons. That is to say, persons can act unjustly, if they have violated a rule, but social patterning which is based on agreed upon exchanges cannot be unjust. The economy is, for Hayek, not about creating justice or injustice, but about creating and distributing services and commodities. A rich country is no more just than a poor country. A rich country may provide more opportunities and a better life, but that has nothing to do with justice. Egalitarian distribution patterns do not indicate anything about the presence of injustice; communist countries which had relatively egalitarian distributive patterns were no more just than capitalist countries with high levels of disparity between incomes and wealth. Social justice activists, on the other hand, conflate material goods and offices with moral qualities and then they arbitrarily select victims and means of redress. Why, for example, should the nation be the adequate means of redress? Why shouldn't affirmative action apply to illiterate, starving people from Africa? Aren't they more in need than the merely disadvantaged in Western states? The answer is obvious, that people wouldn't put up with it, and those who deploy the tool of social justice for their own advantage might very well miss out. The United Nations works with this kind of logic, but there have been few reports of people given jobs through affirmative action programs asking that their position be handed over to a more disadvantaged person whether from inside their own nation or outside.

Hayek's point, then, is that the state and the economy is seriously jeopardised when what may well be an insurance policy, an act of prudent generosity for the genuine impoverished and those who cannot work, is constructed as an issue of national social justice. Once the term becomes enmeshed in government policy as well as finding widespread deployment in the public it is hard for it not to work itself out without damage to other criteria of efficiency and non-arbitrary recruitment. On the other hand, people can see with their own eyes how people manipulate their constructed disadvantages, and thus the 'backlash' occurs which gives the victims something more to complain about.

Against Hayek, it can be argued that where there are pools of impoverishment and alienation and cultural acceptance of lawlessness, then there are, by definition, high incidents of unjust acts. Injustice gets built into cultures, although one cannot say that poverty is the only variable (if it were one would still have to explain why some poor groups are far more lawless than others) and to this extent it is not as absurd as Hayek suggests to talk of social justice. But, it is difficult to see how the kinds of distributive programs suggested by defenders of social justice do much good. What Rawls and social democratic theorists ignore completely is social psychology, and how psychology in turn informs economic activity. Disadvantage, abuse, victimhood and violence once ingrained culturally do not disappear by throwing money at a group. A group will still express its past through its present; an identity is to a very large extent constituted by its behaviours.

The social democratic cast of mind carries its Enlightenment roots in its belief in the malleability of human beings and the possibility of engineering their character. However human beings change not through bureaucratic direction, but through the actions they love to do. Unfortunately some people can love violence, love being in gangs, love raping people, love digesting drugs, love being violated, love hating and would love to seize state power and kill all Jews. Although Nietzsche is a darling of post-moderns his richest insight remains largely untouched by post-modernists: victims are not more just or more deserving, often they are simply bearers of *ressentiment*.[14] The great irony that defenders of social justice rarely acknowledge is that the so called victims frequently don't see themselves as victims. And even then, those that do tend to do so because there may be some advantage to be had in constructing oneself as a victim.

This discussion may lead one to question whether the category of justice is useful at all, if the concept of the victim can be so messy. The answer is that justice is only one aspect of social existence and its preservation and provision is only one purpose of the state. Justice is no more *the* purpose of the state than it is *the* purpose of life. A state which was completely and utterly just - according to egalitarian and pacifist principles - would cease to exist, its enemies would conquer it in a flash. So any potential oasis of 'pure' justice would be fleeting and ephemeral; it would quickly be devoured by predators. A person who is completely and utterly moral does not exist.

The purpose of a state, then, must include conformity to law and justice, but it is in danger when impossibly idealist and incoherent ideas of either take over. Moreover, also in the field of law, the culture is destabilised by a merely instrumental view of the law. If the law is simply an instrument so that whatever group captures the state can do what it will, anarchy will inevitably follow. That is one reason why judges have to try and balance laws against each other, be inducted into a profession which moulds the individual's judgement and reins in caprice by demanding that the judge surrender to precedent or civil law, in much the same way that the legislation of politicians must comply with the constitution. This does not mean that there will not be bad or corrupt judges, or unjust decisions. Nor does it mean that bias may not play a role in passing judgement. But once it is simply taken for granted that a man is a man, a black a black, a woman a woman, a poor a poor, a rich a rich, and that the law should simply serve the interest of this particular aspect of human identity, then the community is being asked to bid adieu to all its past on the basis of its prejudicial formation.

It is obvious that there is no such individual who is merely a rich, a poor, a black, a female, or a male human being - as if these are meaningful entities whose nature can be fathomed without regard for the stories of each individual. But if one enters into the story, one quickly learns the name or nature of the mother and/or the father, possibly the brother and/or sister, possibly the children, the friends, the foes, the ghosts and dreams, the phobias, and regrets: the circumstance, the moods, the characters and whatever else make up a life. To pull every bit of existence through a solitary or even a handful of variables is insane, and to dismiss law itself as merely a patriarchal or racist institution, even when one sees that some laws have been racist and some patriarchal is merely rule application thinking, which is the result of intellectual slovenliness, and ultimately contributes to the replacement of real responses to real dilemmas by the barren dreamscape of the academician's idea of perfect justice. The instrumental view of law which is currently defended by the school of critical legal theory is no less dangerous to the future, than Marxist economics was.[15]

Marxist economics is dead precisely because it was tested by reality and failed. The damage done by critical legal theory is not so visible. Its fundamental premise of social inequality is true, and thus its inferences seem irrefutable. But what is never questioned in the model is the goal itself that it aspires to. Inequality exists for reasons, and some of those reasons may be stronger and more attractive than the alternatives of attempting to eliminate inequality, which may create a far worse social condition than its retention. This is precisely what occurred in the Soviet Union, China and Kampuchea. The value of the options depend upon the particular inequality, and on its particular temporal and spatial location. Equality is a mathematical not a living term, so its value is extremely limited.

Marxist penologists in the 1960s, like Eric Olin Wright, were honest enough to disclose that they wanted socialism, and when that was created prisons would not need to exist.[16] The only thing one had to ignore to accept the truth of Wright's claim, was actually existing socialism with its *Gulag Archipelago*.[17] Critical Legal Theory, on the other hand, proceeds, as does the remaining post-Soviet Left generally to-day, by way of negation. Inequality functions like a talisman to ward off the evil spirits of reality.

Public Works and Public Goods

From the time of the ancients it has been the task of the state to mobilise, direct and administer public works and provide public goods. Through public works and public goods a society's values are made concrete, hence the kinds of public works generated by different societies are invariably a key to their social character. The building of the pyramids in ancient Egypt provided an eternal symbol of the potency of the Pharo's rule -- so much so that the symbol far outlasts the rule. The official drama festivals in ancient Greece, on the other hand, provided a forum in which an artist could display his immortality, his power even transcending the rulers whose tragic lives are captured in his art. The proliferation of public educational goods — art galleries, libraries, museums, orchestras, public universities, radio and television stations — in the nineteenth and twentieth centuries is indicative of the increasing importance that education plays in the developed world.

Of itself the value of works and provisions is neither necessarily enhanced or diminished by whether it is state generated or privately generated, whether they are created by cruelty or public devotion. In the ancient world grand public projects spanning long time intervals required slavery, in Christendom equally glorious and ambitious undertakings reaching over generations such as the Gothic cathedrals could be undertaken by devoted artisans and laborers.

Public works invariably serve a legitimation function. The monstrous statues of Marx, Lenin and Stalin, which were as ugly as they were common throughout the communist world, served the function of drumming unity into the people's heads. A more sublime example which uses gigantic scale to foster the spirit of public unity is the Lincoln Memorial in Washington. Bill Clinton's memorial to Franklin D. Roosevelt is a clever tribute to the social justice ideals which he believes he himself embodies.

Over time the kinds of goods and works which are state administered change. When Adam Smith wrote *The Wealth of Nations* the list of public goods — roads, bridges, canals and harbours — seems small by comparison to the vast range of public goods one finds today in a modern state. It is understandable that people who are on the state payroll may fear such changes as the privatisation of communications systems or airlines or television stations. Likewise, it is understandable that the re-introduction of fees for students in universities, as has happened in Australia, will be condemned by university teachers and students as unfair. But unless one believes that an economy should be entirely state planned, the area of state funding must be frequently reassessed on the basis of affordability, opportunity costs and the government's economic strategy. Although, then, a purpose of the state is to provide public goods and public works, what those goods and works will change over time.

Representation of Interests

The state must also represent the community that it encompasses and not only that which exists, but that which it must ensure will exist in the future. At different times the state will be asked to accept new social claims to political representation and to decide which of them are legitimate. In the early periods of state development these claims were most often mobilised, advanced, pursued and resolved by force. This is the mechanism most commonly used outside the civilised zone today. In the civilised states, however, this mechanism is rarely utilised, although the Irish Republican Army remains one so far unsuccessful exception to the rule. Today new aspiring representations must mobilise ideologically, organisationally and then with votes. That is why these spheres have become such important sites of political mobilisation and contestation.

Although the idea of the general will may be dead it lives on in the more civilised form of a social consensus. The general will of Rousseau was recreated by totalitarians to emerge two centuries later as the Dictatorship of the Proletariat, the State of the Whole People, or the Duce. As societies became more complex such social formations were more difficult to achieve let alone sustain. In the civilised states such a notion was replaced by the idea of an ever adapting social consensus to which new ideas could be admitted by argument or organisation or by political intervention which in the civilised state amount to the same thing. But ideas may also be subtracted from the social consciousness by the same processes.

In the civilised states these two conceptions of core values or a continuing social consensus coexisting alongside other values which are added to and subtracted from it may be discovered in the different components of the state itself. As represented in the annual financial budget, some of the state apparatus is core and remains, while changing over the years, as necessary and accepted expenditure on commonly agreed social goals. Such parts of the state apparatus would include the police, the army, the courts, the legislative arms, the tax gathering bodies and the agencies for distributing state largess to the needy and worthy - including education, welfare and pension programs. These themselves may vary over time with the political conflict but they remain core components of the state. Other parts of the state are transitory and come in and out of existence as the political agenda of the civil society and its demands on the state change. These include universal health provision, child care by the state, environmental protection, university education, agricultural bounties, migration programs, and supporting the established religion.

The general will or core value structure as supported by the state has become (quite properly) a site of political contestation. In this work we have followed the gradual opening of the state to the input of different interests.

Changing Direction

The state cannot be merely the agency for the preservation of things inherited since there do come moments in the evolution of the state when either its society or the state itself encounters such a crisis in its functioning as to require deep restructuring and radical change. The usual agent of dramatic change is war and, to an even greater extent, impending defeat. This condition involves mobilisation and military strategy. But states do also encounter those moments when the direction in which they have been travelling becomes unviable and they must face a substantial overhaul. In point of fact such a crisis rarely emerges for a mature state because it has usually mobilised sufficient antennae to be forewarned of such a situation. Hence most such crises are encountered by authoritarian regimes which have been able to ignore interests that are not represented. Eventually they can face catastrophe if these interests grow sufficiently to mount a challenge. Such states are unable to enact one critical function of the state - avoiding crisis situations - precisely because of these inadequacies.

The most spectacular example of a major state confronting catastrophe in recent times was the Soviet Union. The Soviet state as constructed by Stalin in the 1930s could never function as a civilised society. It depended on a Platonic elite of the *nomeklatura* to run the state and their agents, the state planners in GOSPLAN, to run the economy. This could only work as a storming economy in war, or in post-war reconstruction, or at extremely primitive levels of output. By the late 1950s the Soviet Union was in none of these conditions and a serious reform program in the state and civil society was suggested by Nikita Khrushchev. He started a liberalisation program of censorship and freed millions of people from the labour camps. More seriously a number of plans were hatched for introducing market forces into the working of the economy. These schemes failed.

The attempts to reform the Soviet system in the early 1960s were defeated by the communist party that had itself become the main beneficiary of the dictatorship. Khrushchev was removed in 1964 and criticised for a number of policy shortcomings. But the real reason for his removal was contained in the slogan of his successor, Leonid Brezhnev, 'stability of cadres'. This was taken to mean that the communist party would remain as an avenue of upward social mobility for those who stayed quiet and loyal within its ranks. In other words the interests that had aggregated around Khrushchev and had come to see the need for widespread reform in the system were eliminated by administrative means, a coup, and not accommodated by the political process. The result was atrophy.[18]

By the 1980s the system had moved beyond reform and as the *nomenklatura* recognised their dilemma - or more accurately had it forced on them by international competition - so they had lost the moment to change. The imperial state itself then had to step in and impose reform too late in the shape of Gorbachev's program and then face dissolution into fifteen republics as it lost the capacity to survive competition from its constituent republics. In case of point the Soviet state had been unable to recognise its impending demise because it stifled the reformers and thereby consolidated its own inflexibility. (Boris Yelstin was forced to rise within the structure of the Russian Federation.) It paid the price in the form of its own demise. The former states of the Soviet Union then commenced the transitional task of remaking themselves as civilised democratic states. There was no guarantee this project would succeed in Russia against a backdrop of a collapsed civil society and an economic structure which by the 1990s produced a per capita income at about the level of Thailand.[19]

The case of South Africa is remarkably similar.[20] The White settlers seized the land and progressively established a racist dictatorship after 1913 which was consolidated following the 1948 election triumph of the Afrikaans Nationalist Party. What then ensued was a formal system of separate and unequal racial development - apartheid - which used a strong state apparatus to both enforce economic development and industrial growth and featherbed the Afrikaners by providing employment within it. This system had to be imposed on the African population by dictatorship and the state deployed much the same repressive measures as the Soviet Union - internal passports, detention without trial, murder in custody, censorship, and rewards for the politically faithful included. In the social democratic era, however, the South African state's recruiting method, race, had become completely unacceptable.

This system started to come apart in the 1970s for two main reasons. On the one hand the African population began to resist the system in such a widespread and serious way that internal war became the order of the day. While much of this remained within the African community and its townships, often stirred up by state *agent provocateurs*, or outside the country against guerrilla sanctuaries, and was therefore only of marginal direct concern to many of the Whites, it did start to make the country as a whole ungovernable. On the other hand, the economy started to decline when faced with domestic violence and a strike of capital in the 1980s.

But the state was so rigidly formed around racist criteria it refused to accommodate rising political interests and faced destruction at their hands by the end of the decade. The dilemma for White liberals in this situation is not without interest. Some left the country for exile, probably the only decent avenue available. Others joined the African resistance, a level of heroism few human beings aspire to. Most stayed in South Africa and enjoyed the fruits of the apartheid state without enthusiastically endorsing its policies, the likely choice for most people in such situations. But by the late 1980s the Africans had closed even that option.

In the early 1990s the Nationalists led by F.W. de Klerk finally used the state to begin negotiating their terms of surrender. It got a series of power sharing agreements designed to preserve certain White privileges long enough for them to be consolidated in the civil society alone as the new South African democratic state was formed. The corresponding reaction among the African population was a growing wave of violence which spread from the African townships to encompass the White residential areas. But a realignment of political forces did follow as the Whites, Afrikaner and liberal, and coloureds moved behind the Nationalists and the Africans began to divide along tribal and ideological lines. Whether this emerging pluralism could be channelled into a civilised state or would devolve to barbarism is not clear as the millennium draws to a close.

At such moments of crisis the state has a role to play as the agent of enforced change. To achieve this outcome it must be flexible, attentive to evolving conflicts and able to enforce change on its civil society. It must recognise the moment when stubborn and continued defence of the existing order will do it more harm than will its transformation. Since it is the creation of the existing civil society this is a difficult task to perform. The French *ancien régime* state ignored the warning signs, of which there were many, and played out its hand to its own destructive end. The Tsarist Russian state had more excuse for its demise in the form of its impending military defeat, a condition to which many states have been exposed. The Soviet and apartheid states left their run as agents of change very late and faced wholesale restructuring and social pain as a result. More prescient and flexible states have been able to get their civil societies to adapt to change in a more creative way.

Creating the Future

Just as the successful state must protect the past so must it create the future. In the most elementary sense this involves ensuring that successful processes and procedures initiated elsewhere are made available to the civil society and that it adopts them to its life form. In its more primitive form, in early modern Europe for example, one of the most successful mechanisms for achieving this outcome was warfare. Battle was so common a part of the intercourse between states and as a means of resolving their conflicts about resources with one another that states quickly found that if they were to prosper, indeed survive, they had to maintain front-line military technology and organisational forms. These could not be confined merely to the armed forces since most of production was carried out in the private sector and spread to civilian usage. The result was continuing competition and progress in the methods of production and social organisation throughout the civilised world of Europe.[21]

This conduit was supplemented later by the spread of ideas and commerce. The creation of a European wide intellectual milieu during the Reformation produced a climate for reform in which the ideas and organisational forms of the most advanced societies were offered to the other states and their progress depended in some measure on their capacity to grasp the opportunities offered. Montesquieu urged the English model on France; the Federalists created an updated version of the English constitution; and Napoleon spread the ideals (if not the actual practice) of the Enlightenment throughout Europe. As the industrial revolution gathered pace at first in Britain, this concept of a commercial civilisation started to take hold elsewhere as its evident attractions in the processes of production became so obvious. Many of the later industrialisers had their state apparatuses to thank for the rapidity with which the industrial system spread throughout Europe.

In the mid-nineteenth century the American state also faced a critical moment. Its northern states had created democracy and industrialisation and were set on the path to modern progress. But its southern states continued with the peculiar and archaic institution of slavery, a condition incompatible with modern industrialisation, democracy and civilisation. The state intervened in order to maintain unity on condition of freedom and to this end imposed a military solution to the issue at great cost but without which the crisis of the American state would have become even more intractable and difficult to resolve.

Shortly after the Japanese state made a decision as farsighted and arguably as momentous.[22] When Western power overran East Asia most of the societies of the region were subordinated, mostly to colonial status although sometimes by only informal control as in coastal China. The Japanese feudal elite assessed the situation as involving culturally inferior barbarians with superior organisation and technology. They reinstated the centralised monarchy during the Meiji Restoration of 1868 and then set about using it to create the Japanese future as an industrial and then dominant imperial state in East Asia. To accomplish this the Japanese imported what they assessed to be the most advanced models of each organisational and technological form then in existence. To some degree their own core values were altered but the integrity of the Japanese nation state as a whole was retained.

At the moment of decolonisation, of course, all new states faced a fairly stark choice of how they would create their own future and some of the discrepancies in the performances of the post-colonial states are attributable to the wisdom of those decisions. Many chose options that closed the route to progress by statism, militarism and various local forms of dirigisme described as socialism. These routes were particularly common in Africa. Others chose to emulate the Japanese experience and became the most successful performers, notably Taiwan and South Korea. South Korea was devastated after the Korean War and emulated Japan's drive to industrialise. It did so under a militarist state which enforced labour discipline and used an oligopolistic corporate sector based on the Japanese model to break into the world market in select sectors, like shipbuilding, automobiles, electronics and computers. State intervention led South Korea to the threshhold of civilised status by the turn of the century.

Other states made the wrong choice. The Cubans chose to join the Soviet bloc after their conflict with the United States during the revolutionary process of the early 1960s. Their society was sustained by Soviet subsidies provided for strategic and ideological advantage. With the Gorbachev reforms these were quickly withdrawn and Cuba faced an uncertain and poverty stricken future isolated from the general prosperity around it. Its state should intervene to change course but the grip of Castro on the power structure has prevented this obvious solution. The Vietnamese communists who arrived at much the same position for much the same reasons took advantage of meagre opportunities and shifted from Moscow to ASEAN and the capitalist world and now enjoy substantial growth off a low base.

When civilised states are faced with such choices the chances of a good result are much greater because of the diversity of interests represented and the corresponding increase in the range of political choices made available to the community. In the 1960s the British came to appreciate Dean Acheson's assessment that they had lost an empire but failed to find a new role.[23] They then undertook a vigorous and complicated debate about whether and on what terms they should seek to join the European community. They joined in the 1970s and abandoned much of their old empire and its privileged status in the British market. The British then began long haggling over the pace at which they, and the other member states for that matter, should integrate into Europe. In the main the British were among the more recalcitrant. In this process the British state had indeed lost an empire but also found a new role as a medium European power of some prosperity, against the wishes of the British people who were overwhelmingly anti-Europe at the start of the process and could likely be made so again by any half decent demagogue.

The other side of this process was the difficulties then faced by the former British colonies who found their principal market closed by the European Common Agricultural Policy which had in turn been invented by the French state to protect its farmers. New Zealand was most hard hit. Its Labour Government in the 1980s belatedly produced a market oriented solution that transformed the country from an offshore part of the British economy to a lean and diversified Asia-Pacific economy with little choice and at some social cost.[24]

The state must encourage a continuing debate about its own future and that of the community whose care it must cultivate. In order to generate this debate about the appropriate future it must allow all voices to be heard and all interests to be expressed. Ideally these should be fostered in the national clearing house for political ideas, the national legislature. In this respect some slack in the discipline in party politics is appropriate so that even the more outlandish ideas may receive expression. To prevent a later fracturing of consensus it is better that the consensus itself shifts in time. The civilised and democratic state is best able to achieve that goal.

For this reason the mature state as on display in the civilised world commands the respect of both liberals and conservatives. For liberals, its representative character is such that any interest is able to compete for representation and pursue its vision of the future in a rational manner, and so it commands moral respect and support. For the conservative, the capacity of the mature civilised state to identify new interests legitimately requiring representation and incorporate them into the existing historically determined social consensus, ensures that order will be maintained on a sustainable, organic and consensual foundation. This is a state form commanding support on both moral and pragmatic terms.

Different Powers for Different Moments

The multiple tasks of the mature state also means that for its purposes to be fulfilled different principles inform its different powers. Different powers, although part of the one totality, have different logics. A complex society contains multiple underpinning principles which link up in much the same way that our limbs do. The fit body will be one in which the limbs respond to circumstance and comply with will, but each limb has its own peculiar character, potential dexterity and inherent limitations. This organic theory of the state goes back to the Middle Ages, and it provides a much more adequate metaphor for sound government than the mechanistic metaphors of the seventeenth century, metaphors which derive from the belief that physics could provide the framework for all actions, an idea that does not help a lot with a social phenomenon.

Thus, for example, even in a democratic society, there is no question of an elective military force. Indeed, there are numerous roles of government where the very nature of the purposes to be fulfilled mitigates against democracy: the police force, the bureaucracy, and the judiciary, for example. A democratic government may elect a Police commissioner, but that is not the police force itself. Police officers and soldiers evolve out of the experience of conflict. Conflict comes with its own logic, its own reasons, its own permutations. The enforcement role of the state is separate from its representative function.

Likewise the bureaucrat who works in treasury knows that economic laws have nothing to do with what most people may want them to be; most people want infinite consumption and to work as little as possible. The bureaucrat is not valuable because of popularity, but because of knowledge, performance, quick judgement and other such qualities, and is recruited on merit to acquire and deploy these proficiencies. Just as a democracy needs good (and lucky) generals, so does a democracy need smart bureaucrats. But, to repeat, these needs and the characters which can fulfil such needs are required by any modern state form and they cannot be reduced to the singular principle of democracy. Likewise, an effective and publicly respected judiciary is not a luxury of a modern state, it is indispensable. If a nation is to enjoy economic prosperity, highly skilled people trained in the law are necessary for the mediation of interests and the resolutions of economic conflicts. The judiciary, like the bureaucracy, is the modern day equivalent to the ancient philosophers' conception of the aristocracy. Its role in the state is meritocratically based, even if individual appointments are partisan and their talent somewhat limited.

When Plato provided the first typology of regimes, he distinguished between good and bad forms of government; for each good form there corresponded a bad equivalent. Thus he saw six kinds of government: monarchy, tyranny, aristocracy, oligarchy, mass rule with the law, and mass rule without it. In the *Laws* he combined the best likely elements: law is represented as the divine monarch, and then aristocratic and democratic elements are combined. In presenting the problem the way he did, it appeared as if Plato had settled for what he considered to be the second best form of government, and that is what he believed. But what he did not grasp is that each of the moments he describes has a reason for existence, and that even the oligarchic and dictatorial and mob rule moments may have value.

The different forms of government are merely different expressions of human capacities and human interests, their evolution takes place over time, and at different times different powers emerge as dominant. Thus, it is a sign of a state's strength that it has tyrannical, oligarchic and mob like characteristics. The tyrant is merely the dictatorial energy which dominates in a time of crisis. If it dominates at the wrong time, it will bring misery on its people. In modern times dictatorial power may be the only way to stop civil chaos if there is barbaric ethnic conflict, or if drug lords have a hold of a country, or terroristic zealots are out of control. But dictatorial rule ultimately becomes economically inefficient. If a people know that their produce will be plundered, then their energies will not be harnessed to generating wealth and dreaming up new ideas, investors will stay away, and incentives will grow in the population to bring an end to the dictator; it may take a lot of time for its downfall, but the regime will be out of time. On the other hand, when a state faces terrorist attack it must deploy emergency powers, which are essentially dictatorial by nature.

Finally, consider the oligarchic purpose of the modern state. The wealthy few are not dispensable in modern commercial societies.

Their wealth provides them with economic opportunities and enables them to undertake adventures which will have all sorts of spin offs throughout the community. Whereas the meritocratic nature of a judge and jury is assessable through qualifications and the like, the oligarch's sign of success is wealth. The most conspicuous example of oligarchic leadership in modern civilised states is in the example of the media. Although there may seem something intuitively plausible about the wrongness of a small elite having so much input into the acquisition and communication of information, the fact is that because information is a commodity, it is in the interest of the oligarchic to provide a great variety of it, in all shapes and sizes from its most trivialised versions to highly sophisticated forms. Information societies are invariably oligarchic in important respects, and this is no accident. The oligarch is neither elected, nor meritocratically appointed, nor dictatorial. The oligarch is a wealthy opportunist and, in a modern economy, wealth is maintained by providing what people like as commodities. The intelligentsia invariably hate oligarchs, and treat their existence as a moral issue. But this Platonistic moral view like all idealist view points, is out of time. Thus it is not very useful to us who live in time.

Notes

1. Catherine MacKinnon, *Towards A Feminist Theory of the State*, Cambridge, Mass, Harvard University Press, 1989, pages 178-79.
2. Charles De Gaulle, *War Memoirs*, Vol. 1, London, Collins, 1955, page 9; and *Memoirs of Hope: Renewal 1958-62, Endeavour, 1962-66*, London, Weidenfeld and Nicolson, 1971.
3. Hugh Thomas, *The Spanish Civil War*, London, Readers Union, 1962.
4. Sophocles, *Antigone; Oedipus the King; Electra*, trans. H. D. F. Kitto, Oxford, Oxford University Press, 1994.
5. L. L. Fuller, *The Law in Quest of Itself; The Morality of Law*, New Haven, Yale University Press, 1977; and 'Positivism and Fidelity to Law - A Reply to Professor Hart', *Harvard Law Review*, 1958,

page 593.
6. See Harold Berman, *Justice in the USSR: An Interpretation of Soviet Law*, Cambridge, Mass., Harvard University Press, 1966; Peter H. Juviler, *Revolutionary Law and Order; Politics and Social Change in the USSR*, New York, Free Press, 1976.
7. R. Grunberger, *A Social History of the Third Reich*, London, Weidenfeld and Nicolson, 1971.
8. Leslie Holmes, *Politics in the Communist World*, Oxford, Oxford University Press, 1986.
9. Friedrich von Hayek, ed., *Collective Economic Planning: Critical Studies on the Possibilities of Socialism*, London, Routledge, 1935; Ludwig von Mises, *Socialism: An Economic and Sociological Analysis*, trans. James Kahane, Indianapolis, Liberty, 1981; Von Hayek, *The Road To Serfdom*, [1944] London, Routledge, 1976 ; and *The Constitution of Liberty*, Chicago, Chicago University Press, 1960.
10. F.Von Hayek, *Law, Legislation and Liberty,* Three Volumes, London, Routledge, 1973-1979; John Rawls, *A Theory of Justice,* Oxford, Oxford University Press, 1971; and his later *Political Liberalism*, New York, Colombia University Press, 1993.
11. Susan Moller Okin, *Justice, Gender and the Family*, Basic Books, USA, 1989, chapter five, pages 89-109.
12. Josephine Hart, *Sin*, New York, Viking, 1994.
13. Thomas Sowell, *Civil Rights: Rhetoric and Reality*, New York, Quill, 1984.
14. Friedrich Nietzsche, *The Genealogy of Morals*, trans. Walter Kaufmann, New York, Vintage Books especially third essay section 15.
15. See, for example, Roberto Unger, *Law in Modern Society: Toward a Criticism of Social Theory*, London, Collier, MacMillan, 1976.
16. *The Politics of Punishment: A Critical Analysis of Prisons in America*, New York, Harper and Row, 1973.
17. Alexander Solzhenitsin, *The Gulag Archipelago,1918-1956,* trans Thomas P. Whitney, Fontana, 1974.
18. David Lane, *The Socialist Industrial State*, London, Allen and Unwin, 1980, provides an optimistic account but Paul Dibb, *The*

Soviet Union: The Incomplete Superpower, London, 1985, proved more accurate.
19. Daniel Yergin and Thane Gustovson, *Russia 2010 and what it means for the world; the CERA report*, New York, Random House, 1993.
20. Allister Sparks, *The Mind of South Africa: The Story of the Rise and Fall of Apartheid*, London, Mandarin Press, 1990; and *Tomorrow is Another Country: The Inside Story of South Africa's Negotiated Revolution*, London, Mandarin Press, 1995.
21. For two interesting discussions of this process see, Paul Kennedy, *The Rise and Fall of the Great Powers*, London, Fontana Press, 1989; and Hedley Bull, *The Control of the Arms Race*, London, Weidenfeld and Nicolson, 1961.
22. W. H. Beasley, *The Meiji Restoration*, Stanford, California, 1972.
23. John Lamberton Harper, *American Visions of Europe: Franklin D. Roosevelt, George F. Kennan and Dean G. Acheson*, Cambridge, Cambridge University Press, 1994.
24. See Bob Catley, *Globalising Australian Capitalism*, Melbourne, Cambridge University Press, 1996.

4 Philosophy Dreaming: Idealist Approaches to the State

> "all the while the beast drank there was no noise in the beast's belly"
>
> Sir Thomas Mallory, *Morte d'Arthur*

Ancient Philosophy and Christian Activism

It is a fateful fact that the first full blown political theory is idealist in character. A theoretical grasp of the political body was, for Plato, inseparable from the probings into the nature of truth, the good, being, the gods, the one god, and knowledge itself. When Plato argued that in order to have knowledge of any being, no matter how mundane or sublime, we must intellectualise the idea which illuminates its character, he was making the mind's eye and ideas the benchmark of all existing things.[1] The philosopher *sees* (the word idea derives from *eidein*, to see) the reality behind the appearances, the unity within diversity. He puts together the real story, the *logos*, about truth and the good.

The Platonic dialogues are one vast encounter with all those who do not know reality and thus who lead the Greek souls along the false roads, the false roads of rhetoric (Gorgias is guilty), of statesmanship (Pericles is guilty), of poetry (Hesiod, Homer, and indeed all the poets are guilty), of sophistry (Protagoras is the main offender).[2] Against all these practitioners of falsehood, Plato presents a man who not only outwits the orators, and poets and sophists whenever he encounters them, but a man who calls himself the one true statesman - Socrates.

The irony of this claim is that Socrates held no political office. But irony is the currency of the Socratic exchange. Socrates does not claim to teach virtue, but he is the most virtuous Athenian. Socrates is ugly, but he is (unsuccessfully) enticed by the strong and beautiful Alcibiades.[3] Socrates is executed for corrupting the youth and worshipping strange new gods, but Socrates knows what is genuinely divine behaviour and how the youth should be educated, and how, indeed, the poets should be horsewhipped for filling the minds of babes with lewd and impious tales of deceit, treachery, debauchery, as well as all manner of contradictions. Socrates held no political office, but he builds a new political order with a group of inquisitive young men. And his order is not built on the hurly burly of blind and rapacious desires. Nor does it spring from merely following in the footsteps of traditions which have been passed down by the incompetent poets and statesmen and orators. It is built upon the noble inquiry into the good.

The best political organisation may not be able to be realized - and Plato's interpreters have continually wrangled over whether Plato really believed that the *Republic* could be actualised. But what mattered most was that the Platonic Socrates had provided a standard for assessing the degree of corruptibility of worldly regimes. Although Plato has been pilloried by liberal and Marxist academics for his otherworldliness, the real flaw of Platonism, as with every idealism, whether it appears under the guise of Marxism or liberalism (and idealism can move within any political or -- paradoxically enough -- even ontological framework) is this: a real process is to be measured by what by its very nature is not a real process. Even if the concatenations of the real could be completely reproduced in the mind -- something that is highly improbable with the complexity of social behaviour -- action generates events, while reflection follows in their trail. Actions invent; reflection uncovers. Action unlocks and unleashes powers, opportunities and resources which one could not dream of, precisely because in action one enters into unforeseen territory.

This is not to say that philosophical reflection does not provide insight into how to do some things better, but its creative force is largely limited to what material is supplied by action to the reflecting consciousness. This is also not to say that philosophy is not itself a form of action. On the contrary, as Socrates well knew, philosophy is a mode of action. But it is only one mode of action, a powerful mode, but one mode nevertheless. It is a mode which builds slowly and patiently with the rationalisations of known actions; but action is wild as well as patient, dreamlike as well as wakeful, irrational, with all the madness and savagery and exquisite passions that the soul can muster, as well as reflective.

The Platonic dream was to stabilise the political order by making it conform to the most rational pattern of human association that a philosopher could think. The idea of the philosopher king in Plato was not limited to the fanciful schema of the *Republic* where those subjected to a certain curricula would rule, rather it was (albeit all too often unrecognised) the idea at the heart of all Platonic approaches to politics. The Platonist believes that if only political reality could be adjusted to the ideas in his/her mind all would be well.

Indeed, what tempts a philosopher or academic into being a Platonist is not only the egotism of thinking that the reflective consciousness can grasp the total experience of a sphere of action which one is not actually involved in, but the idea that one can avoid error. The life of the Platonist is a life devoted to truth. And it is no accident that Plato presents the philosophical life as a life devoted to the weeding out of error. The strain between the two great cosmologies which cradle Western consciousness is based upon the Platonist aversion to error and the Christian teaching of action. The Christian idea of action is intrinsically linked to the idea of redemption: redemption is the turning around of a soul which has suffered, despaired and learnt through its wayward and sinful acts. The Platonist sees evil as ignorance and ignorance as error. Hence actions based on error are the futile actions which could have been avoided had one had the right cast of mind. The right temperament or nature -- it is no accident in Plato that philosophy can only be for the few -- is to be combined with the right method.

The Christian cosmology, on the other hand, teaches the primacy of action, of discovery through action and of response to one's calling: one's calling is a unique event and there is no attempt to evaluate human action by reference to one solitary human activity such as philosophy. The Platonist will act truly on the basis of a correct philosophy; the Christian understands that all hearts, whether Christian or not, act first and that no life is singular in its expression. No life, for example, can just be philosophical. Correct action is done from purity of heart and simple faith in the power of love; righteous action does not require a great intellect. Indeed, a great philosophical mind is no more to be prized than a good ability to hew wood, catch fish or play backgammon. It is the condition of the heart which reveals the value of an action. Unlike God, we lack the capacity to view the totality of things, to grasp the significance of details. The philosopher may know all of Aristotelian science, and may miss the bacteria that poisons him.[4]

Generally, the academic mind is steeped in the prejudices of Platonism, and academic accounts of political life tend to idealise political processes. Stated this baldly, it may seem as if every one who thought about the state or sought to act on behalf of the common good was a Platonist. To seek insight into the state is to enter into the sphere of reflection, and to become encumbered with the language of philosophy, which is, indeed, the language of political theory. There is, however, a way to seek the common good and engage in political thought yet remain a non-Platonist. That is to see politics as a process and to realise the limited status of the insight one has, precisely because of the reflective role that one occupies. The value of reflection lies in its being a taking stock, a consideration of alternatives on the basis of available known modes of action. The non-Platonist does not prescribe an ideal state, precisely because existence is not an ideal thing, and what is grasped in the process of reflection is but a transitory composite of discernible forces.

To the extent that Aristotle's approach to politics was one of comparing different political forms and their pathologies, Aristotle represents a methodological evolution in the advancement of understanding political organisation. But Aristotle remained sufficiently Platonist to want to represent an ideal state.[5] And he wanted to quibble with Plato over the details of an ideal state, rather than recognise the endeavour as fundamentally wrong-headed. Aristotle, no less than Plato, wanted to be a philosopher king. Aristotle, no less than Plato, rests politics on ethics. And, again no less than Plato, Aristotle ultimately brings politics before the judgment of philosophers.

In doing this he misses an element of thinking about the political which stems from the Judaic and Christian traditions, an element which is essential for a proper understanding of the contemporary civilised world as for the civilised state: Aristotle, like Plato, has no notion of the historical significance of progress. The story of Judaism is a story of a passage from bondage to freedom. In that respect it is the archetypical story of those who have suffered and want to improve their collective lot as a people. It is a story of the social creation of a kingdom through action and response to the revealed word. It has nothing to do with philosophical artifice or argument.

The gospel, not the writings of philosophers, lays the basis for the spawning of a major social movement which will move from the riff-raff living at the perimeters of the Roman empire into the empire itself, while simultaneously expanding the perimeters of the empire. Eventually the man who had the right to be both emperor and god declines his godhood in deference to a Jewish rabble rouser. A new order of time will be established, one which breaks history into two segments, the former being but the movement toward a birth. Before Christ, the other being the movement beyond a birth as all of humanity is to be embraced in one spiritual mode of consciousness, Anno Domini. The imperial polity, through the Church, becomes galvanised into the task of creating the heavenly imperium, an imperium which will then, again via the Church, continue in its expansion even after the earthly imperium is overtaken by the Goths, Visigoths or by other tribes which have no commitment to peace or progress.

The Christian conception of time and the Christian task of unification work hand in hand. Christianity survives the fall of the Roman Empire. When opportunity arises again Charlemagne becomes the Holy Roman Emperor -- his being crowned by the pope is fraught with political undertones which will show just how secular the heavenly imperium really is. But what is unmistakable about this process is that the Church has a mission in time, to bring all times into one time, all calendars under one calendar, all peoples to one banquet.

Whereas empire societies were expansionary and provide an indispensable mode of consciousness for the evolution of the Church, it is the Church itself which turns the actuality of the imperial form of social organisation into a progressive sphere, a sphere which will not be simply based upon bondage and glory, but upon a commonweal which cuts across classes and sexes and races. The king is just another man in the eye of God, a man with a particular task, to be sure, but a man no more sure of God's mercy and grace than the lowliest of the low. By the twelfth century, the very building of a Church will testify to the essential message of Christendom: that love conquers death, that the time of the believers will outlast those who do not believe, that generations of a community willingly (and not just as slaves) build monuments to reflect their participation in eternity. To be sure grand architecture is a feature of all civilised peoples; as Rosenstock-Huessy beautifully put it in one of his lectures on empire societies, all civilised peoples from the first hieroglyph sing out the praises of eternity, but the Christian message was a call to all human beings, for each to express his or her unique talents in service to God's will. Each soul is to be a brick in the universal Church, thus there can be no salvation outside the Church. The Church was to be the living spirit of peace, because it promised to liberate people from the barbarism of ceaseless conflict.

The Catholicism of the Church's mission stands in stark contrast to the mission of the great Platonist creation, the Academy. The Academy was not an attempt to integrate all non-sinful ways of life into a universal realm, but to develop one aspect of life, the intellect, and the rather narrow interests of those people who found fulfilment in an intellectual life. Just as intelligence (*nous*) is the highest faculty of the soul, philosophy is seen by the philosophers as the highest of all human activities. Political organisation ultimately exists in the Platonic universe to serve the academy, and the academicians ultimately exist to observe the divine intelligence. Society itself is a means for promoting a particular, that is the philosophical, way of life and the interests of a particular group of people. The ideal polities of both Plato and Aristotle have this as their real objective, a point that Leo Strauss and his followers have emphasised in their readings of the ancients.⁶ When Luther raged against the schoolmen, he saw that philosophers had captured the Church for their own ends. In modern times, the academic mind generally accepts Feuerbach's claim that the attributes of the divine are merely the alienated parts of the species.⁷ The modern academicians ultimately exist only to contemplate their own intelligence.

The master stroke of philosophical idealism was to equate the interests of a political group of people with the common good and then to make argument, the one skill philosophers excelled in, the standard for attesting what the common good was. And underpinning the whole show was the vicious circle that since the good is what is intelligible, therefore the good is recognised by those who intellectualise existence. Because philosophy is only a part of life, its program was always going to be politically limited as long as the philosophers were the few. But, it was never going to be clear to holders of power and resources that because they were oafish they should be servants to philosophers.

Concomitantly, while idealism presents a seductive, but highly dubious approach to understanding reality, it was never a great danger in the ancient world. Indeed, in so far as philosophy develops a *modus operandi* which is first practised in the law courts, philosophical thinking would find its most valuable and appropriate political niche in the law.⁸ This was not only true in ancient Rome where the Stoics directed their political ambition to enriching the body of law, but also in Western Europe in the late eleventh and early twelfth century where, on being rediscovered, Aristotle became a vital element in the curricula of the law schools. The great legacy of philosophy to thinking generally, and law in particular, is the systemic gathering of elements into principles, and conversely, the ability to break down principles into their subordinate elements.⁹

It was not merely the fact that someone reflected philosophically upon the nature of the state that made a theory idealist, but the extent to which the philosophising consciousness sets itself up as the benchmark of value. Machiavelli, Hobbes and Locke, for example all philosophised about the state, but they do not attempt to set up a state which will be the expression of a philosophical idea. Rather, they survey the social dynamics of their time and seek to know how their respective objectives - political unification and imperial expansion (Machiavelli), peace (Hobbes), securement of personal property (Locke) - can be politically attained. There is a recognition by all of the limitation of the reflecting consciousness. One may well be an advisor, one may desire political power, but the end for them is not to protect and subordinate political aims to philosophy.

Further, the ancients' idealism was built upon the premise of natural inequality, and with both Plato and Aristotle one's nature was firmly fixed. A contingency could deplete one, an accident may disable one, but the idea that a person could redeem his or her nature was foreign to them. The idea of a radical moment of salvation is, again, Christian not Greek. The tandem relationship between feudalism and Christianity would wear down that way of thinking. From the side of feudalism, the relationship between serf and noble was contractual and with the proliferation of diverse power relations, due partly to shifting power allegiances made possible by the schism brought on by the investiture conflict, and partly to the emergence of towns, power relations were more fluid than in a slave society. From the side of Christianity, although Christianity did not proffer a doctrine of secular egalitarianism, it fostered a culture in which each task, when done in service to the Lord, was the fulfilment of God's plan. In this all important respect it was fundamentally anti-elitist, even though other social and worldly pressures and traditions would emphasise hierarchy, even, or should one say especially, in the Church.

The major legacy to civilisation of these forces was the eventual embracing of various modes of egalitarianism, but most notably judicial, that is, formal legal equality and with it the possibility of civic rights of the individual.[10] Modern idealist theories of the state thus bore the traces of the anti-idealist legacy of the Christian religion within them.

The Moderns

The three great modern theories of the state which have strong idealist components are those of G.W.F. Hegel, Karl Marx and Immanuel Kant. The idealist status of Kant's state theory is not in dispute. But those of Hegel and Marx are. Marx certainly did not think of himself as an idealist and he presents himself as a bitter opponent of idealism and as more politically allied with Machiavelli. While there is a Machiavellian component within Marxian theory, Marxian state theory and its epigone is strongly idealist. Much of it, in turn, derives from Hegel.

G. W. F. Hegel

The case of Hegel is complicated in so far as Hegel's philosophy is one of the most self-consciously idealist philosophical systems there is. Part of the reason for this is that Hegel holds that all philosophy is idealist: that the idea (*Idee*) is the end purpose of a thought process, the *realisation* of the meaning of the constitutive elements of a thought. The objects of philosophy are always *Ideen*.[11] Even materialism is a mode of idealism for Hegel, because the ascription of any content to the term material requires reference to intuitions, representations (*Vorstellungen*), concepts (*Begriffe*) and ideas. A materialism that was not expressed with ideas would simply not be a philosophy, it would be an empty predicate able to muster only a gaping stare. Further, Hegel makes philosophy itself the greatest repository of culture, above art and religion. In this respect, Hegel is very much in line with Plato, although some scholars claim that he breaks too much with the Socratic profession of ignorance in his claim that a philosopher must possess wisdom, and not just love it.[12] Few philosophers have had more hubris than Hegel. He claims that his system fulfils philosophy by realising: (a) that logic must replace metaphysics; (b) that his system is the culmination of the entire history of philosophy; and (c) that he is able to demonstrate and provide the categorical and generic unity of all the sciences.[13]

It would seem, then, that Hegel is an idealist. And some of Hegel's *Philosophy of Right* is insufferable in its formalism, particularly the section on abstract right, which gives the impression that Hegel is playing a huge game by trying to satisfy his own criteria of demonstrating the generic relationship between the elements of justice or right. But there is one enormous difference between Hegel and other political idealists, a difference that makes it inappropriate to classify Hegel as a political idealist at all. Hegel's philosophy of the state is an attempt to depict the social dynamics of his day and how substantive freedom is institutionally achieved by constituents of the modern state. Hegel is bitterly opposed to any social or moral philosophising which substitutes what the particular mind wants, what he repeatedly calls the 'empty ought', with those actual freedoms that have evolved through the balance of social forces and institutional arrangements. In keeping with this, Hegel persistently attacks the Jacobin philosophies of Rousseau, Kant, Fichte and the German romantic philosopher Friedrich Jacobi as well as the ultra nationalism of Jacob Fries.[14]

To this considerable extent, one may even go so far as to say that the most self-consciously idealist philosopher of modernity belongs with the most anti-idealist political and state theorists. And like that other idealist, Karl Marx, Hegel is a great fan of Machiavelli. Further, the Hegelian philosophy does defend a conception of political progress not too dissimilar to that defended in this book: that civilisation represents an advance in people's freedom.[15] That freedom is realised not through any group having absolute power, as if it were possible for all the people to have absolute power, but through a balancing of social interests via a diverse institutional array of sites of representation and articulation of claims.

Karl Marx

If there seems to be great irony in the fact that such a self-professed idealist as Hegel was an opponent of contemporary political idealism, it is an even greater historical irony that he should be the major philosophical inspiration for the most influential of all modern political idealists. Marx attacked philosophical idealism mercilessly for hypostasising real social processes.[16] Ontologically, Marx persistently claimed that he examined real social relations and concerned himself with the material conditions of social existence. At his crudest he would sweepingly deprecate a philosophical position on the basis of the class interests he believed underpinned the philosophy. Thus Kant's categorical imperative was merely a philosophical smoke screen for the interests of the German bourgeoisie.[17]

Marx not only claimed to have uncovered the hidden laws of capitalism, but the social form that lay embryonically within it. Yet the entire project of Marx was idealist from start to finish. Only his persistent denial that he wasn't saying what he was saying has managed to blind legions of Marxist idealists after him to his and their own political idealism. At the start of his intellectual career Marx was a law student who fell in love with philosophy. Philosophy, though, needed to come down to earth. The young Marx's philosophical studies of politics, history and political economy became a search for the true meaning of human nature and history. A short time after he had realised that Ludwig Feuerbach had understood that man is a species being, and that is the clue to his nature, he went on to find the answer to 'the riddle of history.' It was communism. Only in a communist society could the powers of man's species being be unlocked. Just prior to celebrating his discovery of communism, Marx was bitterly attacking Hegel's idealist theory of the state.[18] The problem with Hegel, who wrote the *Philosophy of Right* in 1821, was that he was a constitutional monarchist and not a radical democrat. Indeed, Hegel did not realise that the people were the real source of political authority and all power had to stem directly from the people. Hegel, on the other hand, had allowed himself to defend the interests of the landed aristocracy by rationalising the practice of primogeniture. He had also defended what Marx believed was an outdated representative body for skilled craftsmen.

This critique by the young Marx actually proves the opposite of what he wanted to demonstrate. That is to say, in his critique of Hegel it is Marx not Hegel who emerges as the idealist and Hegel who emerges as the political realist. The reason Hegel does not wax lyrically about the people is because he sees politics as the art of resolving conflicting interests. It is not a question of eliminating conflict. That is not a possibility. Societies are, of necessity, composed of powerful forces pushing in contrary directions. The compromise between forces that is reached through the extended creation of political institutions is better than the bloodbath of classes trying to wipe each other out. In his *Phenomenology of Spirit* Hegel had brilliantly, although with an ellipticism typical of that work, written on the dialectic of the Terror of the French revolution.[19] The attempt to externalise and superimpose upon the world the unsullied purity of the rational conscience, leads the moral fanatic to resort to Terror in order to become real. The Robespierre formula - 'virtue is terror' -

symptomises the reality of political idealism, for Hegel. That different social forces would rather, indeed, would have to compromise after all the bloodletting of the Jacobin experiment was, for Hegel, a sign that real reason had triumphed over the folly of political fanatics. Hegel, then, does not prattle on about the people in the *Philosophy of Right* because 'the people' is not a unified political actor; it is not a meaningful political term.

Marx would later concede this when he had to dispense with any talk about liberating the people, while instead making the working class become the agent of historical destiny. In sum, in his critique of Hegel, Marx really chastises Hegel for trying to fathom the real reason in the institutional balancing act of the modern state.

For Marx, Hegel's identification of the most powerful political forces and their institutional articulation was merely protecting vested interests. Marx would become obsessed with one thing, the elimination of private interests. Having discovered that history as it had hitherto been experienced was the expression of class conflict, he came to see all social relations and institutions as pathologically infected by the existence of private interests. Thus Marx declares that with communism there will be no division of labour, no property, no law, no money, no state, no religion, and no alienation. The degree of one's freedom seems to be proportional to the negations one embraces. That property, law, the division of labour, the state, and religion were not the artifacts of capitalist society but the very elements which emerge wherever there is any moderately large scale, settled social organisation or nation did not bother Marx or his followers. Indeed, when the occasion arose they would denounce the very idea of nation as a repressive ideological construct. Further, at the same time as Marx is declaring that the elimination of all known forms of social organisation, apart from voluntary communal co-operation, will provide so much abundance that alienation stemming from the division of labour, capitalist oppression and poverty will be eliminated, he persistently attacked the Saint Simonians and Fourierists, who were engaging in voluntary non-violent social co-operative experiments, for being utopians. Unlike them, Marx believed he had proof that capitalism would break down, but before it had done that it would sufficiently socialise and expand the means of production so that socialism and communism would occur.

Compared to this fantastical idealism, Plato's idea of the Guardians having common wives and communal property and taking their orders from a bunch of philosophers pales into insignificance. But throughout all of his life Marx never deviated from his belief that communism is 'not an ideal to which reality will have to adjust itself. We call communism the real movement which abolishes the present state of things.'[20] Communism was not an ideal, it was an Aristotelian *telos* immanent in the form of capitalism. It is one of those great, barely appreciated tragic ironies that whereas Aristotelianism had been expunged from the natural sciences, it was alive and kicking in the most disastrous pseudo-scientific social theory of modernity.

That Marx and his followers could pass themselves off as the enemies of idealists is one of the most remarkable historical self-misunderstandings. His followers would continue to pit themselves against idealists even when Lenin and Stalin made speech after speech declaring communism was an act of will, and of faith;[21] even after Gramsci, the most Hegelian and the most realistic of all Marxist theoreticians of the twentieth century, had said that socialism was a religion;[22] and even when communist states imprisoned and executed people merely for the ideas they held. But there were a number of aspects to this form of idealism which were completely lacking in the classical idealist tradition. First, Marxism was essentially an eschatological doctrine. And precisely because of that, it provided moral orientation for a social group, the intelligentsia, who had lost faith in the gods of religion and mere ethics, and were themselves largely lacking in political power.

The potency of its eschatology was also derived from the fact that the essential components of its symbols were the stock in trade of Judaic/Christianity teachings anyway. There was a promised land; there was a historical journey; there was a prophet; there was an agent of sacrifice; and there was an underlying truth and meaning to the drama of existence. Of course, all these symbols take on a different potency when secularised, but they nevertheless form a pattern which will evoke a response in a mind that sees the congruence of the elements as existentially significant.[23] In believing in the secularised version of the symbols one also is morally sanctioned by a conscience that believes science discloses truth, and that truth is only in this world. Again, when Marx repeatedly points to the scientific rigour of his analysis, even though he did not do one single model study of the mechanics of a modern large scale economy under communism, he is really making a moral point to shore up the eschatology.

Marxism was also the modern way of making philosophers, that is academic social theorists, rulers.[24] But they could rule with a clear egalitarian conscience. For the whole enterprise of Marxism was to reproduce in secular society the religious dream of an unalienated life, and that included the attainment of substantive equality. As much as Marx avowed, and yet again denied that he had no interest in equality, the whole *moral* force of communism lay in its promise of the elimination of inequalities of resources, by virtue of its elimination of classes.

Old style Platonists would no doubt baulk at the idea that Lenin, Lukács and Bukharin, not to mention the hack academic Marxists, were Platonists. But this is what they were, although not so philosophically sophisticated as their master. This point had, of course, been made by Karl Popper in *The Open Society and Its Enemies*, and Platonists had rallied to defend Plato from the charge of being a totalitarian.[25] But the point of Popper's critique is somewhat misplaced in that it focuses too much on comparative details which tend to divert attention away from the obvious fact that Plato was writing in a time of non-free states, and that much of what he proposed already existed in one form or another in Greece. This latter point was made by Hegel (also an enemy of Popper) who insisted that *The Republic* was not an empty prescription.

The real continuity between Platonism and Bolshevism is better appreciated not if we think in terms of two similar social programs, for the programs were sufficiently dissimilar for Platonists to show Popper had not been fair to Plato, but rather in terms of their shared belief that a society could be rationally co-ordinated by planners in the first place. There is a most revealing passage in *The Republic*, brought to attention in a transcript of a lecture by Rosenstock-Huessy, a thinker who frequently spoke of the Platonist roots of Bolshevism. In the *Republic*, Plato refers to Apollo, who is said to be 'sitting in the middle....at the very navel of the earth' interpreting reality.[26] The sentence sums up the philosophical dream: to occupy a place where the totality of reality can be disclosed. The social engineer is like

Apollo. He or she believes that there is a hub from which social reality can be grasped in its entirety, just as Marx believed that capitalism could be reduced to a number of laws which the critic of political economy could uncover.

It is no accident that the theoreticians of Marxism came from the academy, that institution which was founded by Plato, just as it is no accident that academic Marxism was still alive and kicking in social science and literary departments all over the Western world up long after it ceased to have any real social support anywhere else in the actual material world. It is equally indicative of the idealist nature of the entire Marxist approach to understanding the state that academic Marxists would claim that the actuality of communism had nothing to do with Marx. Idealism never lets reality sully the purity of what the contemplative intellect experiences in its beatific moment.

While Marx's political idealism was advanced by way of a denial of its own nature, the effect of the denial meant that Marxists could also be free to grab power anyway they could in the name of the working class, without being held back by moral scruples. To be sure, the entire legitimacy of the enterprise involved Marxists in a moral substitution racket: the critics and opponents of Marx or the communist party were the enemies of the working class, and the enemies of the working class were the enemies of humanity, and all future generations who would live in peace and prosperity if only communists would be victorious. Since the stakes were so high, Marxists could not be bound by moral scruples. Further, Marx had shown that morals were simply the ideological expression of class interests.

Nevertheless, in spite of the absurdity of bearing a goal so thoroughly out of fit with the motivations, processes and forms of social action, and in spite of its monstrously idealist political base, Marx's thinking did spill over into one non-idealist dimension of state theory. It did provide a way of looking at the state as responsive to the social forces of labour and capital, although it tends to downplay the multiplicity of different interests that are contained under the rubrics labour and capital.

Immanuel Kant

Unlike Hegel who is a philosophical idealist but a political anti-idealist, or Marx who is a philosophical anti-idealist but a political materialist, Kant is both a philosophical and political idealist. Philosophically his idealism amounted to attempting a systematic examination of the sources and scopes of the elements of reason. Politically the major components of his idealism were: (a) a defence of the possibility of human freedom and the consequent legitimacy of moral judgements; (b) the grounding and systematic development of a metaphysical doctrine of justice and ethics based upon the moral law; and (c) legitimating constitutional government. His philosophy was largely a reaction against dominant philosophical trends. His defence of freedom was directed against the philosophical view that man was merely a natural being driven by his instincts, appetites and other natural determinants. His moral theory was directed against the Aristotelian, Epicurean and utilitarian doctrines which made happiness, however differently these three philosophies construed it, the end of human moral endeavour. His political theory was directed against supporters of the *ancien régime* and political absolutists, such as Hobbes, and radical democrats who wanted majority rule unconstrained by law, like Babeuf. His view of human nature, however, is every bit as bleak as Hobbes' and he accepts and attempts to integrate Hobbes' solution to the danger of divided sovereignty.[27]

As a moralist, Kant saw himself as a direct descendent of Plato and in the *Critique of Pure Reason* he cites Plato's *Republic* as providing a rich philosophical insight into the archetypal character of moral example.[28] Kant argued that no person or social form can be empirically represented as a pure example of morality. What is moral is by its very nature an ideal, a benchmark in the beyond. In assessing morality, empirical actions are to be measured by a standard which is the product of reason, not on their own terms. The whole point of the *Critique of Pure Reason* is to demonstrate that our belief in moral freedom cannot be *known/proven* to be mistaken and we should try to act in accordance with moral laws.

There are also some significant differences between Plato and Kant which are worth mentioning as they highlight some of the core differences between ancient and modern idealism. First, Plato's idealism is ultimately grounded in character; the virtues are construed in terms of types of behaviour and types of men and regime: the courageous action/ man/ regime; the temperate action/ man/ regime; the wise action/ man/ regime; the just action/ man/ regime; the pious action/ man/ regime. Being grounded in character there is never the remotest suggestion in Plato that the key to the good life is to be found by acting in accordance with rules. It is difficult to assess what Plato would have made of Kant's categorical imperatives. Although, unlike some recent anti-Kantian Platonists such as Strauss and Bloom,[29] we think he would have been envious of the Kantian insight that there is a common form to moral judgements and that the moral worth of an action is to be evaluated in the very form of law. Plato could never, however, have started from the same position as Kant because Kant's entire conception of experience is based upon Newtonian physics, and his transcendental idealism is built upon it and another science which had not developed in Plato's time, the science of logic.[30] Plato had an idea of the law of non-contradiction, and his philosophy makes much use of the *species/genera* distinction, but it is not until Aristotle that logic becomes a science. Plato could see that there were different species of arguments, but the kind of distinction Kant made between moral and experiential judgements could not have occurred until after Aristotle and Newton.

Kant, however, as has been indicated, praises Plato's idealism, while breaking with the Platonic search for happiness as the proper human purpose. Like Aristotle, Kant believes that the Platonic idea that happiness is the necessary accompaniment to goodness, even if one suffers, violates the concept of happiness. But Kant's radical distinction between natural inclination and laws of reason leads him to defend a position whereby the natural inclination to be happy is subordinated to the moral demand to be worthy of happiness.

There is another highly significant difference between Kant's and Plato's idealism which is indicative of the very different *ethoi* by which they are informed. In focusing on character, Plato is starting with the model of a particular human type. This may seem strange in light of what has just been said about Kant's debt to Plato; it is also odd in light of Plato's insistence that forms/ideas are the truth, while mortal things have a lower ontological status. Yet, as any reader of Plato quickly grasps, Plato's entire moral doctrine is bound up with the character of Socrates. To be sure, Plato would say that the goodness of the behaviour and character of Socrates is rationally compelling, thus the standard is reason. There is an obvious circularity here which Aristotle formulated in the *Ethics* when he said 'the good is what the good man deems to be good.' But the formulation of the circularity indicates that goodness inheres in the man. This is consistent with the entire tenor of classical Greek philosophy which sees character as inherent, so much so that Plato has the auxiliaries of the *Republic* running around farming out and switching babies if there are early signs of character defects in the children of the Guardians.[31]

The fact that the moral doctrines of the ancient philosophers is grounded in character rather than rules partly explains why their ethics is so consistently elitist, although it would only be a matter of time before Epictetus would, through his own life, demonstrate that a slave could be a philosopher. Kant, on the other hand, is living in a society where Christianity has thoroughly moulded the human understanding of roles and social relations. While status differences were consistently taken for granted, by Kant as much as anyone, the spiritual difference of the inner worth and dignity of human beings was not something that one simply assumed was translated into moral terms. Or to put the matter slightly differently, whereas Plato and Aristotle make the philosopher a higher moral type because they see a necessary link between goodness of character and wisdom being good means, first and foremost, having knowledge Kant sees that there is no link whatever between intellect and goodness: the most simple minded person can be a moral hero; the most gifted intellectual can be a selfish sneak.

In an environment where the Christian teaching of the blessedness of the pure simple heart and St. Paul's admonition of Greek hubris has been so thoroughly absorbed into mass consciousness, Kant is naturally more drawn to a way of framing moral matters which confirms the essential dignity of all persons. Kant always said that he was not inventing a morality, but simply clarifying the rules which are displayed in the morality which everyone in the main knows. The framing of morality by way of rules thus has as its basis a way of dealing with morality that bypasses the classical idealist priorities of character and social status.

The fact that Kant deploys a rule based morality does not mean he is always fair or consistent in how he applies morality. Christianity did not eliminate, nor did it ever try to equalise social status in this manner. For example, while Kant's categorical imperative has as its essential justification that it is a derivation of duty from a purely cognitive source,[32] he defends women's disenfranchisement on the basis of what he claims to be their natural , that is empirical character. Kant simply ignored the fact that his whole philosophy was premised upon reason being a cognitive process which operates transcendentally, and hence cannot have any empirical characteristic such as gender attached to it, and declared women to be irrational.[33] Nowhere does Kant sound more like Aristotle than when he is defending disenfranchisement.

It is not the purpose here to attack Kant yet again for carrying in his mind the typical eighteenth century distinction between civic rights, which liberals such as Kant argued should be available to all, and political rights, which were restricted according to what now seem to be indefensibly irrational criteria and allocated on the ability to perform certain political obligations. Rather, the point is simply this. From classical to modern Kantian idealism a major transformation had taken place: rules had replaced character as the basis of moral reasoning, and this was also translated into the political sphere. Because the reasoning was rule-based rather than character-based, and because the context in which this was happening was one in which there was widespread acknowledgement of the spiritual worth and dignity of every person, the whole tenor of the idealism was more egalitarian. That egalitarianism did, however, have limitations. And the limitation was that the moral rules did not provide any particularly novel criteria for allocating political power. What Kant did was simply to rationalise the existing barriers to social power. Later thinkers would find these rationalisations to be completely unconvincing, but a number of features of the Kantian legacy have remained deeply embedded in civilised thinking about political life.

The first is the belief that political behaviour should conform to moral rules. To a large extent this is a simple proceduralist reformulation of the Christian approach to statecraft which so annoyed Machiavelli. It is also a belief which tends to conflate the separate domains of politics and justice/right and law. The conflation of justice/right and law and politics is a central tenet of all idealism, whether classical or modern. Ultimately the idealist wants a world in which right reproduces right, law reproduces lawfulness, and politics is but the extension of lawfulness. While it has just been pointed out that the ancients grounded their moral theory in character not moral rules, it is also the case that the ancients could see that the kind of character which provided them with the ideal of justice was not only exceptionally rare, but stood little chance of holding political power. Or to put it slightly differently, while Plato and Aristotle ultimately wanted philosophers to be kings, they did not think there was much chance of such a lucky accident occurring. Given that, the next best thing was to let the law, which is meant to be the social expression of the ethical, rule, in so far as it was possible. The natural social niche towards which idealism gravitates is law.

In Kant, the relationship between morality, law and politics is such that the latter two spheres devolve from the first which is the purest expression of freedom. Justice is a secondary derivation of freedom in so far as it is freedom only in its external aspect that must be considered. What Kant means by this is that one is just so long as one does not disobey the law of the land even if one desires to break it, whereas morality requires that the pure will should be the guide of action. For justice to occur one may be in violation of the inner moral law, but that is not for anyone to judge. One has the right to one's own heart, whether it be dark or not. The rules of justice, on the other hand, must ultimately conform to the moral. Likewise, no legitimate political action that is performed in a free state can be in violation of the moral law. The state, then, is ultimately merely the moral sphere externalised, and its main moral limitation lies in its externalism.

The unique contribution of Kantian idealism to state theory lies in the grounding it provides for constitutional government. One might say that Kant's political idealism provided the most satisfying intellectual solution to the liberal casting of the problem of political obligation.[34] The position was first presented with the essential elements of liberalism by Hobbes when he stipulated that the reason one is obligated to the sovereign is not because God has appointed him, but because the subjects desire to leave the rapacious environment of mutual terror and enter a terrain where they can live in security. The sovereign is sovereign by virtue of a voluntary desire to form a society. The liberal elements in the posing of the problem are equality (understood by Hobbes in the sense of the equal capacity of people to inflict injury), voluntariness, and the natural right to pursue whatever one desires, a right that is foregone in any civil space where the sovereign has lain down a law. As liberal as these core elements of the problem of political obligation were, they did not find a liberal solution from Hobbes. Here it suffices to say that the reason for this is that liberalism is ultimately a political doctrine of peace; the more warlike the condition within society or between states the less possible liberalism becomes. Liberalism requires a number of stable social conditions to be present before it exists.

With Locke the problem of political obligation is picked up in the context of a negotiated stability between social forces, and there is a recognition that the diffusion of sources of power does not have to lead to civil war. Further, whatever one makes politically of Hobbes' solution to the problem of political obligation it is philosophically unsatisfying. Hobbes is essentially offering a circular solution to the problem of political obligation, but the circularity of the argument involves a generic cross over from liberal to absolutist elements. The ground of political obligation is the subjects themselves, their own will. The proof, however, that the subjects have endorsed the sovereign is their very existence within civil society and their continual desire to be ruled. But that desire cannot be separated from the fact that when subjects are not in a state of civil war, they are under the rule of a sovereign. Ultimately, no matter how subtle Hobbes' solution to the problem of political obligation is, the club is what legitimates political power.

Apart from this, Locke sees all too clearly that Hobbes' tale of political obligation is a tale about a fictitious compact. The compact needs to be real and the sovereign's actions need to be regularly assessed and validated if subjects are to be obligated to him/it on the basis of their will. To back up his case, Locke adds a fictitious account of his own about the innate co-operativeness of people prior to the existence of civil society. Government is chosen by the people to advance themselves beyond a condition which is satisfying -- and not horrific as Hobbes maintained -- but limited. For Locke, as opposed to Hobbes, the greatest political crimes stem from political absolutism. Each has a good point: Hobbes reacts to the terrifying disorder of civil war; while Locke reacts to the horror of unrestrained political power.

With Locke the political theory of the liberal-democratic state finds an eloquent and refined defence. But there is one crucial problem of the liberal-democratic state which stood in need of a philosophical justification and which is answered by Locke in a philosophically unsatisfying manner. The problem is how to justify curtailing the will of the majority if it makes unjust claims by intruding on the rights of a minority, or single person. Locke's entire theory of the state is built around the need to defend a right, the right to property. But where comes this right? He answers, it appears in the state of nature in our labouring acts or in our discoveries of the unowned bounties of nature. But why should we respect the right of a discoverer to lay claim to what he or she comes across, and why should we respect the right of the labourer because he or she has worked upon nature? This kind of question has a metaphysical ring to it that may seem arid to the political mind. But it is a legitimate question, and it is one which leads Locke himself to fall upon a religious defence of natural law.

The problem with such a solution was that the stringent methodological criteria of the new doctrines of physics, which had reached their high point in Newton, were inevitably going to be turned toward any metaphysical and theological doctrines. The residual elements of Locke's traditional Christianity were to be tested in the growing critical climate. Further, while Locke had provided a political answer to the problem of natural right by asserting the value of property, he had not come up with an answer to another problem which took its spin from yet another way to look at the state of nature.

Rousseau was able to tap a rich vein in the spirit of his times by addressing its moral conscience. And he shamed his readers by getting them to reflect on whether progress in the arts and sciences was tantamount to progress in virtue. Rousseau, himself a hot candidate for the most selfish, personally irresponsible, manipulative, self-pitying philosopher of all time, was able to hold up a mirror to reveal the despicable greed of the European *Zeitgeist*. And this was to be contrasted with the noble savage, the savage who was being slaughtered, raped and pillaged in the name of civilisation and Christianity. Rousseau believed he had located the source of the moral degeneracy of his contemporaries in the act of the founding of private property. Unlike Marx, though, Rousseau knew that his attack was a moral attack on private property, and not an argument about the superior productivity of collectivism. However, if Rousseau were right and property, while contributing to accumulation of wealth contributed to moral impoverishment, the Lockean legitimation of the state as the protector of private property, far from conforming to any higher natural right, would represent a violation of natural right.

The Rousseauian twist on property throws the problem of political obligation and the purpose and form of the state into new relief, and Rousseau raises the problem of human freedom in a much sharper light than Locke. Yet the difference between Rousseau and Locke does not undermine their common opposition to political absolutism of the Hobbesian variety. Rousseau, like Locke, asserts the right of the people to be sovereign of themselves, yet he is aware to a much greater degree than Locke of the need to find a ground of natural right which compels philosophical agreement. To be sure, the imprint of the Platonist approach to politics as an action which needs to legitimate itself before the philosopher's bench is all too evident, and the problems thrown up by Rousseau may appear to be abstruse and remote from the cut and thrust of political action. But the eighteenth century is a time of the cultural flourishing of philosophy and the increasing importance that philosophical ideas will play in a political process which was increasingly absorbing the middle classes. Rousseau himself will be widely read and discussed in the *salons* where members of the most vital political force of the day will meet and plot.

The political genius of Rousseau lay not only in articulating a widely held moral response, particularly among the educated class, to the effects of civilisation, a nostalgia for an idealised and more simple, less competitive, more co-operative smaller scale, rural form of life. It also lay in providing a rule -- the general will -- for assessing whether a right such as the right to private property was a right.

Rousseau had provided a rule for determining which state commands should carry moral obligations with them. To the extent that Rousseau had sought a measure to assess the legality of the law, he is a typical natural law theorist. Where he differs from the Medieval natural law theorists is the heightened role he concedes to the human will in the process of legitimation. A natural law theorist such as Aquinas saw natural law as built upon rational precepts, that is precepts that one could rationally accept without any need to refer to a higher being - although such a position equally sees the idea of God as a natural idea of reason.[35]

But what Rousseau does is define freedom as the compliance with a law that we give ourselves. Man becomes a mini-god. It is this power Rousseau gives to man in his role as legislator combined with Rousseau's collectivist sentiments that have led many liberals to see Rousseau as providing a legitimation strategy for the tyranny of the majority. Although Robespierre is one of Rousseau's fate, Rousseau saw himself more as providing an irrefutable rule for identifying rights and testing laws: no law which would not conform to the general will could be legitimate. Concomitantly, any law had to be applicable to all. The sovereign was not above the law; the sovereign was the law. More radically, the law was sovereign. The whole enterprise could be interpreted as a great piece of modern idealism, and it is.

While Rousseau's *Social Contract* was rightly read by his contemporaries as an attack upon the basis of the European *ancien régime* political structures, it is also a new play for power by the philosophers. For it takes the entire question of political legitimacy away from the Church, a move that was also bound to find sympathy with the intellectual classes who found their interests in science and the world around them threatened by the religious dogmas that suited that class of intellectuals who had built their reputations and livelihoods on the pickings of Aristotle. Rousseau's great contribution to modern state theory is to make the human will in a general sense the basis of constitutionality and constitutionality the single most important feature of the modern free state. As brilliant as Rousseau's manoeuvre is in the history of modern political philosophy, Rousseau is a scrappy metaphysician. One moment he is all heart and sympathy, the next he is duty devoid of impulse. That he could simultaneously be the greatest precursor to Kant and the German romantic movement is indicative of the contradictory strains which the solitary dreamer and political collectivist carried in his head. Kant, on the other hand, is the greatest systematic metaphysician since Aristotle.

For Kant, Rousseau's contribution to our understanding of the moral landscape is as radical and profound as Newton's was to our understanding of the physical world. It is no exaggeration to say that Kant's moral and political thought is simply a more rigorous attempt to secure once and for all the basis and moral scope of human freedom. Kant's defence of the republican constitution as the single political model of human freedom is pure Rousseau. Where he passes beyond Rousseau is in the way that he locates the essence of morality in the simple cognitive act of inferring, and in how he identifies the respective transcendental elements of the entire cognitive process, thus enabling him to employ sharp divisions between different modes of judgements. Whether one is making judgements about the world, God, the soul, rights and political duties or the beautiful, Kant supplies the elements for assessing whether one is respecting the formal boundaries of the claim -- if not, one cannot defend one's claim before the tribunal of reason. Kant is ultimately trying to find a way to channel all the speeches of a culture which would lay claim to exercising authority into their proper spheres. Rational speeches -- speeches which conform to the transcendental conditions and respective proof structures -- should rule. Prejudice has had its run, now is the time to dare to know and for man to free himself from his self incurred tutelage.

The laws of reason, then, for Kant, offer the key to answering the main problems posed by human existence. The discovery of our natural being lies in the laws grounded in theoretical reason, that is, those laws of nature which conform to the elements of pure reason, intuition, understanding, and reason. Freedom is found by conforming to the moral law, because the moral law is itself the expression of the freedom of reason. The answer to our ultimate hopes becomes revealed as a rational answer by providing a scientific metaphysic and accepting the practical existence, but experientially unverifiable ideas, of God and the immortal soul. Kant believes that through this solution he has managed to retain belief in God and cosmic justice as the cornerstone of what is to be a rational society. Had Kant had any appreciation of Pascal, who had so bitterly attacked the God of the philosophers, he may have seen that the anemic nature of his ideas of God and the soul only helped prepare the philosophical culture for nihilism. In attempting to provide a *Religion within the Limits of Reason alone*,[36] Kant has established an identity between divine and human reason. Reason is the middle term between the natural being we are and the divine being we believe in, for either the heuristic purposes of seeing our laws of experience as conforming to an absolute system which we cannot directly experience, or as a necessary idea of moral reasoning. This is not because our morality stems from God. We can't prove that. But we also cannot, according to Kant, understand how we can reconcile our natural desire for happiness with our moral freedom unless we introduce the concepts of God and immortality in order to reconcile our natural end/*telos* (happiness) with our moral reason.

The Kantian problematic and the theology that derives from it, only has plausibility if one is already committed to the philosophical form of life and if one surveys the world through the conundrums of metaphysics. Even then, Kant has few philosophical defenders of his theology. Kant's philosophy, as Hegel tirelessly, but correctly points out, is systematically built upon the truth of empiricism. Hence the non-empirical dimensions of his philosophy can only be authenticated once the metaphysical boundaries of experience have been established. The danger is, even from an empiricist driven philosophy, that when human experience is put together in a different way from the Newtonian orientation, then the *a priori* elements of Kant's philosophy of experience, and thus the entire *Critique*, can no longer be said to contain a scientific metaphysic. This was recognised by Kant's earliest philosophical idealist critics, and has been confirmed by the development of post-Newtonian physics and the deployment of non-Euclidean geometries in the physical sciences.

Kant's contemporaries such as Hamann and Herder, and the brightest philosophical stars of the next three generations, Schelling, Hegel, Kierkegaard and Nietzsche all rejected, in different ways, the Kantian transcendental subject, and the purely cognitive character of that subject. In Kant's overarching scientific and rationalist approach to experience, was a very limited appreciation of the experiential wisdom that gets built up in the language (the essence of Hamann's and Herder's 'meta-critiques' of Kant) and the multiple practices which are developed within a community.

If we pause just a moment longer on the significance Kant's philosophy has for appreciating the character of religion, that is for appreciating the central way in which moral behaviour and the meaning of human purpose and association had heretofore been diffused, the position that Kant holds toward the religious traditions and experiences is that what is good in it is what is philosophically rational and what remains is superstitious and should be eliminated. In this respect Kant, while not a rabid anti-cleric, like some of his French counterparts, is a typical Enlightenment philosopher. And as Hegel said of the Enlightenment in *The Phenomenology of the Spirit*, in its 'approach...to faith...it interprets any determinateness it discovers as wood, stone, etc. as particular real things.'[37]

The point of this excursion into the inadequacy of Kant's grasp of the religious experience is not to make a blanket criticism of the Enlightenment. On the contrary, the Enlightenment heralded one of the greatest steps in civilisation: it broadened the space for critical social involvement in a way that had never before existed. It was a time of tremendous energy, of exploration of the diverse and rich global cultures, of historical and social analysis, of feverish discussion of human possibilities. Modern democracy is unthinkable without it. Yet, it is also true to say that the horrors of twentieth century Marxism equally have their roots in the Enlightenment. And Marx himself, in *The Holy Family*, when tracing his scientific pedigree sees in the Enlightenment the birth of his method.[38]

For the Enlightenment wanted to elevate human reason to such an extent that it made the mistake of underestimating what Pascal would call the reasons of the heart, those reasons which the head cannot fathom, or what Burke, in his brilliant predictions about the inevitable horror that lay in waiting within the French revolution, would call prejudice.[39] Prejudices, in Burke's meaning of the word, invariably have a reason, a reason that is associated with the proven life ways which make social reproduction possible. It is true, though, that some prejudices may no longer conform to the life ways that are operative due to major new social forces; whether cultural, technological, economic, or whatever. That is when the philosopher's reflection may play an invaluable role in disclosing the dangerous consequences of a culture's contradictions. The dangerous side of the Enlightenment, though, lay in the elevation of the rational mind to a place where it was to be a directive force in social life. Socialism is a pure product of the Enlightenment's moral conscience combined with the belief in the power of reason to find a solution to human scarcity and alienation.

The place of Kant's philosophy in this was the brilliant sense of the philosophical conundrums and aspirations of his time. His conception of freedom when properly understood remains one of the most intuitively acceptable forms of freedom of modernity, though it is presented in a philosophy that was always too technical for the general public. Further, within appropriate limits, it provides an invaluable contribution for providing rules of interaction in political environments where rules are possible (this is a qualification that Kant himself overlooks) and necessary.

The starting point of Kant's conception of freedom, as has been indicated repeatedly, is the moral imperative. The imperative is not derived from any experience, but it springs from the inwardness of reason itself. The dualism that the Kantian philosophy creates between form and content, reason and experience, noumenon and phenomenon, seems, on first encounter, to be completely bizarre. People don't generally think of themselves as phenomenal and noumenal beings, or as having a reason that is divorced from experience, or of forming moral judgements devoid of sentiment and inclination. Yet what Kant has grasped and then proceeded to work on with an iron-cast logic is that people do have ideas about what they should do and hope for. Kant tapped into the idea that we are capable of thinking of our own behaviour and society as a whole as if it were something capable of infinite improvement. There is an asymptotic conception of the good life that is at the heart of the whole philosophy, and it is why Kant thanks Plato for making the good an idea, an archetype which cannot be existentially realized in its entirety.

In this sense, the freedom we experience in our lives is always a deficient form of freedom. Or to put it slightly differently, our lot is to strive for a freedom we can never completely realise. Kant's depiction of our existential condition, as Hegel saw far more clearly than Kant did himself, is one of infinite striving, of the search for an unrealisable perfectibility. This works both on a personal level, where we should always strive to better ourselves, and socially, where we should always strive to improve society. Stated this baldly, it is obvious that the metaphysical roots of the social democratic cast of mind have their clearest and most thorough philosophical explanation in Kant. On the negative side, this particular mode of idealism has as its consequence that it is always looking to improve modes of interaction which may be workable and provide mutual benefits, but which from a purely moral point of view are seen as somehow deficient.

Thus, for example, the family is the most enduring of all human institutions, but its very existence is premised upon unequal tasks, responsibilities and distribution of power. A child has few, if any responsibilities. When the workforce was mainly populated by men, and the women in it tended to be single, this also impacted upon the way in which property was divided within the family. There would be a negative impact for other members of the family when the wage earning man would abandon his sense of duty, and spend money on gambling, drink, hookers or girlfriends. In dysfunctional families, the issue of fairness of roles and opportunities takes on a moral relevance that is lacking when the roles are fulfilling. The moral act, as Kant so rigorously followed through on, is a generalising act: it sets to work on justice issues by asking general questions and providing general solutions to issues such as fairness, equality, dependency, violence and so on. Thus from the moral point of view, an institution like the family is simply another form of human association, and the moral rules deployed for assessing its value or the value of behaviours conducted within it are no different from assessing the value of a voluntary mode of association.

When one starts from the purely moral point of view, the sociological role of the family in the general landscape of the reproduction of social life is not a matter for consideration. The question is 'are the actions which take place within the family moral?' If not, and if it can be found that the very pressures of family life contribute to the immoral behaviours (e.g. children are in danger of sexual or physical abuse because the family is a private domain which is more resistant to public rules), then this type of mentality may conclude that the institution of the family is itself of morally dubious value.

It may even, as Plato did, dream up some scheme for child rearing which excludes the family. The moralising conscience, then, takes its idealisation of what it wants to exist, finds examples of deficiencies in actual existing institutions, and seeks to turn the culture against the very institutions which sustain it. This was precisely the danger that Burke saw in Rousseau, and Hegel in Kant's idealism.

The problem with the conservative defence of existing rules for the reproduction of existing institutions, however, is that changes in the life ways may mean that some features of the traditional institutions become increasingly unbearable for a larger number of the population.

The Kantian conception of freedom, then, has a positive and a negative role. On the one hand, it may alert people to cultural or institutional pathologies which no longer have any legitimacy; on the other hand it introduces a rule of legitimation which encourages oversimplification in the assessment of the constitutive features of an institution or process, and it encourages a culture of substitution of unreal possibilities for real processes. The Kantian spirit is a restless one, one that encourages critique of all institutions and social processes. It is because of this that Hegel equated the philosophies of Rousseau, Kant and Fichte, with the terror of Robespierre on the other.

Kant himself argued that rebellion could never be justified, although by a dubious piece of legal reasoning he argued that the French revolution, which he then placed so much hope in, was not strictly speaking a revolution. Politically, Kant's horizons were rather moderate. He did endorse the republican constitutional state as the morally legitimate form of the state. But he insisted that only the means of reason were morally legitimate for achieving it. He also argued that natural necessity would force states into a republican constitutional mode.

The idealism of Kant, then, was moderate to the extent that it provided rules for the assessment of the immoral behaviour of persons and states, but its very moralism led it to prohibit rebellion as a means of change. Ultimately, the idealism of Kant rests upon the liberal insistence that persuasion is the superior mode of political action, for it represents a willed law and willing compliance with it.

Further in its very generalism its moralism is construed in terms of universal benefit, and that benefit, unlike the communist construction of universal benefit, cannot be purchased by a slaughter of those who impede it. Again, it is the consistency of Kant's idealism that saves him from endorsing Machiavellian means to realise an idealist political end. One might say in passing that the worst possible political combination is the deployment of non-idealist means for unlimited idealist ends, for the ends achieved this way will have to carry within them the processes that made them real. On the other hand, the deployment of non-idealist means in the context of limited objectives may spawn long term stable and broadly beneficial, though perhaps not universally beneficial, consequences.

A large part of the greatness of Kant's philosophy lay in the sheer consistency with which he followed through what he was doing. And thus in marrying an idealist politics with a such a systematically developed idealist philosophy, he presents an idealist best case. Perhaps this is nowhere more evident in his political theory than when he turns his mind to the idea of historical progress and the ideal relationship he envisages between states.

In asking the question 'what may we hope for?', Kant realises that the search for happiness, however impossible it is universally to define happiness, and however elusive it may be, is deeply rooted in the human condition. Likewise, when he reflects upon freedom, he knows that the moral dimension of freedom, while perhaps disclosing the essence of its possibility, and conferring us with dignity, is not the only aspect of it which people value. Generally, people also envisage a connection between freedom and happiness. Though like Rousseau, Kant knows that people may be happy in slavery and miserable under the burden of freedom/responsibility. Kant thus believed that there was a deep desire in the species to bring about a state form which was based upon the power of people to choose what they wanted to do with their beliefs to make them happy. This was closely related to his realisation that there was no universal way to create happiness. In this respect, Kant, again, shows the influence of his Christian culture and his departure from the classical idealist understanding of happiness, which wants to make the achievement of the philosopher's happiness a major criterion in assessing statecraft.

The liberal conception of freedom as the freedom to pursue what one wants provided it does not interfere with the freedom of others, is not only a central rule of the republican concept of justice, as defended by Kant, but it becomes the *telos* of the history of political and social experience. Kant, then, sees the republican constitutional state not only as the most moral form of state, but also as the result and sign of historical progress. The republican constitutional state is both the inner and outward expression of freedom: freedom in its moral aspect and freedom in its empirical aspect. History, itself, though, can be seen as purposeful and as contributing to our self-understanding. There is, for Kant, a happy convergence between what we know is right as moral beings, which is that we should be ruled by our own freedom, and the lessons we learn from grim necessity in the struggles of nature. Necessity will drive man to realise that the republican state is the state least likely to initiate wars for wrong purposes. The people will not be willing to pay the costs of an unnecessary war with their own lives and out of their own pockets when given a choice. Moreover, the spoils of war will never match the more general and long term benefits of commercial prosperity. War is ultimately not good for a commercial society.[40]

The idealist vision of Kant culminates, not as with Marx, in a world where there is no money, no state, no religion, no classes, no scarcity, no alienation, no crime, and no law, but in the federation of republican constitutional states (and not others) interacting according to international rules grounded in moral freedom. The Kantian political philosophy moves, then, from an idealist inner law to an international law grounded in that inner law. Law reproducing law converges with necessity forcing us to appreciate the value of law. The consistency of the idealism protects Kant from wanting to jettison the irreplaceable discovery of the judicial and philosophical cast of mind: that a law that people will most willingly obey is a law that finds general acceptance, and for that to happen it must have general appeal that can be rationalised. It must be rational. Kant's political philosophy begins and ends in reason. It may be abstract reason and it does ignore the reasons of the heart and social processes which have tacit approval and benefits not always transparent to the philosophising, legalising or moralising mind. But it does provide a common ground of rationalisation, and when one must go to court

152   This Great Beast: Progress and the Modern State

that is invaluable. But all of life is not the court room, and that is especially the case with political life, as no one knew better than Machiavelli and Hobbes.

Notes

1. *Parmenides*, 129-131. All references to Plato are to the Stephanus pagination system which is included in the margin of almost all translations of Plato's works. Publication details of philosophical and literary works which appear in various editions will only be given if a specific translation or edition is being quoted from.
2. *Gorgias, Protagoras* and *Republic,* books 3 and 10.
3. *Symposium*, 217-218.
4. Cf. St. Augustine *The City of God,* trans J. Healy, London, Dent, 1962, Book XIX, ch. 4.
5. Aristotle, *The Politics,* books 7 and 8.
6. Leo Strauss, *What is Political Philosophy?*, Chicago, Chicago University Press, 1959; *Liberalism, Ancient and Modern*, New York, Basic Books, 1968; and *Platonic Political Philosophy,* Chicago, Chicago University Press, 1983.
7. Ludwig Feuerbach, *The Essence of Christianity,* [1841], trans. George Eliot, New York, Harper, 1957.
8. See the discussion of the origins of philosophy in E. Rosenstock-Huessy, *Soziologie,* Vol. 1, Stuttgart, Kohlhammer, 1958.
9. Harold Berman, *Law and Revolution: The Formation of the Western Legal Tradition,* Cambridge, Mass., Harvard Universoty Press, 1983
10. Henry Maine, *Ancient Law,* London, J. M. Dent, 1917.
11. Wayne Cristaudo, 'Theorising Ideas: *Idee* and *Vorstellung* from Kant to Hegel to Marx' in *History of European Ideas,* Vol. 12, No. 6, 1990.
12. Stanley Rosen, *G. W. F. Hegel: An Introduction to the Science of Wisdom,* New Haven Yale University Press, 1974.
13. See the Preface to the Second edition of Hegel's *The Science of Logic,* or the 'Introduction' to Part One (i.e. *The Logic*) of Hegel's *Encylopaedia of the Philosophical Sciences.*
14. See Hegel's *Faith and Knowledge,* trans. Walter Cerf and H. S. Harris, Albany State Uni. Press of New York, 1977, and *Natural Law*

trans. T. M. Knox, Philadelphia, University of Pennsylvania Press, 1975, the Preface to G.W.F, Hegel, *The Philosophy of Right*, trans T. M. Knox, Oxford, Oxford University Press, 1967.
15. G. W. F. Hegel, *The Philosophy of History*, trans J. Sibree, New York, Dover Publications, 1956.
16. See W. Cristaudo, 'Hegel, Marx and the Absolute Infinite', in *International Studies in Philosophy*, Vol. 24, No. 1, 1992.
17. *The German Ideology*, Moscow, Progress, 1976, pages 208-211.
18. *Critique of Hegel's Doctrine of the State*, 1843.
19. G.W.F. Hegel, 'Absolute Freedom and Terror' in *Phenomenology of Spirit*, trans A.V. Miller, Oxford, Clarendon Press, 1977.
20. Karl Marx, *The German Ideology*, Moscow, Progress Publishers, 1976, page 57.
21. See *Lenin: Selected Works*, Moscow, Progress, 1963-64, Vol. 2, page 611, Vol. 3, p. 520; *Stalin Foundations of Leninism*, London, Lawrence Wishart, 1940, p. 81.
22. 'History, Philosophy and Culture' in *The Young Gramsci*, Pedro Cavalcanti and Paul Picone, eds., St.. Louis. Telos, 1975, page 70.
23. See the discussion of Marx in Eric Voegelin, *The New Science of Politics*, Chicago, University of Chicago Press, 1951; *From Enlightenment to Revolution*, Durham, North Carolina, Duke University Press, 1975; and Albert Camus, *The Rebel*.
24. George Konrad and Ivan Szelenyi, *Intellectuals on the Road to Class Power*, trans. A. Arato and R.E. Allen, New York, Brace and Janovich, 1979.
25. Karl Popper, *The Open Society and Its Enemies*, London, Routledge, 1945, Vol. 1. For subsequent defenders of Plato, Ronald R. Levinson, *In Defense of Plato*, Cambridge, Mass., Harvard University Press, 1953.
26. *Republic*, 427.
27. For Kant's critique of Hobbes see sect. 2 *On the Old Saw: "That May be Right in Theory but it won't Work in Practice"*, trans. H. B. Nisbet, from *Kant: Political Writings*, Hans Reiss, ed., Cambridge, Cambridge University Press, 1991.
28. Kant, *Critique of Pure Reason*, [1781] trans. N. Kemp Smith, London, MacMillan, 1978, page 316.
29. Strauss, op. cit. and Allan Bloom 'Interpretative Essay' in *The Republic of Plato*, New York, Basic Books, 1968.

30. See Ernst Cassirer, *Kant's Life and Thought*, trans. James Haden, New Haven, Yale University Press, 1981.
31. *Republic*, 412-415.
32. The categorical imperative, stipulated 'Act only according to the maxim by which you can at the same time will that it should become a universal law'. *Foundations of the Metaphysics of Morals*, trans. Lewis White Beck, Indianapolis, Bobbs-Merrill, 1959, page 35. Kant then proceeds to derive other formulaions of the imperative from this.
33. Susan Mendus, 'Kant an Honest but Narrow Minded Bourgeois' in *Women in Western Political Philosophy*, Ellen Kennedy and Susan Mendus, eds., Brighton, Wheatsheaf Books,1987.
34. See Patrick Riley, *Will and Political Legitimacy: A Critical Exposition of Social Contract in Hobbes, Locke, Rousseau, Kant and Hegel*, Cambridge Mass., Harvard University Press, 1982.
35. See Thomas Aquinas (1266-73), *Summa Theologiciae*, ed. T. Gilby, London, Blackfriars, 1963-1981, esp. I, II, q93, article 3 and conclusion.
36. Kant, *Religion Within the Limits of Reason Alone*, [1793] trans. T. M. Greene and H. M. Hudson, New York, Harper and Row, 1960.
37. Hegel, *The Phenomenology of Sprit*, [1807] trans. A.V. Miller, Oxford, Clarendon. 1977, page 340.
38. K. Marx and F. Engels, *The Holy Family: or, Critique of critical Critique*, trans. R. Dixon, Moscow, Foreign Languages House, 1956.

    For the down side of Enlightenment see Eric Voegelin, *From Enlightenment to Revolution*, J. Hallowell, ed., Durham, Duke University Press, 1975.
39. Pascal, *Pensées*, trans. A. J. Krailsheimer, Harmondsworth, Penguin, 1966; Edmund Burke, *The Political Philosophy of Edmund Burke*, I. Hampsher-Monk, ed., London, Longmans, 1986; and *Reflections on the Revolution in France*, C. C. O' Brien, ed., Penguin, 1968.
40. Kant, 'Perpetual Peace', trans. Lewis White Beck, in *Kant on History*, L. W. Beck, ed., Indianapolis, Bobbs-Merrill, 1963, pages 5-135.

5 The Seizure of State Power: Realist and Idealist Approaches

> Wee, sleekit, cow'rin', tim'rous beastie,
> O what a panic's in thy breastie!
>
> Robert Burns, *To a Mouse*

Neither classical nor Kantian idealism take their point of departure from the problem of the seizure of state power or how to introduce order in a situation of war. The non-revolutionary idealist patiently waits for the philosophical or moral legislator. Violent and evil means will only produce violent and evil ends. This way of reasoning is both morally seductive and logically consistent. The only problem is that it is not true — for just as reality is not a syllogism, in many situations to be moral is to be impotent. Or to put this point slightly differently, the idealist conception of morality is, like the philosopher's conception of reason itself, generally timeless. The one major idealist exception here is Hegel and among the epigone of Hegel, albeit for very different reasons and to different degrees, are Marx and Gentile. But the good action of a particular time, may be the bad action of another time. Likewise, the deployment of terrible means in one context may be appropriate where there are other times when the deployment of terror will only create more terror.

Action in a time of crisis is about political not ideal choices. And political choice in a time of crisis necessarily involves resorting to violence or the threat of its possibility. This does not mean that every choice made in times of crisis is a wise choice. The guide to whether the choice is wise or not lies in whether the political means and the political ends are appropriate for the time and for the human character of the times. We are plastic beings; but our plasticity is limited. One of the most essential limitations of our plasticity is the general condition of social reproduction within which we have to function. The general conditions may change, but they rest upon a vast network of behaviours, expectations, goals, and material conditions. The conditions which sustain the will are always more complicated than what the intellect can envisage. This means, among other things, that the wisdom of a political action is not always possible to determine *a priori*. But the converse may not be true. That is to say, it may be obvious from the outset that a political program will not only not achieve the purported end, but that the attempt to implement it will only create a great deal more suffering than another course of action. The reason that this can be determined *a priori* is because the program may consist of abstractions and goals which are wildly out of kilter with historical reality.

Theoretical validations of the seizure of power can be divided into two types: those that contribute to the consolidation and development of the civilised state; and those that don't. In this chapter it is argued that Machiavelli provides a validation of political brutality in the service of the seizure of power that is instructive for any political actors wishing to contribute to creating a civilised state in a time of turmoil. Marx, Lenin, Mussolini, and the fascist ideologues, on the other hand, all tied their Machiavellianism to idealist ends which had to lead to barbarism.

One might counter that the unintended consequences of an action may play a larger historical role in the development of civilisation. Even foolish and madly evil social experiments like the Pol Pot regime in Cambodia may contribute an invaluable and inestimable lesson for future generations. Monstrous folly may contribute to the collective wisdom of the species. When, and if ever, all states are civilised, reconciliation with human folly may be appropriate. But for now it makes more sense to distinguish between those who have used and justified political violence and have contributed to civilisation, and those who have used and justified political violence and only created more violence and discord.

Machiavelli

'The wisdom of the world is the enemy of God.'[1]

These words, probably apocryphal, attributed to Machiavelli on his death bed pithily express the central insight of the first political scientist. Machiavelli is the father of all those who make the seizure of power the object of their study. He places his observations in service to the two great causes which preoccupied him, the unification of his fatherland, and the establishment of a republic.

His orientation stands in the strongest contrast to the classical political philosopher's desire to establish virtue in rulers and citizens by holding up the life of the philosopher as the model of the good life and by providing models of ideal societies as a standard for assessing actual societies.[2] For Machiavelli the classical philosophical approach to politics is not only a waste of time and effort, it also leads to bad statecraft. It encourages a ruler to adopt impossible and self-defeating behaviours. The world is not ideal, and ideals cannot be actualised without losing their character. Those who live by ideals will be chewed up and spat out. If one wants to be virtuous in the sense that the classical philosophers conceived it, that is to say if one wants to be just, temperate, wise, courageous and pious, stay out of politics. Machiavelli not only does not want a philosopher to be king, but he indicates that a state would be ruined if it were run according to principles of philosophy.

If one wants to achieve anything through politics, one must know how to seize and preserve power. In the first instance that means one must understand the most fundamental materials of the political. Most importantly, one must grasp the nature of human beings. We can, says Machiavelli in *The Prince*, 'say this about men in general: they are ungrateful, changeable, simulators and dissimulators, runaways in danger, eager for gain; while you do well by them they are all yours; they offer you their blood, their property, their lives, their children...when need is far off; but when it comes near you they turn about.' Once one knows this, then one can manipulate the material to the desired outcome. Provided that outcome is not something contrary to the reality of circumstance and human nature generally, then it may be achieved. One will always have to contend with fortune, but fortune likes to be wooed by the vigorous and courageous, by men of action willing to plunge themselves into the tumult of political life.

Nothing could be further from the philosophical life than the political life. Not reflection but action, not temperance but guile, not the stability of contemplation, but the ceaseless life of manoeuvring and calculating, not justice but the willingness to deploy violence for something beyond oneself, not self-knowledge, but the willingness to sell one's soul for the fatherland — that is what separates the political life from the philosophical life. For Machiavelli *virtù* has nothing to do with the philosopher's idea of virtue, love of the good, it is essentially strength of will, the capacity to pursue something through to the bitter end and not be overpowered by the dreadful means one may have to deploy to see the act through. The prize trophy is glory, a condition which Aristotle says is not a philosophical virtue because it is bestowed on one by others and not one's own creation. But, for Machiavelli, it is precisely this recognition and value by one's subjects that is proof of the success of one's achievement. There is always the risk of one's deeds being labelled as infamous. Success is the dividing line between infamy and glory. The deeds of someone who wants political power must contravene the boundaries of traditional morality or virtue — this is not because anyone wishes power operated this way, it is just the way the world is.

Whereas the philosopher loves wisdom for its own sake, the successful ruler is motivated, then, by worldly things. Yet it is this very worldliness that makes it possible for the ruler to be of benefit to the community. Whereas the philosophical life values intelligence above the body — dying to the world is the Socratic formulation of what a philosopher must do[3] — the successful ruler must be strong in the world, and knowledgeable in the ways of the world. The strength of the lion and the cunning of the fox are the necessary attributes for acquiring and holding onto power. Given how cowardly and untrustworthy most people are, those who want power must be more ruthless and more cunning than their subjects or political opponents.

The prince must learn how to create fear in the hearts of men, only then can he be sure that they will remain constant. It is better to be feared than loved is the Machiavellian maxim which guides the prince through the labyrinth of conquest and rulership. But the prince's subjects might then go on to love him. That is useful. But love is as fickle as human beings; fear is more constant. The wisest prince knows how to blend admiration and awe.

In order to be awesome, the prince must learn how to be more evil and less good, the prince must be trained in the ways of beasts. The model teacher of princes is for Machiavelli, Chiron, the centaur, the teacher of Achilles. Chiron is half man and half beast. Because men are the way they are, the prince must know when to act like a human and when to act like a beast. Unless a prince is capable of breaking promises, breaking with established religion, breaking with morals, knowing when and how to be cruel, when to sacrifice others to his purposes, he will never be able to rule well. Yet because men, while bad, generally believe what they have been told about good and evil, they want their leaders to be good, even though if their leaders were good, the state would easily be conquered either by enemies from within or without. Rulers must then know how to *appear* good, know how to pay lip service to promises, know how to earn people's trust, appear to be religious and devise other artifices. The ruler must know how to manipulate appearances and get on with the bloody acts of state while allowing people to preserve their pious little dreams about goodness.

With Machiavelli, then, the problem of violence moves to the centre of statecraft. Politics is about conflict, about warfare. Peace is not the natural order of things, but an imposition, a momentary and artificial paradise in the flux of hell. The rationalist idealists marginalise the problem of violence, treating it as if its deployment were exceptional, dealing with it as if it were something that need not happen. And when they treat it at all, they are most concerned how to limit and legitimate its deployment, as if in the rational state it will be deployed much less because people will conform to reason. But the Machiavellian insists, solve the problem of violence first, then live by law. And in the *Discourses* he makes it clear that he supports the rule of law. But the law is not secured through itself or philosophy. Its security depends upon something outside itself, a strong state.

Statesmen must be prepared to resort to the greatest illegalities when they combat those who refuse to respect the boundaries within which law can operate. The law does not reproduce itself without power, and statecraft always requires a willingness to lay lawful behaviour aside and demonstrate ferocity to the enemy. The wise prince must ever be on guard against his enemies. He must know his borders. He must know all the possible inlets of the enemy, and he must make sure that his borders are secure. He must have the strength and know how to demonstrate his knowledge.

The most graphic example in Machiavelli of this mastery of appearances is found in chapter seven of *The Prince*, in his example of the case of Messer Remirro de Orco.

> Having conquered Romagna, Cesare Borgia, found a province badly governed and in complete disunion. His henchman Remirro ruthlessly and autocratically cleaned up the province, bringing peace and stability. Then the Duke decided there was no further need for such boundless power, because he feared it would become a cause for hatred; so he set up a civil court in the midst of the province, with a distinguished presiding judge, where every city had its lawyer. And because he knew that past severities had made some men hate him, he determined to purge such men's minds and win them over entirely by showing that any cruelty which had gone on did not originate with himself but with the harsh nature of his agent. So getting an opportunity for it, one morning at Cesena he had Messer Remirro laid in two pieces with a block of wood and bloody sword near him. The ferocity of this spectacle left those people at the same time gratified and awestruck.

Like Borgia, then, the ruler must not only know how to be violent, he must also know exactly how to stage violence. He must know when to be ruthless, when to be merciful, when and how to make the people quake with fear, when and how to make them sing his praises. If he lacks the will and the power to be awesome he will meet his ruin. But if he only creates terror, at the least sign of weakness he will also meet his ruin. If he secures strength and stability within the kingdom, then there will be a convergence of interests: his glory will also be the people's glory. Without wise rulership, the people will never have the peace and prosperity they seek.

While, then, Machiavelli, instructs the prince in the art of rulership, ultimately he seeks a good life for the people. *The Prince* is as much a salutary warning to the prince not to be foolish enough to simply plunder the goods of his subjects as it is a manual of power. Gain and consolidate power, build a strong imperial order with devoted subjects and then riches and glory will come flooding in.

Although Machiavelli's most famous book advises a prince, ultimately, Machiavelli believes it is the people, or at least the best of them, who must learn the art of politics. For even if a prince is wise, there are inherent problems with the principality which can be avoided in a republic. In a republic, unlike a monarchy, the interests of the people are seen to converge with the interests of the state.[4]

The issue of military strength and civic responsibility is closely tied up with that of glory. For while in a princedom, glory is often bestowed on loyal subjects, it is also invariably jealously guarded by the prince. For the prince it makes sense that no one should become so loved by the people that his authority may be challenged. In a republic, however, citizens involved in politics compete for glory, thus simultaneously serving the people as well as their own political ambition. That this service will be bound up with successful imperial expansion was well grasped by Machiavelli, who saw imperialism as the natural outlet of youthful political vigour.[5] In addition, princedoms found it harder to maintain military loyalty; they more easily degenerated into tyrannies, and they fostered disunity. According to Machiavelli, the power of a prince best thrives on a degree of disunity amongst his most powerful potential rivals. Moreover, for Machiavelli, princes are more fickle than the people. They have less genius to draw upon than in republics and hence are less adaptable. Also, the danger of political succession is greater in princedoms. Two weak princes in succession, says Machiavelli, greatly endanger state security.

The choice, then, between a monarchy and a republic is between a form of state which is less likely to succeed in its imperial aspirations, which is more prone to lapsing into tyranny, and which is more likely to be subject to the contingencies of fate and the whims of personality and a form of state which could avoid these problems. If, though, a republic is to endure, it must be built upon a strong and vigorous culture, and Christianity cannot, for Machiavelli, supply that. Rome had the culture to sustain a strong imperial republic because its religion taught a much more worldly range of virtues than Christianity. In the second chapter of Book two of *The Discourses*: Machiavelli says 'our religion, having taught us the truth and the way of life, leads us to ascribe less esteem to worldly honour.' He continues by contrasting the religion of Christianity with the religion of the ancient Romans:

> compare the magnificence of their sacrifices with the humility that characterizes ours. The ceremonial in ours is delicate rather than imposing, and there is no display of ferocity or courage. Their ceremonies lacked neither pomp nor magnificence, but, conjoined with this, were sacrificial acts in which there was much shedding of blood and much ferocity; and in them great numbers of animals were killed. Such spectacles, because terrible, caused men to become like them. Besides, the old religion did not beatify men unless they were replete with worldly glory: army commanders, for instance, and rulers of republics. Our religion has glorified humble and contemplative men, rather than men of action. It has assigned as man's highest good humility, abnegation, and contempt for mundane things, whereas the other identified it with magnanimity, bodily strength, and everything else that conduces to make men very bold. And, if our religion demands that in you there be strength, what it asks for is strength to suffer rather than strength to do bold things.[6]

Machiavelli is undertaking what Nietzsche would later call a transvaluation of values. What 'has made the world weak', 'effeminate', and unpatriotic are the virtues of delicacy, lack of ferocity, humility, contemplation, abnegation, contempt for mundane things, and a condemnation of the strength that is needed not only to experience but to inflict suffering. What the world needs is love of glory, magnanimity, ferocity, courage, men of action, bodily strength and boldness. Given his assessment of Christianity, it is, then, no wonder that in Christendom his name became synonymous with evil itself. But the fates of political philosophers are invariably paradoxical: Kant finds himself approvingly quoted two centuries later by Adolph Eichmann to justify genocide,[7] and the anti-idealist imperialist defender of the state, Machiavelli finds himself a favourite of the most influential political idealist of modernity, Karl Marx. But, then again, paradox breeds paradox. Marx, as we have said, believed he was no idealist, and that he had provided a purely scientific basis for socialism which would first occur in the most industrialised countries of the world. Instead he had provided an impetus to the two most unlimited modes of political voluntarism this century: Leninism and fascism. In both cases, Marx's ideas turn into their opposites through their encounter with the world, one via a purported implementation, another via a rejection by a former disciple. But it is always the fate of unrestrained political idealism to turn into opposite through its contact with the world. Burke and Hegel had both learnt that from the French revolution.

Marx (again) and Lenin

Marx prided himself on grasping political reality. But his grasp was from the first infected by a contradiction that was to ricochet through the ideology which bore his name. On the one hand, he presented a story of political conflict in which ideas and ideals were but the expressions of interests grounded in the economic and political power that a group exercised. On the other, he sought to locate, and he believed he had located, an agent whose interests would coincide with the interests of all. On the one hand, then, Marx had presented a model of political power in rigidly non-idealist terms, on the other hand, the solution to the riddle he had given himself, was completely idealist. The working class had a historical mission. It did not matter that they neither saw that mission, nor wanted it. According to Marx their place in the social totality of capitalism made them the bearers of communism, and communism was to be the social system of universal emancipation.

In *Das Kapital* Marx claimed he had proven with scientific certainty that there was a central contradiction within capitalism which would necessarily lead to the break down of the system. The reasoning was very simple, and the central flaw with it was a fundamental economic error. But if one accepts the false premiss, then it appears plausible. The false premiss was that all value which was accrued in the process of exchange derived from one singular source — the power of labour. The entrepreneurial role of the capitalist class was denied entirely and the interplay between consumer and the marketplace was reduced to an epiphenomenon. Having dogmatically asserted that the capitalist class could not create value and that value was like a congealment of labour power which could be measured on an homogeneous time scale, Marx then argued that, on the one hand, the capitalist class lives off labour power, but on the other, the drive for profits leads the capitalists to discover labour-displacing technologies. The technologies, however, do not generate profits, the workers do. Capitalism is thus a system devouring itself.

The genuine problem Marx and Engels saw was that the capitalist economy goes through periods of boom and depression; the problem with their solution was that if labour was simply one factor of production, then it made no sense to treat it as *the* source of value. Marxism, however, could not condone the idea that labour was not the sole source of value, and non-Marxist economists could readily be dismissed as mere lackeys for the ruling class. The Marxian system was a closed system in so far as each of the elements played a protectionist role within the system as a whole. Any idea which contradicted its economic theory could be dismissed on ideological grounds, and any ideological contradictions could be dismissed on economic grounds as serving the interests of the capitalist class. It was hermetically sealed.[8]

Within this system, then, Marx sought to present the struggle of politics as a struggle between groups each trying to protect their own economic interests. In doing this, Marx did make an enduring sociological contribution, but even though he allowed for a variety of classes in his description of power struggles, the economic model he constructed was based on two variables: capital and labour. Thus all other classes were constructed along the capital/labour vector, and their only relevance was whether they gravitated toward labour or capital. Marx held that the struggle between labour and capital must lead to massive poverty, on the one hand, and, on the other, a technology all geared up and ready to go, but unmanned because it can't be used profitably by the capitalist class. Perceiving this contradiction the working class will seize power, run the factories, and society will now be governed by need rather than profit. Marx believed that the contradiction would play itself out in the most advanced industrialised countries because that would be where the technologies and competencies would be most socialized, and thus where the workers would lead the revolution.

This theory was wildly out of line with what was actually happening in the industrialised world. He and his friend and collaborator, the factory owner, Friedrich Engels, both survived to see the living conditions of English working men and women increase on a scale unprecedented in history. Engels, when writing a new Preface to his *The Conditions of the English Working Class*, had to concede this and proffered the highly implausible explanation that the discovery of gold in California had a great deal to do with it.[9]

Marx himself who had always insisted that capitalism was the precondition of socialism completely abandoned any semblance of consistency when he conceded to Russian socialists that it may be possible in Russia to bypass the capitalist phase on the way to socialism. At that point Marx had made it clear to anyone who knew the least bit about his theory of 'scientific socialism' that he was more interested in revolution than his own science. For how could socialism possibly exist unless the technological conditions for its existence were in place?

While Marx had conceived of political struggle between economic interests, he had no strategy for the seizure of power, and his emancipatory agent was not living up to its historical mission, being bribed, as he and Engels and later Lenin would all (incorrectly) say, by the wealth generated in the colonies.[10] As vague as Marx was about the politics of transition from bourgeois society to communism, he was prophetic in two ways: first, as we have said, he indicated that communism might occur in industrially backward Russia, and secondly, he said that in the transitionary period, the political form would be dictatorial. There would, he said, be a dictatorship of the proletariat to make sure that the bourgeoisie and their agents would not regain political power.

The lack of concern with political organization in Marx and Engels stemmed from their remoteness from any genuine revolutionary struggle. In England they were left alone to get on with their writings and go along to political meetings, meetings where the rhetoric of revolution was strong but they were held in a thoroughly secure and tolerant state. In the less liberal backlands of Russia, revolutionary politics meant something altogether different. First and foremost, the lack of development of civil society in Russia went hand in hand with the lack of development of a tolerant state resting on pluralist institutions. Ideas of modernisation in Russia had invariably come from France and Germany, and the political ideas that were being circulated and taken seriously among the Russian intelligentsia were the ideas that were undergoing significant transformation in Europe as the working classes were gaining increasing economic and political power.

In industrialised England, the trade union movement had created its own parliamentary Labour party, which at first allied with the Liberals to achieve legislative successes before 1914 and then formed its own government in the late 1920s. But in Russia, the lack of an industrial proletariat meant that there was no strong sociopolitical base to moderate the radical dreams of the intelligentsia.

The intelligentsia could speak on behalf of the Russian masses precisely because the masses were mostly illiterate peasants whose very livelihoods were not conducive to mass political organisation. Thus the ideas of Marx which were the ideas of a philosopher could have more impact: there was less chance of their being dissolved and defused within the actual political experience of the group they purported to represent; that is there was less chance of them becoming social democratic. Concomitantly, whereas Marx and Engels were radical democrats and eschewed secret political organisations because they could openly denounce capitalism in the tolerant atmosphere of Great Britain, in Russia radical political ideas usually meant clandestine political activity.

The Leninist strategy, then, for the seizure of political power was bred out of the experience of transposing a radical social and political doctrine from a liberal and tolerant political context in a society with a broad industrial base onto an economically backward society with a small working class with very limited political experience in a highly illiberal state.[11] In 1913 only one fifth of Russia's national income was generated by industry and only five percent of the total work force were employed in the industrial sector. This was a lower level of industrial development than Indonesia in the 1990s. Lenin's strategy for seizing power was exactly what the conditions in that type of environment required if one were going to try and implement such a radical social program as communism. In keeping with the role the Russian intelligentsia played in absorbing and acting upon European ideas, Lenin denied the historical validity of the consciousness that the Russian proletariat had managed to gain from its own experience. Following the German Marxist Karl Kautsky, Lenin correctly argued that if left to their own devices, the working class would only ever reach trade union consciousness and their political strivings would stop at desiring parliamentary representation. He insisted that the proletariat's liberation must follow behind the developed consciousness of the revolutionary party who would in turn guide the masses in their best interest.

The Platonism of this way of seeing the world is all too palpable. Though, one must add at once, Plato was no revolutionary and Lenin was as oafish a philosopher as has ever put pen to paper. In *Materialism and Empirio-criticism* Lenin tries to show that the central philosophical problem is whether the world has an independent existence, and whether matter exists outside of the head or not.[12] The work is a boorish and tiresome polemic directed at any thinker who has had the temerity to explore the part the mind plays in the formation of data. To be an appalling Platonist, however, is still to be a Platonist. What Lenin owes to Plato is the belief that a society can be planned, that an ideal kind of human society can be engineered.

The Leninist tactic for the seizure of power — a close-knit revolutionary political organization governed by strict party discipline willing to apply terror to achieve its objectives — provided the model for all revolutionary groups wanting to rapidly transform the social base of an undeveloped society through political means. The trajectory of the revolution only compounded the anti-democratic elements which lay latent in Marx's radical democracy. The trajectory had, however, been predicted in Marx's lifetime by the Russian anarchist and fellow associate in the Workers International, Bakunin. For Bakunin, Marx's thought was a recipe for red bureaucracy. Marxism was, he said, the vilest lie of the century. Marx responded with typical vitriol insisting that Bakunin was a voluntarist, which meant he made the will the basis of revolutionary action, while he, Marx, had a scientific understanding of revolutions and a proletarian revolution could not occur in Russia.[13] In other words, Marx's rebuttal was as speculative as any reasoning process one would find in a Medieval monastery discussing the nature of angels.

Having seized power through their willingness to be more manipulative and brutal than any of their opposition, the Bolsheviks were set on rapidly developing the Soviet industrial base ostensibly to prepare the ground for communism. In 1917, the secret police, the Cheka, was set up in a political meeting, without any statutory backing, and was empowered to sentence and execute suspected counter-revolutionaries without trial. When the Cheka was criticised, Lenin bit back at the 'narrow minded intelligentsia...who sob and fuss over mistakes made by the Cheka.' From the start the total entwinement of legality and politics was built around Marx's idea that justice, law and the state are nothing more than instrument of a ruling class. In keeping with this Soviet justice was built upon the elements of 'the class enemy', 'class traitors', 'enemy to the revolution' and 'enemy of the people.'[14] With its program of rapid economic development, any activity which was seen as slowing up the economy (apart from the Bolsheviks' own economic stupidities) was interpreted as sabotage by the class enemy. In a pamphlet entitled 'To the Population' Lenin urged:

> Establish the strictest revolutionary law and order, mercilessly suppress any attempts to create anarchy, by drunkards, hooligans, counter revolutionary office cadets...and the like. Arrest and hand over to the revolutionary courts all who dare to injure the people's cause irrespective of whether the injury is manifested in sabotaging production (damage, delay and subversion) or in hoarding grain and products or holding up shipments of grain, disorganizing the railways.[15]

After the abysmal economic failure of war communism, some latitude was given to market mechanisms, with Lenin's warning that any abuse of concessions was 'to be countered with every means including the firing squad! Against officials accepting bribes, Lenin urged ten years imprisonment plus ten years of compulsory labour. Against the kulaks, priests, and white guards Lenin's solution to their obstruction was 'ruthless mass terror.' The purpose of the law courts, for Lenin, was the creation of terror, as he explicitly stated in a letter discussing the 1922 Russian Criminal Code, where he says:

> The courts must not ban terror — to promise that would be deception or self-deception — but must formulate the motives underlying it, legalise it as a principle, plainly without any make believe or embellishment. It must be formulated in the broadest possible manner, for only revolutionary law, and revolutionary conscience can more or less widely determine the limits within which it should be applied.[16]

What Lenin had done for the communist movement as a whole was to establish the revolutionary reign of terror as the norm of the political process. The legal system was geared up as an instrument for the scouting out of class enemies. By 1926 the criminal code had introduced article 58, which was to be the legal justification constanty invoked during the great purge. Article 58 was not so much a new principle but the summing up of where the Bolsheviks had been moving since they had seized power. Not only speeches, but even thoughts were to be considered acts.

The strategy which had led to the 1926 Criminal Code had been perfected by Stalin. He had had the insight to see the significance of the idolatry shown toward Lenin by the party. He was able to turn the leader of the party into the all knowing, all wise embodiment not only of the nation but of all working people. Thus every new political proposal by the state was a matter of life and death, any objection could be seen as a sign of bourgeois consciousness. The statecraft of communism proceeded by way of the most amazing sequence of inverted substitutions. All humanity would be emancipated if it would but be led by proletarian consciousness. However, the victory of proletarian consciousness required that it be led by the vanguard of the party, and the success of the party required that it deliver ultimate authority to one man. Universal emancipation thus became reducible to the triumphant will of one man. What had been instigated as a supposed materialist approach to power came to reveal itself more and more as an exercise in controlling the consciousness of those who were to be liberated. Any speech that hinted that there might be some doubt about the wisdom of the party leader could lead to imprisonment or execution. The wisdom of the leader extended far beyond politics itself. Culture was also political. Thus the leader had to dictate to the people what was culturally progressive and what was not. Stalin not only interfered in music and literature insisting upon the exclusively appropriate aesthetic forms for a communist, he also prided himself on being able to determine the truth to be followed in the sciences of linguistics, anthropology, biology and physics.

The story of the trajectory that leads from Marx to Lenin to Stalin and on to Mao to Pol Pot is the story of the collision between idea and reality, of an idea which initially distorts reality, and then becomes the means to force reality into an impossible mould. At each step of the way there is parody and absurdity: a forced labour-camp society that is supposed to be a workers' paradise; people deprived of legal protection because the ideology has exposed the law as the instrument of the ruling class; the most underdeveloped country in Europe becoming the spearhead of the socialist revolution, then having to spread into Asia and Africa before it is supposed to make a comeback into Europe; the cosmopolitan theory of socialism transformed into the doctrine of socialism in one country. All presided over by the smiling face of Stalin (or Mao, Tito, Honecker, Hoxha, Castro, Kim Il Sung, Deng) as philosopher-king.

The brutality of the communists is invariably the measure that is used to condemn the ideology. But it is the case that in most of the nations where the communists were victorious (as opposed to the satellite states) a degree of brutality was inevitable if nations were to rapidly modernise. The circumstances in which the Bolsheviks found themselves in 1917, for example, were ones that required a steel will and iron fist for any party which wished to keep power and change the economic and social base. The above citations of Lenin on the law are, then, completely understandable - though not morally laudable - in light of the task that faced a political party wanting to drag Russia into the twentieth century. But the extent of the brutality is exacerbated by the idealism that feeds the politics.

A contrast of Machiavelli and Lenin will serve to clarify our point. With Machiavelli, as with Lenin, violence is at the heart of the state and law. With Machiavelli, there is also an acceptance that this is the way things will always be. Human nature is constant, so even though one may contrast how different characteristics are spawned by different cultures, one should not expect to live in a society where the threat of warfare will have ceased. On the contrary, too much peace creates self-indulgence and laziness of spirit, and this, in turn, will make one vulnerable to one's enemies. Politics will never cease for Machiavelli, because power and violence are existential constants.

Contrast this with the ideology Marx and Lenin were weaving. On the one hand, they, like Machiavelli, present a view of politics which is not to be infected by mere moralising. On the other hand, they promise a world without state and without politics — politics will become a purely administrative affair. They foster the belief that the conflict between human beings can cease, that human beings can live their lives in such thorough co-operation that the political institutions can one day be dissolved. One day people will all be genuinely moral, provided social and economic conditions are correctly organized. Because the end is so moral, every political battle takes on cosmic proportions. Political battles are always about the fate of the species and the contribution that can be made to the end of exploitation. Thus any opposition to those who are bringing about this great end can only come from monsters. Concomitantly, when there are enemies of the state, it is not enough to shoot them as the enemy, they must sign confessions and abase themselves before the world as parasites and enemies of humanity. At the mass trial of Bessonov, Bukharin, Rykov and others, the Soviet prosecutor Vishinsky screeches with moral indignation:

> Our people and all honest people throughout the world are waiting for your just verdict. May this verdict of yours resound through the whole of our great country like a bell calling to new feats of heroism and to new victories! May your verdict resound as the refreshing and purifying storm of just Soviet punishment!
> Our whole country, from young to old, is awaiting and demanding one thing: the traitors and spies who were selling our country to the enemy must be shot like dirty dogs!
> Our people are demanding one thing: crush the accursed reptile!
> Time will pass. The graves of the hateful traitors will grow over with weeds and thistle, they will be covered with the eternal contempt of honest Soviet citizens, of the entire Soviet people, But

over us, over our happy country, our sun will shine with its luminous rays as bright and as joyous as before. Over the road cleared of the last scum and filth of the past, we our people, with our beloved leader and teacher, the great Stalin, at our head, will march as before onwards and onwards towards Communism![17]

The effect of this psychology upon Western intellectuals was extraordinary: the communist party idealised the working class and berated the intellectuals as bourgeois lackeys, yet it provided a class of intellectuals with a historical mission, a purpose for their intellect, a purpose bigger than just having a luxurious life style with greater leisure time and opportunities than most working people. They could have a bourgeois life style and at the same time be better people than the bourgeoisie. For some, like the idealists who went to Spain to fight Franco, only to be betrayed by the Soviet communist party, this idealism translated into a willingness to engage in political action. Generally though, the intelligentsia who played with communism happily defended the latest position of the Soviet Union. When news came out about the extent of the massacres in the Soviet Union under Stalin, the first reaction of the fellow travelers was to deny its validity. But once Khrushchev himself denounced Stalin, there was no escaping the reality. While this event induced a crisis of faith for many, many more saw this as a further test of their faith, and if humanity was to be saved now it was necessary to dig in harder, be more vigilant in one's good will. With the Soviet-Sino split a golden opportunity had arrived, one could ditch the Soviets and side with Mao. Again the same reasoning process went on as news came out about the millions killed by the Great Leap Forward and then the Cultural Revolution. There was always a reason why error had occurred or why a group of people were counter revolutionaries. And China was so vast what did thirty million people matter?

Underneath the moralising defence of communist dictatorships was a huge and elementary methodological flaw: one system (capitalism) was judged by its actuality (and not very fairly); the other (socialism), was judged by its potentiality (and not very critically). No matter how bad communism was, capitalism, from this idealist perspective would always be worse. The Soviet Communist Party, then, consistently relied upon the moral conscience of intellectuals outside the Soviet Union, while it imprisoned and executed the best minds within its own borders. The moralising idealist mind was the collaborator with the most murderous regimes in the twentieth century, but it was able to be so murderous because it was hidden from itself. It neither acknowledged its murderousness nor its purely moralistic abstractness.

It was this deadly combination that separated it so sharply from Machiavelli. For a Machiavellian, the actual experience of communism was a verification of the Machiavellian way of looking at the world. Behind the smoke screen of justifications about building the new world was simply a struggle for survival and power by a group of political actors. Their ideal of changing human nature would have been scorned by Machiavelli because human nature was, for him, not that malleable. As much as the idealism of Marxism would have repelled Machiavelli, no doubt he would have appreciated the discipline of the politics, the sheer tactical ability of Leninism.[18] But it did not spill over into anything durable. The politics only depleted the vitality of civil society.

While Machiavelli would have not only not been impressed by the ideology of communism, and would have seen it as merely a means of political manipulation of the gullible, Machiavelli, nevertheless had a strong appeal to the communist mentality. The reason for this was best expressed by the one time apologist for Stalinist terror who then went onto become a founding philosopher of the New Left, Maurice Merleau-Ponty.[19] If one sides with the victims of the earth — something alien to Machiavelli but essential to the moral starting point of Marxism, provided the victims are not the class enemy — then one cannot simply stand on a moral condemnation of injustice. For Merleau-Ponty, the central message of Machiavelli — which was, in fact, the central message of Moscow — was that those who want to keep clean hands and pure moral consciences in a world which is the way it is are guilty of allowing the worst to continue ruling. Thus by one of those amazing ironies of world history, the teachings of the first political scientist and the great anti-idealist were to be absorbed into the psychology of one of the most moralising, idealist and vicious form of politics in human history.

As ironical as this is, it is no more ironical than the dialectical twist that took place between Marxism and fascism. The central element of dialectic, as taught by Hegel, is that underlying a polarity there is a fundamental unity that makes the polarity possible. That is to say, in the case of the relationship between fascism and Marxism, in spite of the fact that these two ideologies seemed to be the most bitterly opposed ideologies of the twentieth century, they form an intellectual and historical continuum, a continuum that would result in the partitioning of Poland. Bluntly, without Marxism, there would have been no fascism. Both ideologies were generated out of a perceived failure of liberal democracy to provide people with their most important life needs (naturally, these needs are reinterpreted differently in the ideologies of fascism and Marxism). Both of them became adopted by states in countries where the cultural soil needed for stable liberal democracy was not present. But the evolution of fascism involved the reaffirmation of the major negations — the nation, the state, private property, classes — that occurred in Marx's political idealism. The theoretical reaffirmation of fascism, however, in spite of the vastly different ideological rationalisations, of the nation, the state, the preservation of classes, of hierarchy, were barely different in practice from the actuality of Marxist-Leninism. The reaffirmations, however, all led to an overtly, but highly *irrationalist*, idealist philosophy which was as blind to the limits of idealism and the complexity of human social evolution as was Marxism.

The Political Philosophy of Italian Fascism

The evolution from Marx to Lenin had involved a major philosophical inversion, which, was theoretically acknowledged by the Italian Marxist Antonio Gramsci. He had emphasised that what was vital in Marx's thought had to be prised from the economist and mechanist residues of Marx's model of social evolution. Gramsci insisted that the activist and idealist elements of Marx's thought had to take priority over the 'contaminated and naturalistic encrustations' of his thought.[20] What is valuable in Marx, said Gramsci, lies in his continuation of the idealist thought which makes man - not brute economic facts - as the supreme fact of history: the society of men who draw close to and understand each other, who develop by means of these contacts (civilisation) a collective, social will. They comprehend economic facts, evaluate them and adapt them to their will so that this will becomes the propelling force of the economy.[21]

What Gramsci had said was, in fact, simply a theoretical acknowledgment of what was involved in accepting the task of attempting to modernise an underindustrialised country along socialist lines. The philosophical primacy given to the human will was the exact opposite of Marx's teaching that while the will was a core category of the political, social transformation was created by economic and not politically willed conditions. What Gramsci had articulated in broad philosophical terms was identical to what Lenin was saying in more pragmatic terms in speeches such as the following.

Large scale machine industry...calls for absolute and strict *unity of will*, which directs the joint labours of hundreds, thousands and tens of thousands of people. The technical, economic and historical necessity of this is obvious, and all those who have thought about socialism have always regarded it as one of the conditions of socialism. But how can strict unity of will be ensured? — by thousands subordinating their will to the will of one.[22]

The voluntarist ideas of Gramsci and Lenin, although the *opposite* of Marx's materialism, were, however, widespread enough to represent the *dominant* political strain of Marxist orthodoxy. The French Marxist George Sorel had taken the voluntarist philosophy to its logical conclusion, in *Reflections on Violence*, written in 1908.[23] He had grasped that just as the heroic will was the source of political transformation, it was not merely a reactive power to objective forces pushing upon it, rather it was a creative force. Sorel, following Henri Bergson,[24] grasped that reality was a creation not a given. Further, the power of the working class, for Sorel, lay precisely in its dynamic capacity to transform the material and social worlds around it. What was most important in this process was the spur to action. In this respect, another inversion of Marx's thought took place.

Marx was wrong, Sorel thought, to insist that the significance of the working class was essentially due to its objective place in the industrial process. On the contrary, the value of the working class lay in the power of its belief, in the role it saw itself as fulfilling. The working class was not so much a reality as a belief in action. What mattered most of all was the energies that it generated through its actions. The value of class warfare lay, then, as much in the energy that was generated through the violence of its encounter with the bourgeoisie as anything. This was an idea later that Sartre would defend in his Preface to Franz Fanon's paean to violence, *The Wretched of the Earth*.[25] It was also to be applied to the theocratic revolution in Iran by its admirer Michel Foucault.[26] The working class was, then, for Sorel, a force driven on by the power of its myths.

The emphasis upon the potency of myth, the central role of the heroic will, the integral need for iron discipline to unify and co-ordinate the revolutionary will, and the value of violence in aiding that process was the political stock of the anti-bourgeois revolutionaries in the early part of the twentieth century. It was Marx's location of a singular source of enmity, the bourgeoisie, which had made it possible to synthesise the mechanistic and vitalistic, the scientistic and voluntaristic, the economistic and the political, the radical democratic and the dictatorial in the quest for social transformation. Such contrary intellectual forces could remain broadly united under the rubric of Marxism so long as they remained an oppositional movement. But the tensions were not able to remain reconciled when a group wanting rapid social transformation could no longer accept either the general diagnosis of poverty or the cure that Marx had provided.

It was the experience of a number of Italian radicals which was to lead to the creation of fascism.[27] It is no accident that the most significant fascist had been a Marxist. Benito Mussolini had been the editor of the Italian Marxist newspaper *Avanti!*, and he had been highly esteemed by Lenin himself. When Mussolini left the Italian communist party to found the fascist party, he was able to find so much support among the Italian radical intelligentsia and the more radical sections of the working class because he had seen that Marx's thought did not provide an explanation of, nor solutions to the Italian situation. It was the combination of the voluntarist political direction of communism as exemplified above in Sorel, Gramsci and Lenin with the perception of the following lacunae or errors in Marx's thought which is at the core of fascist political philosophy.

The first error of Marx was, as the Leninists had realised, that Marx's analysis had been directed at the industrial world, because the entire published theory (as opposed to his private correspondence) from the *Manifesto* and through to *Das Kapital* had been premised on the material advancement of productive forces leading to such an increase in socialisation that socialism was the natural heir of capitalism. Yet the countries which were most fertile for revolution were not the industrial countries but those countries where the productive forces were undeveloped, and where wages and living conditions generally were low. Because of the way that Marx conceived the trajectory from capitalism to socialism he had no programme for industrial development, as the Leninists did. While the fascists would jettison Marxism, they would retain their essentially Leninist conception of the party.

The second major error of Marx was to believe that the working class had a common interest that cut across national barriers. Mussolini, on the other hand, had the experience of the First World War, the experience of having to choose between fatherland and class. He saw that Marx was wildly wrong in his belief that in the time of economic crisis, the working class will see its real interests and act in cosmopolitan solidarity; workers will arise in unison to overthrow the bourgeoisie irrespective of national barriers. The war showed Mussolini that people, irrespective of their class, saw themselves first as French, or English, or Italian. Even the Social Democratic parties of France and Germany showed that they too believed in the tangible reality of nation more than the intangible idea of international solidarity when their representatives had voted for the war credits which financed the conflict. Indeed, it is not too strong to suggest that the war was the watershed between Marx's idealist cosmopolitanism and the reality of nationalism as a mobilising force.

There was nothing politically innovative in an appeal to patriotism, but what fascism married was the feeling of patriotism with a programme of industrialisation. That in turn involved a much more socially directive role for the state. Fascism's patriotic standpoint had a strong appeal to conservatives who saw that their social role was embedded in the traditional national institutions. But fascism made a radical departure from the conservative view of the state. By introducing what A. James Gregor has perceptively called a series of substitutions, fascism identified the nation with the state, the state with the party and the party with the leader.[28] Thus the conservative connection between nation and state, which sees the latter as the servant of the former, is reversed, as the nation becomes the creation of the state. 'It is not nationality that creates the State', says the fascist philosopher Giovanni Gentile, 'but the State which creates nationality, by setting the seal of actual existence of it.'[29] Once the state is seen as the creator of the nation, it is inevitable that there is no sharp divide, as there is in liberal and even in conservative thought, between the private and public spheres. Long before feminists were decrying the split between the public and the private, Gentile wrote of 'the fallacious distinction between the "public" and the "private" life of an individual.'[30] And as he also wrote, in another work published under Mussolini's name: 'for the Fascist, everything is in the State, and nothing human or spiritual exists, much less has value, outside the state. In this sense, Fascism is totalitarian, and the Fascist State, the synthesis and unity of all values, interprets, develops and gives strength to the whole life of the people.'[31]

The central ideological ingredient of fascist politics is unity. It is the demand for unity that requires that the state be controlled by only one party, just as it is the desire for unity that demands that the party's will be given singular expression through the will of its leader. Before Stalin had grasped the psychological significance of the cult of the personality, Mussolini had seen that the connection between leader, state and nation had to be all embracing if people were to undertake sacrifices for nation building. Just as it was to be the state which would forge the nation, the state would be the expression of a singular will, a will that would be both directive and yet expressive of the collective aspirations and connectedness of the people. From within this schema, the party is the link between leader and state, just as the state is the link between party and people. One of the ten maxims of fascism expressed the theory of the state with brutal elegance: 'Mussolini is always right.'

In its insistence upon unity fascism was essentially following the Platonists' dream, just as it was every bit as idealist as Marxism had been. But unlike Marxism its practice was not encumbered by the contradictions of having an idealist politics rest upon an ostensibly materialist basis. Fascist theoreticians had no difficulty in accepting the idealist roots of their ideology, even when their ideology was fundamentally pragmatic. They insisted repeatedly that the ideology was about belief and faith, that it was grounded in will and action not intellect,[32] and that it was pragmatic, and it was primarily engaging in a moral revolution by political means. Further, unlike Marxism, it did not seek to make its dictatorial practice appear democratic. Democracy was divisive because it expressed a multiplicity of points of view. Therefore it had to be rejected. The egalitarian doctrine of liberal democracy also placed severe limits upon the leadership. If the nation was to be mobilised it must see its leader as the expression of its higher self, and it must see itself as dutifully bound, as ready to make the ultimate sacrifice for the nation, the state and its leader.

The fascist mentality took the military model of social hierarchy as the appropriate model for building a society. Homogeneity of thought and purpose are absolutely essential for creating an obedient and loyal people to the fascist cause. The combination of the need for unity and the identification of the leader's will with the nation's will meant that it was a matter of indifference whether the subjects had voluntarily agreed to a particular course of action. Such a distinction between the commands of a democratically endorsed legislature and dictatorial fiat stems, according to Gentile, from a failure to appreciate force as an essential attribute of will, and the basis of political morality. Moral unity, in other words, was not something that emerged out of the rational individual moral will, as Kant, would have it, rather the moral is forged by the triumphant heroic act of power and will which builds nations. As Gentile says, in an infamous passage,

> Distinctions in this field are dear to those who do not welcome the concept of force, which is nevertheless essential to the state, and hence to liberty. And they distinguish moral from material force; the force of law freely voted and accepted from the force of violence which is rigidly opposed to the will of the citizen. Ingenious distinctions, if made in good faith! Every force is a moral force, for it

is always an expression of will; and whatever be the argument used — preaching or blackjacking — its efficacy can be none other than its ability finally to receive the inner support of a man and to persuade him to agree to it. The material force to which I attribute a moral value...is not that of a private person but of the state. The blackjacking of fascist squadrons was intended to be and actually was, the vindicating force of a state whose constitutional powers were renounced and denied by its own central organs.[33]

In most of these respects, fascism simply articulated in a more theoretically rigorous and honest fashion the practice that was also being conducted by the Leninists. To a large extent both political forms were trying to do the same thing: rapidly modernise. Marxism and fascism were both to become the state form commonly adopted by nations in their attempt to industrialise rapidly. Concomitantly, they were also the political consequence of an industrial state. Since they correspond to that period of development they died with it. But there was one fundamental area which divided the two ideologies theoretically as well as practically, and that came back to the conscious ideological role that had been assigned to the problem of national unification by the fascists. Bolshevism was always tactically as well as theoretically internationalist in its scope. The Bolsheviks in spite of their appeal to nationalism were also always tactically reliant upon the good will of the international working class or its intellectual spokesmen.

For Mussolini, Marx's general lack of interest in the problem of swift industrial development was the reason he had not focussed upon the nation as a mythic entity for social mobilization. For Marx, the capitalists were uprooting social relations swiftly enough (though, given how little of the world was industrialised when Marx was writing, it is remarkable that he and his followers thought that communism was but a short time away). Nevertheless, for Marx, the whole mission of the bourgeoisie was the global development of productive forces. But the question of what to do when the bourgeoisie weren't developing things swiftly enough, became a critical question within the history of Marxism.

What Mussolini saw, then, was that the establishment of national unity meant eliminating the very thing that gave Marxism its meaning in the first place, class war. To the Marxist the most common working class tactic in that war, the strike, was a minor victory. It depleted capitalist profits and thus was a small step toward overthrowing the bourgeoisie. As soon as the Leninists seized power, the strike was the embodiment of class treachery and sabotage. To Mussolini and the fascists, the strike was an erosion of national capital and hence of national resources. The experience of the Soviet Union only confirmed for Mussolini what was clear to anyone who thought about what a political attack upon the bourgeoisie meant, a major economic setback as production all but ceased. The fascists thus roamed Italy blackjacking strikers and forcing the working class to cooperate with their bosses. Both capitalists and workers were subjected to the party.

Although Marxists have invariably presented fascism as just another bourgeois ideology, this is overly simplistic. The ideology of fascism was essentially militaristic. Whereas the mature bourgeoisie flourish within a market driven society - provided it is politically stable - where the values of the society like the commodities which are produced within it are publicly circulated and considered within civil society, and not, for the most part, state directed, the fascist state was a corporatist state, which controlled the bourgeoisie and viewed its members with suspicion. A fundamental distinction was made between productive and unproductive capital and it was up to the state to make the distinction. Thus although fascism accepted the necessity of private enterprise, the scope of state powers were such that civil society was not primarily the expression of voluntary associations and commercial transactions as they are in liberal democracies. The role the party played in daily life was such that private property was extremely limited in its potency. The entire ethos that was being sponsored by the state was also contrary to a large domain of freedom for entrepreneurs and consumers, thus contrary to the primacy of commercial activity in daily life. Mussolini's model of the good society was ancient Rome, not America nor England. For the fascists, liberal societies were weak and feminine, their institutions corrupt and ineffective. In sum, fascism eroded the very environment which made the bourgeoisie such a potent force for freedom: civil society.

There is one last ideological component of fascism which should be touched on further, and that is the role of violence. Unlike liberalism and Marxism, which espouse the value of peace as an end, the militaristic dimension of fascism was so strong that it continually emphasised soldierly virtues. Like Machiavelli, whom Mussolini greatly admired, fascist theoreticians generally interpreted the world as a struggle of powers. Whereas Machiavelli, however, had not had the experience of the superior benefits of trade to warfare, Mussolini had so focussed upon the militaristic that he rejected outright the value of taking Italy down a liberal democratic track. It may have been the case that the social and economic conditions were not ripe in Italy for liberal democracy, but there was also little chance of its being tried since the most powerful political activists and theoreticians in Italy had been imbued with much more radical dreams, and their parameters had been set by a combination of Marxism, the syndicalist movement, the First World War, and Italy's relative underdevelopment.

Just as fascism was the transformation of Marxism into its opposite, fascism was also the inversion of Platonism. What it retained from Platonism was the core belief that it was possible for a wise leadership to engineer politically an entire society and to enforce a unitary vision of life upon that society. Yet its foundations were also the antithesis of Platonism in a number of important respects. In place of reason, argument, contemplation, and the academy, it celebrated the irrational, the will, culture, race (as a concession to Hitlerism), and military might. But although Mussolini might look a million miles from the philosopher king, his dream was also the dream of philosophers and social scientists such as Gentile and Michels.

While Plato's politics had involved him in a battle with the poets, by the time of the twentieth century idealism was the common disease of the intelligentsia, shared by writers, painters and philosophers alike. If one takes fascism and National Socialism as a pair, it is revealing to see just how many of this century's most important intellectuals and artists sympathized with or supported these ideologies while expressing their contempt for the bourgeois philistinism of liberal democratic cultures and the spill and sprawl of liberal democratic politics. Its apologists and sympathizers include the futurist school of artists, D'Annunizio, Ezra Pound, W. B. Yeats, the poet Gottfried Benn, the German playwright Gerhardt Hauptmann, Carl Jung, Carl Orff, the noble prize winning Knut Hamsun, the film maker Leni Riefenstahl, the French novelists Louis Ferdinand Céline and Drieu la Rouchelle, possibly the most important philosopher of this century, Martin Heidegger, the painter and writer Wyndham Lewis who wrote a book on Hitler, and Ernst Junger, to name just some of the more well known. Indeed if one took out the artists and philosophers of the twentieth century who were interested in politics and did not sympathise with the irrationalist idealists of fascism and National Socialism or the more rationalist idealism of Marxism (rationalist because of its insistence upon universality) there would be but a handful. What this suggests is the vast gulf that separates the real political conditions for peace and prosperity in everyday life, and the poetic and philosophical imaginings of how power can achieve what the good life is. The twentieth century intellectual idealists who supported fascism and Marxism reproduced the Platonic fallacy. Just as Plato in his dreams wanted to make philosophy rule, and ended up with the disappointing reality of the tyrant Dionysos of Syracuse; the intelligentsia wanted to create a more just (the Marxists) or more heroic (the fascists) social world, but what they got was Stalin and Hitler.

Notes

1. Sebastian de Grazia, *Machiavelli in Hell*, London, Picador, 1992, page 341.
2. For an essay on the many Machiavellis see Isaiah Berlin, 'The Originality of Machiavelli' in *Against the Current: Essays in the History of Ideas*, London, Hogarth Press, 1979, pages 25-79.
3. Plato, *Phaedo*.
4. Niccolò Machiavelli, *The Discourses* in *The Prince and The Discourses*, intro. Max Lerner, New York, Random House, 1950, pages 282-3. For the significance of Machiavelli in the republican tradition see J. G. A. Pockock *The Machiavellian Moment: Florentine Political*

Thought and the Atlantic Republican Tradition, Princeton, Princeton University Press, 1975.
5. *Ibid.*, pages 128-129.
6. *The Discourses*, trans. Leslie Walker, London, Penguin, 1983, page 278.
7. Hannah Arendt, *Eichmann in Jerusalem: A Report on the Banality of Evil*, Harmondsworth, Penguin, rev. ed., 1994, pages 135-137.
8. See Eugen von Böhm-Bawerk, *Karl Marx and the Close of His System*, an edition of this classic refutation of Marx's theory of value has been published with Rudolf Hilferding's (unsatisfactory) Marxist reply, *Böhm-Bawerk's Criticism of Marx*, Paul Sweezy, Philadelphia, Orion, 1984.
9. Friedrich Engels, *The Condition of the English Working Class*, trans W. O. Henderson and W. H. Chaloner, Oxford, Blackwell, 1971.
10. *Karl Marx on Colonialism and Modernisation*, S. Avineri, New York, Doubleday, 1969; V. I. Lenin, *Imperialism, The Highest Stage of Capitalism* in *Selected Works*, Moscow, Foreign Languages Publishing House, 1950.
11. Lenin's views on this are in *What is to be Done?* [1902] trans. J. Fineberg and G. Hanna, London, Penguin, 1988.
12. Lenin, *Materialism and Empirico-criticism: Critical comments on a Reactionary Philosophy*, New York, International Publishers, 1970.
13. 'Conspectus of Bakunin's Statism and Anarchy' in Karl Marx, *The First International and After: Political Writings Vol. 3*, David Fernbach, Harmondsworth, Penguin, 1974. For Bakunin on Marx see *Statism and Anarchy*, trans. Michael Sihatz, Cambridge, Cambridge University Press, 1990.
14. Peter Juviler, *Revolutionary Law and Order: Politics and Social Change in the USSR*, New York, Free Press, 1976.
15. 'To the Population', 5 November 1917, *Pravda*, No 14 in R. W. Makepeace, *Marxist Ideology and Soviet Criminal Law*, London, Croom Helm, 1980.
16. Makepeace, page 108.
17. *Report of Court Proceedings in the Case of the Anti-Soviet Bloc of Rights and Trotskyites*, Moscow, People's Commisariat of Justice of the USSR, 1938, page 697.

18. For a clever assessment of how various political events and leaders might be summed up by Machiavelli see Edward Pearce, *Machiavelli's Children*, London, Gollancz, 1993.
19. Maurice Merleau-Ponty, *Humanism and Terror*, trans. John O'Neill, Boston, Beacon Press, 1969. On Machiavelli see *Signs*, trans. Richard McCleary, Evanston, Northwestern University Press, 1963.
20. 'The Revolution Against *Capital* in *History, Philosophy and Culture in the Young Gramsci*, Pedro Cavalcanti and Paul Piccone, ed., St. Louis, Telos Press, 1975 page 123.
21. *Ibid*, pages 123-4.
22. Lenin, *Selected Works in Three Volumes*, Moscow: Progress, 1963, Vol 2, page 611.
23. George Sorel, *Reflections on Violence*, trans. T. E. Hulme and J. Roth, New York, Macmillan, 1950; and *The Illusion of Progress*, trans. J. C. Stanley, Berkeley, University of California Press, 1969.
24. Henri Bergson, *Creative Evolution*, [1907] trans. A. Mitchell, London, Macmillan, 1911.
25. Franz Fanon, *The Wretched of the Earth*, Harmondsworth, Penguin, 1967.
26. These sentiments can be seen in his newspaper reports for the Italian *Corriere Della Sera*. See James Miller, *The Passion of Michel Foucault*, New York, Simon & Schuster, 1993, pages 306-309.
27. For an extensive and in depth study of the circumstances leading to the creation of the Italian fascist state see, C. Seton-Watson, *Italy: From Liberalism to Fascism*, London, Methuen, 1967.
28. A. James Gregor, *Young Mussolini and the Intellectual Origins of Fascism*, Berkeley, University of California Press, 1979.
29. Giovanni Gentile, *Genesis and Structure of Society*, trans. H. S. Harris, Urbana, University of Illinois Press, 1960, page 121.
30. *Ibid.*, page 177.
31. See Mussolini's contribution to the *Enciclopedia Italiana* called 'The Doctrine of Fascism' in Vol. 14, 1932, republished as *Fascism: Doctrine and Institutions*, New York, M. Fertig, 1968.
32. *Ibid*.
33. Herbert Schneider, *Making the Fascist State*, New York, Oxford University Press, 1928, page 347.

6 The Preservation of Order: Leviathan and Behemoth

> From ghoulies and ghosties and long legged beasties
> And things that go bump in the night,
> Good Lord, deliver us!
>
> *Scottish Prayer*

The initial function of the modern state is the preservation of order. Such a task requires a strong state, a state capable of ensuring that all warring factions cease from their violent encounters. So long as violent factionalism is part of the social world, civil society is thwarted, if not completely destroyed. It was Thomas Hobbes who first provided an apology for the benefits of the absolute power of the state. For him, the benefits can be expressed in one word: civilisation. Whereas Machiavelli had required that political leaders be beast like, Hobbes insisted that the state itself must be a great monster mighty enough to instill fear into the hearts of all its subjects so that they would cease from their violent strivings and pursue their private interests in peace. The monster, Leviathan, was thus a blessing. But Hobbes also conceived another monster, Behemoth, which he saw exemplified in the Long Parliament, which was a curse, a chaotic beast who fostered anarchy and terror to no peaceful end. In a time of political crisis, the beastial nature of the state reveals itself in its most gruesome guise. In contrasting Thomas Hobbes's defence of political absolutism with Carl Schmitt's attack upon liberalism and subsequent apology for National Socialism we can see the extremely thin, but all important, line between a rationalisation of the beast that preserves civilisation and a rationalisation for a beast that threatens to destroy it.

Thomas Hobbes: Leviathan

Thomas Hobbes's entire political philosophy was a meditation upon the political convulsions that took place in England between 1640 and 1660, the English civil war.[1] Hobbes's response to those convulsions was a theory of the state which guaranteed order above everything else.

To fully appreciate Hobbes' theory of the state we must, however, make a historical detour which simultaneously casts light on the historical origin of the modern liberal constitutional state and the bloody legacy of the idealism of classical political philosophy which Hobbes believed had created such devastation for all of Europe.

In *Behemoth* Hobbes traces the origin of the English civil war to what may at first seem an unlikely event: the schism between pope and emperor generally known as the investiture conflict dating back to the eleventh century. The 'initial impulse' for that schism can, as Rosenstock-Huessy argues in *Out of Revolution,* be traced back to the Synod of Sutri in 1046.[2] Having deposed three rival popes and installed another, the Holy Roman Emperor, Henry III, offended sections of the clergy who believed it their right to appoint the pope, and who saw the independence of the papacy under threat. The very existence of a church which saw itself as responsible for the soul's orientation and final destiny, had already contained an imminent sphere of sovereignty untouchable by human legislators.

But Henry III's diminution of the powers of the clergy in the appointment of the pope, was to have a costly price. Not only did the offended members of the clergy demand that the imperial and other secular powers had no right to appoint the pope, that it was a matter for the cardinals, but the right of the 'investiture' of bishops became a major political issue between Pope Gregory VII and the next emperor, Henry IV, sparking off centuries of protracted violence in Christendom. With the papal dictates of Gregory VII in 1075, it was clear that the spiritual struggle was saturated with secular implications and consequences. Amongst the twenty-seven dictates of Gregory were the following claims made on behalf of the papacy: the

Roman bishop alone is by right called universal; he alone may depose and reinstate bishops; he may depose emperors and other significant powers.

In effect Gregory had proclaimed 'the legal supremacy of the pope over all Christians and the legal supremacy of the clergy, under the pope over all secular authorities,' including emperors. The Church, which had always claimed to be universal, had become synonymous in this dictate with the papal will. The emperor was now no longer a universal power, he was the moon in the sun's, that is the pope's, orbit. He was just another secular power who himself, like other kings and other men generally, had to take their ultimate orientation from the pope. The claim that the pope could absolve 'unjust subjects of their fealty' in a social world held together by a cross of fealty oaths, was an invitation for civic strife. Oaths of loyalty to the emperor were now null and void.

The conflict between pope and emperor was thus a conflict which reached into the entire social basis of mediaeval Christendom testing the interests and loyalties of kings, vassals and serfs. The pope's declaration that the papal court was 'the court of the whole of Christendom' was an opportunity for disaffected Christians to bring their grievances against their bishops and priests, thus further enforcing the centralising aspirations of the papacy and undermining the legal, political and spiritual role of the emperor. Likewise, with Gregory calling for the excommunication of married priests, the struggle within the clergy pushed all members of the clergy into one of the two competing sphere of influence. Equally significant in this struggle was the beginning of the crusades, whereby the secular power of the papacy was enhanced as Christians were encouraged to actively bring all disbelievers into the sphere of the church, and hence under the authority of the papal will.

The various stages of the papal revolution, the different balances of power and concessions made by each party in the turbulence of bloody skirmishes, and the tumult of changing alliances do not concern us here. What is of importance is that the character of politics within Christendom and the nature of political philosophy was profoundly changed by this division between two sovereign powers each in constant tension with the other. Feeding into this tension was the classical doctrine of natural law which was first philosophically developed by Plato and Aristotle.[3] That doctrine had argued that there was a standard of justice over and beyond that articulated by human legislators. In their different ways, Plato and Aristotle had sought to demonstrate the source and nature of this standard. Plato had devised an ideal city based upon the Idea of the good. Aristotle had appealed to the distinction between the common necessities of just laws and healthy political associations, and the contingencies of regulations and different punishments for injustices within different regimes.

In the teachings of Plato and Aristotle this doctrine had never been an incitement to rebellion, but merely a way of assessing the pathologies of particular regimes. This is mainly because of the importance of temperance as a virtue for the classics, and a belief that violent rebellion unlocks destructive passions of the soul. Plato, for example, can make it clear in the *Republic* that Athens is an unjust and inferior regime and that its condemnation and execution of Socrates is the ultimate proof of its degeneracy, but Socrates will refuse to disobey the law of Athens by fleeing for safety, because it may encourage others to disobey the state and its laws.[4] But in the violent struggles between pope and emperor, the classics took on a radical significance. Thus we find the emergence of a doctrine in Christendom not taught by the ancients, the doctrine of tyrannicide. The earliest defender of this doctrine, John of Salisbury in *The Policraticus*, is a supporter of the papacy and he builds upon the classical natural law teaching of Aristotle.[5] While Aristotle provides the idea of natural law, the pope provides a specific site of articulation of power that can be appealed to as higher than any merely earthly power. The earthly power, in John, is merely a hangman, someone who carries out the dirty necessities of political life, but whose main contribution to good is the elimination of the worst men and their actions. When the earthly ruler oversteps the mark and when he creates more misery through misapplying his powers, a subject has the duty to disobey, and in the most extreme cases to kill him.

Although more circumspect than John, Thomas Aquinas also argues for the legitimacy of tyrannicide.[6] He too invokes the classical natural law theory in dealing with a situation that had no parallel in the ancient world. For John of Salisbury and Aquinas the pope is God's earthly representative and hence a force for good in a way that the emperor can never be. Both, then, contribute to maintaining the divided sovereignty that the papal revolution had created. Both recognised that such a situation was politically unstable, and the resolution of the problem involved a hierarchical arrangement which ultimately results in the superiority of one of the sovereigns. In their case, the ultimate earthly sovereign had to be the pope.

Exactly the same strategy of subordinating one sovereign power to the other is followed, although leading to the opposite conclusion, by Marsiglio of Padua. In the beginning of *Defensor Pacis* Marsiglio presents the most despairing account of the effects that contestation between papacy and emperor has had on Italian political life.[7] Marsiglio blames the constant battles in Italy on the papacy. And he states specifically that the existence of the church creates a problem unknown to Aristotle.

For Marsiglio, the most pressing political problem is peace, and the key to the establishment of peace is the establishment of a unified form of sovereignty. Peace, for Marsiglio, will only come if the spiritual power subordinates itself to the earthly power. And while Marsiglio works closely with the natural law doctrine of Aristotle, he is a major pioneer of the legal theory which will be developed further by Hobbes and be known in the twentieth century by the name legal positivism.[8] Law is a coercive command issued by an earthly authority: that and that alone is the real law.

The problem of war caused by divided sovereignty and the anti-papist solution is also treated in Dante's *De Monarchia*. And, finally, the problem of the linkage between classical natural law and the power play of the papacy is also a major concern of Machiavelli. While it would be wrong to see peace as such as the major political goal of Machiavelli, he makes it clear that the specific cause of the political chaos in Italy is the papacy's meddling in politics and the divided loyalties that the papacy creates. Machiavelli's disparagement of political idealism is also a thoroughgoing attempt to discredit the classical source which supporters of the papacy had drawn upon for their own legitimation.

Although the problem of divided sovereignty undoubtedly caused massive and bloody political instability throughout Christendom, the struggle between pope and emperor, when combined with other transformations spreading through Europe, eventually had a very positive unintended consequence which was to provide the basis for the modern liberal democratic state. The uneasy equilibrium reached between pope and emperor meant that each power was in competition with its actual and potential subjects. The arbitrary use of power by either authority was an incentive for kings and lords and their subjects to switch allegiances. Because of the essentially contractual nature of feudal society, the struggle between rulers created a more dispersed system of power than had ever been found in any empire in human history. This was of huge importance for the development of the modern sovereign state. The possibility for shifting alliances was also exacerbated by the proliferation of urban centres, the development of commerce and the evolution and entrenchment of legal systems, facilitating a much more diversified flow of political power than had ever been experienced in human history, particularly in social organisms of similar size.

By the time, then, that Hobbes was writing about the English civil war and cursing the seditious doctrines of Presbyterians and the dangers of universities, the conduits of a pluralist political and legal system already existed. But, what Hobbes had witnessed was not so much a plurality of powers in a taut but stable condition, an agreed upon standoff where differences between competing interests could be settled peacefully, but the violent unspringing of those pluralities as the two major power blocks of the time struggled unto death.

For Hobbes the attempt to find a solution to the problem of disorder carried with it the need to deal with the passion that both fed the disorder and was the necessary response to it. The passion was fear. As we observe how Hobbes deals with fear we witness the careful construction of a rhetoric of legitimacy which is meant to be more terrifying and frightening than the fear from which it is supposed to deliver its subjects. Yet, the strength of that state does not so much lie in its unleashing the forces of terror, but rather in the people's knowledge that the forces are at the ready and will be unleashed if there is danger of disorder. Hobbes, then, wanted a state strong enough to terrify men into the cessation of violent quarrels. But Hobbes also knew that states are not just sustained by their underlying ferocity and strength, they are also sustained by a willingness of subjects to accept them. The perpetuity of the state requires its legitimation. States also have the task of dispensing right to their subjects: of providing and enforcing the rules of social intercourse.

The dominant tradition of legitimation had been provided by the classical philosophers and they had, as we have seen, fed the schism which Hobbes saw as leading to the English civil war. Hobbes well appreciated that the idea of natural right was widely believed in and why the Hebrews as well as the Greeks defended it. Its appeal lay in its establishing rational common guide lines of human conduct. But, as we have also said, Hobbes saw natural right, especially in the context of the power struggles within Christendom, as a subversive force. For Hobbes, nothing could be more subversive than the public cries for the execution of unjust kings, when the word 'unjust' can be so lightly applied in different ways and applied to such disparate actions. In adopting this perspective, Hobbes defends what Plato had considered to be an erroneous premise spread by his enemies, the sophists. This is the belief that the goodness of what we hold valuable depends, not on its own intrinsic nature which touches and opens up some power in us, but in our deeming something valuable. In the latter case, the naming is based upon the disposition of the subject. And because, for Hobbes, people have vastly different dispositions one cannot expect the same actions to be evaluated in the same way: 'the opinions of men differ concerning meum and tuum, just and unjust, profitable and unprofitable, good and evil, honest and dishonest, and the like, which every man esteems according to his own judgment.'[9] He goes on, 'men by giving names, do usually not only signify the things themselves, but also their own affections, as love, anger, hatred and the like. Whence it happens that what one counts an aristocracy, another esteems an oligarchy; and whom one titles a king, another styles him a tyrant'.

Hobbes, then, in confronting natural right is dealing with an idea that has deep cultural roots, widespread acceptance and explosive political consequences. There is, for Hobbes, no way that one can simply ignore dealing with the attractions of natural right, as Machiavelli does, who also undermines the doctrine without naming it. Hobbes thus undertakes a most delicate operation on natural right. He will clarify its power, at the same time he will remove the unstable elements which make it so troublesome. He will be able to undertake this operation by placing it in the context of what he takes to be absent from 'the babbling philosophy of Aristotle and other Greeks': a correct understanding of the nature of the species.

One cannot emphasise enough that what Hobbes understands by nature generally is vastly different to what we find in Plato and Aristotle.[10] These ancients see nature as purposeful, and hence the nature of something is the proper alignment of its constitution with what brings that constitution to fruition. Thus, while for them, it is not natural, but an accident within nature, to be blind or deaf or cruel and heartless, Hobbes sees nature in non-teleological terms. What nature does is natural, even if we desire it were otherwise. Nature is neither purposeful, nor errant; it is merely a constellation of powers. And for Hobbes, as for the other pioneers of the new science generally, the proof of the failure of teleologist lay in the barren legacy of scholastic science: it provided a vast array of logical definitions which did nothing to enhance our ability to make nature serve our purposes.

Just as the picture of nature differs so does the representation of the nature of man. Because, for Plato and Aristotle, man's fruition is dependent upon political life, they saw political life as natural. Conversely nothing would be more wrong-headed for them in trying to fathom the nature of man than constructing an image of him outside of the social. As Aristotle says, only gods and beasts live in isolation. Hobbes, on the other hand, studies man as if he were able to be placed in a laboratory. Hobbes' depiction of the nature of man, then, involves considering him removed from the force, society, which gives an artificial dimension to his character. Further, for Hobbes, humans in the state of civil war reveal what they are like when unconstrained by a central authority. This is the key to our true nature. Hobbes finds the clue to our natural or asocial character not in what brings us together, but in what tears us apart. It is our vices, not our virtues, our propensity for selfishness, not our altruism which reveal what we are underneath the veneer of civility. As he says 'it may be perceived what manner of life there would be, were there no common power to fear, by the manner of life, which men that have formerly lived under a peaceful government, use to degenerate into, in a civil war.'[11]

War, then, is the natural condition of man, and the traits that lead to war are the real building blocks of human character. Thus Hobbes writes 'I put for a general inclination of all mankind, a perpetual and restless desire for power after power, that coasted only in death.'[12] And 'during the time men live without a common power to keep them all in awe, they are in the condition which is called war; and such a war, as is of every man, against every man.'[13] It is not hard to see, as Rousseau did, that the view of human nature which is presented by the dispassionate mechanist is in fact a passionate observation of a political partisan who feared what, in fact, is the product of social conditions. What for the ancients was a crisis typifying a most dangerous departure from our nature is, for Hobbes, the standard condition of our nature which requires an intrusive, artificial force for its correction. To be sure, then, Hobbes is in contradiction with himself in that he traces the source of the English civil war to a social, not a natural conflict. Yet this contradiction is understandable, given that Hobbes sees the most pressing political problem of his age as the cessation of war.

Perhaps equally as understandable is the liberty Hobbes takes with the truth in his emphasis upon self-preservation and fear as the natural drives of those in the state of war, while ignoring other qualities which are the concomitants of war — courage and the preparedness to die for one's side. It should also be noted in passing that while Hobbes is usually allied with Machiavelli as one of the seminal pioneers of political realism, there is a very big difference not only in the respective passions they ascribe to the foundation of statecraft, but in the meaning that those passions play for subjects within the state. Although Hobbes demands of political subjects a compliance with authority much stronger than anything one finds in Machiavelli, he is much less of a patriot than Machiavelli. For Hobbes, loyalty inevitably, naturally, ceases when one's own life is imperiled by the actions of the sovereign. Further, unlike Machiavelli, Hobbes, while recognising that glory and the reputation that comes from it are valued by many, sees glory as but a trifle in the scheme of things. The virtue he always prizes above all else is security. Not for Hobbes is the appeal to the wild, even reckless, virtue of youthful manhood which Machiavelli so prized, when it was married with cunning, for the overcoming of fortune. It is the overarching fear which possesses those living in the ever imminent battles of the state of nature which lead, for Hobbes, both to natural right and to the conception of the state as a great beast, the biblical sea monster, Leviathan.

The subsequent conflict between natural right and the authority of the earthly sovereign, then, is resolvable, for Hobbes, by seeing how they both derive from a common source - the passion of fear, and then defining the appropriate scope of each of these forces in light of that common source. That will, for Hobbes, lead to a theory of sovereignty which will keep natural right claims in check. The result is the reversal of classical natural right teaching: whereas for the classics, natural right provides a standard for assessing the legitimacy of a ruler's decrees, for Hobbes, natural right must yield ground when the ruler lays down the law: it is only in the spaces where the ruler is silent that one can rely upon natural right for providing a proper guide and rule of conduct. The Hobbesian end is already discernible in the very way that natural right is construed. In keeping with his construction of human nature, Hobbes's definition of natural right is thoroughly at variance with the classical and scholastic natural right theorists. He announces in the commencement of his chapter on natural laws that, 'The Right of Nature, which writers commonly call *jus naturale*, is the liberty each man hath, to use his own power, as he will himself, for the preservation of his own nature; that is to say, of his own life; and consequently, of doing anything, which in his own judgment, and reason, he shall conceive to be the aptest means thereto.'[14]

While Aquinas, for example, speaks of self preservation as a natural law, nowhere does he suggest that the pursuit of good and the avoidance of evil, the principle he sees as embedded in natural law, should be subordinate to self preservation. Far less does he suggest that one should deploy any possible means to achieve that aim. Further, for Hobbes, prior to the establishment of any arbitrating power, and because of the vast difference in dispositions, desires and characters of people, there is no general agreement about right or wrong which has the authority to restrain people in their pursuits. As far as right goes, 'every man has a right to everything; even to one another's body.'[15] Right within nature, then, is boundless, and its pursuit is inherently antagonistic - it is a right which encompass murder, theft, rape and slavery. The only impediment to such rights is the power of the other to obstruct. In so far as each person in the state of nature is driven by licentiousness, there is a kind of equality which is characteristic of this state of being: the powers of the species which enable desires to be pursued are distributed in such a way that anyone, either through their own strength, or 'by secret machination, or by confederacy with others may possess sufficient of them to pose a danger to another'. Brute force may triumph sometimes, but cunning and stealth may overpower force. 'And therefore, as long as this natural right of everyman to everything endureth, there can be no security to any man, no matter how strong or wise so ever he be, of living out the time, which nature ordinarily alloweth men to live.' In the prospect of a violent and premature death, the species finds its common vulnerability. It is our vulnerability which forces us to recognise our fundamental equality, something that the veneer of civilisation conceals from us.

If the ground of natural right is power and passion, Hobbes equates the law of nature with the restraint of natural right. Hobbes makes no secret of the fact that the opposition he makes between natural law and natural right is a departure from the classical natural right doctrine: 'For though they that speak of this subject, use to confound jus, and lex, right and law: yet they ought to be distinguished; because RIGHT, consisteth in liberty to do or forbear: whereas LAW, determineth, and bindeth to one of them: so that law, and right, differ as much, as obligation, and liberty; which in one and the same matter are inconsistent.'

The clash between law and right is indicative of an unhappy and divided self that occurs again and again within modernity: a self that strives to conquer all, a greedy, rapacious and inconsiderate being, who is doomed to be frustrated as it moves from one desire to the next — and this is what Hobbes calls felicity, 'a continual progress of the desire, from one object to another' — but who is thwarted by others who are similar. Law is seen by Hobbes as the only way out of this predicament. But it is an unhappy solution, for it requires sacrificing one's nature, laying down one's liberty. Passion, just as it will do for Kant, submits to reason, though reason itself, for Hobbes, is little more that a cautious calculation of the limitation of one's power, a limitation which is most sharply brought to visibility through the fear of death. Natural law, the law which one constructs in the state of nature, is little more than a trade-off brought about through mutual fear and necessity for survival. The contradiction between law and right leads to the shrinking of natural rights through the necessary surrender of liberty. Freud's idea that civilisation is the great artifice of human discontents built upon the superego's constraint of the id is pure Hobbes. But such libidinal restraint is the very condition of the bounties and liberties that require sociality.

That there is no point in divesting oneself of one's power and natural right to be the predator unless others do likewise is, again, a fundamental departure from Greek, classical and Christian thinking about the purpose of life, the nature of goodness and natural law. Yet he presents his teaching on natural right as compatible with the gospels: 'This is the law of the Gospel; whatsoever you require that others should do to you, that do ye to them.' The fact that the law of the gospels is built on love and not mutual fear, the fact that the gospels teach the necessity of being ever prepared to make a sacrifice of one's own life to preserve the law of love, and the fact that the gospels teach that the self who is driven by nothing more than the power of its own appetites is not in any way free, but lost, should make clear that Hobbes is using old words to do something different. It is not that Hobbes does not want people to treat each other well. It is not, as it was with Machiavelli, that Hobbes has a deep antipathy to the Christian virtues because they deplete man's vital powers — the task of the state is not to foster heroic qualities, it is to terrify men into behaving themselves. Hobbes simply does not believe that statecraft can be founded on idealised understandings of the passions which drive men into cooperation. Human selfishness is the source of conflict and the resolution must take that into account.

Just as natural law is elevated through the diminution of natural right, once Hobbes has the element of natural law to work with, it is necessary to diminish its natural component, precisely because nature makes us dangerous, fearful and unhappy. The conditions of social cooperation, such as trust, mutual purposes, honest communication, compassion are, from the Hobbesian perspective, too fragile, too dependent upon the fleeting moments of contiguous felicities to provide a basis of statecraft. Fear on the other hand is all pervasive and it makes good sense, for Hobbes, to take our bearings from this passion. Only someone who forgot how vulnerable everybody is in the state of nature, i.e. only a fool, would not be afraid in the state of nature. Likewise, within civil society, only a fool would dare to challenge the mighty power of the Leviathan. But that is also why, for Hobbes, the power of the Leviathan must be mighty. As soon as the authority of the sovereign can be challenged, the destructive powers of the species are baying at the gates, ready to throw us back again into the frightening terror of the state of nature. It is much better to fear Leviathan, and then build a life, than to fear everyone and everything and live a life without letters, commerce, culture and civilisation.

For Hobbes, the articulation of the law as the expression of the state's unity, as the guarantor of peace, cannot be left to powers who take their orientation from any other authority than the sovereign, whether that be scripture, philosophy, a church leader or the conscience. Although Hobbes has made the will of those in the state of nature the basis of state authority, it is a mistake to see Hobbes' primary concern as the freedom of subjects, as it is, say, for Locke. Hobbes' subjects in the state of nature make a choice out of desperation. And just as a slave who having foregone death is obligated to his master, up to the point where protection from death is guaranteed, the subjects who have preferred the artifice of the state to the carnage of their own freedom are obliged to obey their ruler. Having been saved, having willed to be alive in civil society rather than dead or living in ever imminent fear of death in the state of nature, and because subjects have handed over power to the one who wields the sword, 'it follows, that whatsoever he doth, it can be no injury to any of his subjects; nor ought he to be by any of them accused of injustice.'[16]

What, then, is grounded in fear, provided it continue to allay the greatest of fear - death - is reasonable, just, immutable, and, for all intents and purposes, omniscient. Hobbes is, in effect, saying that the subjects have created a cage for themselves when they abdicate responsibility out of fear. Though, for Hobbes, humans need to be socially caged precisely because of their nature. Left without a master who wields a club or sword big enough to scare them, they will devour each other. For Hobbes, the acceptance of paternal authority means that the fear of the subjects is rational, yet they should be able to live pleasantly enough, living their lives in fear of God and ruler, but at least in relative freedom from fear of their fellows.

The question that must arise when considering Hobbes' attack upon natural right and his defence of political absolutism is whether Hobbes is providing a defence of tyranny, providing a defence of rapacious rulership and dictatorial terror which will only perpetrate a ceaseless reign of terror. Hobbes is aware that just as he must convince the subjects of Leviathan to surrender their natural rights and judgments about the content of law to the sovereign, he needs to entice the sovereign to see the good sense behind the old standards and principles of justice which people see as naturally right. The security of the sovereign is best preserved by the attempt to deliver a justice that is compatible with the desires and perceptions of his subject s, that his law is always just goes by virtue of the nature of law itself. The sovereign is just a man, or group of men, and although he wields the sword, he must be careful that he does not incite others to forge new swords and wield them against him. Likewise, the sovereign has fears. The sovereign's fear will be best alleviated if, and to the extent possible, he acts according to the laws of nature, above all if he makes 'the safety of the people . . . the supreme law'.[17]

Although Hobbes, then, provides a theory of statecraft in which subjects only have rights either directly through the sovereign commands of law, or indirectly through the silences and omissions of the sovereign's commands, it was never Hobbes' intention to write a handbook for rapacious rulers. Peace, the deliverance from the hell of civil war, and 'delightful' living, in so far as that is possible, was always the goal. But where the ruler refuses to comply with the dictates of reason, with natural law itself, he is confronted with a necessity, that he could have and should have avoided had he followed better counsel. The ruins of the commonwealth and perhaps the loss of his own head will be his reward.

But the imbalance of power between ruler and subjects means that the risk taking sovereign has better odds. If a dictator uses absolute political power for the creation of better living conditions for the people, if the imposed order leads to prosperity, then the absolutist moment of rule will be vindicated. When there are only violent means available, those means which secure less violent and fruitful ends prove to be the right ones. In the case of England, the transition from the civil war to civil peace was relatively quick and by the time of Locke, it was clear to see that the diffusion of sovereignty did not have to mean violent political sites of instability and carnage.

Hobbes' theory of the state makes sense in the chaos of civil war. What also is important about it is that it is not attached to any ideological political program which is wildly out of kilter with the social conditions of its time or the possibilities of human prosperity. It is also attached to a vision of government as limited to the preservation of peace. When, however, a defence of political absolutism finds itself harnessed to a political program that has insidious ideological goals which will necessarily draw it further and further into war, when the creation of peace, national security and prosperity is not the end of state, then the defence of political absolutism takes on a very different meaning. This mismatch was to be the fate of one of this century's greatest legal and political theorists, Carl Schmitt, a thinker who called Hobbes 'the greatest and perhaps the sole truly sytematic political thinker,' but a thinker who rejects all of the the liberal elements of Hobbes' thinking.[18]

Carl Schmitt: Legitimising Behemoth

The political art involves the ability to read the time and know the day, that is to know the act required by the moment, which also means knowing what futures are pregnant, and adopting the appropriate course of action which will create a more fruitful future. One must know precisely when to compromise, when to crush one's enemies, when to be merciless, when to be merciful, when to embrace the devil and when to reject him. Crisis offers the greatest opportunity for the statesman to acquire the trophy of glory by inscribing his name in the future. In hell one can't avoid devils. Churchill is a great statesman because he knew that he had to sup with Stalin, and he did it well, but his greatness was diminished by conceding too much in 1945. The stakes and burdens of political action are so much higher than the stakes and burdens of individual action. That is one reason why the application of ordinary moral standards is irrelevant to politics. To choose to live the political life is to choose to leave the moorings of human decency and enter into the darkest chambers of the heart. As Machiavelli knew, if one is not prepared to do that, one will never achieve anything in politics and one will bring ruin to one's people.
    There are two great dangers that one must avoid in the moment of crisis: one is being too weak, and that includes lacking the backbone to violate morality; the other is backing the wrong cause. If one does the latter, then all the moral violations will be in vain, and

one will then be condemned to infamy. The worse case is when one supports the momentarily victorious cause which is devoid of future. To place oneself in service to the barbaric cause because one believes one is staving off barbarism even borders on the pitiful. The terrible choice that faced the German intelligentsia in the early thirties was between the known unstable edifice of liberalism, the known barbarism of bolshevism, and the promises of stability offered by the conservative nationalists and Nazis. The unforgivable crime of the intelligentsia who supported the Nazis was that every available sign indicated that the Nazis would lead the nation into barbarism. The Nazis offered order but created infinitely more suffering and death than what preceded them.

The story of Carl Schmitt is a salient example of a theorist who in seeking to stave off crisis contributed to a far greater crisis by throwing his considerable abilities behind a political program of barbarism. Schmitt was a man of enormous intellectual ability, a constitutional lawyer who had received international accolades in his twenties. In the moment of crisis he seized his opportunity by joining the Nazi party just prior to the Nazi's decision to place a ban on new members. He publicly endorsed Hitler's ascension to power as leader of the Reich, the suspension of parliament, and the purge of the SA. Once the Nazis were in power his writings became openly and viciously anti-Semitic. For example, in 'Die deutsche Rechtswissenschaft im Kampf gegen den jüdischen Geist,' he urged his readers to read 'every sentence of Adolph Hitler's *Mein Kampf* on the Jewish question, particularly his statements on Jewish dialectics.'[19] In that same piece he calls Jewish thinkers parasites. And, again specifically invoking Hitler, he calls Jews the deadly enemy of all genuine creativity in another people. His final sentence of that piece reads 'In so far as I defend myself against the Jews', says our leader Adolf Hitler, 'I struggle for the work of the Lord.'

Schmitt's early misgivings about the Nazis combined with his late decision to join the party, his Catholic background, and personal associations with figures such as chancellors Brüning and General Schleicher, who was murdered during the Röhm purge, as well as General von Fritsch, Chief of the General Staff, who was mistakenly accused of planning a coup, gained him a number of political enemies. He was publicly attacked in the SS weekly newspaper, *Das Schwarze*

Korps, which followed Heydrich's virulent anti-Catholic line.[20] It was largely through the intervention of Göring that Schmitt was able to survive the animosity directed at him by his enemies and retain his university post. After the war Schmitt was interrogated by the Allies, but he was released without trial and he continued publishing and trying to vindicate himself until he died in 1985. Schmitt was a survivor, whose reputation was severely tarnished by his association with Nazism. In spite of the SS attack, Schmitt had unequivocally placed himself at the service of National Socialism. But that has not prevented attempts to rehabilitate him and in the last decade, his work has, curiously enough, been embraced by a number of Left wing academics. The journal *Telos* has devoted an entire issue to him[21] and articles on or by Schmitt appear regularly. Schmitt was also appreciated by some prominent Left wing theoreticians in the 1920s and early 1930s such as Franz Neumann and Otto Kirchheimer.

If Schmitt was an opportunist, he was also one who had been driven by a major conviction which proved to be true: that the Weimar Constitution and the liberal principles which sustained it could not endure against the kinds of enemies working against it. Germany was too divided about its ultimate purposes and future political directions for any resolution to be supplied through liberal means. The severity of political factionalism, most conspicuous in the willingness of fascists and Marxists to resort to any political means to secure their ends, was indicative, for Schmitt of the severity of the crisis and the need to embrace a political force that would guarantee cohesion, unity and direction.

In so far as Schmitt's major political motivation was an end to factional conflict and the establishment of political order, Schmitt has frequently been called a disciple of Hobbes. But disciples can never be completely faithful to their masters, because the challenges posed by the world change. In Schmitt's case, he was writing at a time when the conditions of the peace, and hence of the political room to manoeuvre had been imposed by a foreign power. Thus there is a dimension of nationalism in Schmitt which is thoroughly absent in Hobbes. While it may simply be that Schmitt's character made him a nationalist — and he was an ardent nationalist — the fact is that the civic strife of the Weimar republic could not be separated from the widespread national bitterness toward the victors and their terms of victory. Thus no one who wanted to see peace in Germany could dispense with the issue of nationalism. What also separates Schmitt from Hobbes is the ideological contestations which confronted him. With Hobbes there is a curious amalgam of liberal elements and illiberal political solutions. Hobbes is writing prior to the complete emergence of liberalism. The catastrophe he sees around him is thus not traceable to liberalism as such, but to political forces and currents which antecede liberalism. With Schmitt, on the other hand, the political turbulence of Weimar Germany is seen as the result of liberalism as a tested ideology. And, for Schmitt, his experiences led him to an overwhelming conviction: liberalism was a failure. It could not contain the antagonistic political forces which would destroy the Weimar republic.

There are a number of reasons why Schmitt believed that liberalism is too ill equipped for the task of providing peace and social order and why he thought the fragile institutions of Weimar Germany would collapse. In the first instance, Schmitt believed that the very end of liberalism is non-political: liberals dream of a world where people are merely economic competitors and individual moral agents. But, argues Schmitt, politics cannot be reduced to either economics or morality, nor can it be reduced to a combination of the two. The political exists precisely because the possibility of collective action involves more than economics and morality: according to Schmitt it involves the identification and elimination of the power of the enemy. That is to say, the starting point of politics is not unanimity, but conflict, conflict of goals and means. The enemy is one whose goals are of such a fundamentally different order that compromise is out of the question. Enmity is not something that is at the margins of the political, a contingency which interrupts the smooth flow of political life; enmity is the essence of the political. The distinction between friends and enemies is to politics what the distinction between good and evil is to morality, beautiful and ugly is to aesthetics, profit and loss to economics — the fundamental polarities of evaluation of the field. As Schmitt so elegantly puts it: 'Political thought and political instinct prove themselves theoretically and practically in the ability to distinguish friend and enemy. The high points of politics are simultaneously the moments in which the enemy is, in concrete clarity, recognised as the enemy.'[22]

The corollary of this is that the problem of the permanent possibility of warfare cannot be shirked. 'War is neither the aim nor the purpose nor even the content of politics. But as an ever present possibility it is the leading presupposition which determines in a characteristic way human action and thinking and thereby creates a specifically political behaviour.'[23] Yet, even after the experience of the First World War, Schmitt believed that liberals were blind to this fact. According to Schmitt, liberals are foolish enough to believe that problems can be traded away or talked away, that reason, the point of view of the liberal, will win out, and then everyone will be a winner. Further, because of the primacy liberalism accords to the freedom of the individual, the liberal state, at least when it is consistent with its first principles, foregoes the right to demand the ultimate sacrifice.[24] Liberalism does not, then, deal with the reality of the possibility of conflict until death. This makes it vulnerable to any ideology where political things are important enough to die and kill for. If liberalism is too stupid to appreciate that wherever there is politics there are enemies, that war is a permanent possibility, that speech is not the paradigm of political action, that a regime which cannot demand death from its subjects in its preservation will rot, then it deserves to perish in the hands of its enemies. The continual street skirmishes between para-military organisations, the uprisings and agitations by communists and the National Socialists, as well as the representation given in the Reichstag to the parties which made no secret of their desire to destroy the Weimar constitution and the liberal state — all made it clear to Schmitt that the enemies of liberalism were simply waiting for their moment to seize power. And the myopic and impotent doctrines of liberalism were no match for its enemies.

The critique of liberalism is, then, one that emerges by examining its nature through the optic of crisis. Like Machiavelli and Hobbes, Schmitt's entire political (and legal) orientation is built upon the moment of crisis, the exception, that unpredictable contingency which eludes the rule, and hence what can only be dealt with in a moment of new decision. Good statecraft and legal theory require providing a place for crisis in the general scheme of things, acknowledging its imminent arrival, and having a solution in waiting. In keeping with its impotence and myopia, Schmitt saw that the one place where liberalism touches the nerve of the problem of sovereignty and provides itself with the opportunity to deal with the exception in a time of political crisis — that is in the constitutional reference to emergency powers — it immediately negates the problem by making the sovereign power subject 'to a division and mutual control of competencies.' This problem for Schmitt was highlighted by Article 48 of the German constitution of 1919 which simultaneously allowed the exception to be declared by the President of the Reich, but the Reichstag can at any time demand its suspension. Pointing to the constitutional tension in this provision Schmitt says:

> But only the arrangement of the precondition that governs the invocation of exceptional powers corresponds to the liberal constitutional tendency, not the content of article 48. Article 48 grants unlimited power. If applied without check, it would grant exceptional powers in the same way as article 14 of the [French] Charter of 1815, which made the monarch sovereign. If the individual states no longer have the power to declare the exception, as the prevailing opinion on article 48 contends, then they no longer enjoy the status of states. Article 48 is the actual reference point for answering the question whether the individual German states are states.[25]

In other words, Schmitt argued that in Germany there was a constitutional shambles, and that the failure to resolve the problem meant that Germany was not a real state. Or, to state his case less rhetorically, the reality of the German state could not be guaranteed over time because it lacked the capacity to allocate unconditional authority in the moment of greatest danger.

For Schmitt, the constitutional problem which he saw as a grave political one, one which would lead to the demise of the liberal state itself, was not even noticed by liberal jurists. The dominant trend, one which he saw himself fighting against, was to collapse the distinction between the law and the state. Hence the rule of law would be (mis)construed either as the expression of a collective ethos, a position advanced at that time by the Dutch theorist, Hugo Krabbe,[26] or as the systematic reproduction of underlying norms, the position defended by the neo-Kantian legal positivist, Hans Kelsen.[27] Liberal theorists like Kelsen lead, says Schmitt, to the conclusion 'the state is nothing else than the legal order itself.' Schmitt, however, does not, at least for the great bulk of laws dealing with the routinisation of everyday life, deny that the sovereign should operate by the rule of law. But for the rule of law to exist one must, for Schmitt, accept the true nature of law. The law, and hence the rule of law is derived from a decision. The law, and the state do not reproduce themselves *sui generis*. Decision must precede rule, and this means that the sovereign, by virtue of the very nature of holding political power and being sovereign, is beyond the law. Further, without there being an ultimate power behind the law, there would be no law. All law is 'situational law.' The sovereign produces and guarantees the situation in its totality. He has the monopoly over this last decision. Therein resides the essence of the state's sovereignty, which must be given a correct judicial definition, not as the monopoly to coerce or to rule, but as the monopoly to decide. The exception reveals most clearly the essence of the state's authority. The decision departs here from the legal norm, and (to formulate it paradoxically) authority proves that to produce law it need not be based on law.

In spite of Schmitt's polemic against the liberal trend in state theory and jurisprudence to conflate politics and law, the pivotal role he allocates to the moment of decision also conflates politics and law. Although unlike his liberal enemies, his conflation requires the subsumption of law into politics, and not vice versa. This is what makes Schmitt so attractive to those on the Left who argue that law is merely a political instrument.[28] But it is also the reason why he is such an enemy of liberal democratic state theory. Liberal democratic states preserve the distinction between law and politics to the extent that the law acts as a brake on the political actor, while the political actor revitalises it through new legislative acts. There is in liberal democracy a reciprocal relationship between law and politics, but they are not interchangeable.

The stark alternative that Schmitt believed confronted anyone who wanted genuine political stability was the alternative between decision and discussion. The latter, however, was, according to Schmitt, essentially useless in liberal states because the social cohesion and collective purposes which made discussion a fruitful component of political life were absent. Further, in spite of the fact that liberalism was built around the centrality of discussion, parliamentary democracies were, he argued, caught up in a necessary contradiction between factional interests which emerged through the democratic process and liberal procedures which reduced genuine political talk to a mere formality.[29] Parliament was full of prattle and lacking in real decision. The political impotence of the liberal state and the political terror that lay in waiting for those too weak to act had for Schmitt long been understood by earlier 'decisionist' critics of the liberal state: the Catholic political philosophers, de Maistre, Bonald and, in particular, Donoso Cortés.[30] It is worth pausing upon Schmitt's discussion of Cortés, because it is such a powerful expression of Schmitt's own psycho-political orientation.

Like Schmitt himself, Cortés identified the complete inappropriateness of liberalism in the struggle between good and evil, as manifest in the nineteenth century in the 'bloody decisive battle' between Catholicism and atheist socialism, as laying in liberalism's abdication of decision. Further, Schmitt applauds Cortés's insight that the bourgeoisie was by its very nature a 'discussing class.'[31] In making discussion take priority over decision, the decisions the bourgeoisie did take were fraught with compromises: 'Although the liberal bourgeoisie wanted a god, its god could not become active; it wanted a monarch, but he had to be powerless; it demanded freedom and equality but limited voting rights to the propertied classes in order to ensure the influence of education and property entitled that class to repress the poor and uneducated; it abolished the aristocracy of blood and family but permitted the impudent rule of the moneyed aristocracy, the most ignorant and the most ordinary form of an aristocracy; it wanted neither the sovereignty of the king nor that of the people.'[32]

For Cortés liberalism was and could only ever be an interim politics. The decision of ultimate questions could not be evaded forever, and as soon as liberalism found itself confronted with demands by those who were strong enough and who would not compromise, who would not allow themselves to be disarmed by the seduction of a lengthy conversation, that is by those who saw liberalism as representing, or at least abetting, a genuine evil, it would be overthrown by its enemy. Liberalism tries to postpone indefinitely the day of decision. But Schmitt sees Cortés as implying that the postponement only prolongs the agony, and makes the evil to be confronted so much the worse. For Cortés, there was no way that the real political problems of the day could be solved by liberalism, and to delay the day of decision any longer was madness: 'Donoso Cortés was convinced that the moment of the last battle had arrived; in the face of radical evil the only solution is dictatorship, and the legitimist principle of succession becomes at such a moment empty dogmatism.'[33]

Schmitt does not say outright in *Political Theology* that he desires dictatorship. But the intense presentation of Cortés' argument combined with the strong parallels between Cortés' criticism of liberalism and Schmitt's own, leaves the reader with no other conclusion: a dictatorship is not just inevitable, it is desirable: it is the only way out. Indeed it is a characteristic of Schmitt's writings that he presents his work as scientific, as if he were not urging anyone to do anything. But as one places Schmitt's writings in the context of their times, his very formulation of the problems as well as the logical conclusions of his analysis betray a partisan, albeit a partisan who was reluctant to take responsibility for his decisions, and who could and would repeatedly represent himself as a servant of whatever state he was serving. That Schmitt and his defenders could argue that he was trying to save Weimar during the early thirties, while in real life he joined the Nazis immediately on their coming to power, is only a mystery if one fails to understand that Schmitt was a man whose entire political philosophy not only deferred to authority, but who craved authority. Authority provided him with his intellectual and indeed existential *raison d'être*. He was a jurist whose central idea is the need to locate and then justify the necessity of a decision-maker. Had the liberal state been more dictatorial, that is, had it not been a liberal democratic state, but a police state, he would not have needed to turn against it.

The real paradox of Schmitt's thinking lies in his reason for preferring dictatorship to liberalism. Schmitt wants a dictatorship because, it will be more authentically legal. This seemingly bizarre conclusion which ignores the enormous extent of legal arbitrariness in convictions, sentencing and the appeals process which characterises dictatorships[34] logically follows from Schmitt's theoretical insistence that the key element in understanding the character of law is the point and moment of decision, just as the key element in understanding the state is the sovereign. Schmitt's solicitation of a dictatorship is, from his own point of view, a solicitation not for arbitrary despotic rule, but for a genuine legality. This is a legal authority which is not blind to its own power and hence its own responsibility, but an authority which is not hampered by the liberal doctrine of the separation of powers, which Schmitt sees as having created spaces for the spread of subversion.

The difference between Schmitt and Hobbes on this point does not so much stem from their respective appraisals of the doctrine of the separation of powers — both were hostile —, but from the respective time in which they were writing. For Hobbes, there had been no experience of liberalism. By Schmitt's time, liberalism had been well and truly tried and while it had severe difficulties in Germany, it had been most successful elsewhere in a limited number of advanced countries. What it needed, above all, to succeed in Germany was support from the middle class and public servants, i.e. it needed the support of people like Schmitt himself. Lacking the belief in the very desirability of liberal democracy, the middle class and leading German intellectuals aided and facilitated the Nazis in every step of the way to Auschwitz.

It is instructive to note that Schmitt's attack upon liberalism is not presented by Schmitt as an attack upon democracy. The reason for this lies in Schmitt's understanding of democracy as mass political involvement, and not as a system based on universal suffrage or legal guarantee of rights and the provision of voting mechanisms for adults to express a political preference. For Schmitt, a democracy was not only within its rights to exclude certain sections of the population from having political rights, but, he argued, democracies invariably practiced political exclusion and the maintenance of political inequalities. For example, England was not anti-democratic because it did not grant voting power to the colonised. It was, he argued, liberalism, with its cosmopolitanism and jurisprudential idea of the abstract person that had created unreal and undesirable strains upon democracy.

Given the disjuncture Schmitt introduced between the individualistic and formalist dimensions of liberalism and the substantive and collectivist struggles of democracy, it is easy to see how Schmitt could simultaneously present himself as a supporter of democracy and dictatorship. Indeed, from within Schmitt's perspective dictatorship and democracy are more compatible than liberalism and democracy. As he writes in his 'Preface to the Second Edition' of *The Crisis of Parliamentary Democracy*:

> Bolshevism and Fascism...are, like all dictatorships, certainly antiliberal but not necessarily anti-democratic...The will of the people can be expressed just as well and perhaps better through acclamation, through something taken for granted, an obvious and unchallenged presence, than through the statistical apparatus that has been constructed with such meticulousness in the last fifty years. The stronger the power of democratic feeling, the more certain is the awareness that democracy is something other than a registration system for secret ballots. Compared to a democracy that is direct, not only in a technical sense, but also in a vital sense, parliament appears as an artificial machinery, produced by liberal reasoning, while dictatorial and Caesaristic methods not only can produce the acclamation of the people but can also be a direct expression of democratic substance and power.[35]

Schmitt's conviction that liberalism was incapable of dealing with the political chaos of Germany was prophetic, but it is not simply a case of Schmitt being a prophet. Schmitt was not merely a disinterested intellectual announcing that liberalism in Germany was falling apart. He was providing direction to those who would listen on the basis of his understanding of the past and the present. To be sure, the Nazis did not need Carl Schmitt to come to power, but given the theoretical conclusions Schmitt had been drawing it is difficult to see why some scholars have treated Schmitt's move to Nazism as out of character. Schmitt and his defenders have argued that he wanted to save the prevailing constitution and that he was equally afraid of Nazism and communism.[36] It is true that before they had won power in 1933, Schmitt had thought the Nazis lacked political maturity and would probably lose power to the Bolsheviks if they took office. But once the Nazis had won power, he was impressed by their willingness to act swiftly to destroy their enemies. Ideologically, there was nothing significant about the Nazis that contradicted the theoretical net Schmitt had been weaving for the previous decade. The Nazis, did not lack the friend/enemy distinction — they had enemies aplenty: Jews, Marxists, homosexuals, trade unionists, Christians, liberals, social democrats, gypsies. Nor did they have any qualms about the centrality of decisions in the scheme of things. Hitler's will was the law. The task of a judge was to rule not merely in conformity to the letter of the law, as a stringent legal positivism would require, but to be a vehicle for the expression of Hitler's will. Nor was there any danger that National Socialism was going to fall into the liberal error that law was created by the self generation of principles.

For Schmitt the relationship between the judge and the law was the central theoretical and practical issue for German jurists.[37] The problem, of course, was at the heart of the schism between legal positivism and natural law. In Hobbes, as we saw, the problem is resolved by recasting the nature of nature so that natural law is subsumed under positive law. In spite of Schmitt's debt to Hobbes, he could not abide twentieth century legal positivism any more than he could accept a variant of natural law which would delimit the state's power. The reason for his deviation from Hobbes on this issue lies in the alliance that legal positivism had with liberalism, an alliance that had become firm in England, at least, with Jeremy Bentham and John Austin. Both had seen natural law as a judicial doctrine defended for political advantage. And Austin's definition of law as the command of the sovereign backed up by sanction was entangled with a defence of the parliament as the representative of the people and hence the belief that the people were sovereign.[38] The connection between liberalism and legal positivism was also important to Schmitt's main enemy in the field of jurisprudence, Hans Kelsen. Kelsen's legal positivism went hand in hand with a fundamental mistrust of philosophical and political absolutism and a faith in pluralism which he saw as an essential characteristic of liberalism. For Schmitt, then, there was no way that an anti-liberal politics could succeed were it to retain a liberal jurisprudence.

Further, for Schmitt, one of the most important scientific insights of Nazism was its overcoming of dualisms 'between matter and spirit, blood and soul, word and sense.' The Nazi movement, for Schmitt, had overcome the natural law/legal positivism dualism via the establishment of a spiritual communion between Führer and judge. Whereas in legal positivism, the judge is a servant of positive law, under Nazism, the judge was to play an active role in concretising the Führer's will. In turn that meant being responsive to the movement and what it was the movement was wanting to achieve. Thus if there were a conflict between National Socialist ideals and laws which had not been specifically overturned, but which sprang out of an earlier constitution, this in no way meant that the judge should be beholden to a law that rested on ideals alien to National Socialism.

Schmitt had left himself with few possible allies after identifying the vast alliance of forces that were rotting the 'decisionist' basis of the political. In *Political Theology* he equated anti-politicism with modernity itself, claiming that 'nothing is more modern than the onslaught against the political.' And in one fell swoop, on the penultimate page of *Political Theology*, Schmitt unites American financiers, industrial technicians, Marxist socialists, and anarchic-syndicalist revolutionaries. In an almost post-modernist allegation, they are all accused of dissolving the political into the technical-organisational and the economic-sociological. In other words, in surveying the major political forces vying for global or domestic domination, Schmitt had put together liberals, communists and conservatives, just as the Nazis had, thus ruling out all but an ultra-nationalist dictatorial style of politics.

Ironically, for Schmitt, these modern cold calculators of the spirit are essentially identical to the backward looking aesthetes, the romantics who dissolve politics into culture and see 'everlasting conversation' as the way to self-realisation.[39] Even more ironic though is the fact that Schmitt, who had written a conservative polemic against romanticism, should have supported a party so obviously indebted to romanticism with its fusion of community, myth, spirit, blood and soil. Schmitt's emphasis upon decisionism closely mirrors on the political plane the characteristic of 'occasionalism' which he uses to blast the political romantics: the capacity to exercise one's will without any extrinsic restraint.[40] One could say that the romantic is to art what Schmitt's sovereng is to the political.

On joining the Nazis Schmitt also added a new theoretical formulation to his work, one which created a perfect bridge between his own state theory and that of his new political friends: state, movement, people were 'the three spheres and elements of ... political unity.' The formulation of the unity of these three elements was thoroughly in keeping with Nazism. Once Schmitt had given his seal of approval to Hitler's dissolution of the Reichstag, the typical fascist identification of people, movement, state, leader was complete.

The journey that began with the fear of liberal weakness in the face of social fragmentation, led Schmitt to defend a politics that could only deal with difference by resort to imprisonment or death, and which demanded the service of the whole person. It is also not surprising that in making this journey, Schmitt would settle accounts with his master, Hobbes, criticising him for tolerating private religious convictions.[41] For Schmitt, Hobbes was not sufficiently aware of the dangerous powers that could be unleashed if Leviathan allows people to choose for themselves what it is that they hold sacred. The dangerous individualistic residues which Hobbes's teaching had left were, said Schmitt, to become the main focus of 'the first liberal Jew', Spinoza, who preserved the essential elements of Hobbesian state theory but reversed their respective weightings so that the individual conscience finds its protection in the freedom of expression, while the power of Leviathan is diminished. Further, Hobbes' tolerance, which Schmitt claims was exploited by Spinoza and his followers, had contributed to the proliferation of very different, even mutually hostile cults and secret societies such as Rosicrucians and freemasons. Also, they had found a public safeguard for 'the restless spirit of the Jews.' The equation of the origins of liberalism with Judaism and secret societies such as the freemasons was a standard piece of Nazism. Schmitt's analysis of Hobbes was, in spite of the somersault that he had made in the 1965 postscript to that work, a critique of the shortcomings of Hobbes' authoritarianism from the perspective of a jurist in service to a state that was not going to repeat what Schmitt believed had been Hobbes' mistake of being too liberal. By 1965 Schmitt was defending Hobbes from the accusation that he was a totalitarian whereas in 1938 he was criticising him for not being totalitarian enough. By leaving open the loophole of private religious conviction, Hobbes had defended a theory of the state in which the state was extrinsically powerful, but intrinsically weak.

Interestingly, Schmitt's argument for a total state, which was in fact a restatement of the central position he had been advancing since the Nazis came to power, came after the attack that had been made upon him by the SS. And one of the points that the SS had made against Schmitt, and which has subsequently been raised by those who diminish the extent of his commitment to Nazism, was that in his formulation of 'state, movement, people' he had given a priority to the state which although fascistic was out of character with Nazism.[42] However, Schmitt was always a supporter of a strong state and that position was completely consistent with the party leadership in their first two years of rule. In his book, *State, Movement, People*, Schmitt had made the movement the dynamic element of the state, and the state the static political part is the expression of the movement. As Franz Neumann succinctly put it in *Behemoth*: 'Carl Schmitt sharply distinguishes his theory of the tripartite structure of the state from the dualistic theory of liberalism, in which the state and society confront each other as two separate entities. In the new theory, the state has no monopoly of political decisions. Schmitt concludes that the state no longer determines the political element but is determined by it, that is by the party.'[43]

Like all political movements, Nazism was driven by its own antagonisms and contradictions. The contradictions within Nazism, however, like everything else about the movement, were of an extremely violent nature. A faction could find itself out of favour with the Führer and still consider itself loyal to him — those in the SA who were giving Hitler salutes as they were being shot by men obeying Hitler's order is perhaps the clearest example of this lunacy. One could despise Himmler and still be a Nazi, just as one could see the SS as counterproductive to Nazism. Indeed, if, as Schmitt himself indicates, there is any hidden message in his *Der Leviathan*, one could see Schmitt again adopting an oracular role and warning the leadership that if the state is not totalistic enough it will be torn apart. It is possible to see this as an oblique critique of the SS who did see themselves as a law unto themselves. Though it could just as easily be argued that the SS were the key to creating a state which would not allow the residual elements of dissent to be left unchecked. That its meaning could run in such contrary directions is typical of Schmitt's tendency to serve whatever power required him.

But, to repeat, the fact that one was threatened by a faction within Nazism was not in any way a sign of anti-Nazism. Schmitt himself liked to blur this distinction, so much so that he could refer to himself after 1936 as being like Melville's fictional character, Benito

Cereno, a hostage who waited for the moment to escape. But even Schwab, who makes the very dubious distinction between Schmitt's Catholic anti-Semitism and Nazi anti-Semitism, concedes,'Schmitt did not contemplate emigrating from Germany, nor did he consider actively undermining the Nazi regime.'[44]

The Nazi state had, as Franz Neumann suggested, taken on the appearance of that other biblical beast, Behemoth. Ironically, Schmitt, the man who hated political factionalism owed his life to the fact that the SS did not have complete control of the Nazi state. It is as if Schmitt spent so much energy trying to prevent disunity, that he spent too little time reflecting upon the much more fundamental question: what are the desirable characteristics of a sovereign power? Unity itself is no guarantee of anything. How that unity is achieved and what is achieved through that unity are more important than the unity itself. But Schmitt was too busy attacking disunity to be self-critical of his own goal.

Schmitt was afraid of mobs who clashed in the street, so he supported a party that made street brutality legal provided it was the designated enemy who were brutalised. Schmitt was afraid that liberalism had no way of dealing with the exception, and he abhorred legal positivism, so he supported a regime in which due process could be suspended at will, where retrospective legislation was typical, where the distinction between secret orders and public law was meaningless. Schmitt was afraid that liberalism was incapable of recognising the enemy, so he not only supported a party which made enemies of almost everyone who did not agree with or fit into the National Socialist world view,[45] he himself became designated as an enemy by one of the strongest factions. Schmitt was afraid of communism and the dangers it posed to Christianity, so he supported a party which was the avowed enemy of Christianity and which, for a time at least, made a pact with the Soviet Union to conquer other nations. Schmitt was afraid that there could be a civil war, so he supported a party which led its country into a world war. His fear led him to embrace things and defend acts whose consequences were far more frightening than what he was trying to avoid. Schmitt had spent over a decade expressing his fear of the weakness of liberalism. While he had correctly seen that it was suicidal for the Weimar republic not to have sufficiently strong constitutional safeguards against communists or National Socialists assuming power, he was more afraid of liberalism than Hitler.

The problem of the preservation of order is at the centre of politics. Hobbes was correct to see that without order provided by the state, there can be no secure enjoyment of the fruits of liberty and cooperation. Schmitt had attacked the very element in Hobbes, the freedom left to individuals, which makes the order provided by the state worthwhile. Hobbes knew that the good life is to be had outside of the grim realm of the political. Because people can never all agree to the existence of an ultimate good, it is impossible to reach it through politics. The bounties of civilisation rest upon the state providing order, but the state itself cannot provide great culture. Nazism tried to politicise all facets of a culture. In doing that Nazism, like communism, demonstrated that if the state becomes an instrument in the hand of brutal people who will stop at nothing to fit reality into their ideology, then the state will create far more suffering and chaos than statelessness. The brutality will be systematically organised.

Notes

1. Thomas Hobbes, *Behemoth or the Long Parliament*, Chicago University Press, 1990, page 1.
2. Eugen Rosenstock-Huessy, *Out of Revolution: Autobiography of Western Man*, Argo, Norwich VT, 1969, page 530. Also on the investiture conflict see Harold Berman, *Law and Revolution: The Formation of the Western Legal Tradition*, Cambridge Mass., Harvard University Press, 1983.
3. A. P. D'Entrèves, *Natural Law: An Historical Survey*, New York, Harper and Row, 1951; Lloyd Weinreb, *Natural Law and Justice*, Cambridge Mass., Harvard University Press, 1987; Otto Gierke, *Natural Law and the Theory of Society, 1500-1800*, trans. Ernest Barker, Cambridge, Cambridge University Press, 1934.
4. Plato, *Crito*.

5. John of Salisbury, *Politcraticus: of the Frivoloties of Courtiers and the Footprints of Philosophers*, trans. Cary J. Nederman, Cambridge, Cambridge University Press, 1990.
6. Thomas Aquinas, *Summa Theologica*, [1266-73] T. Gilby, ed., London, Blackfriars, 1963-81, Qu. 42, Art. 2.
7. Marsilius, *Defensor Pacis*, [1324] two vols., trans. A. Gewirth, New York, Colombia University Press, 1956.
8. *Ibid*, vol. 1 xii, S1-3.
9. Thomas Hobbes, *De Cive* [The Citizen: Philosophical Rudiments Concerning Government and Society] in *Man and Citizen: Thomas Hobbes*, C. T. Woods, *et al*, eds., New York, Doubleday, 1972, pages 178 and 192.
10. For further discussion of Hobbes' view of nature see Leo Strauss, *The Political Philosophy of Hobbes, its Basis and Its Genesis*, [1936] trans. Elsa Sinclair, Chicago, University of Chicage Press, 1952; Cf. Howard Warrender, *The Political Philosophy of Hobbes: His Theory of Obligation*, Oxford, Clarendon Press, 1957.
11. Thomas Hobbes, *Leviathan, or the Matter Forme and Power of a Commonwealth*, Michael Oakshott, ed., Oxford, Blackwell, page 83.
12. *Ibid*, page 64.
13. *Ibid*, page 82.
14. *Ibid*, page 84.
15. *Ibid*, page 85.
16. *Ibid*, page 115.
17. *De Cive*, page 258.
18. See Leo Strauss, 'Comments on Carl Schmitt's *Der Begriff des Politischen*' in Carl Schmitt, *The Concept of the Political*, trans. George Schwab, New Brunswick, Rutgers University Press, 1975.
19. *Deutsche Juristen-Zeitung*, 15 Oct 1936, page 1198.
20. For a general overview of the content of Das Schwarze Korps see Charles Wighton, *Heydrich: Hitler's Most Evil Henchman*, London, Odhams, 1962, chapter 8.
21. *Telos*, Special Section, No. 71 Spring 1987, and entire issue No. 72 Summer 1987.

22. Carl Schmitt, *The Concept of the Political*, trans. intro and notes by George Schwab, New Brunswick, Rutgers University Press, 1976, page 67.
23. *Ibid*, page 34.
24. Carl Schmitt, *Political Theology: Four Chapters on the Concept of Sovereignty*, Cambridge, Mass., MIT Press, trans. George Schwab, 1985.
25. *Ibid*, page 11.
26. Hugo Krabbe, *The Modern Idea of the State*, trans. G. M. Sabine and W. J. Shepard, New York, D. Appleton, 1922.
27. On Hans Kelsen see, *General Theory of Law and State*, trans. A. Wedberg, Cambridge Mass., Harvard University Press, 1945.
28. For example, Paul Hirst in 'Carl Schmitt's Decisionism' writes, 'His concept of 'sovereignty' is challenging because it forces us to think very carefully about the conjuring trick which is 'law'', *Telos*, Summer, 1987, page 19.
29. Carl Schmitt, *The Crisis of Parliamentary Democracy*, trans. Ellen Kennedy, Cambridge, Mass., MIT Press, 1985.
30. *The Concept of the Political*, pages 61 and 64-65.
31. *Political Theology*, page 59.
32. *Ibid*, pages 59-60.
33. *Ibid*, page 66.
34. For an excellent picture of the legal system under Nazism see Ingo Muller, *Hitler's Justice: The Courts of the Third Reich*, trans. Deborah Schneider, Cambridge, Mass., Harvard University Press, 1991.
35. *Crisis of Parliamentary Democracy*, pages 16-17.
36. See, for example, George Schwab's *The Challenge of the Excepton: An Introduction to the Political Ideas of Carl Schmitt between 1921 and 1936*, Berlin, Duncker and Humblot, 1970; Joseph Bendersky's *Carl Schmitt: Theorist for the Reich*, Princeton, Princeton University Press, 1983; Guy Oakes' introduction to the English translation of *Schmitt's Political Romanticism*, Cambridge, Mass., MIT Press, 1986; Paul Gottfried, *Thinkers of Our Time: Carl Schmitt*, London, Claridge, 1990. Against this see Jerry Muller's 'Carl Schmitt, Hans Freyer and the Radical Conservative Critique of Liberal Democracy

in the Weimar Republic' in *History of Political Thought*, Vol. XII. No. 4. Winter 1991 and the succinct but extremely sharp chapter on Schmitt in Stephen Holmes's *The Anatomy of Anti-Liberal Thought*, Cambridge, Mass., Harvard University Press, 1993.

37. See 'Der Weg des deutschen Juisten,' *Deutsche Juristen*-Zeitung, 1934 Vol. 39, page 692.
38. John Austin, *The Province of Jurisprudence Determined Lecture* (London 1832) Hart's edition London: Weidenfield and Nicholson, 1954.
39. *Political Theology*, page 53.
40. *Schmitt's Political Romanticism*, trans. Guy Oakes, Cambridge, Mass., MIT Press, 1986. The point about Schmitt's romanticism has been made by Karl Löwith in 'Der okkasionelle Dezionizmus von Carl Schmitt' in *Sämtliche Schriften*, Vol. 8, Stuttgart, Metzler, 1984, pages 32-71 and Richard Wolin in 'Carl Schmitt: The Conservative Revolutionary Habitus and the Aesthetics of Horror', *Political Theory*, August 1992.
41. Schmitt, *Der Leviathan in der Staatslehre des Thomas Hobbes: Sinn und Fehlschlag eines politischen Symbols*, [1938] Koln, Hohenheim, 1982 pages 85 and following.
42. See Gunther Maschke in his apologetic commentary, *Der Leviathan in der...Symbols*, pages 186-191 and 227-241.
43. Franz Neumann, *Behemoth: The Structure and Practice of National Socialism*, London, Victor Gollancz, 1942.
44. *The Challenge of the Exception*, page 134-141.
45. *Ibid*, page 141.

7 The Legitimate Representation of Interests: The People

> The multitude: that numerous piece of monstrosity,
> which, taken asunder, seem men, and the
> reasonable creatures of God; but, confused together,
> make but one great beast, and a monstrosity more
> hideous than Hydra
>
> Sir Thomas Browne, *Religio Medici*, II, 1,

Between the polarities of the serenity of the mere idea of the best political and/or social form, and the brute necessities of the struggle for power and the imposition of order, lies the middle term. This is the situation where there is a convergence between the issue of legitimacy as something more than the sovereign's sheer force and the real compromise that emerges through the actual contestations of groups. Here the normative questions of statecraft revolve around legitimacy and power. Generally, these two issues have worked in tandem.

Historically, the most common pattern of state formation is the transference of power from the tribe to the chieftain who then becomes a king in his role as legislator and mediator of disputes.[1] His function is initially to provide military protection, justice within the domain he presides over, and that in turn means providing internal protection and administering the rules of exchange and ownership, both of property and persons. Such a task invariably occurs when a society reaches a certain size, when it ceases to be nomadic and usually when, in the first instances, it has an agrarian base. This in turn coincides with the relative proliferation of the division of tasks and specialisations so that some people engage in providing implements, others in working the land, others administering and others protecting the society.

The oldest and most original form of a complex state is a variant of the monarchy. In his role as military protector, legislator and administrative overlord, again usually as a result of the increasing size of the domain over which he presides and the proliferation of tasks within it, the monarch must replicate his powers. The family heads who serve the king in this way are originally the more wealthy and the more powerful. The secondary form of the state is thus usually some kind of aristocracy.

The democratic form of the state is usually a more derivative state form, representing an expansion of public offices to the rest of the property holders within the city-state or *polis* - for it was in the Greek city state where this form of government first arose. Classical democracy, was not a form of government for the representation of all adults: women and slaves did not have political power.

Although the democratic state form is a relatively late state form, the monarch was, in the first instance, chosen by the tribe to hold it together. The monarch is invariably either an emperor/god (the pharaoh) or (as in Mesopotamia) servant of the god, that is to say a priest, who is at the same time there to provide justice for his people. All the earliest records of states including the Bible, the Code of Hamurabi and other Mesopotamian and Assyrian law fragments, and Egyptian writings point to this.

The very scale of the society and the complexity of social organization plus the existence of a military caste may have made it inevitable that the monarch or emperor would invert this role and thus the subjects would be seen to exist for his glory. The emperor's or king's glory would symbolise the glory of the society as a whole. The same is equally true for aristocratic states as well as ancient democracies. Further, all ancient states discriminated between free men and slaves, and men and women - slavery itself may have started with the enslavement of women and it becomes integrated into the pattern of social reproduction even within larger tribal societies.² Political power originally rested upon unequal status between human beings. Once the state was formed nothing was more remote from the political agenda for thousands of years than the idea of equality.

The Ancients

Plato and Aristotle both divide the forms of government into monarchy, aristocracy and democracy with law, and tyranny, oligarchy and democracy without law. In this breakdown the modalities of government are represented as three polarities of which one is a legitimate and the other a perverse political form. The tyrant is a perverse monarch, the oligarch someone who wants wealth alone to grant him political power, and the lawless democrat someone who wants to exercise political power unconstrained by law. At the basis of this division, then, is a recognition by Plato and Aristotle that the good ruler(s) preserves more than the immediate self-interest. He or they must preserve the whole order over which he or they preside and that order must ultimately be dedicated to the pursuit of higher things. The good ruler, then, is portrayed as representing the good of the whole society (at least as the good was interpreted by the philosopher). The bad ruler, on the other hand, represents a narrower interest. The part takes precedence over the whole, and the part is the baser part of him or their self.

Both Plato and Aristotle preferred the monarchical form to the democratic form, if one could find a wise enough monarch. In the case of Plato, he saw the democracy as responsible for executing Socrates. Plato is merciless in his description of the arrogance and foolishness of his contemporary democrats. They are represented as selfish, as hedonistic, as easily swayed by demagogues, as superficial, as vindictive, as dilettantes and dolts. He presents the democratic polity as the preparatory step for tyranny. The excessive demand for equality will enable rabble rousers from the lower classes to rise to power, once having attained power they will be uncontrained in their appetites and will the tyrannise the class from which they sprang.

As critical as Plato was of democracy, he did see that if it were tempered by law, it was the least bad of the negative kinds of state. And in the *Laws* he presents a state form which has democratic components mingled with the rule of law. As aware as Aristotle was of the dangers of the poor using government to rob from the rich (not solely because he was on the side of the oligarchs, but because such action would inevitably lead, as it had done in the struggle between the thirty and the democrats, to much bloodshed), he saw a number of advantages in letting the many have a part to play in the political process. Most importantly, Aristotle recognized that there are advantages to the collective use of intelligence. Although many minds do not amount to one genius, the sheer fact that each person, although of limited intelligence, may see different things means a better picture of the whole may emerge through the collective. The political form which Aristotle called the polity combined aristocratic and democratic elements with the rule of good laws.

We have been critical of much of the legacy of Plato's idealism. It cannot be disputed that Plato and Aristotle brilliantly elucidated the major flaws of democracy and that their political compromise of a mixed constitution has largely been the way in which the flaws of democracy have been kept in check.

While Plato and Aristotle present a critical appraisal of the respective forms of ancient regimes, the most eloquent apology for democracy is found in Thucydides *History of the Peloponnesian War*, the first account and theory of international relations.[3] Pericles's 'Funeral Oration' is a panegyric to the great civic spirit which he believes is generated through democracy. He describes a political form in which there is equal justice for all and a strong civic ethos based upon a willingness to serve. In addition, there is orderliness produced from good will and mutual respect for citizens, refined living, cultivated taste, strong military training, and an openness to ideas from the outside world. Where Plato saw dilettantism and selfishness and envy (he points out in the *Gorgias*, that although Pericles built harbours and roads, he was exiled from Athens), Pericles praises versatility, grace, tolerance and generosity of spirit. To die for such a city is, for Pericles, a great honour. Whatever motivated the Athenian enemy in their battle could not, for Pericles, compare with what the Athenians were fighting for. According to Pericles what men love most is what belongs to them, and the greatness of the democratic form of the state derives from this. Pericles has put his finger on a fundamental truth about democracy that will be repeated time and time again in one form or another by its defenders. One can also see that as true as this realisation is, it does not negate the enduring problems of democracy.

Indeed, as glittering as Pericles' speech is, Thucydides' narrative ultimately reveals that the funeral oration is the selective self-image of an imperial leader. The reality of the Athenians is that in warfare they showed no generosity of spirit to the Melians who had wanted to remain neutral during the war with Sparta. Before being slaughtered the Melians are 'invited' to join the Athenians by being informed that justice is merely about power, and where there is not equal power, appeal to any higher principle of justice is futile and a pathetic exercise. Likewise in the debate between Diodotus and Cleon about what should be done to the Mitylenians, the issue of whether to punish or spare them for having the temerity to revolt against their Athenian masters is over the priorities of imperial power: the demonstration of might as a warning to other potential rebels (Cleon); or the virtue of more moderate chastisement in producing future revenue, for the dead cannot provide a profit (Diodotus).[4]

Finally on this point, the Athenians whom Pericles presents as moderate and unostentatious are seduced by Alcibiades to undertake the Sicilian expedition. Thucydides' tale of the collapse of democracy through imperial overexpansion is a salutary warning to those who, like Pericles, overidealise the virtues that come from civic involvement. For what Plato, Aristotle and Thucydides and Machiavelli, after them, all realised is that the form of government is ultimately a representation and cultivation not only of a particular group of men, but a particular range of passions and human characteristics. The democratic constitution is always in danger of being driven by its own self-righteousness and thus of confusing its idealised self-image with its reality. (This is why there is no more dangerous form of idealism than a democratically based idealism. That is one reason why Marxism was always an infinitely more pernicious form of idealism than the rational elitism of Plato's idealism.) However potent we still find Pericles' oration, it nevertheless misses the point that the reason the Spartans are just as ready to die in the war as the Athenians is that they too stand to benefit from the spoils of empire.

Given that a political form will be the expression of human passions and characteristics, the perennial political philosophical problem is to identify the best and most appropriate blend of self-preserving, ordering, and civilizing institutions. A concomitant of this is that the best contributors to the democratic theory of the state have always advocated a limited rather than an unlimited role for the *demos*, and they have been conscious of both the strengths and the limitations, both technical and psychological, of democratic involvement. Conversely, radical democratic theorists have invariably endowed the *demos* with ideals that have no basis in what most people actually want to do with their lives, which is to make money, get on with their hobbies, relax with family and friends and enjoy the fruits of civil society. Radical democrats find it hard to believe that most things political are deadly boring for most people.

Marsiglio of Padua

One of the earliest philosophical appeals to the sovereignty of the populace as a whole comes from Marsiglio of Padua. His *Defensor Pacis* (1324), as we said in the previous chapter, was written as a reaction to the bloody mess that had been caused by the clergy having secular power. Having realised that the spiritual power could only be a power in so far as it was represented on earth, the central political problem of the day was to contain the power of the clergy by subordinating it to a secular sovereign. And in a move which is striking in its anticipation of Rousseau, Marsiglio claims that the sovereign is the people.

On first consideration, this may appear to be a complete reversal of the dominant mode of Medieval thinking about statecraft: that the sovereign was a servant of God, and thus power flowed from God down to the people through the sovereign. It is true that the Medieval model of power was a top down model, but the church had established a power relationship between all people and the clergy, making the former dependent upon the latter for their own salvation. In this respect the conflict between the imperial and the papal powers could be seen as expressing the more fundamental struggle for sovereignty between the clergy and the laity. Because the purpose of the clergy was to serve God and the congregation, it was perhaps inevitable that the move, which was to be made again and again in the Reformation, to make the priest an elected representative of the congregation would occur. This is exactly what Marsiglio proposed by arguing that all priestly powers, and this included powers on matters of Christian doctrine and coercive powers over apostates and heretics, had to be authorised by the people. The clergy was to be elected by the Christian laity, and the priest, the bishop, the cardinal and even the pope himself was the political representative of the people. Thus Marsiglio assigns to the population as a whole the most important political power for bringing about peace.

Marsiglio justifies making the people the sovereign on the following grounds. No one will make laws that will harm themselves and the common interest will tend to emerge as each is given the opportunity to reflect upon his own interest under the burden of public responsibility. People will be more inclined to obey laws which they have given themselves, thus there is a greater guarantee that the legislator will be effective and its laws obeyed. And the people need to know the dangers and benefits that may befall it, thus there is a need for public discussion about them. At the same time as Marsiglio grounds sovereignty within the people, he does not see the mechanics of its operation as desirable or possible without the people transferring power to a ruling element that can take on dictatorial powers in a time of crisis. That ruling element whether monarchical or aristocratic is, nevertheless, an elected element. What Marsiglio grapples with in his doctrine of popular sovereignty is a form which blends the interests of the people as a whole with the necessity of prudential and firm leadership. Marsiglio frequently draws upon Aristotle in *Defensor Pacis* and there are strong similarities between his proposed political solution and Aristotle's solution to the problem of the conflict between oligarchs and democrats, the polity.[5] But the Christian soil upon which he is working as well as the violent problems that are peculiar to Christendom mean, as we have seen, that there is a radical shift of emphasis from Aristotle[6].

Marsiglio begins with the legitimacy of the sovereign being the whole people and then seeks to refine the mechanics of leadership so that the people will be most benefited. In this respect, there is a strong indication of the shift to a much more egalitarian ethos that has been brewing within Christendom. Although, then, Marsiglio anticipates modern democratic theorists, the cultural soil and the problems that inform his political theory are thoroughly Medieval.[7]

Benedict de Spinoza

The first modern philosopher to advance an overt defence of democracy was Benedict de Spinoza.[8] Spinoza's philosophical starting point is the radical separation that must be made between scripture and philosophy: each one must be allowed to function without subordination to the other in its proper domain. In so far as this is a major problem for Spinoza, and it is the central subject of his *A Theologico-Treatise* (1670), Spinoza's political problem is largely, though not exclusively, centred around the issue of freedom of speech. Note that the problem of freedom of speech was, to put it mildly, not a major concern of Aristotle nor of Marsiglio. What makes it so important for Spinoza is the huge shift that has taken place in the understanding of the natural world.

The development of the new scientific worldview, which gets its major impetus from the physics of Galileo and the philosophical writings of Francis Bacon and René Descartes (1596-1650), was severely handicapped by the Church wanting to forbid these new doctrines being taught in universities - a fact that leads Spinoza to say 'Academies that are founded at the public expense, are instituted not so much to cultivate men's natural abilities but as to restrain them.'[9] The success of the new science required that scientists and philosophers could communicate the results of their experiments without fear of persecution. Descartes had expressed the aspiration of the new wave of scientific thinking in *The Discourse on Method* when he spoke of a new 'army' of scientists who would pool their results and help man become master over nature as discoveries would be made which would ease the burdens of labour and advance the health of the species. Spinoza saw himself as a philosophical member of such an army. But, given the nature of his philosophical speculations, the issue of free speech was a matter of personal survival. He knew that while he was safe in the commercial republic of Holland, because of the perceived dangerousness of his atheistic philosophy, he was not at liberty to live in various other parts of Europe.

Like Hobbes, Spinoza begins with a view of nature as governed by scientific laws. Also, like Hobbes, Spinoza's understanding of all natural beings is premised on the simple idea that they are what they do. Nature is what it does, and what it does is its right. As he succinctly puts it in *A Theologio-Political Treatise*: 'Whatsoever an individual does by the laws of its nature it has a sovereign right to do.'[10] There is no extrinsic standard of right. This is one of the significant consequences of Spinoza's initial rationalist premiss of the *Ethics*, that substance is by its nature unified, and there is only one substance or else it could not be unified. Thus Spinoza made a heretical equation that was to make his name a byword for infamy (even Hobbes whose philosophy of nature is essentially the same as Spinoza's did not want to be mentioned in the same breath as Spinoza): the power of nature and the power of God are the same power.

Because, then, there is no wrong in nature, because mankind is only one other species of nature and no less subject to its power and the laws through which that power is expressed than any other species, the wise have no rights over the fool: each has the sovereign right to do what he will. The egalitarian basis of the philosophy, then, exactly as in Hobbes stems from equating man's right with his essence, and if that means one will use reason, another cunning, another brute force, so be it. Each is simply exercising its domain in the particular way that is peculiar to its character. And to repeat there is absolutely nothing that a human does that is contrary to nature, and because God and nature are one, therefore there is no human action that has or ever will be performed that is contrary to God. We cannot see the totality of existence, and 'man is but a speck,' 'If anything, therefore in nature seems to us ridiculous, absurd, or evil, it is because we only know in part, and are almost entirely ignorant of the order and interdependence of nature as a whole, and also because we want everything to be arranged according to the dictates of human reason; in reality that which reason considers evil is not evil in respect to the order and laws of nature as a whole, but only in respect to the laws of our reason.'[11]

Spinoza's cool prose somewhat disguises the real meaning of such teachings, but that meaning was expressed in its full clarity by a disciple of a much less philosophically gifted exponent of the mechanistic philosophy, Julien la Mettrie, author of *Man as Machine*. The disciple was the Marquis De Sade who time and time again, in *Justine*, in *Philosophy in the Bedroom*, in *Juliette* defends murder on the basis of the interdependence of nature as a whole. To astute contemporaries of Spinoza's time, however, there would be no surprise that a philosophical line could be drawn between Spinoza and a libertine's philosophy of murder. For his part, Spinoza's passionate enthusiasms were primarily cerebral and he believed he had really just expressed what was the logical implication of the new way of seeing nature as a vast continuum of cause and effects. Spinoza's entire philosophy, in fact, had emerged from an initial acceptance of Descartes's equation of matter and extension.[12] But Spinoza saw that Descartes' metaphysical division between mind (a non-extended substance) and matter threatened to undermine its fundamental insight. And, for Spinoza, this was most evident in the Cartesian concession to freedom of the will. According to Descartes the evidence of the free will lay in language, and language is essentially, from this perspective, a mental act.[13] For Spinoza, Descartes's philosophy thus undermines its greatest insight, the vision of nature as a continuum of laws.

Spinoza, then, begins with an appeal to the recognition of human beings as being completely under the dictate of nature. He also perceives that in its immediate interactions nature is full of great discord as sovereign beings each strive to exert their power. Like Hobbes, he sees that this struggle of power and preservation is an anxious state and that the only way to exchange fear for security is for individuals to forego some of the power that they have by nature and allow reason to provide the measure of law. The move from the state of nature is pure Hobbes, but whereas Hobbes races from the transfer of power from those in the state of nature to dwell upon the absoluteness of the power received by the sovereign in order to keep the mob in check, Spinoza takes a different turn. He calls into question the passion of fear as a solid enough foundation for the continuity of the state and obedience to the law.

Like Hobbes, Spinoza sees that no one would make the sacrifice of surrendering their powers unless there were to be a greater good. Hobbes' sovereign cannot guarantee this. For while Hobbes, as we have seen, clearly concedes that the sovereign's right to obedience ceases when he threatens the life of the subject, the act of transfer of powers and rights which one exercised in the state of nature to the sovereign means that the imbalance of power is always stacked in the sovereign's favour. For someone who is in the state of nature and who aspires to find protection in the Hobbesian state, the price of order may well seem worth the price. But to the insider, that is not so obvious. One may often feel that one has simply traded one intolerable condition for another. Further, Spinoza implies that the danger of Hobbes' resolution is that the Hobessian citizen will invariably be looking for an opportunity to regain his powers because the loss of power is extracted under fear. As soon as a better opportunity presents itself to the subject he will take it. The Hobbesian kingdom is, from this perspective, held together by a pretence of loyalty. This may suffice for as long as Hobbes' sovereign is strong, but the citizen body will not be contributing anything to shoring up the state. On the contrary, there is an incentive to look for weaknesses in the sovereign's armour, so that one can regain one's freedom.

The virtue of democracy, then, when considered from this perspective is that it will create the strongest possible sovereign. For the sovereign will be the people as whole. Thus the act of transference is a mutual act of transference whereby the citizens are the body politic; they are not merely subjects, as in Hobbes, but they are reconstituted in their role as sovereign legislators. Interestingly, the very thing which most other (non radical) democratic theorists fear, the excessive potency of the *demos* is what Spinoza endorses, when he defines a democracy as 'a society which wields all its power as a whole. The sovereign power is not restrained by any laws, but everyone is bound to obey it in all things; such is the state of things when men either tacitly or expressly handed over to it all their power of self-defence, or in other words, all their right.'[14]

In this respect one might say that Spinoza endorses a radical form of democracy. Nevertheless, for Spinoza, the potency of any sovereign form is only to be feared when the power is used for ends which are contrary to the public good for it is its own good. And, says Spinoza, a democracy is least likely to ignore the public good for it is its own good. A democracy is, in terms of Spinoza's philosophy, dedicated to compromising between the different powers which can come into collision. The very focus of its concern tends to diminish the irrational. Of course, if by rational one stands by a Platonic or Aristotelian sense of reason as directed toward a transcendent or immanent form of the good, then Spinoza's defence of a democracy makes no sense. For sheer numbers do not necessarily lead to a greater understanding of the good and hence the fact that a policy is reached through democratic consensus does not mean it will be good. However, Spinoza has dispensed with any extrinsic standard of the good: for, from his position, such a standard is always the imposition of one form of life upon another, or as Nietzsche, who identified Spinoza as his one great precursor, will say, morality is always the expression of a particular will to power.

From this perspective, the philosopher's concept of reason as expressed by Plato and Aristotle is simply a pattern of rationalisations which spring from a particular nature wanting to exercise its sovereignty over its domain. Thus it would be absurd to expect a *demos* to come up with policies which are commensurate with what the philosophers hold as good. From this perspective, then, it is thoroughly understandable why the classical philosophers were so opposed to democracy. The members of the *demos* would be generating laws consistent with their own desires, and what was rational for their nature was irrational for the philosophers. Hence Plato's mission of making the world safe for the likes of Socrates, not to mention himself, led to his vision of philosopher kings. The only person that Plato allows to speak at length on the virtue of democracy is Protagoras, the sophist who held that there are no absolute truths, and that 'man is the measure of all things.' In the Platonic dialogue the *Protagoras*, this view is presented as a sophistic endorsement of the idea that each man knows his own interest, and men are credited with possessing an intuitive knowledge of what is their own interests, thus a democracy is seen as the best form of government for men's nature.

One of Plato's responses to Protagoras is that this doesn't get very far, that the relativist has to concede that the believer in absolutes is entitled to his position thus he extinguishes his own maxim. Politically, this amounts to the fact that the relativist has to concede that his position has no intrinsic superior moral merit, and where power and the numbers go against him he must just accept it. Spinoza's whole conception of rights is thoroughly consistent on this point. He never for a moment suggests that a ruler doesn't have the right to rule in the most violent manner, indeed he explicitly says that a ruler has this right, as well as the right 'to put citizens to death for very trivial causes.'[15] For Spinoza the proper rejoinder to the charge that relativism may endorse tyranny is not to look for a transcendent rational solution, but to locate a cause of the same nature. In other words, only force counters force, not reason. Thus while a tyrant has as much right as any other individual to exist, and a tyrant's very existence is the demonstration of his right, tyrannical actions ultimately imperil the doer. In all likelihood, the tyrant will find himself at the limits of his power, and his own vulnerability in the face of the scale of enmity he has created will ensure his demise.

Spinoza's justification of democracy, then, proceeds along purely relativist lines and has nothing to do with any search for an ideal standard of right or the creation of a virtuous person in the Platonic sense. For what is rational to the democratic constituents is simply the mediation between their self-chosen ends. To repeat, there is no form of the good to which the mind may turn. Rather, each nature is driven by its own passions and needs. Reason is a surface for nature's self-reflection. The good, then, is always relative to the nature of the sovereign power. A democracy simply provides an opportunity for all the adult male sovereign powers to provide laws that enable them to articulate and pursue their interests in so far as that is feasible. It should be noted that Spinoza specifically excludes from exercising political power: slaves, criminals, children, wards of the state and women, the latter because of their weakness and the fact that because of man's lustful, jealous and proud nature there would be chaos.[16] What democracy also preserves, which the Hobbessian state does not, is the power of the subject which is reconstituted in his role as a member of the sovereign body.

Spinoza's defence of democracy rests on a thoroughly realist foundation, and the virtue of democracy rests in its fusion of the potency of the convergence of more numerous sovereign forces and the greater opportunity each power has in presenting the reasons behind his own liberty. As he says: 'The object of government is not to change men from rational beings into beasts or puppets, but to enable them to develop their minds and bodies in security, and to employ their reason unshackled; neither showing hatred, anger, or deceit, nor watched by the eyes of jealousy and injustice. In fact, the true aim of government is liberty.'[17]

For liberty to be attained, however, means allowing, to as large an extent as possible, that natures be let be. 'He who seeks to regulate everything', observes Spinoza, 'is more likely to arouse vices than to reform them.'[18] The reason for this is that, for Spinoza, we have no choice over our nature. We are what we are. Some may be able to develop powers through their reason, but that development inheres in one's nature anyway. There is no such thing as a contradiction in nature; such an idea is merely the difference between an idea of the understanding and the order of nature. The latter is always the proper benchmark for the former. In prohibiting men's natures, the state will simply encourage a multiplicity of other passions including anger and resentment, and behaviours based on those passions may lead to social chaos.

The fact that some natures will have to be controlled because some behaviours are too disruptive to social life is a fact of political life, thus some natures will be branded criminal, and will be treated as such. But it is in the best interests of the sovereign to limit those curtailments as much as possible. This is the corollary of making liberty the aim of government. But the area Spinoza singles out as being of most importance for the preservation of liberty is the area of free speech. For free speech 'is absolutely necessary for progress in science and the liberal arts.'[19] Further, the sovereign body that tries to suppress free speech cannot succeed in the long run. People will think what they can and they will not surrender their judgment because someone wills it. Indeed, argues Spinoza, it is precisely the best people, the most upright and tolerant who most respect and value free speech. And it is thus the best people (like Spinoza himself) who are branded heretics, and whom the censors wish to silence. Further, when what men firmly believe to be true is being unfairly branded as criminal, they will, for their own honour, be tempted to conspire for seditious purposes.[20]

In a democracy, freedom of opinion is vital for the people to discuss the advantages and disadvantages of any piece of legislation, thus enabling it to overturn old laws if their disadvantages outweigh their benefits. While, then, Spinoza indicates that no ruler is acting in his best interest if he suppresses free speech, in a democracy such a suppression would be most contrary to the best interests of the sovereign body itself.[21]

If Hobbes' deep mistrust of religious freedom is born from his perception of the impact that inflammatory speeches of the Presbyterians and rabble rousing university teachers played in bringing about civil war, Spinoza's celebration of freedom of speech is born out of his experience of the prosperity and tolerance of Amsterdam. [22]

While Spinoza may well merit the title of the first philosopher to provide an elaborate defence of modern democracy, and while he makes a strong case for the value of religious tolerance and freedom of speech, the legitimation he provides of democracy provides few of the hallowed conceptions of man which are usually associated with the great documents of liberal democracy. Indeed, as we have seen, Spinoza's conception of rights and powers deeply contradicts the notion of rights which is ingrained in the whole constitutional tradition and incorporated in such documents as the American Declaration of Independence and the French Declaration of the Rights of Man. That tradition draws upon the language of rights as a moral and, where possible, legal bulwark against the excesses of government power. Spinoza's conception of democracy is more ancient than modern — and therein lies its radical democratic character: it does not deal with the problem of the dangers of the congealing of sovereign power in any singular source, regardless of whether that congealment be of a monarchical or democratic character. The first modern political theorist who can be credited with providing a liberal as well as a democratic account of state theory is John Locke. Interestingly, he saw himself as in no way indebted to Spinoza, let alone Hobbes, both of whose writings he said he barely knew, and both of whom, he said had been 'justly decried.'[23] Whether he was telling the truth is open to question, but given their reputations it was a wise political move for Locke to distance himself from them.

John Locke

Where Hobbes and Spinoza both equate human nature with rapaciousness which is only constrained by fear and force, Locke sees human nature as civil, reasonable, tolerant, industrious, and essentially equal in its distribution of talents and opportunities. The symmetry that Hobbes establishes between scarcity and brutality is counteracted in Locke by a symmetry between nature as bountiful and people as cooperative in their distribution of those bounties. Seen from this perspective, what Hobbes had done was to take a pressing moment — the struggle for survival in the face of scarcity — and transformed that into the general human condition where strong rulership is lacking. With Locke, on the other hand, as long as one is not struggling to survive, there is a natural tendency to realise the advantage that comes from mutual respect of the rights of all to preserve their life, liberty, health, limbs and goods. It is this natural benefit that flows from the recognition of the advantage of respecting in others what one wants for oneself that forms the essential difference between the Hobbesian and Lockean concepts of rights. Thus whereas Hobbes had created a cavern between natural rights (whatever one could lay one's hands on) and natural law (the golden rule), Locke already imputes a normative dimension to the concept of right — that it is a rational constraint. Hobbes brings reason into the equation only once a counter force of equal power is introduced. In this respect, Locke is much more in tune with the traditional pre-mechanistic and pre-determinist thinking on natural right, though the elevated status he ascribes to property and the vision he has of commercial society is as alien to the classical and Medieval natural right tradition as Hobbes' singling out of self-preservation as the ground of natural law.[24]

Nevertheless, Locke does preserve a distinction between natural right and natural law, the latter of which is distinguished by its enforceability. But the legitimacy of that power derives from the right that everyone has to preserve their basic rights. No one has the right to invade the rights of others and 'every one has the right to punish the transgressors of that Law [of nature] to such a Degree, as may hinder its Violation.'[25] We have, then, the reverse of the Hobbesian and Spinozian understanding of natural power: force rests upon reasonableness. Even when a wrong occurs in the state of nature, the right one has to punish the wrongdoers is not absolute or arbitrary but restricted 'by calm reason and conscience.'[26]

If Hobbes writes in the anticipation and then the actuality of the civil war, Locke writes in the context of the English Bill of Rights, passed in the year that Locke submitted his *Two Treatises of Government*. His Preface states that he hopes his work is sufficient to 'establish the Throne of our Great Restorer, Our present King William; to make good his Title, in the Consent of the People, which being the only one of all lawful Governments, he has more fully and clearly than any Prince in Christendom: and to justifie to the World, the People of England, whose love of their Just and Natural Rights with their Resolution to preserve them, saved the nation when it was on the very brink of Slavery and Ruin.'[27]

Given that England had been so close to the brink, it may seem odd that Locke should assume that peace is the norm of politics and thus imply that the civil war had been but a violent irruption in an order which has now been restored. But the key to Locke's position lies in the very title of William, he is a Great Restorer. The rights he concedes are the rights that go back to the *Magna Carta*, the rights that are (to use Burke's phrase) 'time out of mind'. It is a peculiar phenomenon of English history that the parliamentary revolution was advanced as the restoration of ancient rights.[28] In this respect, Locke's state of nature with its original natural rights and fundamental human civility succeeded in crowning the parliamentary revolution by cementing the fiction that natural rights did indeed precede the formation of the state. And he does so by transforming 'the issues of a predominantly historical, highly parochial political controversy of this sort into a general political theory.'[29] There was a double consequence of this brilliant strategy of adopting a virtual silence on the particular historical controversy while providing a general theory which was derived from his experience. (Anyone familiar with Locke's theory of knowledge should know that whatever truth the *Two Treatises of Government* contained would only be because they were empirical and not merely logical relations.[30])

On the one hand, its ahistoricism meant that it could be appealed to anywhere at anytime, and it could thus later be transposed with great success as a defence for founding new institutions in America. On the other hand, and this has always been a seduction of the liberal conscience, the disciple of Locke can argue as if the institutional balances which were the product of over four hundred years of intense and often bloody struggles can simply be imposed on terrains that have no organic dispositions toward liberal democracy. Such a transposition stands in the gravest danger of creating more bloodshed in the long run than a more dictatorial order which will enforce conditions for long term commercial stability and prosperity. Locke's story of the state of nature and the institutions he described to best protect the rights of civil society were peculiarly English. And as enviable as they might have seemed to others, without an ethos which was already steeped in rights of 'life, health, liberty and possessions', or possibly a traumatic event which engraves such an ethos into a people, the configurations of state power which Locke legitimises would be as unsuitable for long term human dwelling as the cardboard buildings of a film set.

But Locke does not present the state of nature as if it were built upon the English experience, rather it is the experience of reason itself: that where respect for liberty prevails so will prosperity. Further, he argues that his conclusions are drawn from the everyday experience of the international community: 'all *Princes* and Rulers of Independent Governments all through the World, are in a State of Nature.' And

> other Promises and Compacts, Men make one with another, and yet still be in the State of Nature. The Promises and Bargains for Truck, &c. between the two Men in the Desert Island, mentioned by *Garcilasso de la vega*, in his History of *Peru*, or between a *Swiss*, and an *Indian*, in the woods of *America*, are binding to them, though they are perfectly in a State of Nature, in reference to one another. For Truth and keeping of Faith belongs to Men, as Men, and Not as members of Society.[31]

When viewed from the darker corners of a Machiavelli or Hobbes or Spinoza this sounds extremely naive. From their perspective, it may appear as if Locke takes what is a consequence of forces in equilibrium as a foundation for the state. But Locke makes it clear that the right to self preservation is not renounced. In the state of nature every person commences with a right to use force against a transgressor of the natural order. He concedes that the preservation of executive power by each member of the state of nature raises problems where people do not live in good faith, and where their passions get out of control. Likewise, there is a danger of impartiality to oneself. Thus a transfer is justified, but only insofar as the civil government preserves the essential rights which were possessed in the state of nature and only insofar as the civil government is reasonable in its deployment of the executive power. It cannot mean, for Locke, that the reason which men share to their mutual benefit becomes monopolised politically by a singular power, who invariably will seek to expand his interest by misusing the powers at his disposal. Hobbes had given total power to the sovereign because he did not see that the mutual benefits that flow from good faith, property, industry, and the protection of natural rights will produce a much greater surplus than mere force. Hobbes knows that the greatest goods can only be held if order is imposed, but Locke holds that the benefits of that order are sufficiently transparent and that there is no need to hand over absolute power to one who may destroy the very fruits of civilization which Hobbes argued were unattainable without strong government.

For Locke the danger to the peace is not the licentious and grasping natures of men pursuing their own interests, but the rapacious behaviour of the monarch and his contempt for natural rights had forced men to move from the calm state of nature to the state of war to protect their property and their rights. The lesson of the civil war was not, for Locke, the one Hobbes or Locke's adversary in the *First Treatise*, Robert Filmer drew, viz. the need to defend the absolute power of the monarchical sovereign. Rather, the lesson was that the monarchy lost, and it had to devolve its stolen powers if the institution were to continue. The power of the reasonable wrath of free men in the state of war was superior to the power of the thieves Charles I and James II. Thus from Locke's perspective there was nothing fanciful about his distinction between the state of nature and the state of war, nor was there anything fanciful in recognizing that people who have rights will resort to force to be free from the slavery and tyranny of absolute power.

The attempts to squeeze excess revenue out of a people and to ignore the parliament and the will of the people in the process, is from a Lockean perspective a recipe for keeping the nation poor; for it drains the faith and good will that is necessary to generate commercial prosperity. That is another reason why, from this perspective, the legitimation of absolute legislative and executive power is bad for the commonwealth. More bluntly, Locke, the economist, cannot abide the Hobbesian insistence upon the primacy of politics.

The point raised in the previous chapter was that Hobbes takes a social conflict which emerges from two sovereign claimants in conflict as disclosing the essence of nature. From Locke's position this was a pernicious misinterpretation of the truth. In the political conflict the natural civility of human intercourse is exploded and replaced by 'enmity, malice, violence and mutual destruction'.[32] Further, as we have said, for Locke the cause of the conflict is due to the violation of the very liberties which Locke sees as natural and widely held. The people who fought against the thieving monarchs had only acted to protect what was reasonably and rightfully theirs. Further, it was through their natural respect for the rights and reasons of each other that the wealth which the monarch sought to extract through taxes was able to be created. A king does not generate prosperity; industry, cooperativeness and exchange do that. And, again, Locke argues that the nature of production and the way its bounties should be distributed is plain to anyone who sets their mind to it.

The exercise of freedom and reason and their industrious deployment is thus, for Locke, the natural disposition of man. The role of government is not to change this disposition, but merely to assist its facility and development by providing for a neutral judge when disputation occurs. Government is based on the reasonable recognition that people cannot be expected to be impartial when they are parties to a dispute. This very fact that disputation is the reason for the transition from a state of nature to political or civil society (Locke uses these terms interchangeably) suggest that the state of nature is not so harmonious a place as it may first appear. But, nevertheless, while Locke concedes that everyone must obey the legislator, the legislature's authority simply extends to protecting the freedom and the reason that people already had prior to the legislature's existence. Or to put it slightly differently, the transition to political society is an evolutionary one based on increasing factors of social complexity, including money, private property, and the free exchange of labour and wealth. Because of that increasing complexity, there is an increasing likelihood of private passions and interests disturbing the fairness of reason. There is also greater opportunity for criminals. The state, then, evolves to solve problems brought about through increasing sociality and mutual reliance. Its purpose is only served if it facilitates the benefits that stem from sociality and the free exchange of labour and wealth. The government is in its inception, its end, and its perpetuity a creation of the people whose interests it is there to serve.

While Locke grounds the entire theory of government upon reason, and thus he may be considered an idealist, there is nothing particularly ideal in the end of government. As Locke frankly puts it 'Government has no other end but the preservation of Property'[33], by which he means 'Lives, Liberties and Estates.'[34] Locke does not seek to subject private property to a radical critique because he sees that the greatest prosperity ever achieved in history had occurred with its existence. But at the same time he sees that private property is a corollary of social evolution. In addition, Locke does not in any way seek to make philosophers kings. The government must represent what the majority of the people desire. Though, in the first instance Locke assumes that what binds the majority is the protection of their own liberty. In the *Two Treatises of Government* Locke does not agonise over the question that Aristotle posed, whether the majority will seek to rob from the rich. There is no suggestion that the majority is meant to include any but landed property holders. There is ambiguity to the extent that property in Locke can mean wealth and even capacity as well as land. But Locke does not go into any detail about who is to have the franchise. It is reasonable to assume that Locke, like so many liberal theorists even into the nineteenth century, did not automatically equate political and civic rights. Likewise, given that the general thrust of the *Two Treatises of Government* is so congruent to the English parliamentary model and the tenor of the 'Bill of Rights', it is also reasonable to assume that Locke believes that the criteria for representation in the parliament is, to a large extent, already sufficiently refined. On the other hand, the justification of 'political and civil society', for Locke, rests upon the consent of 'All Men', 'Mankind' and 'the People.' He also points out the need to have 'fair and *equal*' representation and to make sure that electorates are not numerically distorted.[35]

The most probable reason, then, why Locke does not trouble himself with the dangers of a democracy allowing the poor to take the property of the rich is that he sees no reason to believe that the poor will acquire political power. Yet the very definition of property he gives, combined with the points just made indicate that Locke could easily be invoked by those wanting to expand the franchise. By so thoroughly grounding the theory of government on the right of private property, Locke may have hoped that whoever constitutes the governing body would be aware of the sacrosanct nature of this right. His political solution to the preservation of the right of property is that there can be no taxation without the support of the majority and the government has no right to deprive people of their property. Indeed, if it attempts to do so, then the people have a right to rebel. For whenever the government tries to deprive the people of its natural rights, the people have the right to rebel. As dangerous an option as this may seem, Locke thinks that regular elections will rid people of the need for the feeling of rebellion. By and large, though, the problem of property deprivation is filtered through the conflict of the English civil war and the danger of the abuse of prerogative power by the monarch in his usurpation of property. Thus the problem of the struggle between rich and poor is not addressed. In retrospect, it is tempting to say that Locke had so much faith in the virtue of industry and the institution of private property that he thought it would become evident even to the poor that the way to material advancement was not through deprivation of the wealth of the rich. Economic progress could be achieved through saving, industriousness, and risk-taking, and by deploying one's property, one's talents and labouring capacity to generate wealth.

Locke's theory of government does not solve all the problems of a democracy. But it does clearly set forth the doctrine of government as essentially a representative body of the people's rights and interests. The potency of Locke's theory of government largely arises from the generality of its principles. The benchmark for Locke is 'calm reason', and as we have seen, the *Two Treatises of Government* is meant to be a reasonable exposition of the base, purpose and scope of reasonable government. Locke knows that in exceptional circumstances such as war the usual conventions linking the public, legislature and executive are disrupted so there is no need to conflate the moment of absolute decision in a time of crisis with the regular conduct of government when social intercourse generally proceeds with respect for natural rights. When that is not the case then force and 'the will of heaven' are the judge. But Locke's general principles for the proper basis, conduct and limits of government is singularly striking in its omission of regard for the historical circumstances in which both a people and a government finds itself.

For Locke, it is as if the circumstances of the Great Restoration are the typical circumstances in which all peoples of the world find themselves, and as if all governments could readily slip into their natural role. This way of thinking is still the major bane of all natural rights based theories of government.

Notes

1. For discussions of patterns of the political formations of the earliest civilizations see Charles Redman, *The Rise of Civilization: From Early Farmers to Urban Society*, San Francisco, Freeman, 1978; H. W. F. Saggs, *Civilization Before Greece and Rome*, New Haven, Yale University Press, 1989; Elmore Service, *Origins of the State and Civilization: The Processs of Cultural Evolution*, New York, Norton, 1975.
2. Gerda Lerner,*The Creation of Patriarchy*, New York, Oxford University Press, 1986.
3. *Thucydides History of the Peloponnesian War*, trans. Rex Warner, rev. ed. Harmondsworth, Penguin, 1972.
4. *Ibid.* See Book 3, chapter 1,'Revolt of the Mytilene.'
5. Leo Strauss 'Marsilius of Padua', Leo Strauss and Joseph Cropsey eds., *History of Political Philosophy*, Chicago, Rand McNally, 1969.
6. Discourse One of *Defensor Pacis*.
7. Another Medieval legitimation of popular sovereignty was devised by Nicolas of Cusa in the *Catholic Concordance*. For a more extensive discussion of Medieval treatments of popular sovereignty see Otto Gierke, *Political Theories of the Middle Ages*, trans. Friedrich Maitland, Boston, Beacon, 1958.
8. For a more detailed discussion of Spinoza's politics see Robert McShea, *The Political Philosophy of Spinoza*, New York, Columbia University Press, 1968.

9. 'A Political Treatise' in *The Chief Works of Benedict de Spinoza Vol. 1*, trans.R. H. M. Elwes, London, George Bell and Sons, 1891, page 369.
10. *A Theologico-Political Treatise, ibid.*, page 201.
11. *Ibid.*, page 202.
12. See Spinoza's *The Principles of Descartes' Philosophy*, trans. Halbert Britan, Illinois, Open Court, 1905.
13. Spinoza, *The Ethics*, part II, Prop. XLIX, and part 5, Preface, in *Works of Spinoza*, Vol 2, trans. R. H. M. Elwes, New York, Dover, 1955.
14. *A Theologico-Political Treatise*, page 205.
15. *Theological-Political Treatise*, page 258.
16. *A Political Treatise, ibid.*, page 387.
17. *Ibid.*, page 259.
18. *Ibid.*, page 261.
19. *Ibid.*, page 261.
20. *Ibid.*, page 262.
21. For a useful survey of what Hobbes's contemporaries thought of him see John Bowle, *Hobbes and his Critics: a study in seventeenth century constitutionalism*, London, F. Cass, 1951.
22. *Ibid.*, page 264.
23. See Peter Laslett's 'Introduction' to his edition of John Locke, *Two Treatises of Government*, Cambridge, Cambridge University Press, 1963, page 73.
24. A point well made in Leo Strauss's *Natural Right and History*, Chicago, University of Chicago Press, 1953.
25. John Locke, *Two Treatises of Government*, page 312.
26. *Ibid.*, page 312.
27. *Ibid.*, page 171.
28. Eugen Rosenstock-Huessy, *Die europäischen Revolutionen und der Charakter der Nationen*, Moers, Brendow, 1987, ch. XIV and XV and *Out of Revolution*, ch. VI.
29. Laslett's 'Introduction' *ibid.*, page 91. For an ambitious attempt at a reconstruction of the circustances forces, and ideas to which Locke is responding see Richard Ashcraft, *Revolutionary Politics and Locke's Two Treatises of Government*, Princeton, Princeton

University Press, 1986. Also see John Dunn, *The Political Thought of John Locke: An Historical Account of the Argument of the Two Treatises of Government*, Cambridge, Cambridge University Press, 1969.
30. *An Essay Concerning Human Understanding*, Oxford, Clarendon Press, 1975.
31. *Two Treatises*, page 318.
32. See *ibid.*, page 321.
33. *Ibid.*, page 373.
34. *Ibid.*, page 395.
35. *Ibid.*, pages 419-20.

8 Separating Powers or Willing Unity?: Montesquieu vs. Rousseau and Paine

> Now the serpent was more subtle than any beast of the field
>
> *Genesis*, 3, 1.

The reality of English liberalism had generated two primary kinds of reflection about liberty. One continued much further down Locke's track of searching for the general principles of liberties. Those who continued down that idealist track included Rousseau, Paine, Jefferson, and Kant, and even that arch anti-rights theorist, Jeremy Bentham, whose utilitarianism is just a variant on *a priori* social engineering. The other response, although broadly in agreement with the Lockean view of representative government, took its lead from Montesquieu, and it included Burke, Hume, the American Federalists (particularly, Alexander Hamilton), Benjamin Constant and Hegel. From the perspective of the first group, the latter can be accused of allowing reality to temper their allegiance to right, and thus of being guilty of acquiescing with existing injustices. But from the perspective of the latter group, the former group make the mistake of thinking that society consists of parts that can be moved around at will. They give an exaggerated importance to the political will in the role of human affairs which is fraught with consequence: what begins with a will to freedom may become the need to tyrannise over those who do not conform. Concomitantly, the former group ultimately want to eliminate individual or partial interests; the latter group tend to see that personal interest and partiality is an inescapable component of the human condition, and that any attempt to brush this aside by trying to place too much emphasis upon legal directives of the social will lead to a great spillage of blood.

Baron de Montesquieu

The first great theorist of the modern state who raised the relevance of the question of the social character and degree of social evolution for exploring how government expresses the interests of its people is Charles Secondat, Baron de Montesquieu (1689-1755). His profound importance as a state theorist also rests upon his inquiry into the connection between the commercial base of a society and its institutions of government and the doctrine of the separation of powers.

The methodological starting point of Montesquieu's *The Spirit of the Laws* (1748) is that what constitutes good governance will very much depend upon the 'humour and disposition of the people in whose favour it is established.'[1] While Locke had relied upon natural reason to safeguard natural rights and delimit the nature of government, in Montesquieu, reason is always to be filtered through the complex layers which constitute a particular nation. Thus while Montesquieu follows Locke in seeing the conjunction between law and reason - 'Law in general is human reason, inasmuch as it governs all the inhabitants of the earth' - his inquiry will differentiate 'civil and political laws' to the extent that:

> They should be in relation to the nature and principle of each government: whether they form it, as may be said of politic laws; or whether they support it, as in the case of civil institutions.
> They should be in relation to the climate of each country, to the quality of its soil, to its situation and extent. To the principal

occupation of the natives, whether husbandmen, huntsmen, or sheperds: they should have relation to the degree of liberty which the constitution will bear; to the religion of the inhabitants, to their inclinations, riches, numbers, commerce, manners, and customs.[2]

That insight alone rightly makes Montesquieu, as Durkheim recognised, the founder of political sociology (the other contender for that title is Vico).[3] But before Montesquieu delves into the geographical, historical, and sociological dimensions of the different 'spirits' of the nations and laws he examines, he dissects the different forms of government and the principal spirits which differentiate the monarchy from the republic from the aristocratic and from the despotic. In depicting the respective virtues of each governmental form, Montesquieu provides his readers with the opportunity of seeing what benefits the people receive from different forms of government and what each form of rulership has to contribute to the human spirit as a whole.

That Montequieu's seemingly neutral observations about the different spirits and different laws has a specific political purpose behind it can be gleaned from the opening gambit of *The Spirit of the Laws* where Montesquieu urges caution, appealing to the general public to appreciate the complexity of what makes for the reality of the nation and its government, by encouraging 'every man to love his prince; his country, his laws,' while simultaneously trying 'to persuade those who command to increase their knowledge in what they ought to prescribe.'[4] Aware of the perterbating energies of the rising commercial class he indicates that reform will be best achieved if it is gradual and in conformity with the general character and habits of France. The lesson of the English revolution was that 'when the country had undergone the most violent shocks, they were obliged to have recourse to the very government which they had so wantonly proscribed.'[5]

Thus, any attempt at too radical a leap from the human imagination to political and social reality will not succeed, and much energy will be squandered to no avail. Unlike Rousseau whose high esteem of the virtues of the ancients was in inverse proportion to his contempt for the real world of modernity, Montesquieu, although a keen student of the ancients, in no way indicates that there should be an attempt to return to ancient virtues. There is one and only one model society which provides Montestquieu with the benchmark of what he most esteems: the most politically civilised country of the period, England. Indeed, one may say that through all the zigzagging of *The Spirit of the Laws*, its core teaching is that France should follow England's lead. For it is England which is the most prosperous, most free, most tolerant nation on earth, and it is England which has the most advanced form of government.

One of the extraordinairy achievements of England, which Montesquieu, grasps, is that its political instituitions embody all the major spirits of the respective modes of government. Further, as it turns out when Montesquieu comes to his treatment of commercial society,[6] England was able to take full advantage of a despot who did not just fill his own coffers, but whose ruthlessness promoted the fundamental virtue of industriousness, a virtue without which England would never have been prosperous. More seemingly humane regimes may help foster indolence and real poverty which in the long term may have more devastating effects than the despotic acts which lead to the creation of a prosperous commercial society

> when the nation is poor, private poverty springs from the general calamity, and is, if I may so express myself, the general calamity itself. All the hospitals in the world cannot cure this private poverty; on the contrary, the spirit of indolence, which it constantly inspires, increases the general and consequently the private misery.
>
> Henry VIII, resolving to reform the Church of England, ruined the monks, of themselves a lazy set of people, that encouraged laziness in others, because, as they practised hospitality, an infinite number of idle persons, gentlemen and citizens, spent their lives in running from convent to convent. He demolished even the hospitals, in which the lower people found subsistence, as the gentlemen did theirs in the monasteries. Since these changes, the spirit of trade and industry has been established in England.
> At Rome, the hospitals place everyone at his ease except those who labor, except those who are industrious, except those who have land, except those who are engaged in trade.[7]

Thus Henry's despotism had opened the way for a virtue which had helped create a free and prosperous country and which in turn carried 'prosperity along with it' in all its colonies. By contrast France was still burdened by the fact that its commercial class had far less political power than the unproductive classes of the clergy and the nobles. And ancient and Medieval prejudices against usury were still widespread in Catholic France.

If England had, through the actions of Henry VIII been even able to turn to good use the spirit of despotism, it had also permanently achieved a blend of the monarchical, arsitocratic and republican virtues throughout the evolution of its constitutional system. It had achieved this blending of powers through a long period of struggle, compromise and insitutional devolution. The powers of the monarchy had been checked by the nobles with the *Magna Carta;* and the Glorious Revolution had further checked it and the House of Lords by making the House of Commons the legislative spring of the nation. To this extent, the institutions of England all bore political testimony to the realities of social power.

Thus Montesquieu saw England's institutions combined the republican virtues of equality and consistency in the rule of law with the aristocratic virtue of moderation, and the monarchical virtues of ambition and honour. Because of the power of the House of Commons, however, republican virtues will dominate, but, they will also be filtered through the experience of its success as a commercial and trading power. In France, on the other hand, there was a dangerous lacuna between social and political power, and the distribution of political power only contributed to a worsening of the general prosperity of the nation. Further, the aristocracy in France had done exactly what Montesquieu believed was indicative of a corrupt aristocratic form: it had assumed 'the nature and principle of the monarchy, by exercising prerogative powers and claiming special personal privileges distinct from those of their body.'

Montesquieu's admiration of England's achievements as a power for liberation in its colonies would suggest that he thinks that the English model may work in other parts of the globe provided that the ethos of the people as a whole is effected by the experiences of trade and commerciality. Montesquieu believed that there was a strong correlation between the spirit of liberty and trade. 'The spirit of trade', he said, 'produces in the mind of a man a certain sense of exact justice, opposite, on the one hand, to robbery, and on the other to those moral virtues which forbid our always adhering rigidly to the rules of private interest, and suffer us to neglect this for the advantage of others.' Trade also is said to be a cause of peace. The spread of the commercial ethos is the biggest social force for change. But where a lifestyle can continue without having to become industrious then that ethos is unlikely to be adopted. The corollary of this is that the success of the English political model rests upon the degree of success it has in reproducing the core social characteristics which sustain the political model. It is, for Montesquieu, not merely a matter of applying the political model *a priori*. That would never work.[8]

What Montesquieu esteems is a real entity which has a real history. He sees that what all governments have in common is the performance of a number of fundamental tasks. What he also grasps is that social and political power is something that emerges in response to the various environmental and social circumstances that surround a people. In this respect he is at a similar starting point to figures such as Adam Ferguson and others who are usually credited as being forefathers of historical materialism.[9] It is also understandable why Marxists such as Louis Althusser and Franz Neumann hold him in such affection.[10] If people want liberty, religious tolerance, and prosperity then they should follow the English model. If they do not want these things then they will not follow. English political experience may have created the series of lucky accidents which gave birth to the model, but others may be able to learn from those accidents.

The most important insight that Montesquieu was to pass on to posterity, and one which was absorbed into the American constitution was the insight that all government consists of three constitutive elements - 'the legislative; the executive in respect of things dependent on the laws of nations; and the executive in regard to matters that depend on the civil law'- and that liberty can only be had when the legislative and the executive powers are not united in the same person, or in the same body of magistrates.

Although republicans have generally followed Harrington's formulation that a commonwealth is 'an empire of laws not of men',

Montesquieu had no illusions about the fact that disregard for liberty could occur under any system of government and that republics were not immune from this. Indeed, he singles out the republics of Italy as providing 'less liberty than in our monarchies' because they fused all three branches of power in one body. Montesquieu knew, as did Plato and Aristotle before him, that to place all power in the hands of 'the people' meant in practice to give power to a portion of the population with a partial interest and a partial vision. By dispersing the powers of legislature, executor, and judiciary that vision would still be subjected to something larger than itself, that is the law itself and the historical interests that were sedimented in the customary dimension of law. It is not that Montesquieu was opposed to social change, but for change to be enduring, it had to accommodate the complex of realities that made up the nation. And one part of the nation could not lay claim to embodying that entire complexity.

For Montesquieu, the value of having a legislator elected by the people meant that there was a dynamic component to the law, enabling the eventual elimination of archaic and oppressive laws through the process of parliamentary debate. That debate, though, could not be conducted by the whole body of the people. And thus while 'the legislative power should reside in the whole body of the people', Montesquieu sees that the sheer scale of public participation will require the election of representatives.

But, for Montesquieu, once there is a representative he cannot be beholden to his electorate on each specific issue on which he must make decision. It is inevitable that each group will want its interests represented. But that is why, for him, the legislature must not be entirely governed by the representatives of the common people. The social and economic strength of the aristocracy must have political expression. For it would be ridiculous to think that if the common people wanted to sap their power, they would simply acquiesce without a fight. Thus he says that 'the share they have, therefore, in the legislature ought to be proportioned to their other advantages in the state.' In this respect, Montesquieu well knew that if common liberty was to be blended with peace and prosperity, political compromise was essential.

For Montesquieu, the executive power should be in the hand of the monarch because 'this branch of government, having need of dispatch, is better administered by one than by many.' The English retention of the monarch, for Montesquieu, is thus seen as the logical solution to the problem of a legislature which were it to have executive powers would be unlimited. The separation of the executive from the legislative power, then, enables, the monarch to keep the legislature in check. It is the executive power that must deal with the exigencies of the day, with the urgencies and immediacies of war and threats to order. The executive power is inherently limited by the fact that it does not introduce legislation. Nor does it have the right to enter into public debate, nor to raise money. For Montesquieu, the crown and the nobility, through the legislative power exercised in the upper house, have a power of veto over the laws issued by the majority of representatives of the people.

The whole theory of liberty defended by Montesquieu in his doctrine of the separation of powers is based upon the insight that the national interest can only be preserved by allowing those strong social and economic interests which already exist to have political power, and that the deprivation or prohibition of political power to a strong interest will be calamitous for the common good. Thus Montesquieu perceived that the English House of Commons had to accept limitations upon its power, just as did the House of Lords and the monarch and the ministers to the crown. On the other hand, the implication for France that flowed from this doctrine was that it had not come to grips with accepting that there is a grave risk of denying political power to a strong social and economic power. In this respect, *The Spirit of the Laws* is full of foreboding. For those who were more intent upon rectifying that situation, who saw the beneficiaries of the *ancien régime* as mere parasites whose excision from the body politic would be nothing but a bonus, Montesquieu seemed to be merely an apologist for tyranny. For thinkers such as Hélvetius, Voltaire and Rousseau, the Montesquiean problem of the balancing of interests seemed a vast waste of time. What mattered was putting an end to an unjust oppressive social and political order. But their singleness of focus and their self-assuredness about their own high moral ground helped foster a climate where there was little choice but to exterminate the enemy.

Montesquieu's theory of a mixed constitution evolved because he thought deeply about the links between the social and the political, and about the benefits that would flow from necessary compromises. It was not that he loved liberty any less than a Rousseau or Voltaire, but that he preferred a drop of real liberty to an ocean of wild imaginings.

The Idealist Democracy of Rousseau and Paine

Earlier we discussed the historical and philosophical roots of idealism, and here we see that there is an intrinsic political idealist wing to liberalism. We are not disputing that liberal societies would be unimaginable without that wing — without the great idealist legal documents and idealist philosophies which rationalise their underpinning principles. But the real endurance of liberal democratic societies is based upon a continual compromise or watering down of its idealist elements. Without such a compromise the advocates of liberalism would never have survived in a world which is also woven of values generated within ancient institutions such as the family and religion. What we want to emphasise here, though, is that the less willing the compromise with reality, the more pronounced the contiguity between the rhetoric of freedom and the reality of tyranny. Nowhere is this contiguity more conspicuous than in Jean Jacques Rousseau.[11]

On the one hand, as we have indicated earlier Rousseau's contribution to the self-reflexivity of the liberal conscience stems from his locating the source of constitutionality in the general will. The writer of *The Declaration of the Rights and Man and of the Citizen* of 1789 paid tribute to Rousseau by stipulating: 'The law is the expression of the general will. All citizens have the right to concur in prison or through the representatives in its formation. It must be the same for all whether it protects or punishes. All citizens, being equal before it.'

In passing one should say that while the *Declaration* does service to Rousseau by employing his idealist formulation as the cornerstone of the law, it does equal disservice to Montesquieu's doctrine of the separation of powers by decreeing that where the separation of powers is not laid down, there is no constitution at all. This is something that Montesquieu never would have dreamed of saying, for that is tantamount to saying that anything that does not conform to the one spirit of the version of law arrived at in the *Declaration* is not law at all. The absoluteness of the claim reeks of Rousseau, not Montesquieu. That the *Declaration* could so attempt to house the spirits of both Rousseau and Montesquieu was indicative of its intrinsic and extrinsic tensions.[12] The manifestation of that tensionality was the necessity of its violation. The situation that had brought forth the document was the very situation that made for its systemic violation, nowhere more evident than in its practical denial of the rule of law and the separation of powers. The French revolutionaries were driven by circumstance to retain their own power by fusing the very powers they insisted should be separate. In effect, they were simply more consistently Rousseauian than Montesquieuean.

If Rousseau's genius lies in his location of an ideal source of constitutional right in the general will, the cost for this great insight is that the political reality of different interests is avoided. Politics is reduced to morality, worse, to a single moral principle, a principle which enables its adherent to dismiss as illegitimate the entire historical experience of nations. Civilisation, according to Rousseau, was built upon false and pernicious foundations — private property and self-interest. With Rousseau begins the disastrous attempt to use political means to attain a vague, indeed, indefinable form of social freedom which is supposed to be in tune with both our primordial nature as well as our moral conscience. The Rousseauian political agenda is built around exchanging the tangible liberties of partiality for the intangible ones of generality. In place of the private happiness that comes from pursuing one's own interests, one should, for Rousseau, take one's place within the community; in place of the appreciation of the fruits borne of the advancements of science, one should experience self-disgust; in place of the project of increasing commercial society, one should live a life of subsistence; in place of esteeming the achievements of liberty secured at great cost within modernity, one should esteem the ancients; in place of endowing different social interests with political power, one should eliminate social divisions and interests; in place of civilisation, nature; in place of industriousness, carefreeness.

It is not that there is nothing that may be appealing about some of the values which drives Rousseau's vision. On the contrary,

Rousseau's appeal derives from the nostalgic and idyllic sentiments which he expresses so forcefully. But Rousseau turns these sentiments into a mood of great despair. The depth of that despair is expressed perfectly in that most powerful and famous of all his many memorable sentences: 'Man is born free, and everywhere he is in chains.'

Rousseau is both the most political and least political of men. On the one hand, he endorses a kind of politics in which the sovereignty of the people has no restraint bar the principle of generality.

> The clauses of this contract...rightly understood, can be reduced to the following only: the total alienation of each member, with all his rights to the community as a whole. For, in the first place since each gives himself entirely, the condition is equal for all; and since the condition is equal for all, it is in the interest of no one to make it burdensome to the rest....

> And that is justified by the principle that each individual, by giving himself to all, gives himself to no one; and since there is no member over whom you do not acquire the same rights that you give him yourself, you gain the equivalent of all you lose, and greater force to preserve what you have.[13]

Whatever one may think of the value of such a formulation of the general will, what is clear is that it totally politicises community experience. It is as if the purpose of community is political existence itself, a far cry from the Lockean or Hobbesian notion of politics as a necessary means for our own ends.

On the other hand, Jean Jacques is a solitary dreamer, lost in his own sentiment, happiest when alone with nature.[14] The paradox is somewhat resolved, however, when we consider the opening of his *Confessions* with his claim 'I wish to reveal to my fellow beings a man in all the truth of nature, and this man will be myself! myself alone!'[15] Rosenstock-Huessy in *Out of Revolution* beautifully captures the significance of this opening: 'Rousseau had the courage to exhibit himself as the first individual of the new society, the citizen of the future earthly city.'16 Or to say it slightly differently, Rousseau's collectivism is really the expression of his egoism. He wished to create the collective in his image and he holds out the illusion that such a collectivity is possible, a collectivity of egos, each with nothing to lose. In Rousseau we have the modern bohemian who, not content with dropping out of society, wants to take society with him. Even though he does not know where he is going, he is sure that nothing could be worse than where he is right now. In a more modern form again, he wants to drop out of society into a tenured and superannuated academic position funded and defended by the society he so despises which was created by the compromises he cannot permit.

The civilized world is the repository for all the world's guilt; it is badness incarnate. The depth of its depravity can be gauged by the innocence of its 'other': the noble savage, simple in desires and sympathetic by nature, uncorrupted, and harmless. Rousseau oscillates between wanting to be an ancient Lawgiver for the modern world and wanting to be a noble savage. Unable to be either, one of his fates was to be the philosophical law giver for the more savage moments of the French revolution. Another, was to be treated by the intelligentsia as one of the more noble hearts of the eighteenth century searching for liberty and seeking to put an end to civilized savagery. He was, however, only able to retain such a reputation for those who did not know him. To those, like Diderot and Hume, who did, Jean Jacques was a self-obsessed hypocrite. 16

Exactly the same blend of egoism and collectivism is found in the thought of Edmund Burke's great adversary, Thomas Paine. Thus, as if deliberately echoing Rousseau's *Confessions,* Paine exclaims 'I saw an opportunity, in which I thought I could do some good, and I followed exactly what my heart dictated. I neither read books, nor studied other people's opinions. I thought for myself.'17 But, as with Rousseau, what this really means is that Paine saw himself, his own heart and his own reason, as the measure of reality, and what did not conform to those standards was inhuman, unreasonable, and undeserving of existence. What he saw as most undeserving of continued existence was any form of government based upon hereditary titles. Paine divided government into those built on hereditary succession (monarchy and aristocracy thus get equated) and those on election and representation (republics). For Paine, unlike the ancients, representative government is built upon reason, and all men, for Paine, have reason: it is common sense.

Paine's thinking is that where hereditary government is overthrown so will fundamental social differences be overthrown - then man will return to the egalitarian use of his reason which pertains to his character. For Paine, politics is simply a technical matter of applying the people's will. It is extraordinary that in a work built around the reality of revolution, that outside the problem of the conflict between the men of reason and those of hereditary privilege, the problem of factionalism - that is a conflict of interests - is invisible. Although that extraordinaryness dissolves if we take *The Rights of Man* for what it is, not an inquiry into the complexities of government or rights, but a political pamphlet of government based upon ideal moral principles. Like Rousseau, Paine's defence of the age of reason is tantamount to the recreation of the first, and therefore uncorrupted, man and the world. 'The present generation', he says, 'will appear to the future as the Adam of the new world.' In America that way of thinking was not so out of place, at least to the non-enslaved and non-indigenous peoples, for America was a new world; in France, the attempt to rediscover Adam would mean butchering those who had departed too far from the first man.

Paine vehemently rejected the idea of a mixed constituition as a compromise where everyone could pass on the blame and act as a committee. Instead he idealised the unity of a republic. In a republic, he says, 'the parts are not foreign to each other', 'as there are no discordant distinctions there is nothing to corrupt by compromise or confound by contrivance.' 'As there is but one species of man, there can but be one element of human power, and that element is man himself.' The unity of man, of reason, of the common good is, for Paine, unproblematic. In *Common Sense*, Paine had provided the methodological principle which informs his understanding of government: 'I draw my idea of the form of government from a principle in nature that no art can overturn, viz. that the more simple anything is, the less likely it is to be disordered.'[18]

The Rights of Man is prophetic in its making social welfare for the poor a rights based issue, although Montesquieu had also insisted that a government must provide for its poor, provided it did not encourage indolence. Paine was also a man ahead of his times in his objection to the property qualification for the franchise. Like his friend, Thomas Jefferson, Paine's rights based vision of the political was drawn with clear and simple lines and derived from his faith in the power of reason and the willingness of the world to conform to it. To Paine it was incomprehensible that such a faith could be seen as highly dangerous. The greatest refutation of Paine was not any single person, but reality itself. Paine and Jefferson had played a major part in the American revolution. And then Paine had gone on to France to sing the glories of the French revolution. That the trajectory of the French revolution would move not only into Terror, but to an expansionist dictatorship before a restorationist compromise enforced by English bayonets would be met, was something that the rationalist writer of *The Rights of Man* could not have imagined. But it happened. Again, to any careful reader of Montesquieu, that would be no surprise. It was fortunate for America, that the writers of *The Federalist Papers* were closer in their outlook to Montesquieu than to Rousseau.

Notes

1. Charles de Secondant, Baron de Montesquieu, *The Spirit of the Laws*, trans. T. Nugent, New York, Hafner, 1949, Book 1, page 6.
2. *Ibid.*, page 6.
3. Emile Durkheim *Montesquieu and Rousseau*, Ann Arbour Michigan, University of Michigan Press, 1960. Also see Raymond Aron, *Main Currents in Sociological Thought*, Vol. 1, trans. R. Howard and H. Weaver, New York, 1968, pages 13-72.
4. *Ibid.*, page lxviii, Preface.
5. *Ibid.*, Book 1, page 20.
6. David Lowenthal correctly says that Montesquieu is 'the first great political philosopher to consider commerce worthy of expansive empirical treatment within his major work.' David Lowenthal 'Montesquieu' in Leo Strauss and Joseph Cropsey, eds., *History of Political Philosophy*, Chicago, Rand McNall, 1969, page 485.
7. *Ibid*, vol. 2, Book 23, page 26.

8. For Montesquieu's low esteem of idealism see his comments on James's Harrington's republican utopia, *Oceania* [1656], *Ibid,,* vol 1, Book 22, page 162.
9. Adam Ferguson, *An Essay on the History of Civil Society*, [1767] Duncan Forbes, ed., Edinburgh, Edinburgh University Press, 1966.
10. Louis Althusser, *Politics and History*, trans. B. Brewster, London, New Left Books, 1972.
11. J. L. Talmon *The Origins of Totalitarian Democracy*, London, Secker and Warburg, 1955.
12. Norman Hampson, *Will and Circumstance: Montesquieu, Rousseau and the French Revolution*, London, Duckworth, 1983.
13. *Social Contract*, trans. M. Cranston, Baltimore, Penguin, 1968.
14. Jean-Jacques. Rousseau *Reveries of a Solitary Walker.*, trans. C. E. Butterworth, New York, New York University Press, 1979.
15. Rousseau, *Confessions*, trans J. M. Cohen, Harmondsworth, Penguin, 1953.
16. E. Rosenstock-Huessy, *Out of Revolution*, London, Jarrolds, 1938, page 180.
17. Thomas Paine, *Rights of Man*, [1791-2] Harmodsworth, Penguin, 1984.
18. Thomas Paine, *Common Sense*, [1776] I. Kramnick, ed., Harmonsworth, Penguin, 1976.

9 The Extension of Representation

> A beast that wants discourse of reason
>
> *Hamlet*, 1, ii, 150

In Europe the assertion of the rights of man and the sovereignty of the people was inseparable from the fate of those classes who had acquired social and political privileges in a feudal political system and an agrarian economy. Thus any constitutional overhauls in Europe were unthinkable without violent resistance. The teachings of a Rousseau were so dangerous in Europe — as his opponents only too well appreciated — because the implementation of the general will required the elimination of privileges which were not going to be readily surrendered. In the Old World, the material expression of the doctrine of natural rights was the blood dripping from the axe-head or the blade of the guillotine.

In the New World matters were very different. Once the British had defeated France in the Seven Years War (1756-63), the fundamental basis for loyalty among the predominantly English speaking settlers in the Thirteen Colonies — i.e fear of the French — was also destroyed. The 'reason' of the American social-scape bore no resemblance to that of the Old World. Moreover, the hatred that Englishmen held for a rapacious monarch in the seventeenth century was to be replicated by Americans in the eighteenth century. But unlike England, the monarch did not have any 'natural' social allies to rally to his defence as he did in England. Likewise, because there were no archaic classes to contend with, the achievement of independence brought with it an opportunity for a completely new political framework. Two great currents of political thought recommended themselves to the architects of the new constitution: the natural rights tradition which had already been absorbed in the Declaration and the thought which had evolved by reflecting upon experience.

Britain may have belonged to the Old World, but its commercial and military might suggested that its institutions had much to recommend them, provided that the relevant principles of those institutions could be extracted from the very different social interests which fed into them. Because of his own interest in guiding France toward liberty, Montesquieu had already distilled the principles of the British constitution. A careful reader of Montesquieu could quickly gauge that he had taught that it would be possible for a nation to replicate the core characteristics of the diffused sovereign powers, provided the nation in which this were to take place had a healthy cultural soil. It was as if *The Spirit of the Laws* had been written for the Americans.[1]

The extent of Montesquieu's authority in the framing of the new constitution can be measured by the fact that he is invoked by anti-Federalists and Federalists alike. The anti-Federalists contended that Montesquieu had argued that a republic which extended over too large a territory would come unstuck. The Federalists (Alexander Hamilton, James Madison and John Jay) responded by arguing that Montesquieu had seen that the way to overcome this obstacle was to establish a confederation of republics. Hamilton and Madison also cited Montesquieu in their argument that representation should be proportional to the size of the population. Madison also underscored the huge debt that the architects of the new federation owed to Montesquieu when he said that Montesquieu 'has the merit of displaying and recommending' the doctrine of the separation of powers 'most effectually to the attention of mankind.' The other equally important debt that the Federalists owed to Montesquieu was the insight that politics is about the balancing of social forces. That very approach to the problem of politics explains the extremely different character of *The Federalist Papers* from the Jeffersonian *Declaration of Independence*. The latter document is a general statement about rights and their grounding, about the wrongs perpetrated by the British monarch, about the assertion of power, and it concludes with a pledge. It is a brilliant rhetorical performance which speaks to the patriot's love of freedom. Its power lies in the generality of its sentiment and the unswerving faith in man's mind and in man's right and ability to act from righteousness. It is a document celebrating an event where there is no room for scepticism or hesitation. It is a document which is intrinsic to the character and style of American politics. Its aspirations have spilled over into all the free states of the world. But, unlike *The Federalist* it is not a document which is capable of providing direction for the routines of the political or for dealing with the conflicts of interests. Whereas the power of its rhetoric emanates from the reverence it pays to the unifying subject, 'the people', the power of *The Federalist* lies in its rigorous and more truthful analysis of conflict, compromise and cooperation.

Jefferson and The Federalists

The character and concerns of the major architect and dominant personality of *The Federalist Papers*, Alexander Hamilton(1757-1804), could not have been more different from Thomas Jefferson (1743-1826).[2] Jefferson's politics is essentially driven by a republican conception of honour, by a deep faith not only in man but in revolutionary action itself, by a mistrust of commercial society, by a desire to preserve an agrarian economy,[3] and by an essentially populist mistrust of institutions. Despite his belief in the equality of man he nonetheless kept slaves and probably had children by one of them, Sally Hemings. Hamilton's politics, on the other hand, is governed by the desire to create peace and commercial prosperity, to provide a strong industrial base for America and thus to make her a strong military power, to provide institutions which can mediate conflict by providing a balance between local and national interests. He is as practical as Jefferson is romantic, much more mistrustful of human nature, and as afraid of democratic abuses as of monarchical abuses. One of the remarkable achievements of *The Federalist* was that Hamilton could cooperate so closely with Madison whose Southern roots and social vision was to make him Jefferson's ally in the Republican party, as well as Jefferson's successor as president.[4]

An important indicator of the deep differences between the Jeffersonian and Hamiltonian approaches to politics can be gleaned from their different responses to a popular uprising in Massachusetts. Jefferson wrote to John Jay's son-in-law, Colonel William Stephen Smith,

> God forbid we should ever be twenty years without such a rebellion. The people cannot be all, and always, well informed. The part which is wrong will be discontented, in proportion to the importance of the facts they misconceive. If they remain quiet under such misconceptions, it is a lethargy, the forerunner of death to the public liberty.... And what country can preserve its liberties, if its rulers are not warned from time to time, that this people preserve the spirit of resistance? Let them take arms. The remedy is to set them right as to facts, pardon and pacify them. What signify a few lives lost in a century or two? The tree of liberty must be refreshed from time to time, with the blood of patriots and tyranny. It is its natural manure....[5]

Hamilton, on the other hand, points out in the *Federalist* #21 that the rebellion could easily have created a form of despotism. And whereas Jefferson sees virtue in rebelliousness, Hamilton sees 'unceasing agitations and frequent revolutions' as the scourges of petty republics' (#28). But he addresses the problem in pragmatic terms, weaving between when to set example, and when to act with clemency. Given the scale of sedition in Massachusetts, Hamilton indicates (#75) that clemency is politically expedient, but it has nothing to do with any faith in the people spilling their blood. It has to do with the contingencies of the moment, with preserving lawfulness to the extent that that is possible and doing so in a way that will create as little damage as possible. And although *The Federalist Papers* admits the right of rebellion (#28 and #3), Hamilton generally sees 'seditions and insurrections' as 'maladies as inseparable from the body politic as tumours and eruptions from the natural body.' Further, he stresses his departure from 'the reveries of those political doctors' who want to control force by law by stressing that force is the only remedy to deal with insurrection, as he stresses that 'insurrection, whatever may be its immediate cause, eventually endangers all government.' (#28)

For his part, Jefferson would charge Hamilton for his aristocratic desire to exclude the people from holding political power, and for interpreting politics in terms of force and interest. According to Jefferson, Hamilton was not only a monarchist, but in favour of 'a monarchy based on corruption'. He frequently repeated the story that he had attended a dinner where a discussion had arisen about the British constitution. '[John] Adams observed 'purge that constitution of its corruption, and give to its popular branch equality of representation, and it woul d be the most perfect constitution ever devised by the wit of man'. Hamilton paused and said, 'purge it of its corruption, and give to its popular branch equality of representation, and it would become an impracticable government: as it stands at present, with all its supposed defects, it is the most perfect government which has ever existed.'

Two points are pertinent here. First, Jefferson's claim that Hamilton was a monarchist is an interesting indicator of the rhetoric of the day. For the writer of the *Declaration* to brand a man a monarchist was a smart ploy, but it overstated the reality. The one thing that united the founding fathers was the recognition that the problems of the New World could not be solved by the power configurations of the Old World. The hostility toward the British crown spelt out in the *Declaration* was a sentiment shared by the revolutionaries. Further, it had been a commonplace for the revolutionary generation to generally construct monarchical government as given to warlike behaviour and wasting the people's money, and Federalist papers by Jay and Hamilton both expressed this sentiment.[6] But while the Federalists accept the standard critique of the day of the monarchy, Hamilton has no illusions about the innate peacefulness of republics. Hamilton had read too much history to hold such an idealist sentiment. Nor did he believe, as Paine, for example, did, that commerce was intrinsically peaceable.[7] Hamilton's republicanism, then, was not borne out of a belief in high minded ideals, but out of the reality of the American situation. There was no point in being a monarchist, for the monarchy was not relevant to the American situation. But that did not mean that some of the roles fulfilled in Britain by the monarch were not necessary requirements of government in a modern commercial society.

The other criticism expressed above by Jefferson, that Hamilton favoured government based upon force and interests, well captures the underlying methodology behind *The Federalist*. Politics *is* about force and interests, not about saints and sages. Hamilton's view of human beings is far closer to that of Hobbes and Machiavelli than Locke. 'Why', asks Hamilton in *Federalist* #15 'has government been instituted at all?' And he answers, 'Because the passions of men will not conform to the dictates of reason and justice, without constraint.'[8] Hamilton not only does not hold any great faith in the people, he sees the idea of the people as a dangerous demagogic device. Society is composed of different interests and the task of politics is to provide stable institutions so that those interests can co-exist. Nothing is easier than for a particular interest to claim that its interests are those of the people's. But the geographical and sociological reality of America presented the Federalists with a society with a multiplicity of interests, and the interests of classes had to be multiplied by the regional interests.

This situation of competing interests presented a fundamental contradiction which the Federalists deal with. On the one hand, there is a grave danger of factionalism. Factionalism is recognised in *Federalist* #10 by Madison as a vice to which popular governments are particularly prone.[9] The vice stems from the virtue of liberty which provides the rationale for the form of government in the first place. The close connection between factionalism and interests is spelt out beautifully by Madison. While liberty is at the root of faction: 'it could not be less folly to abolish liberty, which is essential to political life, because it nourishes faction, than it would be to wish the annihilation of air, which is essential to animal life, because it imparts to fire its destructive agency.' Madison also saw the diversity of occupations, and the diversity even in social groups of similar circumstances. The Federalists knew that they were charting new political territory. Instead of pursuing the idealists dream of unity - Madison dismisses those 'theoretic politicians who...have erroneously supposed that by reducing mankind to a perfect equality in their political rights, they would, at the same time, be perfectly equalised and assimilated in their possessions, their opinions, and their passions' - their treatment of factionalism rested on the recognition that the faculties of men, from which the rights of property originate, is so vast in America that, with the right style of government, the interests would be relatively diffused. In a society where there were fewer opportunities for occupation and fewer life options, interests groups would be fewer and much more likely to be involved in recurrent conflicts in which the majority would regularly triumph.

The solution, then, did not lay in a political elimination of the diversity that sprang from the dispersal of interests, talents, desires and sentiments, that is 'the faculties of men, but in realising that a large distribution of interests would, in general, counteract the danger of factionalism itself. 'Extend the sphere, and you take in a greater variety of parties and interests; you make it less probable that a majority of the whole will have a common motive to invade the rights of other citizens.' Or, as was said in *Federalist* #51 of the federal republic, break the society 'into so many parts, interests and classes of citizens that the rights of individuals, or of the minority, will be in little danger from interested combinations of the majority.'

The argument about the dispersal of factional interests was also a way of defending the Federalists program of a confederate republic. For a confederate republic would also aid this process of dispersion by adding another geographical layer to the interests that would be formed at either a local or state level. Thus linkages of interests could be formed between social groups which constituted a minority in some states while being a majority in others. Further, alliances of social interests cutting along geographical lines would tend to protect minority groups. At the same time, interests based upon geographical factors might take on greater relevance at one time, while another time, social factors which were operating nationally may dominate. The great value of confederalism, then, was that the polymorphic nature of factionalism would aid the minority.

But while the Federalists argued that the large territory of America combined with 'the multiplicity of interests' and 'the multiplicity of sects' made it highly unlikely that a majority would share a common cause of injustice, Hamilton and Madison neglect to mention that that is only true with respect to those peoples whom are included in the franchise. The lack of franchise would mean that those people without political representation — particularly indigenous Americans and slaves — would be every bit as endangered by a system in which they were just one interest among many, but where they lacked political rights. Thus it would take almost 80 years and a war before the ambition articulated in the Jefferson Virginian Ordinance, that slavery be abolished, would be realised. And the diversity of interests would not help the indigenous American as the railways moved West and the expansion of the frontier meant that Indians were driven off to reservations and treaties became routinely broken.

It is, however, difficult to believe that another constitutional form would have made things any better for black slaves and the indigenous peoples. The indigenous peoples of South America fared no better than those of the North, but then again, those Indians who were ruled over by the Mayans, the Aztecs and the Incas had also fared terribly. Indigenous people were treated with similar scant regard by Russians in Siberia, Australians in Tasmania, Chinese in Tibet and Rwandans in Burundi. No political system can protect the most vulnerable members of a territory where the ethos of humaneness is not deeply woven into the social consciousness. But the lesson of history is that 'humaneness' has tended to be branded in the collective memory by a synthesis of spokespeople from the dominant group and social resistance by the disenfranchised. While it is now a commonplace for tenured radicals wanting to make a career out of other people's suffering to lump together disparate groups who were once politically disenfranchised and who are said to be still socially disadvantaged, at the time of the formation of the Union, white women, blacks and Indians had very few social or political affinities. Political rights still belonged to those classes that had had successful victories in their fight for them.

Nothing is more difficult for the idealist intellectual to accept than the harsh truth that political power is something that has exploded into reality, that it is won in the act of creation, that it did not fall from the sky as a gift divided into equal packages, and that its creation initially involves imposition, force, and cruelty, (a point made by Nietzsche, but ignored by post-modernist Nietzschean moralists.) Respect and recognition are late products of creation. They may be beautiful. We may wish it were otherwise, but civilisation was not built by the wishful thinkers. And the reason for this is not that there was once upon a time where there were all these good people living in perfect harmony who became prey to the evil ones. Every social group acts from the conditions which are thrust upon it, and the more conscious the groups become of the opportunities they have for exercising their power, the greater their aspirations. This is not to say that we may esteem some qualities more than others, but there is nothing admirable in either lack of opportunity, impotence or lack of imagination. We all start with the accident of circumstance and build from there.

Nothing, then, is easier to do or more methodologically unsound than to apply retrospectively the conditions which have evolved through the expansion of the franchise to assess the value of the framers of the American constitution. Without a constitutional and political framework which sought to 'break down' interests and provide representation there probably would not have been an end to slavery in America, without the extension of the franchise to non-property holders women would not have got the vote, and, to repeat, as terrible as the fate of indigenous peoples has been, imperial expansion is the inevitable companion of large scale, militarily strong societies prior to the modern global economic system.

While, then, the Federalists saw that the sociological and geographical conditions of America eroded the danger of factionalism, much of their attention was directed to dealing with the different aspects of government, and ameliorating the dangers that lay lurking in the respective powers of government. The foremost danger lay within the legislature, the spring of the people's will. Not only was the legislature the site where the majority could 'legitimately' suppress or rob the minority, but, as Montesquieu had previously recognised, the legislature would see any restraints upon its power as restrictive, as merely the resistance of vested minority interests. 'There is', says *Federalist* #15, 'in the nature of sovereign power, an impatience of control, that disposes those who are invested with the exercise of it, to look with an evil eye upon all external attempts to restrain or direct its operations. The legislative department is everywhere, extending the sphere of its activity, and drawing all powers into its vortex.' The *Federalist* also saw the danger of this tendency to be 'almost irresistible' in 'governments purely republican.' But just as the government could be oppressive by its use of the legislature, so could untempered brute factionalism. There was also the problem of having to balance the power of the states and the power of the federal government. Hamilton saw the states as tending to be in constant battle with the national government, as each would assert its interests at the expense of the whole. Because of the danger this created for the whole, the Federalists repeatedly emphasised the higher priorities that must guide the national government. But at the same time, the states serve as a useful buffer against the legislature's tendency to overextend.

With their doctrine of the separation of powers, the Federalist provided a reworking of the ancient idea of the mixed constitution. They understood that there is an appropriate time for each modality of government - that each mode brings with it a particular characteristic of power, and that each modality has arisen for a reason, and this is true even when a modality such as dictatorship may frequently be bloody. A strong government is strong because it is constituted by the full range of possible expressions of political power. The moment in which each modality must be exercised cannot be known *a priori*, it is dependent upon the issue of the moment. But there are circumstances when a singular act of executive leadership is required, others when the populace must decide, others when their representatives must legislate, others when the more powerful social interests of the time will rightfully react to the legislature's attempt to extend the interests of the majority, others when the judiciary must intervene to protect an individual's or a group's rights from legislative interference. Because any such problem can occur at any time, the government must carry within it monarchical/dictatorial, aristocratic, and populist tendencies.

This dynamic conception of the state was to be vindicated by the creation of a strong defensive capacity; a strong central government, able to provide commercial and political stability for a vibrant industrial society; and a form of government in which local interests still had strong representation, and in which more people than ever in history had freedom. It was that freedom, as Alexis de Tocqueville saw, which was to provide the energy for this dynamic creature. The creature was still a Leviathan, but a Leviathan whose bestial nature was not so obvious. By being more responsive to the wishes of the citizens, and more restrained by the principle of natural rights, as well as the blending of constitutional safeguards and the checks and balances of the monarchic, aristocratic and democratic forces, the Leviathan of the Federalists had taken on a more humane countenance, at least for an expanding pool of law abiding citizens. To be sure, against its enemies, it was no less terrifying. On the contrary, the fact that the beast was being fed by the energies of free people only meant that its capacities were expanding. But what the beast had acquired through vitality and civility was not necessarily at the expense of it ferocity. Its terrifying energies were now in much greater check, but the very constraining of the energies only made them more focussed when America finally revealed its strength in the twentieth century as the strongest commercial and military power the world had ever seen.

Alexis de Tocqueville (1805-1859)

> American institutions, which for France under the monarchy were simply a subject of curiosity, ought now to be studied by republican France. It is not force alone, but rather good laws, which make a good government...
>
> While all the nations of Europe have been ravaged by war or torn by civil strife, the American people alone in the civilised world have remained pacific. Almost the whole of Europe has been convulsed by revolutions; America has not even suffered from riots. There the republic, so far from disturbing them, has preserved all rights. Private property is better guaranteed than in any land on earth. Anarchy is as unknown as despotism.
>
> Where else can we find greater cause of hope or more valuable lessons? Let us not turn to America in order to slavishly copy the institutions she has fashioned for herself, but in order that we may better understand what suits us; let us look there for instruction rather than models; let us adopt the principles rather than the details of her laws....But the principles on which the constitutions of the American states rest, the principle so for order, balance of powers, true liberty, and sincere and deep respect for law, are indispensable for all republics; they should be common to them of all; and it is safe

to forecast that where they are not found the republic will soon have ceased to exist.[10]

Thus wrote Alexis de Tocqueville after visiting the United States in the early 1830s. Tocqueville had seen the republican future, and it was America. While Montesquieu had looked to Britain to urge the French monarchy to change its way, Tocqueville urges republican France to follow America's lead. Whereas the Federalists had looked to a comparative sociologist who had studied the most advanced constitutional arrangement for the securement of liberty, Tocqueville looks to the New World for the most advanced constitutional arrangement for securing liberty and equality.[11] For what America taught Tocqueville was that the future of civilisation rested upon a necessary combination of democracy, liberty and equality. This triumvirate came at a price, and Tocqueville frequently laments the cost, but he saw that the passions of the modern soul demanded a more equal, a freer and a democratic society. And these demands were being expressed in revolutionary activities throughout Europe. In words that (no doubt, unwittingly) conjure up the spectre of Hegel's vision of history as the tale of the unfolding expression of the spirit of freedom, he writes that 'the effort to halt democracy appears as a fight against God Himself, and nations have no alternative but to acquiesce in the social state imposed by Providence.'

In the same year, Karl Marx was urging that overthrow in *The Communist Manifesto*, 1848, Tocqueville warned fellow representatives of the French Chamber of Deputies that France rested on a volcano and that the working classes would overthrow the 'foundations' upon which society rests unless property were distributed on a more egalitarian basis.[12] But Tocqueville believed that social processes and change eventually resulted in political development and was urging the extension of representation within the liberal state to encompass the enfranchisement of the working, non-propertied classes as was occurring in America. That is the great lesson of America, in the eyes of Tocqueville. In the main, it had successfully combined the individual freedoms with egalitarian social conditions. The two exceptions, for Tocqueville, were African and indigenous Americans. Women, on other hand, says Tocqueville, had a different situation and 'although the American woman never leaves her domestic sphere and is in some respects very dependent within it, nowhere does she enjoy higher station.'[13] With the African and native Americans things are very different. Tocqueville writes of the blacks that, 'in one blow oppression has deprived the descendants of the Africans of almost all the privileges of humanity. The United States Negro has lost even the memory of his homeland; he no longer understands the language his fathers spoke; he has abjured their religion and forgotten their mores.'

While the oppression of blacks stems from slavery, Native Americans live on 'the edge of freedom.' Their life way has been destroyed through the possession of their lands, the dwindling of wild game and their adoption of new tastes such as firearms, iron, brandy, cloth. He describes their condition thus, as they are forced to leave the soil of their birth:

> It is impossible to imagine the terrible afflictions involved in these forced migrations.
>
> The Indians leaving their ancestral fields are already worn down and exhausted. The country in which they intend to live is already occupied by tribes and who regard newcomers jealously. There is famine behind them, war in front, and misery everywhere. In the hope to escape so many enemies, they divide up... each one of them in isolation tries furtively to find some means of subsistence, living in the immensity of the forest like some outlaw in civilised society. The long-weakened social bond then finally breaks. Their homeland has already been lost, and soon they will have no people; families hardly remain together; the common name is lost; the language forgotten, and traces of their origin vanish.[14]

The progress that has developed in America in combining liberty and equality has, then, come at a terrible price for blacks and native Americans. Tocqueville's portraits of African and Native Americans are drawn with great compassion and sensitivity. He does not try to justify the fates of these people by an appeal to an evolutionary scale of races - he was horrified by his friend's, Gobineau's, theories on race, which he could see would have devastating consequences.[15] Nor does he just gloss over their fate. He dwells at length on the cruel legalities and philanthropic approach to extermination, pointing out how much more pernicious was this kind of treatment of Indians in North America than what the Spaniards had done. The latter were savage and merciless in their initial treatment of the Indians but 'they did not succeed in exterminating the Indian race and could not even prevent them from sharing their rights.'

Tocqueville sees that what is good and progressive is not good and progressive in all respects, that America has opened up a future for the world, but it has done so by robbing the Indians of their lands. While his description of native Americans is full of admiration, he sees that there were only two choices for the Indians when the Europeans arrived: to be victorious in battle or to enter into the civilisation. For the former possibility, they were not only not sufficiently unified in their opposition to the conqueror, but they lacked the technology. On the other hand, the difference between 'civilisation' and hunting peoples is that the condition of the former is a settled, agrarian life style. For Tocqueville, it was a great pity that the more well meaning whites who sought to bring enlightenment did not realise that 'the first problem was to turn the Indians into cultivators.' But had they tried, he asks, why should the Native Americans want to exchange the 'idle' and 'adventurous life of hunting' for 'the constant and regular demand of labour'? Tocqueville points out that the natives of North America consider 'labour not only an evil, but also a disgrace.' The native American 'thinks hunting and war the only cares worthy of a man.'[16]

As terrible as the fate of the native Americans is, and it would get even worse, Tocqueville, while acknowledging this, saw something inevitable about the clash of cultures. Had the Indians been conquered by a people less sophisticated in its technologies and social organisation, they would have had a much better chance, for, says Tocqueville, when barbarians conquer civilised peoples they eventually change the tastes and habits and institutions of their conquerors. But this will not happen when the conquerors have more complex social arrangements and institutions. Tocqueville's bleak picture of the fate of the native American peoples carries with it something of the air of inevitability. Conquest may be morally reprehensible, but hunting peoples and settlers rarely co-exist, and to the settlers, the vast regions within which the Indians hunted looked infinitely more than was necessary for their needs. The experience of the Indians powerfully depicts the dilemma of liberty which Tocqueville saw with such clarity: that liberty can easily be tyrannical, as can the condition of social equality. The fate of the American Indians, for Tocqueville, was so bad because the very conditions of the New World were such that they would smash to bits the way of existence and the more 'aristocratic' virtues and aspirations of the original inhabitants.

As Tocqueville sees it, the inequality between blacks and whites is not only as devastating in its effects as the inequalities of Indians and whites, but it threatens to tear apart the very fabric of American society. The principles of liberty and equality are both violated in the institution of slavery, as is the religious basis of American society. Further, he points out that slavery was an economic liability, as could be proven by comparing the living standards in the agrarian South with the industrialised North. For Tocqueville that should hardly be surprising, for the difference between the progressive prosperity of modernity and the stagnant societies of the ancients rests on the respective virtues which are fostered in a society where idleness rests upon the work of others whose intelligence, dexterity, and ability are not rewarded, and in a society in which the same abilities can be turned to profit. He further points out that slavery is far from being provided free and that the slaves' upkeep must be paid. But because the 'master spends his money little by little in small sums to support his slave' he does not notice that he has paid more for a less economically productive worker than the capitalist.

Slave owning societies are less dynamic, less industrious, less prosperous, less capable of harnessing the abilities of the species to the general prosperity so that even the direct beneficiaries of slave labour can never achieve the same levels of prosperity as the entrepreneurial purchaser of free labour. In spite of this, Tocqueville sees that there are a number of factors which contribute to the continued existence of slavery in the South. These included the fact that the crops grown in the South, 'tobacco, cotton, and especially sugar cane, need continual attention.' Slave labour is more suited to such crops than those which can be largely left alone. If slavery were abolished, comments Tocqueville, either the South would have to change their system of cultivation 'and would find themselves in competition with the more active and experienced northerners', or 'they must grow the crops without slaves in competition with other southern states still keeping their.' Also, whites are less inclined to want to work in the tropics. In addition to the economic loop which locks the South into the system of slavery, Tocqueville believes that because of the relatively large numbers of blacks in the South their emancipation could easily lead to a backlash, as there would be a relatively large section of the population free but lacking in material advantages.

The social inequalities brought on by slavery have, he observes, proven to be a curse - all options for the South point to trouble. He conjectures that a way out of the impending danger would be for the races to mingle, but he does not see that as a possibility. Racial prejudice in the North is equally as prevalent — the legal freedoms which blacks receive in the North do not translate into the respect and opportunities that are required for people to enjoy genuine social liberty. The only other option for the South is to hang onto slavery. Any intermediate position warns Tocqueville, 'is likely to terminate...in the most horrible of civil wars, and perhaps in the extermination of one or other of the two races.'[17]

Tocqueville was prophetic in seeing that the changing social conditions of North and South could also bring about a rift in the Union. While he argued that all parties to the Union benefited, he saw that the shifting demographic patterns favouring the North, through the increasing Western expansion, meant that the centre of federal power due to changes in political representation was also shifting to the North. The South's response to this state of affairs could very well be to 'turn its melancholy gaze inward and back to the past, perpetually fancying that it may be of the prophets. Noticing that a law of the Union is not obviously favourable to itself, it cries out against this abuse of power, and when no one listens to its ardent remonstrances, it grows indignant and threatens to leave an association whose burdens it bears without share.'

In spite of these insurmountable problems, Tocqueville believes that America is still the most egalitarian and democratic civilised society on earth. This is not based on any starry-eyed love of an ideal,

Tocqueville's temperament is too practical for that. Rather, as with Montesquieu, his assessment is based on a comparative understanding of other European social and institutional arrangements.[18]

In the main, what America has managed to get right is a blend of the pursuit of private interests and public freedom. This blend does not mean that everything about the American political institutions is perfect, but what matters for Tocqueville is the overall liberty and well being for most of the inhabitants that is based upon the core principle running through American society, that each person is the best judge of his interests. In government, administration and in private life, this way of looking at things is seen as inculcating a dynamic, responsible, daring, and energetic spirit. Technically, it may not always produce the best results. Thus, for example, Tocqueville praises the decentralisation, dynamism and public participation in municipal administration, while conceding that 'it is no good looking in the United States for uniformity and permanence of outlook, minute care of details, or perfection of administrative procedures.' Yet he adds immediately 'what one does find is a picture of power, somewhat wild perhaps, but robust, and a life liable to mishaps but full of striving and animation.'[19]

Tocqueville grasps that the ethos of the New World is one which factors in danger and willingness to learn from mistakes. Dynamism and paternalism are socially exclusive qualities, if one wants the former qualities then one must be free to be mistaken about one's real interests. Paternalism 'monopolises all activity and life to such an extent that all around it must languish when it languishes, sleep when it sleeps, perish when it dies?'[20] All the anti-paternalistic philosophies of science and religion are carried over into the New World. For Tocqueville the Americans are (without having read Descartes) instinctive Cartesians, as well as disciples of Luther, Bacon, and Voltaire. They are pragmatic and self-reliant, because their world demands it, everything is treated as if it has begun anew.

American laws and political institutions work in tandem, according to Tocqueville, with the American character. And there tends to be a generally beneficial convergence. Thus, for example, when Tocqueville, considers the economic conditions contributing to equality in America, he praises the inheritance laws, which commenced with a 1786 statute in New York and which broke with the English law of property succession. That statute decreed that the estate of the deceased was to be divided equally, regardless of gender, by all surviving heirs, unless otherwise stipulated in the testator's will. The result of this division of property, says Tocqueville, is that not only do large family estates not remain in the one family over time, but large properties are divided into ever smaller units. Families themselves become more disconnected over time, as the large property no longer serves as a gravitational force binding common interests. Landed property is thus readily discernible as a saleable commodity, and all members of a family stand to inherit wealth.

Unlike Marx and Rousseau, Tocqueville does not see inequality, as such, as a problem. It is only a problem if it is stagnant, if it continually rewards the idle rather than the industrious, and if it blocks the energies of the population — in America the rapid circulation of wealth is bound up with enterprise and creativity in a manner that has never previously been experienced. Tocqueville's approach to inequality is, then, pragmatic: it brings with it certain characteristics, but there is nothing valuable about it as such. Being pragmatic, he is able to scrutinise the advantages and disadvantages of American democracy with detachment.

At the time of writing *Democracy in America*, in the states of Missouri, Alabama, Illinois, Louisiana, Indiana, Kentucky, and Vermont there was no property qualification for voters while in the other states of the Union, property qualifications varied considerably. In Tennessee, Tocqueville points out that 'any property at all is enough', while 'in the states of Mississippi, Ohio, Georgia, Virginia, Pennsylvania, Delaware, and New York, if you pay taxes you can vote'. In those states, as well as in Connecticut, which required a property 'with a revenue of seventeen dollars', performance of militia duty also gave one the franchise. All states made twenty-one the voting age, and all carried a residential time requirement. But Tocqueville sees that the trend is toward eliminating restrictions upon voting requirements and expanding the franchise.[21]

The fact that democracy is an infectious political form would suggest that there is something intrinsically desirable about it for the majority of people. But that fact does not mean that it is a perfect form of government, or even the most adequate form of government for achieving a range of goods. Tocqueville sees just as much as Nietzsche does after him that the egalitarian ethos of a democratic society carried a levelling tendency, but the levelling effect is seen by Tocqueville as eliminating the worst of the extremities which plague other regimes.[22] For Tocqueville, the most important negative in the trade off between aristocratic and democratic societies consists in the diminution of glorious achievements. Great culture tends to require that a society is placed in service to the ambitions, tastes, and talents of a group who see their deeds as the *raison d'être* of society. But the most significant gain is the energy that gets unleashed through the mass participation in political affairs.

Tocqueville also concedes that democracy will not produce a more noble kind of human being, nor a more spiritual or austere type, nor a more profound type, nor a more refined or cultivated or glorious type. He also believed that a democratic society will probably not have a powerful military influence over other nations, thus seriously underestimating the extent of prosperity that America would achieve and how its commercial strength would also be accompanied by military strength and the power of example and demonstration. Nor, he says, will it leave behind the historical achievements of more aristocratic or despotic regimes, but it will 'provide for every individual therein the utmost well-being, protecting him as far as possible from all afflictions.' And he adds, that there is really no choice in the matter anyway, the democratisation of the civilised world is inevitable.[23]

While Tocqueville sees equality of social conditions as an inevitable and generally advantageous process, he is also aware that democratic societies can devour themselves.[24] In particular, Tocqueville, like the Federalists, feared the danger of the tyranny of the majority. As much as the architects of the constitution had hoped to balance the respective social forces by following the English conception of a mixed government, Tocqueville believed that it was inevitable that the power of the majority would dominate. He did not believe that theories of mixed governments adequately described political realities. In any society, he argued, one finds in the end some principle of action that dominates all the others.'[25] The Montesquiean reading of England as a mixed constitution is rejected by Tocqueville as mistaken. Eighteenth century England, he says, 'was an aristocratic state, although it contained within itself great elements of democracy, for laws and mores were so designed that the aristocracy could always prevail in the long run and manage public affairs as it wished.' According to Tocqueville no matter where one turned to find a force to counter the will of the majority in America, one always found the idea of the majority as its determining principle. 'When a man or a party suffers an injustice in the United States, to whom can he turn? To public opinion? That is what forms the majority. To the legislative body? It represents the majority and obeys it blindly. To the executive power? It is appointed by the majority and serves as its passive instrument. To the police? They are nothing but the majority under arms. A jury? The jury is the majority vested with the right to pronounce judgment; even the judges in certain states are elected by the majority.'[26]

Tocqueville takes care to emphasise that American democracy is not tyrannical, rather what he sees is that there is no inherent political check against the dangers that he sees latent in majority rule. 'Custom', he says, 'is spreading more and more in the United States which will end by making the guarantees of representative democracy vain.'[27] As the power of the majority inevitably increased Tocqueville saw that the innate vices of democratic government would likewise increase.

One such problem was the instability of laws and public administration. Laws would be far more likely to be rapidly introduced, and just as rapidly dropped, as some new idea took the public's attention. A more insidious feature of the power of the majority, according to Tocqueville, is the power over thought. Whereas, says Tocqueville, in monarchies, the monarch is not able to compel moral authority, this is precisely the ground which the majority tries to occupy. In democratic republics, says Tocqueville, tyranny 'leaves the body alone and goes straight for the soul.' 'No monarch', observes Tocqueville, 'is so absolute that he can hold all the forces of society in his hands, and overcome all resistance, as a majority invested with the right to make the laws and to execute them, can do.' And 'I know no country in which, generally speaking, there is less independence of mind and true freedom of discussion than in America.'

Tocqueville's regrets about the 'lack of virile candour and manly independence of thought,' is to be taken as a warning that a democratic society endangers itself by its tendency to demand conformity to the majority opinion. Tocqueville believes that what counteracts this tendency in America is the federal system which mitigates against the power of the central government, and communal institutions 'which give the people both a taste for freedom and the skill to be free.' He also sees that the legal profession which plays such an important role in American politics serves as a brake upon the democratic mentality. 'Hidden at the bottom of a lawyer's soul', says Tocqueville, 'one finds some of the tastes and habits of an aristocracy.' Also of great significance, is the underlying principle which Tocqueville sees as underpinning democracy itself, 'self interest.' Americans are more driven by commercial passions than political passions, as most people are far more desirous of material prosperity than political power.

Tocqueville's assessment of the inevitability of democracy, then, is matched by a cautious appreciation of the values of democratic society. The precarious balance achieved in America between liberty and equality is praised by Tocqueville, but he grasps the tension that exists between them. America is fortunate in having the cultural roots which sustain this balance. Tocqueville knows that those roots are different from other countries, including France, which he saw were destined to go down the pathway of democracy. Thus there is a deep sense of foreboding that democracy will not be as smooth in the Old World as in the New World, that there the pull toward equality could easily tip the balance toward an egalitarian despotism, an entrenchment of mediocrity and paternalism. The European creations of communism and fascism (although non-egalitarian, nevertheless, an ideology of mass mobilization) indicates how right he was.

The dilemmas raised by Tocqueville were also being grappled with in England by a liberal philosopher, John Stuart Mill who was to review *Democracy in America*, praising it as 'the first philosophical book ever written on Democracy, as it manifests itself in modern society; a book, the essential doctrines of which it is not likely that any future speculations will subvert, to whatever degree they may modify them; while its spirit, and the general mode in which it treats its subject, constitute the beginning of a new era in the scientific study of politics.'[28]

Notes

1. Charles Sherover calls Montesquieu 'the godfather' of the American constitution. *The Development of the Democratic Idea: Readings from Pericles to the Present*, Washington, Washington Square Press, 1974, page 99.
2. Fawn Brodie, *Thomas Jefferson: An Intimate History*, New York, Norton, 1974. John Miller *Alexander Hamilton and the Growth of the New Nation*, New York, Harper, 1959.
3. Henry Dethloff, ed., *Thomas Jefferson and American Democracy*, Heath, Lexington, 1971.
4. For the compromises between Madison and Hamilton see Gary Wills, *Explaining America: The Federalist*, New York, Doubleday and Co., 1981.
5. Adrienne Koch and William Peden, eds., *The Life and Selected Writings of Thomas Jefferson*, New York, Random House, 1944, Introduction, page 436.
6. Thomas Paine, *Rights of Man*, Harmondsworth, Penguin, 1984, page 161. *The Federalist* #4, and # 34.
7. *The Federalist* # 7.
8. Morton White, *Philosophy, The Federalist and the Constituition*, New York, Oxford University Press, 1987, part 5.
9. On the intellectual background to Federalist #10 see Douglas Adair, 'The Tenth Federalist Revisited', Trevour Colbourn, ed., *Fame and the Founding Fathers*, New York, Norton, 1974 and James Conniff, 'The Enlightenment and American Political Thought: A Study of the Origins of Madison's *Federalist* Number 10', in *Political Theory*, Vol. 8, No. 3, August 1980. For the most thorough commentary on *The Federalist* see Gottfried Dietz, *The Federalist: A Classic on Federalism and Free Government*, Baltimore, John Hopkins, 1965.
10. Alexis De Tocqueville, *Democracy in America*, trans. George Lawrence, J. P. Mayer and M. Lerner, eds., New York, Harper and

Row, 1966, pages xiii–xiv.

11. On Tocqueville and the founding fathers see Bernard E. Brown 'Tocqueville and Publius' in *Reconsidering Tocqueville's Democracy in America*, S. Eisenstadt, ed., New Brunswick, Rutgers University Press, 1988, and Thomas G. West 'Misunderstanding the American Founding' and James Schleifer 'Jefferson and Tocqueville' in *Interpreting Tocqueville's Democracy in America* Ken Masugi, ed., Littlefield, Rowman, 1991.
12. *Democracy in America*, pages 752-3.
13. Ibid., page 603.
14. Ibid., pages 323-4.
15. *The European Revolution and Correspondence with Gobineau*, trans. John Lukacs, New York, Double Day, 1959. Also see James Schleifer, *The Making of Tocqueville's Democracy in America*, Chapel Hill, University of North Carolina Press, 1980.
16. *Democracy in America*, pages 327-8.
17. For more on Tocqueville and slavery see William Richardson, 'Racial Equality in America' in *Interpreting Democracy in America*; Seymour Drescher, *Dilemmas of Democracy: Tocqueville and Modernisation*, University of Pittsburgh Press, 1968, ch. 6.
18. Though, for an attempt to read Tocqueville through Rousseau's influence see Harvey Mitchell, 'The Changing Conditions of Freedom: Tocqueville in the Light of Rousseau', *History of Political Thought*, Vol. IX, No. 3. Winter, 1988.
19. *Democracy in America*, pages 92-3.
20. Ibid., page 93.
21. Ibid., pages 59-60.
22. Ibid., page 15.
23. Ibid., page 245.
24. Jack Lively, *The Social and Political Thought of Alexis de Tocqueville*, Oxford, Clarendon, 1962.
25. *Democracy in America*, page 251.
26. Ibid., page 252.
27. Ibid., page 247.
28. John Stuart Mill, *John Stuart Mill on Politics and Society*, Geraint Williams, ed., London, Fonatana, 1976, page 188.

10 The Development of Social Rights and Social Democracy

> No beast so fierce but knows some touch of pity
>
> *Richard III, I, I, 71*

Tocqueville had seen that equality and liberty were the electric forces of America's social reproduction. In America mistrust of the potency of the state ran through the entire political mind-set. This was as true of the anti-federalist who did not want to see their communities imposed upon by outsiders, as it was of the federalists who laboured so assiduously over a constitutional framework which would ensure the separation of powers. It was as true for Jefferson who wanted to preserve the Lockean right of rebellion, as it was of Hamilton whose mistrust of the legislative power derived from a Machiavellian view of human nature. In spite, then, of the fact that the American constitution derived from a synthesis of Lockean opposition to political absolutism and natural right and Montesquieu's appreciation of the need to balance powers, the state is still conceived as something threatening, something dark, in short, it is still conceived as a monster. Hence constitutional safeguards are needed to protect people, and states from its excesses and potential abuses. The fact that the monster is made up by the people does not change this.

This view of the state is perfectly consistent with liberalism, but changing circumstances in Europe were leading people to be considering the state in a new light. As the labouring classes in Western Europe were becoming politically mobilised against the middle and upper classes, the state was increasingly construed as a force which if properly directed could provide people with the goods that they needed. The push for political representation and social equality became increasingly bound up with this new attitude toward the state. The continual exchange between the experiences of Europe and America meant that America would follow Europe (with the New Deal) and come to adopt a more collectivist view of the state in line with European social democracy.

John Stuart Mill (1806-1873)

Like Jefferson, Madison, Jay, Hamilton, and Tocqueville, Mill was no mere observer of political action. He was elected for a term as a Member of Parliament. Like Tocqueville, Mill was a witness to the synthesis of the continuing triumph of liberal principles with the expanding social power and political mobilisation of the lower classes. Also like Tocqueville, Mill believed that the modern liberal democratic state could not adequately be described as a mixed constitution. Ultimately, in any state there was one sovereign power, and in a democratic state, that was the people. Whereas Montesquieu saw the monarchy and House of Lords as still representing considerable social power, Mill no longer saw this as the case. The burning issue of the day, for Mill, was how exactly the will of the people was to be constituted, and then how it was to be channelled for the greatest political good.

The question of what constituted the greatest good, for Mill, was addressed in what was to become the most important defence of liberal principles since Locke's *Two Treatises on Government*. In that work, *On Liberty*,[1] Mill focussed upon what Tocqueville in *Democracy in America* had seen as the greatest single benefit that democracy had conferred upon the social character of America, a prodigious energy. For Mill, the primary purpose of politics is to unleash the energies of the species. Liberty takes on supreme importance for Mill because it energises those who act in accordance with it. Liberty, then, is not simply an end in itself, as it is for Kant. Liberty is valuable because it is useful. Mill approvingly cites Wilhelm von Humboldt's *Spheres and Duties of Government*,[2] on 'the end of man' - 'the highest and most harmonious development of his powers to a complete and consistent whole.' He continues, 'therefore, the object "towards which every human being must ceaselessly direct his efforts, and on which especially those who design to influence their fellow-men must ever keep their eyes, is the individuality of power and development"; that for this there are two requisites, "freedom, and variety of situations"; and that from the union of this arise "individual vigour and manifold diversity", which combine themselves in "originality."'

If people are free to follow their inclination and left free to build their talents, their activity will serve the dual purpose of their own fulfilment and the creation of a more interesting world that stems from their own abundance. The enemy of the novel deployment of creative energy, for Mill, is invariably custom and prejudice. The danger that constantly faces the great beneficiaries of humanity is the twin despotism of opinion and authority. Again, like Tocqueville, Mill sees that the despotism of the majority is a serious danger in the modern democratic state. There is in Mill a strong aristocratic mistrust of the ability and judgments of the mass. He sees that a major problem of the day is to conjoin the democratic system with procedures and institutions which have a strong meritocratic component, with emphasis being given to intelligence and administrative, political, and judicial experience.

Intrinsic to the development of liberty, for Mill, is the expression of one's wants and the willingness to involve oneself in the interests of the nation. Unless one does this, one's liberty will inevitably be curbed by circumstances which are imposed by interests that have emerged from another group. Mill does not believe that politics is just about the expression of self-interest, partly because he sees the very concept of 'self-interest' as an unclear idea - what is seen as self-interest by an impartial observer and what is seen by the actor are invariably very different things, and what may be in one's self interest in the short term may turn out to be disadvantageous. But he does see that power serves different purposes for different groups. Members from groups rarely notice the interests of different groups, and when they do, they usually do not do a good job of articulating the other's groups experiences and problems. They will invariably introduce their own perception based on their interests and moral concerns, concerns which have evolved from their own particular circumstance. Further, unless a group participates in the decisions which concern it, it is not developing the energies required for its own growth.

Ultimately, for Mill, it is only through our own actions that we come to value what we have. ' The food of feeling is action', says Mill, adding 'let a person have nothing to do for his country and he will not care for it.' And 'leaving things to Government', he says, 'like leaving things to Providence, is synonymous with caring nothing about them.' Thus even apart from the technical difficulties that Mill sees with the notion of a benevolent despot, that it must be all seeing, perfectly informed of the minutiae of every branch of administration,[3] or the inevitable tendency of power to corrupt one's willingness to serve the interests of others, Mill claims that it would never provide the advantages of a system of government in which different social groups articulated their own interests.

Hitherto in Britain, Mill sees that there have been two major social groups that have been deprived of participation in popular government: the labouring class and women.

In the case of the labouring class, Mill sees that they are responsible for a major social transformation taking place. But this transformation is dangerous. For when two classes (viz. the wealthy and labouring classes) are engaging in bitter struggle with each other, the state may become beholden to one of them, and thus become more despotic in its engagement with the other. Ideally, says Mill, it would be best if these respective classes were to hold 'about an equal number of votes in the Parliament.' There are three basic components of Mill's proposal for moderating the potential of one class continually dominating another. The first is to provide as wide a representation of interests as possible. It is based on a similar observation which we saw Madison had used in *The Federalists Papers*: if there are a small number of factions they tend to be more dangerous, but if that number can be broken up, then there is less danger. Mill adopts the scheme of proportional representation which had been developed by Thomas Hare.[4] Voting under this scheme is not limited to a choice between parties due to one's geographic location in a particular constituency, but each voter votes for a series of candidates from all over the country. Once a candidate has a sufficient number of votes, or fulfils his quota, to be elected, the remainder go to a second candidate until he gets a quota, and so on to the third and subsequent candidates until the places are exhausted. Mill believed that this approach would guarantee diversity of representation, and indeed variations of this system have been successfully utilised in Australia.

The second proposal that Mill had for moderating against the danger of self-interest submerging the national interest was the provision of education for all classes. Mill believed that education was indispensable for the viability of popular government. If one could not read, write, or do simple arithmetic then one is incapable, for Mill, of participating in the political process - he even suggests that voters should be tested by being asked to copy a sentence out of a book and doing an exercise from the three times table. The key to good government, for Mill, lay in combining energy and intelligence, spreading political power so that it accurately represented the different interests and energies of different groups, while wisely distilling the common interests which emerged from this system of representation. To that end, Mill proposed that voters who had achieved a certain level of education be granted more votes, and that a second chamber be created on a meritocratic basis. Thus, incidentally, does Mill display that he thinks the British aristocracy has become a political irrelevancy, and that it is just another subsection of the wealthy class and should be politically treated as such.

The other major buffer that Mill invokes for preventing the labouring classes using the government to ensure their advantage at the expense of the nation's prosperity - as was to happen in Argentine under the populist Perón, and arguably Australia under the social democrat Whitlam - is to argue for the principle of no representation without financial contribution. Bankrupts and those who are dependent upon charity (or state welfare) for their livelihood should, says Mill, be excluded from the suffrage. Those who introduce new taxation, suggests Mill, must also feel the effect of it. Mill well knew that public goods come at a price and that one group may be happy for another group to pay the bill, just as one generation may want the successor generation to pick up the tab for its enjoyments.

Mill's solution to the problem of the shift of political and social power is indicative of the strong idealist and realist elements concurrently running through his thought. His insistence that no one else adequately represents one's own interests is strongly in the tradition of Spinoza and Montesquieu, but his belief that education imbues one with greater insight of the common good equally suggests a Platonistic layer in his thought. An indication of how much faith the idealist Mill placed in the intelligentsia can be seen from his comment that he 'had no difficulty in admitting that Communism would even now be practicable among the *elite* of mankind, and may become so among the rest.'[5] Indeed, on the subject of communism and socialism, Mill was sympathetic to the Owenist, Fourierist and Saint-Simonian experiments in socialism. If socialism were to be proven to be the superior form of economic organisation and provided it was commensurate with individual liberty, as it was in these utopian schemes, then, indicates Mill, he would gladly be a socialist. He was, however, deeply suspicious of revolutionary communists who believed that all of society had to be transformed in one sweep for the benefits of communism to be experienced. He was also very prescient in his claim that communism would be most widely supported by the intelligentsia, rather than by the more practical working class for whom its intellectual discoverers had designed it. The more realist side of Mill, was careful to argue that the economic viability of socialism was something that had to be demonstrated in practice.[6]

The intelligentsia, in Mill are conceived much along the lines of Plato's guardian class. Their love of wisdom would, he believed, make them more sensitive to the idea of progress and collective well being. But Mill does not stop to consider that his idealisation of the intelligentsia is largely the self-projection of how the intellectual sees him or herself, not how he or she actually is. Equally as important, he does not consider that the strength of intellectuals, the facility to engage in abstractions, is their greatest weakness. Intellectuals are more prone to take their abstractions as reality itself, thus deluding themselves and others that what is a very partial perspective of the world is the world itself. Ironically, it was on the very issue of communism and its subsequent variations that this weakness of the intelligentsia would become so transparent (at least to most other people but themselves) in the twentieth century.

Mill's belief in the special merits of the intelligentsia, in the potential of socialism combined with his awareness of the inevitable political power that was to fall into the hands of the labouring class, adumbrates the social democratic synthesis of the intelligentsia and the working class. This is certainly paradoxical in light of Mill's perceived need to mitigate the potential despotism of the majoritarian government of the labouring classes and the dangers of statist paternalism, which included inferior performance, depletion of private initiative and energies, and excessive power which would work against the prospect of reform. Yet it was just this prospect of the working class gaining political power that brought out the extent of paternalism in Mill's own thinking.

The other way in which that paternalism presented itself in Mill was in his assessment of liberal democracy as a political arrangement which required a level of cultural attainment which not every peoples had achieved. Like Montesquieu and Tocqueville before him, he was aware of how laws and political institutions may shape a people's character. But Mill specifically rejects elevating 'opinions, tastes, and habits' to the level of being 'necessary conditions' for undertaking a more progressive form of government. At the same time, he concedes that not every attempt to provide progressive government will succeed. In this respect, Mill believed that despotism was justifiable if it prepared a people for self-rule and liberty. Mill's paternalism though, whether intended for the benefit of the working class or conquered peoples, was always premised upon the eventual attainment of liberty for all peoples; his liberalism was global in its scope. The value of the principle of representative government, for Mill, would always hold true; the only issue was whether a group or a people were sufficiently advanced to have the franchise. Mill well knew, though, that inclusion within the franchise must ultimately come from the desires, struggles and victories of the group heretofore excluded.

In Britain, the other group for whom the franchise was beginning to become an issue were women. Amongst the ancient philosophers, it was Plato whose idealism extended to the inclusion of women as capable of having a political input. In the *Republic* he had argued that women should be included in the guardian class. Aristotle, however, had defended the more traditional view of women as incapable of making any contribution to political life. Women, he said, lacked the deliberative faculty. This view was pretty much the standard philosophical view of women in the Middle Ages, not surprisingly given Aristotle's philosophical dominance. Descartes had to a minor extent broken with this tradition by declaring that intelligence was equally distributed between people, and publicly pronounced on the intellectual virtues of his female patron Queen Christina. But generally even the more radical democratic spirits did not desire political power for women. We have already mentioned Spinoza's rejection of the idea of women having political power. And while Locke vigorously argued against paternalism, within the family he believed that it was natural that the male should rule, and by implication political power should fall to him.

Even Rousseau, while working for the removal of man's chains had, in *Emile*, sought to ensure that women's role remained divorced from politics. There he had written that the 'man should be strong and active; the woman weak and passive; the one must have the power and the will; it is enough that the other should offer little resistance.'[7] According to Rousseau women's capacity to charm gives them a power over males. He goes onto say that 'Women do wrong to complain of the inequality of man-made laws; this inequality is not of man's making, or at any rate it is not the result of mere prejudice, but of reason.' 'To cultivate the masculine virtues in women and to neglect their own is evidently to do them an injury.' And, finally, 'What is most wanted in a woman is gentleness; formed to obey a creature so imperfect as man, a creature often vicious and always faulty, she should early learn to submit to injustice and to suffer the wrongs inflicted on her without complaint.'[8]

The significant intellectual exceptions to this traditional way of constructing women were Marquis de Condorçet (1743-1794), Jeremy Bentham, and the woman usually credited as being the first to write a sustained treatise for the emancipation of women, Mary Wollstonecraft. Condorçet in 1790 published an article 'On Granting Civil Rights to Women.' In it he compared the situations of negroes and women, attacking their maltreatment and the institutional discrimination that they had to endure. In stark contrast to Rousseau, (and Kant, whose views on women could have been written by Rousseau), Condorçet insisted that because reason was universal, women could not be denied their rightful status as rational beings. Condorçet argued in *Five Memoirs of Education* that women should be educated just as men are, an issue that Daniel Defoe, had raised almost a hundred years earlier, and the historian Catherine Macaulay was also advocating in her *Letters on Education* (1790).[9] Condorçet's argument for women having civil rights was consistent in its advocacy that such rights should also be accompanied by political rights provided the property qualifications for the vote were also met.

The issue of women's suffrage was also something that occupied Mill's one time mentor Jeremy Bentham (1742-1832). In an unpublished manuscript of 1789 he had objected to equating women with infants and the insane for the purpose of excluding them from the vote. And in a number of published works, *Catechism of a Parliamentary Reform* (1809), the *Radical Reform Bill* (1819) and the *Constitutional Code*, he argued for opening up educational and political opportunities for women.[10]

Whereas Bentham had considered the problem of enfranchisement from a strictly utilitarian viewpoint, Mary Wollstonecraft wrote *Vindication of the Rights of Woman* emphasising the absurd contradiction between Rousseau's conception of rights, which she largely accepted, and the subordinate role of women which he advocated. For Wollstonecraft, the inferior economic, political and moral circumstance of woman had been the result of socialisation, not nature. For her, the transformation of women's role was largely a matter of education. Women needed to acquire new skills so that they would possess the necessary virtues for independence and participation in public life. She had made the same point as Macaulay, whom she admired, only her work was more polemical and overtly political.

Thus, by the time Mill wrote his *The Subjection of Women*, 1869, the idea of gender emancipation was already in the air, philosophically. There also existed a movement for the female suffrage, although to be sure it was nowhere near as strong as the Union movement and the push for political power then being made in England by the working class. But, for Mill, the circumstance of the denial of women's rights is not equivalent to other situations. 'Men', he points out, 'do not want solely the obedience of women, they want their sentiments. All men, except the most brutish, desire to have, in the woman most nearly connected with them, not a forced slave but a willing one, not a slave merely, but a favourite. They have therefore put everything in practice to enslave their mind.'

The circumstance of women, then, for Mill, is different from any other social group — for other social groups are enslaved by fear, not by skewing natural sentiments to create compliant devotion — and this largely explains the complicity of women in their own lack of political powerlessness. Further, Mill believes that the nature of women has been more thoroughly distorted through their relationships than any other social group, including slaves. The duties of women, according to Mill, have been stretched beyond that of slaves, 'no slave is a slave to the same lengths and in so full a sense as a wife is. Hardly any slave, except one immediately attached to his master's person, is a slave at all hours and minutes of the day.' Even a slave is not under obligation as a wife to sleep with a master who degrades and tortures her.

For Mill, 'the moral regeneration of mankind will only really commence when the most fundamental of social relations is placed under the rule of equal justice, and when human beings learn to cultivate their strongest sympathy with an equal in rights and in cultivation.' Closely related to this was Mill's belief that human progress was generated through discontent with the existing order. Each new group who had been through the process of demanding their liberty and articulating their moral discontents were entering into the creative task that lay before the species: its collective intellectual, moral and material improvement. The spirit of liberty was, for Mill, a restless one, but its very restlessness was indicative of the energising character of human freedom. As much as Mill's philosophy is a celebration of liberty, the emphasis it places upon the importance of political representation of different social groups indicates that Mill is also driven by the concepts of fairness and equality.

It was Mill's fate to sit between the opposing tendencies within liberalism, between those who wanted to expand the powers of the state as an agent for achieving greater liberty for groups who remained socially disadvantaged, and those who saw that any such attempt would drag liberalism into the sphere of socialism, and that the emphasis upon social equality would have deleterious effects for individual liberty and social prosperity. Both groups would see Mill's form of liberalism as unsatisfactory: the former because Mill did not provide enough latitude for the state to play a more directive role in opening up the conditions of liberty; the latter because Mill was veering too close to paternalism, straying too far from his belief in the importance of the energies of the individual. It was the former group, however, who were to play the dominant role in shaping the future of the state for well into the twentieth century.

Idealist Social Liberalism: Thomas Hill Green

One of the most influential and eloquent of this new breed of social liberals was the English academic Thomas Hill Green (1836-82).[11] Green believed that a free society would only emerge if the state played a directing role in changing the social circumstances of men and women. In arguing for this, Green reformulated the most fundamental idea of liberalism, liberty itself. Tocqueville, in distinguishing the values of the ancients from the moderns, had succinctly captured the meaning of the modern liberal notion of liberty when he said that 'according to the modern notion of liberty every man is inherently entitled to be uncontrolled by his fellows in all that only concerns himself and to regulate at his own will his own destiny.'[12]

For Green, however, the stock liberal definition of liberty failed to take adequately account of the social good and social justice, two ends highly valued by Mill. But, unlike Mill, Green factored into the very definition of liberty the end that Mill had hoped would be realised, so that an action which did not conform to the end of the social good became, *ipso facto*, an action which could not properly be called free. As he wrote in 'Liberal Legislation and Freedom of Contract': 'We shall probably all agree that freedom, rightly understood, is the greatest of all blessings; that its attainment is the true end of all our efforts as citizens. But when we thus speak of freedom...we do not mean merely freedom from restraint or compulsion. We do not mean a freedom that can be enjoyed by one man or one set of men at the cost of a loss of freedom to others. When we speak of freedom as something to be so highly prized, we mean a positive power or capacity of doing or enjoying, and that too, something that we do or enjoy in common with others. We mean by it power which each man exercises through the help or security given him by his fellow-men, and which he in turn helps to secure for them.'

A large part of what gave Green's position such plausibility was that it was wielded in the language of liberalism. In its inception liberalism had arisen in opposition to the propertied classes above the commercial class, not primarily in opposition to the classes beneath it. Although the commercial class had not wanted to spread political power to those who could soak its own wealth, the language that had been forged in opposition to the aristocracy was the language of universality, right, equality, progress, as well as freedom. Or to put it slightly differently, freedom was only one of the variables in the political rhetoric that the emergent middle class had used in its political struggle. The rising working classes did not need to forge another language in order to make its claims. Indeed, it was one of the constant frustrations of Marx and Engels that trade unionists and socialists outside of their camp would express their political claims in terms of a *just* wage, the right to a *fair* day's work, *fair* working conditions, i.e. all claims that Marx and Engels denounced as bourgeois moralising. Green's philosophical conception of freedom, then, was not contrary to the ideas already embedded in liberalism, in spite of carrying a freight that many liberals viewed as contrary to the kind of society they wanted to build, one based on private initiative free from paternal directions and bureaucratically laden (mis)constructions of what people needed.

Further, what also gave Green credibility was his emphasis upon the delivery of improved living standards. The core argument of liberal political economists had never simply been that freedom was good for the wealthy, but that in a liberal society wealth would be most speedily generated and more people would benefit than under any alternative economic system as commodities became increasingly cheaper. Green does not dispute the central tenets of liberal political economy. Indeed, in England and America those tenets were continually being verified. Nevertheless, the liberal tradition had provided a benchmark for measuring the value of political arrangements: progressively expanding social prosperity. It was the kind of benchmark that was completely absent from the ancient and Medieval conception of the good life, as well as from the more morally driven traditions of Rousseau and Kant. Concomitantly, lack of prosperity was an indication that the society was still in need of growth.

Closely related to this was the connection that had been established within the liberal tradition between the value ascribed to property and the value ascribed to capacities or personal properties. Locke's defence of private property rested upon the fact that a claim had been established through labour. In other words, private property was the expression, as Kant and then Hegel pointed out more clearly than Locke himself, of an action and an act of will. In the *Federalist Papers* (#10), Madison had spoken of 'the diversity of faculties of men, from which the rights of property originate'. The 'first object of government', he said, 'was the protection of these faculties.' Mill's defence of liberty had, for all its warnings about paternalistic government, not primarily been an argument about protecting private property, but an argument about how personal capacities and energies would best flourish.

Thus the path had already been paved within the liberal-democratic tradition for Green to emphasise that the job of the state is to equip its populace with the necessary fundamentals for the exercise and development of their capacities. A state which failed to do this thus becomes seen as complicit in tyranny and the unfair preservation of privilege in much the same way as the pre-liberal state had been complicit in the preservation of privilege for the select few. Private property, then, is justifiable only to the extent that it does not impede the faculties and talents of persons of a particular class. As Green says in *Liberal Legislation and Freedom of Contract*, because 'property' is 'only justifiable as the free exercise of the social capabilities of all, there can be no true right to property of a kind which debars one class of men from such free exercise altogether.' Just as Locke had seen Hobbes' grounding of political obligation was illegitimate unless 'the people' had representative political institutions, the social liberalism of theorists like Green is based on the observation that 'the people' must mean all who are capable of exercising their rights and who have not acted in such a manner that they may be legitimately deprived of them. But having the capacity to exercise their rights means that barriers to them must be removed.

Further, the argument that the state should not intervene in a non-criminal contract freely entered into may seem to be a strong argument to the social liberal position. But as Green well knew, the liberal tradition had explicitly rejected the right of people to voluntary enter into slavery. Rights were inalienable. Beginning from the invalidity of a contract of slavery, Green, goes onto argue that 'no contract is valid in which human persons, willingly or unwillingly, are dealt with as commodities, because such contracts of necessity defeat the end for which alone society enforces contracts at all.' Again, the claim has a strong liberal antecedent, namely Kant's principle that humans as rational beings should never be treated as means, but they are ends in themselves. When Kant had articulated this principle he had conceived it in conjunction with a very minimalist version of public welfare state mentality. But in the case of Green this principle becomes a justification for a range of work related laws. As he writes in the same essay; 'restrictions may be needed to place upon the sale of this commodity which would be unnecessary, in other cases, in order to prevent labour being sold under conditions which make it impossible for the person selling it ever to become a free contributor to social good in any form. This is plainly the case when a man bargains to work under conditions fatal to health, eg. in an unventilated factory. Every injury to the health of the individual is, so far as it goes, a public injury. It is an impediment to general freedom; so much deduction from our power, as members of society, to make the best of ourselves. Society is, therefore, plainly within its right when it limits freedom of contract for the sale of labour, so far as it is done by our laws for the sanitary regulations of factories, workshop, and mines. It is equally within its right in prohibiting the labour of women and young persons beyond certain hours. If they work beyond those hours, the result is demonstrable physical deterioration; which, as demonstrably, carries with it a lowering of the moral forces of society.'

Although, then, Green is justifying increasing state intervention, he did not see himself as a proponent of illiberal ideas. Nor were the elements of his argument for a more active state illiberal. He was, however, well aware that other defenders of liberalism objected to the kinds of interventions he defended on the grounds that too much state interference would concentrate too much power into too few hands and the spirit of liberty would be asphyxiated. To this argument, Green responds, 'we shall probably all agree that a society in which the public health was duly protected, and necessary education duly provided for, by the spontaneous action of individuals, was in a higher condition than one in which the compulsion of law was needed to secure these ends. But we must take men as we find them. Until such a condition of society is reached it is the business of the state to take the best security it can for the young citizen's growing up in such health and with so much knowledge as is necessary for real freedom.'

For Green, protective labour legislation, public health and public education are justifiable because they raise the well-being of those members of the population who otherwise would not be able to exercise their freedom or contribute to the public good.

The philosophy articulated by Green was built upon the synthesis of the liberal ideas of private power, the republican concern with the public good, and the egalitarian spirit of Rousseau. It was, self-consciously so, an idealist philosophy. But it was also built in response to the social and political changes taking place in Britain. Late nineteenth century liberalism had become to a large extent a doctrine as suspicious of the minority of the wealthy bourgeoisie as seventeenth and eighteenth century liberalism had been of the aristocracy. Thus, for example, the liberal politician Joseph Chamberlain would say in a speech of 1885 that 'the great evil with which we have to deal is the excessive inequality in the distribution of riches' and 'the sanctity of private property is no doubt an important principle, but the public good is a greater and higher object than any private interest, and the comfort and happiness of the people and the prosperity of the country must never be sacrificed to the exaggerated claims of the privileged class who are now the exclusive possessors of the great gift of the Almighty to the human race.'[13]

Liberal theorists in the twentieth century, with few exceptions, were to continue further down the path of seeing the task of the state as providing the conditions for social justice, and invariably that meant restraining the liberty of the most wealthy of those individuals.

The most well known exceptions to this were mainly economists such as Ludwig von Mises, Friedrich von Hayek, and Milton Friedman. Among philosophers Robert Nozick also stands out. More typically Leonard Hobhouse (1864-1929) in his classic twentieth century defence of *Liberalism*,[14] would spell out what all liberals had accepted, that 'liberty itself only rests upon constraint'. He further argued that 'the function of the state is to override individual coercion' in order to maintain social justice and such rights as 'the right to work' and the right to a living wage. Wealth and property are therefore treated as social goods.

By the time of John Rawls's *Theory of Justice* (1971) the claim is made that justice is to society what truth is to knowledge. Writing at the high water mark of social democratic political power, the linkages Rawls established between justice as fairness and between the basic liberal rights and freedoms - the right to vote, freedom of conscience, the press, the rule of law - and fair and equal opportunity, and the principle of the greatest benefit to the least advanced member of a society, seemed to be a mere restatement of the basic stock of liberalism. Paradoxically, it came at a time when a growing number of economists had seen that such a conception of social justice, when translated into increasing economic demands upon the state to deliver real resources, was playing a major role in causing stagflation and thus in restraining national prosperity.

Idealist Socialism in France, Germany and England

The roots of socialist thought, whether they be traced to Plato's *Republic*, Sir Thomas More's *Utopia*, (1516) to Rousseau's *Discourses on the Origins of Inequality Among Mankind*, (1755)[15] or to Morelly's *Code of Nature* (1755), are invariably idealist. What all these works have in common is a belief in the fundamental wrongness of private property. In the case of Plato that wrongness is seen as the cause of war, but at the same time he only envisages that a select group of people could forego private property and possessions (in Plato they are conflated.)

The earliest significant modern utopian work is Thomas More's *Utopia*. It is no accident that More approvingly cites Plato's *Republic* for having argued for 'an equal distribution of goods'. But More's book was not written in an attempt to make philosophy safe from the tyranny of the mob, but as a response to the break down of village life, the enclosure of lands for sheep pasturing, and the excessive punishments meted out to the large number of beggars, vagabonds and thieves in sixteenth century England. It is an attempt to devise a society in which poverty will be eliminated. And its attempt to eliminate poverty, like most communist attempts to do so, commences with the vilification of existing wealth and the power that accompanies it: 'when I consider any social system that prevails in the modern world, I can't...see it as anything but a conspiracy of the rich to advance their own interests under the pretext of organising society.'[16] In this one sentence, More has expressed what Marx and his successors will try to demonstrate in a million different ways.

As with More, Morelly's *Code of Nature* asserts that 'where no property exists, none of its pernicious consequences could exist,' and 'if you were to take away property, and the blind and pitiless self-interest that accompanies it you would cause all the prejudices and errors that they sustain to collapse.'[17] Like *Utopia*, the communist vision expressed in the *Code* is frugal, meticulous, tedious and draconian - 'Every citizen between the ages of twenty and twenty-five without exception, will be required to do agricultural work.... In every occupational group, there will be one master for every ten or twenty workers, and it will be his task to instruct them, inspect their work. At the age of thirty, every citizen will be allowed to dress according to his taste.... The senators and chiefs are authorised by this law to punish all excesses in this manner.... Young people between the ages of twenty and thirty will be dressed uniformly with each occupation ...every citizen will have both a work suit and holiday suit.... Every citizen will be married as soon as he has reached the marriageable age; no one will be exempt from this, at least as long as nature or health presents no obstacle.... Within each tribe, all children reaching the age of five will be brought together, and the two sexes will be separately housed and fed in an establishment aside for this purpose.... For periods of five days at a time, groups of parents will succeed one another in taking care of the children in these establishments with as much care as they would give to their own.'

Morelly's *Code* contains many of the core elements of later day communists - egalitarianism, a sagacious bureaucracy, principles of rotation, prohibition of private property, the requirement that all work. But it was Gracchus Babeuf (1760-1797) who is generally heralded as being the first systematic defender of modern communism.[18] Babeuf, who was tried for conspiracy and executed during the French revolution, saw his communist ideas as the natural progression of the Enlightenment. It was, he would say in his defence at his trial, the philosophical poisons of Mably, Helvétius, Diderot and most importantly Rousseau which had corrupted him. For Babeuf, communism was a means for ending injustice. In the *Manifesto of Equals* he wrote, 'We declare ourselves unable any longer to tolerate a situation in which the great majority of men toil and sweat in the service and at pleasure of a tiny minority.' 'Men of all classes', he would write to his partner in dialogue, Dubois de Fosseux, in every country, 'should be accorded the same rights in order of succession to property' and 'an absolutely equal portion of all the goods and advantages that can be enjoyed in this mean world.' And in the *Analysis of the Doctrine of Babeuf*, written by his followers, the egalitarianism of the Constitution of 1793 was invoked against the wealthy. 'The revolution is not finished, because the rich are absorbing all goods and are exclusively in command, while the poor are toiling in a state of virtual slavery.' The way out of this class division was to make everyone work - 'no one has ever shirked this duty without having thereby committed a crime.'

What all these thinkers had in common with each other, and with Marx, is an emphasis upon relieving the suffering of the poorest classes. All of them also fail to do any serious economic analysis of what a communist system would entail. They also conflate ideas for social organisation which ultimately rest upon a moral abstraction — viz, the concept of equality — with ideas about human action, the truth of which have nothing to do with morality, but everything to do with human motivations, capacities, information flows etc. Marx, in spite of the huge smokescreen of political economic problems he surrounds himself with, is guilty of the same conflation.

The same approach is to be found in the most brilliant (if not the most influential nor imaginative, since the latter crown would have to go Charles Fourier) of all socialist thinkers, Claude Henri Saint-Simon (1760-1825). He saw in Christianity the means to preach the amelioration of social divisions. 'God', he wrote, in *The New Christianity: Dialogues Between a Conservative and an Innovator* (1825) 'gave only one principle to men: that He commanded them to organise their society in such a way as to guarantee to the poorest classes the promptest and most complete amelioration of their physical and moral existence.'[19] In the tradition of Condorçet, who wrote *Sketch for a Historical Picture of the Progress of the Human Mind* (1795), and Anne Robert Jacques Turgot, the physiocrat financial official who authored *Reflexions sur la Formation et la Distribution Richesses* (1766), Saint-Simon held that human society was progressing. But progress, for Saint-Simon was not primarily about intellectual evolution and the application of ideas to society, as it is largely in Condorçet, but it entailed the increasing complexity of social organisation and technology. What Saint-Simon brings to this historicist and sociological perspective is the promise of social fulfilment in a unified administrative industrial society: science, industry and the fine arts are seen as conspiring to form a sociological unity which if rightly administered would bring peace and prosperity to all. In Saint-Simon the twentieth century bureaucratic cast of mind with its faith in a planned society finds its unambiguous nineteenth century antecedent, as can be gauged from his phrase, to be repeated by Engels: that the government of persons will be replaced by the administration of things.

In France, it was, however, neither Saint-Simon or Fourier, who would play the most important intellectual role in contributing to working class politics, but Pierre Proudhon (1809-1865). Proudhon's *What is Property?* (1840) succinctly formulated what socialists and communists had all in one way or another been saying. Proudhon answered the question posed in the title of his most famous work: 'It is theft.'[20] But Proudhon's answer, and his rebuke of private property as the economic pivot of society, came with a twist which was to be prophetic, as well as assuring the wrath of communists. Agreeing with the socialists that the accumulation of private property beyond small scale holdings was expoitative, he says: 'Communism is oppression and slavery....communism violates the sovereignty of the conscience and equality: the first, by restricting spontaneity of mind and heart, and freedom of thought and action; the second, by placing labour and laziness, skill and stupidity, and even vice and virtue on an equality in point of comfort.'

Proudhon's solution to inequality was a society composed of small scale property holders, each enjoying an interest-free credit system, and each working their land. Thus, while he insists that he (just like Saint-Simon had done and Marx would do) is merely a messenger who knows the direction of history, his vision, as Marx all too easily saw, was built around a fundamental anachronism, an anachronism, however, which was more likely to appeal to the social conditions of a still largely agrarian France than industrial England or America.

In Germany, Ferdinand Lassalle (1825-64), President of the General German Workers' Association would lay the foundation for what would become the German Socialist Party. Like Marx had done in the eighteen forties, Lassalle identified the interests of humanity with the interests of the working class. This class, which he calls the fourth class, he writes in *The Working Man's Program* of 1862, 'is the last and the outside of all, the disinterested class of the community, which sets up and can set up further exclusive condition, either legal or actual, neither nobility nor landed possessions, not the possession of capital, which it could make into a new privilege and force upon the arrangements of society.' And continuing in a vein that made Marx believe he was simultaneously being plagiarised and betrayed, he exhorts: 'Whoever therefore invokes the idea of the working class as the ruling principle of society, in the sense in which I have explained to you, does not put forth a cry that divides and separates the classes of society. On the contrary, he utters a cry of *reconciliation*, a cry which embraces the whole of the community, a cry for doing away with all the contradictions in every circle.'

The corollary of the belief that the self-interest of the working class would converge with the interest of society as a whole, was the stock socialist belief that the upper class's self interest had to be at the expense of the nation's cultural development. Unlike Marx, but like the first German philosophical nationalist and socialist, Johann Fichte (1762-1814), author of *The Closed Trading State* (1800), Lassalle saw the State as the cornerstone of a nation's development and the heart of its moral development. In this respect he already provides a tenet of Social Democracy. He thought that the nature of the State would be transformed by the political participation of the working class, who would build on the liberal idea of the development of individual powers (although with the socialist opposition to private property), by adding the moral virtues of '*solidarity* of interests, community and reciprocity of development.' It is the State says Lassalle, whose function is to carry on this development of freedom, this development of the human race until its freedom is attained.' He continues by claiming that '*The State* is this unity of individuals into a moral whole, a unity which increases a million-fold the strength of *all* the individuals who are comprehended in it, and multiplies a million times the power which would be at the disposal of them *all* as individuals. The object of the State, therefore, is not only to protect the personal freedom and property of the individual with which he is supposed, according to the idea of the Bourgeoisie, to have entered the State. On the contrary, the object of the State is precisely this, to place the individual through this union in a position to attain such objects, and reach such a stage of existence as they never could have reached as individuals; to make them capable of acquiring an amount of education, power, and freedom which would have been wholly unattainable by them as individuals.'

The concept of the state advanced here, while far removed from the laissez-faire liberalism of Wilhelm von Humboldt, is not much different from the idealist social liberal conception of the state advanced some years later in England by T. H. Green. By the end of the century, Eduard Bernstein (1850-1932), the leading German socialist politician had acknowledged that the Marxian roots of social democracy were no longer legitimate. Socialism was a matter of parliamentary democracy and evolution.

Much the same conclusions had been reached by the English Fabian socialists, who too believed in the historical inevitability of socialism, but neither the necessity or desirability of class war. In 1894 the Fabian socialist, Sydney **Webb** (1859-1947), would proclaim in *English Progress Toward Social Democracy*,[21] 'that there is no anti-socialist party in England', and that 'England is already the most Socialist of all European communities.' The Fabians were convinced that they saw the future and it was socialist. In the case of the leading English Fabian intellectuals, Sydney Webb, his wife Beatrice, (1858-1943) and George Bernard Shaw, they believed, like Bernstein, that socialism could and would be achieved by peaceful and parliamentary means. To this end the Webb's helped form the London School of Economics (LSE) in 1895 and the *New Statesman* in 1913.[22]

This did not mean that the Fabians were necessarily opposed to other methods being used. After Stalin had taken complete control of the Soviet Union, for example, the Fabians believed that the future had been realised and that it was very good. In 1935 the Webbs published the two volume laudatory study, *Soviet Communism: A New Civilisation.*[23] Like so many other observers of the Soviet barbarity they saw what they were shown and what they wanted to see. The Soviets had a whole industry for showing Western sympathisers what they desired, an industry that started ironically with the villages of Catherine the Great. During the Cold War, other Western intellectuals were to see the same thing, including Harold Laski, an LSE Professor, who idealised the Soviet Union in his *Faith, Reason and Civilisation*[24], and the most famous of Australian historians, Manning Clark, who was moved to write *Meeting Soviet Man.*[25]

By that time the central issue of the state in industrial Europe and North America was not about collectivism or individualism. Collectivists had won. Although the United States was still less collectivist than the remaining free states of Europe, Roosevelt and Churchill both presided over collectivist liberal states, while the Hitlerite and Stalinist state forms were collectivist anti-liberal states. But by the time of the Second World War and its immediate aftermath, the major issue in international politics was not whether the state should be more responsive to individuals, but how to prevent first one (the fascist) beast, then another (the communists) from devouring civilisation. The domestic politics of the civilised societies was still governed by the belief that only some form of welfarist collectivisation would protect and civilise members of the liberal Leviathans.

Social Democracy in Power

The political ascendancy of the social democratic movement derived from three main sources: the political claims of the fairly recently enfranchised masses on the product of civil society by using the state as a redistributive mechanism; the intellectual ideas of democratic socialism redirecting the liberal tradition in a social liberalism direction which lessened the political resistance from that source; and the economic ideas of state intervention associated with the doctrines of John Maynard Keynes.[26]

The Great Depression of the 1930s had an impact everywhere in the developed world on political programs. The level of employment became the foremost issue and since classical laissez-faire liberalism appeared to have little to say about this matter, or at least little to recommend that might do something to alleviate the situation in the short term, it faced political defeat everywhere. In its place the movements which struggled for supremacy included fascism, communism and social democracy. The fascists had already triumphed in Italy and the Nazis used the weaknesses of the Weimar Republic to seize state power in Germany. During the next decade most of Europe progressively came under fascist regimes, who used state economic intervention and a terrorist political apparatuses to increase economic activity by supine populations. Their communist opponents had control only in the Soviet Union where the state ownership of the economy enabled avoidance of the Depression at great cost to human liberty.

In the other advanced societies some form of social democracy became more influential, although at differing rates of growth. In the United States President Franklin Roosevelt (1882-1945), President 1933-1945, reversed generations of liberal economic doctrines to inaugurate the 'New Deal' with its emphasis on public works programs and welfare measures to stimulate economic activity. In Australia and New Zealand the welfare state was to be extended in the midst of some bitter political struggles. In Britain (where universal suffrage was achieved in 1928) the Depression only started to recede with the rearmament program of the 1930s. But the political impact of mass unemployment was to later change the political landscape fundamentally. In France the Popular Front governments also pushed the social democratic program in a society close to civil war and soon to be easily defeated. The victorious liberal powers of 1945 were anxious to avoid both another war and another depression.

The end of the Second World War heralded the triumph of social democracy. Fascism had been defeated in the field and survived only in isolated pockets that had managed to avoid a strategic relationship with the Axis powers, like Spain, Portugal and Argentina. Communism acquired considerable prestige in the West, as a result of the Soviet Union's contribution to the defeat of fascism, and the political spectrum in most advanced democracies swung to the Left. The ideas of an uncontrolled market economy seemed unsustainable in light of the experience of the depressed 1930s. The fusion of these tendencies produced the post War dominance of social democratic governments. In Britain the Labour Party led by Clement Atlee (1883-1967), another former LSE tutor, formed its first overwhelming majority government and spent the next five years nationalising many British industries and creating the welfare state. In Australia the Labor government laid the basis for state directed industrialisation. In the United States the Democrat President, Harry Truman, assumed Roosevelt's mantle on his death and was re-elected to carry on the program in 1948. And in liberated Europe the Anglo-Americans devised social democratic style regimes designed at first to crush the forces which had sustained fascism and then supported them against the communists' substantial popularity.

Although not all the social democratic parties stayed in power - indeed the Tories led by Winston Churchill returned in Britain in 1951, Robert Menzies led the Liberals back to power in Australia in 1949, and the Republicans got Dwight Eisenhower in as the President of the USA in 1953 - the impact of their doctrines remained until the later 1970s. In the three decades that followed the war economic growth was strong, the business cycle was minimal and the role of the state in economic management, redistribution of resources and the running of welfare programs was extended. During those decades the apogee of social democracy was achieved - particularly in Western Europe[27] - and with it the possibility of its encroachment on the process of progress because of its greatly expanded state impinging on the activities of economic civil society and the initiatives of individuals. This possibility was only to be seriously considered in the late 1970s when the post-War economic boom ran out of steam.

Internationally this period of social democratic dominance coincided with the emancipation of many of the former colonial territories and with an intense strategic struggle against the communist states. It would not be true to say that the decolonisation process started then, since much of Spanish America achieved independence in the early nineteenth century and the Middle East after the First World War. But the social democrats were less well inclined towards imperialism and after the British Labour government accepted the independence of the Indian Raj in 1947-8, the remaining areas of Asia, South America and Oceania began the accelerated process of decolonisation.

The social democrats also fought against the communists during this period. For the most part they sustained governments which maintained market economies with larger state sectors rather than vice versa. They also joined the Western strategic coalition against the Soviet Union, although some like New Zealand in the 1980s refused to pull their weight.

The social democratic states thus never completely abandoned their liberal heritage. And as the example of the Cold War shows, they knew where their real interests lay. On the other hand, the decline of social democracy historically parallels the decline of communism. The dying gasps of the totalitarian idealist beast were occurring at much the same time as the dying gasps of the more good natured, provider beast of social democracy. It was like those strange twins which nature occasionally produces who are so closely connected that one cannot live without the other.

Notes

1. John Stuart Mill, *On Liberty, with The Subjugation of Women and Chapters on Socialism*, Stefan Collini, ed., Cambridge, Cambridge University Press, 1989.

2. Wilhelm von Humboldt, *The Sphere and Duties of Government*, trans. Joseph Coulthard, London, Trubner.
3. John Stuart Mill, *Utilitarianism, Liberty and Representative Government*, London, Dent, 1910, page 342.
4. Thomas Hare, *A Treatise on the Election of Representatives, Parliamentary, Municipal*, London, Longman, 1859.
5. *Utilitarianism*, page 345.
6. For an excellent study of the different sides of Mill's character and thought see Gertrude Himmelfarb, *On Liberty and Liberalism: The Case of John Stuart Mill*, New York, Alfred Knopf, 1974. Also see Isaiah Berlin, 'John Stuart Mill and the Ends of Life', in *Four Essays on Liberty*, Oxford, Oxford University Press, 1969.
7. Rousseau, *Emile*, trans. Barbara Foxley, London, Dent, 1974, page 322.
8. Ibid., page 333.
9. Catherine Macaulay, *Letters on Education: With Observations on religious and Metaphysical Subjects*, New York, Garland Publications, 1974. See Natalie Davis and Arlette Farge, eds., *A History of Women in the West: Vol. III: Renaissance and Enlightenment Paradoxes*, Cambridge, Mass., Belknap, 1993 and Miriam B. Krammick's Introduction to Mary Wollstoncraft, *Vinidication of the Rights of Woman*, [1792] Harmondsworth, Penguin, 1985.
10. See Lea Campos Boralevi, *Bentham and the Oppressed*, Berlin, De Gruyter, 1984, ch. 2.
11. Thomas Hill Green, *T. H. Green Lectures on the Principles of Political Obligation, and Other Writings*, Paul Harris and John Morrow, eds., Cambridge, Cambridge University Press, 1986.
12. 'Etat social et politique de la France depuis 1789 or Political Science and Social Conditions of France', pages 165-66, *London and Westminster Review*, April 1836.
13. Joseph Chamberlain and others, *The Radical Programme*, [1885] with 'The Future of the Radical Party', by T. S. Escott, D. A. Hamer, ed., Brighton, Harvestor Press, 1971.
14. Leonard Trelawney Hobhouse, *Liberalism and Other Writings*, James Meadowcroft, ed., Cambridge, Cambridge University Press, 1994.
15. Jean Jacques Rousseau, *A Discourse on Inequality*, trans. Maurice

Cranston, Harmondsworth, Penguin, 1984.
16. Thomas More, *Utopia*, trans. Paul Turner, Harmondsworth, Penguin, 1961, page 130.
17. For a useful anthology of socialist thought see *Socialist Thought: A Documentary History*, Albert Fried and Ronald Sanders, eds., New York, Double Day, 1964. In this section, unless otherwise stated all citations from the utopian socialists will come from this anthology.
18. Fried and Sanders, *ibid.*, also Babeuf, 'Manifesto of Equals', trans S. Lukes in *The Good Society*, A. Arblaster and S. Lukes, eds., London, Methuen, 1971.
19. Fried and Sanders, *op. cit.*, also Henri Saint-Simon, *The Political Thought of Saint-Simon*, Ghita Ionescu, ed., Oxford, Oxford University Press, 1976.
20. Pierre-Joseph Proudhon, *What is Property*, ch. 5, in Fried and Sanders, page 223. Also *What is Property?* ed. and tr. Donald Kelley and Bonnie Smith, Cambridge, Cambridge University Press, 1994. For a very useful selection of lesser known French socialists see Paul Corcoran, *Before Marx: Socialism and Communism 1830-1848*, London, MacMillan, 1983.
21. Sidney Webb, 'English Progress Towards Social Democracy', *Fabian Tract No 15*, London, The Fabian Society, 1893.
22 See David Caute, *The Fellow-Travellers: intellectual friends of communism*, rev. ed., New Haven, Yale University Press, 1988.
23. Sidney and Beatrice Webb, *Soviet Communism: A New Civilisation*, 3rd ed., London, Longmans, Green, 1947.
24. Harold J. Laski, *Faith, Reason and Civilisation: An Essay in Historical Analysis*, London, Goolancz, 1944.
25. Manning Clark, *Meeting Soviet Man*, Sydney, Angus and Robertson, 1960. See also Canute, *op.cit.*
26. William E. Paterson and Ian Campbell, *Social Democracy in Post-war Europe*, London, Macmillan, 1974; J. Lauri Karvonen and Jan Sundberg, *Social Democracy in Transition: Northern, Southern and Eastern Europe*, Aldershot, Dartmouth, 1991.
27. Paterson and Campbell, *op. cit.*

11 The Mature Civilised State

> See him the gentle Bible beast,
> With lacquered hoofs and curling mane
>
> Edwin Muir, *The Toy Horse*

The beast of the mature state is strong, flexible, responsive, and even clever. The experience of social democracy has also left it with a capacity to have pity and to provide a minimum of living conditions for all its members. But the experience of social democracy also revealed that the energy of pity when taken too far tended to deplete the very civil society which contributed to material prosperity. The experience of communism also revealed what a terrifying beast the state can become if it is meant to rule and direct all aspects of our lives, if it takes on the task of engineering an ideal world. The beast is just that. It is never an abstraction, it is never free from defects, and it is never so thoroughly civilised that it can lose its claws or its roar. But it is also capable of civil, even gentle behaviour. The end of communism and social democracy in no way meant that the power of the state has been diminished. But it has been deprived of an overbearing paternalistic character. A mature society has, through on-going experience, learnt, and is still learning, how to let the beast serve the initiatives and socially accepted pursuits of a tolerant and vibrant civil society.

    The history of the state reveals that the journey to achieving this condition has been long and arduous. The recognition that there existed a wide range of political interests each of which had a legitimate claim to be heard was an important step, as was the defining of the three major functions of government and the need to keep them separate insofar as practicable. The extension of the suffrage to all adult men and women was a most significant step towards the fulfilment of that process. The demands for suffrage as well as a willingness to comply with those demands by those who already held political power, required a cultural respect for the values of equality and individual liberty. As we have seen, though, liberty and equality are frequently in tension with each other, and the accordance of equal political rights is not the equivalent of equal social conditions. The mature civilised state is not perfect. But it is the best form of state that has yet been attained, and its vitality and value stems from the way that it has been able to harness even (what would normally be seen as) negative characteristics, for positive purposes.

The Modern Liberal Democratic System

The political system of the mature state is a complex of interrelated institutions and associations. The virtue of the system lies precisely in the interrelationship between sites and modes of representation which ensure that the system balances the existing social forces, and yet provides constitutional durability. It is important that it not operate in a way that will preclude the emergence of new energies that will require political flexibility to accommodate them.

The most elementary act of representation occurs at the ballot box, where each citizen gets to choose from the candidates who have put their names forward for consideration, the most significant of which are likely to have been selected by the respective political parties competing for the office of government. That act may be based upon ignorance, it may be done without much thought or concern for the consequence, but although seemingly trivial it is a decisive act. For many of the voters, that is pretty well as much as they ever will do in the political process, indeed as much as they will even want to do. In some democratic states citizens do not even have to do that much, and often a large minority choose not to do that. In other states like Australia, however, there is a legal requirement that citizens at least turn up to the voting booths on election day.

It has always been the complaint of radical democrats that the weight given to the vote is farcical, and that real democracy means that people must participate in a more active way in the political process, and that it is both possible and desirable to extend democratic decision making to other spheres of life, including the administration of the state.[1] In making such criticisms, however, the radical democratic perspective reveals itself as being one-sided in the emphasis it places upon politics in the scheme of life and immature in its vision of democracy. Its one-sidedness stems from the fact that many of the most rewarding activities of life are not political, even though once people make the elementary error of conflating the social with the political everything becomes seen as political. Its immaturity stems from the fact that democracy is not *ipso facto* a good thing.

In the first place, the value of democratic decision making partly rests upon the quality of the intelligence and character of the demos. This was an important point recognised by Mill who, as we mentioned in an earlier chapter, not only espoused public education, but sought to find a way whereby the more experienced and educated people would have political advantages.

Secondly, democracy is not an end, but a means to action. All too often radical democrats defend democracy as if it were itself an end. It may well be the case, as Mill argued, that participation in political affairs energises people and thus a political system will benefit from a greater number of energies being involved in the process. To that extent one might even say that there is a degree to which democracy may be seen as a political end and not just a means. But one must be careful here. Those who become energised through the process of participation are those who want to be in it. Even in the most elementary participatory democratic forums, such as committees, the amount of time and energy expended on a project varies between people and is often no more than a function of the value which they place on such activities. The energetic and capable golf club secretary may become in another context the tyrannical chief executive of the local council.

There is also the inevitable tendency first grasped by Plato in his observation of the democratic assemblies and then presented as a social scientific law by Robert Michels in his study of modern political parties: that the rule of the many invariably becomes oligarchic in character. Michels's *Political Parties* was a work based upon a study of social democratic parties, particularly the German Social Democratic Party.[2] Michels saw that even the social democratic parties who were ideologically committed to participatory democracy were not exempt from this transference of power from the mass to an elite. Michels' insight into the inevitable oligarchicisation of the democratic process is partly explicable, as it was to him, by the fact that the majority of people want, even need leadership, and partly because there is simply a technical problem in the co-ordination of large numbers who would want to put information into the system and place pressures on the decision making system. The idea that all people can have a regular input into all aspects of social existence is fantastical because it defies the possibility of co-ordination. This would be as much of a problem if everyone was a genius devoted to probing the common good, as it is in a society where the common good is itself a hotly contested issue, and the understanding of the means to achieve widely held and differing ends crosses the spectrum of intelligence.

In addition, there is a problem about the incommensurability of values and desires, as well as the hiatus between the particular good and the common good, between private vices and public vices, between private virtues and public virtues. Such incommensurabilities are simply built into the woof and warp of social life and they do not become less real through democratic participation. Consider, for example some of the ends advocated by the more radical wing of the democratic Left: higher living standards, anti-development (usually now called sustainable development), egalitarian distribution patterns, available work for everyone who wants it, maternal and paternal leave from work, provision of state funded child care, public health and education, democratic participation in the work-force, people performing productive work without regard to the profit motive. These aims are either self contradictory, or if achieved would bankrupt the society concerned.

Or, to take some of the ends advocated by the more conservative wing of the political spectrum: private initiative and private acquisitiveness, preservation of religion, and the maintenance of the traditional family. In the modern conservative party the aims of the market economy, with its continuing and indeed accelerating process of technological, economic and therefore social change, sit ill with the simultaneous desire for a stable social environment.

In both these cases of the Left and the Right, the ends are in tension with each other. Provision of high living standards will be seriously effected by a reduction in profit rates which can easily be effected by the higher tax levels needed to fund public welfare or the environmental protection programs which prevent mining exploration. On the other hand, the inculcation of a culture based upon private contracts and personal acquisitiveness tends to erode religious beliefs, and churches have been emptying everywhere in the Western world with the onset of the civilised state. The modern family structure has been drastically effected by the lack of preparedness of people to stick to life-long commitments, as legislation has been passed recognising the rights of individuals to divorce in effect at will. The corollary of this of course has been that fewer of them marry in the first place. When a Newt Gingrich or Bob Dole advocate the rejuvenation of family values their own lives bespeak the contradiction between the ideals and the social reality which they are involved in.

These incommensurabilities stem from the nature of the processes which are constitutive of modernity and will not be ameliorated by more people participating to a greater extent in the democratic process.

This should not be taken to mean that the desires of the people are not represented in the mature state. On the contrary, the apparent passivity derives not from the impotence of the mass electorate but from its institutional empowerment. Just as the state has legitimised interests and integrated their expression as political parties, so in its mature form it has devised ever more sophisticated mechanisms for divining the electorate's wishes in the form of the industry of politics with its opinion polls, group reviews and other ever refined means for testing the government's popularity and the likelihood of its holding office.

It is only the radical democrat armed with the belief that people hold political values above all others who can believe in the virtues of interminable political gatherings. Most people, however, believe to the contrary that politics is a means to an end, and while that end - decent progress - is being achieved, the process of government can be best left to those elected for the task, for the time being. The lack of deep emotional involvement by most of the electorate in mature states in the electoral process, so far, then, from being a sign of their lack of interest in that process, is indication of their satisfaction in the capability of the mature political system to represent their interests within the parameters established.

Insofar as the ballot box is the one area of political life in which all citizens have the opportunity, and in some states the duty to make a political decision, its importance in the political scheme of the mature modern state cannot be underestimated. The voter *qua* voter does not have a daily input into the policies formulated by parties, but the voter must find the package of policies as presented by the parties acceptable. The role of the voter in the mature state is to act as the final unit of acceptability. However while the voter may think he or she is voting for a particular program, the object of the party is first and foremost to gain political power in a legitimate manner, and only secondarily to carry through a package of specific policies. The package offered invariably is a gamble based upon what the party thinks is the best compromise between the interests of its supporters and the majority of the electorate.

The delivery of the election platform then becomes a compromise with a number of factors, such as public opinion, the composition of the parliamentary houses, the constitution and the social, cultural and economic imperatives of growth and cohesion. It is rare that a government can deliver the policies that it presents to the public at election time. Gough Whitlam, Australian Prime Minister 1972-75, was one of the very few political leaders to have consciously ticked off the items in his party's winning election program as each was achieved, in the hope of delivering the entire package. And that was a quarter of a century ago.[3]

It may sound cynical or even nihilistic to say that the public knows that it is being lied to in every run up to an election, but the voter accepts this in the comfort that if the lies are too irritating then he or she can choose from the alternative package of mendacities. The voter knows that she or he is a unit of potential negation, that his or her power lies in being able to vote against the incumbent. It is precisely this capacity to facilitate the rotation of leadership which is one of the greatest strengths of the liberal-democratic system. The advantage of being able to rotate governments without bloodshed is a high point of civilisation. Indeed in mature states this is so taken for granted that the electorate turns out governments, even when they are doing well, *pour encourager les autres*.

Governments can be deprived of their power, programs dismantled, large sectors of the population lose their privileges, even their livelihoods, and no one is shot or tortured. Locke's equation of popular sovereignty with the right of revolution may be seen as a dangerous doctrine in illiberal societies, but it expresses the belief in the right of the power of the people to ensure its representatives do not subject them to conditions which they do not have to accept. In the mature state revolution is unnecessary not, as some radical democrats have suggested, because people have been ideologically repressed but because the institutions surrounding them are open to their in-put at a number of levels. Bloodless defeat and the willingness to surrender power because of a faith in the system of government, rather than in any particular governors, is the norm of civilised democracies. In a mature democratic state - and liberal democracy is the *only* mature form of the state - the vote is the synthesis of the principles of sovereign order and individualist disorder. The voting public are only sovereign for an instant, but that instant is the point of ultimate decision which will probably determine the nation's fate - or more accurately some part of it - until the next election.

The one overriding exception to this is the constitution. The constitution, whether it be written or unwritten also has sovereign status insofar as it delimits the power of the voting population and the representatives they choose. In an election the voter participates in the sovereign power and then enables sovereign power to be shared between the head of state, which executes sovereignty in its particularities, and the constitution which is the stabilising link between present, past and future. But the individual voter also has the power at the time of election to negate the executor of sovereignty. In any case there are limits on the authority of the head of state.

In some states executive sovereignty is shared between the leader of the party holding government and a representative of the crown appointed by the head of the state, such as Australia; in others the head of state and head of the executive are one and the same person, as in the United States; in others again the Head of State, the

President, is elected separately from and may be in opposition to the head of the parliamentary government, as in France. In the former instance the crown's representative is with a few exceptions a ceremonial figure. Whether the head of state be monarchical, presidential or a governor general is a matter of little importance in a mature state. What matters is that the head of state is, as Hegel correctly claimed in the *Philosophy of Right*, the symbolic point of state unity. Sovereignty then has a unifying point when grasped at that level of symbolism.[4]

On the other hand, when one refers to the sovereignty of the people in the mature state one is referring to two aspects of the people. One is the voter's right to express a preference between parties and thus to have the opportunity to endorse a program which is seen as representing him or her, or what he/she conceives as in the nation's interests or, although they are invariably the same, what he/she conceives of as being in his or her interests. The other is the constitutional protection of rights, whether written and codified or unwritten and deriving from customary practise is irrelevant. The voter then is not forced to conform to any general will in selecting policy - the general will is, in this instance, a constitutional foundation and not a policy matter. The voter can be as selfish as he or she wants in choosing the party of his or her choice, precisely because the voter is one of many and there are constitutional limits on the implementation of political selfishness.

Another important feature of mature states is the level of information and education that is available to the voting public. By and large all voters, unless they come from a substantially disadvantaged minority, and these continue to exist in many civilised states, and/or an extremely dysfunctional personal background, have the opportunity to attain a high level of education. In such civilised countries literacy is almost universal. Citizens are also surrounded by all manner of information if they but put in a little effort to such activities as reading books, papers or keeping abreast with current events as reported on the radio or TV. The information age has expanded these opportunities exponentially. There is no excuse for a voter being ignorant, other than the voter's own laziness. Still that does not stop some academicians from claiming that there is a giant conspiracy to keep the population ignorant, when in fact there is not only no such conspiracy but the person writing such nonsense has often been lucky enough, in a commercial society governed by a mature state, not only to say what he or she wants but to find employment, often in a state funded institution.[5]

A mature state is open to the flow of all manner of points of view no matter how out of kilter with reality, because it is strong enough to contain internal contestation and tensionality. Dictatorships exist where social forces and social patterns are fragile, where civil society is weak, where civility toward opponents has not been culturally imbibed, and where people have not learnt to benefit from tensionality. In a civilised society benefits accrue in paradoxical ways through the virtue of tolerance. Thus, for example, a book seller or publisher may stock or publish many books which he or she thinks are complete nonsense, even vile nonsense, but nevertheless receive financial benefits from the enemy. To the moralising mind this is awful. But the moralising mind is rarely, at least when it comes to politics, able to live beyond the contradictions it is involved in, nor to admit its own complicity in its contradictions.

In fact, a major virtue of maturity is a large degree of acceptance. It is not the nonsensical belief that all values are of equal merit. On the contrary, maturity requires heightened judgement and prudent discrimination, discernment between what should be buried and what should have a future. Without it, one's accumulated life's experiences cannot be passed on, to facilitate orientation in the world to the young and immature. But once social life is not solely about self-preservation, and institutions are robust enough to endure those whose views would, under other less hospitable conditions, be a matter of dangerous consequence, then it is a matter of public benefit that people become more knowledgeable as they learn for themselves, and that means by working through their own mistakes.

Widespread access to information and high levels of education, then, are of fundamental importance to the mature state. Where they are lacking a state simply will not be able to be mature. It is not so much that the voters in the mature state are particularly smart, since education and intelligence and smart decisions are not synonymous. But mature states are more ready to tolerate behaviours and attitudes which can be offensive and even subversive for more primitive and dictatorial regimes. A large reason for this spirit of tolerance is that in a mature society people are able to make more social choices. Further, they often have to make them and live with the consequences. The virtue of tolerance is not merely an idea, or rather its social embeddedness was not readily adopted because people woke up one day and felt it was a great idea. It only became embedded into the culture after long and protracted religious, social and political struggles.

There is no mature state which has not inherited a system in which political power is diffuse. The precise form of that diffusion may vary between states, but that depends upon the particular historical forces a state has had to deal with as new institutions arise. As we saw in our survey of the history of state theory, the story of the expansion of the franchise commences after the separation or balance of political powers has already become a reality. The story of diffusion, though, is also usually a continuing story of the struggle between powers. In a federal system, for example, states and the federal government are frequently vying with each other over who has the right to do what as each is pressured into satisfying demands of different constituencies. This tends to create a greater space for liberty. Likewise the House of Representatives frequently finds itself in struggles for power with the House of legislative review, especially when the Houses have different parties in the majority. The House of Representatives will frequently see the upper House as a thorn in its side. In some cases, as in Australia, or other federal systems like the United States, there may be a tension in the upper house between two contradictory grounds of legitimacy. On the one hand the Senate may be more genuinely representative of the people in so far as the voting system provides fairer representation of the different choices made by the voters due to proportional representation; on the other hand it may be constituted along federal lines so that it may provide very disproportionate but appropriate geographical representation.[6]

When the government does not have the majority in the House of review it invariably feels frustrated. An Australian Prime Minister, Paul Keating, when referring to the Senate once spoke of 'that unrepresentative swill on the hill,' neglecting to mention that nearly half of the 'swill' came from his own party. Where the House of review is hereditary as in Britain or even appointed as in Canada, it can be argued that this is anachronistic in a democratic society. But just because its membership is not strictly based upon democratic mechanisms does not mean the actions of a particular organ of government may not function in a democratic manner. The House of review (Lords) in England, for example, can serve to express public concerns about legislation, and the House may be more responsive to the most current expressions of public concerns than the Commons. The Prime Minister, though, knows that the greater source of power lies in the House where legislation is normally initiated and that if an issue is considered significant enough, legislation may get through by calling a joint sitting, or what ever other mechanism the constitution provides for resolving a deadlock. [7]

A tension that is common in those mature states which have a written constitution, as do most of them, is between the judicial interpreters of the constitution and the legislator. The judicial interpretation is able to check legislation when a case comes before it which revolves around the constitutionality of its provisions. Invariably, this process also provides for re-interpretations which amount to revisions or rewritings of the constitution itself in keeping with evolving social mores, or rather the constitutional judges' views of those mores. Again, the legislative house may feel itself constrained by the judiciary, but it is precisely that constrainment which enables a greater degree of discussion, deliberation, reflection and ultimately protection of different rights, particularly the rights of a minority. Protection of the political rights of the minority is one of the greatest benefits of the mature state. As the American federalist authors grasped, the value of a judiciary lies in the 'aristocratic' role it plays in statecraft as it interprets policy in accordance with the spirit and letter of the evolving skeleton of the political process itself.

The fact that there is tension between the respective sites of government is of great social benefit. Usually, political actors and their supporters are inclined to see tension as a negative, and the opposition as the enemy. But a tension which does not lead to the system snapping is the best way for social energies to be productive. A strong parliamentary opposition, a critical House of review, an astute judiciary, (in a federal system) a strong sense of state rights, a critical and investigative media, and a volatile public with persons prepared to pursue their rights in the highest courts of the land are the hallmarks of a healthy political system. The great fallacy of idealist political thought, and of the Left and the authoritarian style of conservatives is the belief that conflict is bad. Conflict is merely energy and pull. As Nietzsche taught, that which does not kill you makes you stronger.

All real creation involves tension, the overcoming of the resistances of the settled and the 'normal'. Even when the 'normal' is rotten, it represents that to which a section of the population has grown accustomed. In the mature state that energy is circulated through institutions, each with their social function delimited and each with a historical, hence real, connection to the society. The test of the strength of reforms and policies is, in the first instance, in the resistances that they can overcome. It is much better for the society that those resistances are first articulated within the respective sites of their representation, than merely tried out as a giant social experiment on the population as a whole. The idea that political freedom can be divorced from institutional channelling is the great deception of radical democrats, a deception that invariably has been used to entrench dictatorships.

In mature states political and judicial offices are frequently occupied by hypocrites, dolts and hacks, by people with drinking problems, mean spirits, poor judgements, gullibility, indeed the entire range of human weaknesses, but all these weaknesses are less important than the solidity of the institutions in which all the deficiencies of human character will enter and people thrash out the policies of the future. It is where institutions are least stable that charismatic leadership is most important, and where institutions are best formed that individual office holders are least important. For such charisma is a form of compensation for the weakness that exists within the social fabric as a whole. America can afford to have presidents with memory loss or relatively low moral or intellectual qualities precisely because the office is stabilised and directed by far greater forces than one man.

In a mature state the continued accommodation of tensionality not only characterises political institutions, but it characterises society. A mature society is not stable because it is classless or because everyone shares the same interests or the same conception of the common good. Its stability comes through the way in which conflict is politicised. The party system originally arose to represent specific interests within an aristocratic but representative system in eighteenth century England. In most liberal democratic states outside of America (and even there but to a less obvious extent), by the twentieth century that took the form of labour versus capital and wealth. There was, however, always a substantial minority of working class people who voted for the party that was supposed to be working for its enemy. What Marxists most hated about the democratic states was that they had managed to stabilise conflict between classes, and it became increasingly clear that the interests between classes was not always mutually exclusive. Indeed, some of the most important social goals, such as high living standards could not be achieved simply through political kow-towing to militant party supporters.

Further, the concept of class easily glossed over even more significant differences in interests between groups. Some workers and some manufacturers, for example, have a vested interest in governments pursuing protectionist policies, others in free-trade. Some workers stand to benefit (and others to lose) from closed union shops which guarantee higher wage levels than would be granted under more open market conditions; so do some firms which are able to afford to pay higher wages and thus remain un-threatened by leaner competitors; other people remain unemployed because of artificially high labour costs imposed by state regulation. Political parties thus can never remain merely representatives of class interests, largely because interests cut in all manner of other ways. Only in the mind of academic Marxists and communists (and the rhetoric of ambitious politicians) who forbid real political differences within the working class does a phrase like 'working class interests' make any sense at all.[8]

In addition, other interests besides socio-economic ones are an intrinsic part of the political process. Issues such as race relations, immigration, (in some countries) treatment of indigenous peoples, abortion, censorship, foreign policy, the environment, women's entrance into the workforce, changing attitudes to the family, and the distribution of resources between young and old, healthy and sick, are areas of social strain that can not be neatly demarcated along the lines of social class. In a mature state the way that these issues are handled is through a conglomeration of interests and lobby groups, the media, in some cases individual consciences of the politicians, and political parties trying to gauge what to choose for electoral purposes. In a mature state, people become conscious of opportunities, partly because of the greater prosperity generated in these states and partly because people know that they can involve themselves in the political consideration of these issues and make a difference to the outcome.

It is at the level of the struggles of interests expressed through pressure and lobby groups and non-governmental organisations where the radical democratic vision retains its relevance. The interests articulated in the struggle between these groups is invariably partial. Groups have to lobby in the first place because there is not a general will about most areas of policy, just as there is a great deal of diversity about life style options. Again, there is a connection between levels of abundance and diversity of interests. This is not a bad thing, but it strains cohesion. That cohesion will only be returnable through the durability of the underlying stabilising institutions. At the same time a society can never be complacent about the mores which dominate its institutions.

It was the Italian Marxist Gramsci who most clearly articulated the strategy for the destruction of the more durable liberal-democratic societies by emphasising the role of the intellectuals in occupying strategic sites of cultural and social reproduction.[9] In the mature state an intelligentsia becomes integral to the transmission of cultural and social values, as an elite to manage the cultural industry, and as administrators with special technical information and competencies. It is not surprising that the universities thus become the breeding ground for ideas stemming from particular interests and that in casting what is a program of partial interests in the language of broader groups, as if there were such a thing as minority interests, or gay interests, or women's interests, or black interests, or white interests, or white middle class interests.[10]

The intellectual advocates of such 'identity politics' may well facilitate the shaping of some government policies, and certainly play a role in coining the language of the culture, which is no small thing, as well as in changing the curricula imposed on the young at school. In all these respects, there is a serious danger of the intelligentsia helping to foster barbarism. Radicals and conservatives are both convinced that each side is barbaric - socialism or barbarism was once the formulation of Marxists as the choice for intellectuals - and the radical thought coming out of universities today frequently supports futureless barbarism.

Nonetheless, in a mature state it is healthy to present a broad array of ideas, to have the public witness the folly of the intelligentsia, to let it know that a philosopher such as Martin Heidegger was a Nazi; that a Paul de Man, a leading theorist of a major movement in literary criticism, deconstructionism, had kept his fascist past from his adoring public; and that a number of this century's most prestigious thinkers in fields of philosophy, law and literature supported communist regimes. But it is just as valuable for the public to learn about the violence defended by conservatives: the CIA's support of Pinochet in Chile; the attempts to assassinate Fidel Castro; the assassination program Operation Phoenix in Vietnam; and the Contragate deception. By vigorous and public debate the public can reach its conclusions about if, when, where and how political murder and violence is necessary, desirable, or tolerable. The mature state thus may benefit from information which one or other political wing is unlikely to disclose. The Left usually said nothing about the Soviet satellite states; conservatives tended to remain silent on dictatorial brutalities in Latin America. In the post-Cold War world it may be possible to combine around a civil rights program, although even here there are differences of nuance.[11]

There is always a danger within liberal society that it remains ignorant of and thus becomes complacent about the more brutal conditions of its existence - its history, its geo-political situation, the necessity of and narrow options in dealing with its enemies. Carl Schmitt was largely correct in seeing that speech is the paradigm of the political in liberal societies. Where speech can provide the best solutions to problems that is a good thing, and this often holds in such domestic societies. And the virtue of the mature liberal democratic state is that it creates an increasing number of pools of speakers, in the sense of vocal proponents of interests, as more and more groups are able to enter into the process of articulating their interests. But while the civilised state is still surrounded by barbaric states it is invaluable for the interests which wish to erode civil society and civilisation to be made public. Values in a community are easily taken for granted, and may be lost sight of amidst the clamour of ideas and the pursuit of individual interests.

The mud fights of the intellectuals provide a valuable role in keeping the public aware of its power and its desires. Public policies initiated in the various sites of social reproduction by some groups may cause public anger at what is happening. But public anger and frustration can be invaluable energies for protecting values. Through the conflict of ideas it is hoped that the best values will be distilled. A political system, which is built upon the representation of interests, is to some extent dependent upon character, but not so much of the particular people who occupy the highest political offices, as of the people spread through the whole strata of society. These are the best reason for keeping radical school-teachers and tenured university lecturers who want to tear down existing society and replace it with their imaginings.

One real danger contained in the very toleration of a mature, modern liberal-democratic society is, as critics and apologists alike recognise, nihilism. The paradox of the mature society is its simultaneous delivery of the highest production and broadest spread of material benefits to humanity, together with a significant lack of intellectual and spiritual faith in the virtues of civilisation. This partly comes from no longer having to fight for what previous generations had to and accepting the freedoms delivered as the natural order of things. They are not.[12]

The Annual Budget

Each year in the mature state the Treasurer, Chancellor or Minister for Finance introduces the annual budget which is a financial statement of what the state intends to do with the economy and civil society over which it presides. This document's projections may prove to be inaccurate, but it is in fact usually correct to within a percent in its forecasts which for a social science is remarkably good. Not only does the document reveal the state's ambitions with respect to deflating or stimulating the economy and other measures of aggregate demand, it also shows the prevailing community attitude towards the disposition of resources, which is another way of testing the community's attitude towards political priorities. It also reveals the way in which the revenue will be raised to pay for such programs.

These annual budgets vary considerably in the proportion of the Gross National Product they consume. Among the Organisation for Economic Cooperation and Development (OECD) countries, which generally means the civilised states, this varies from the low zone in North America, Australia, New Zealand and Japan, whose governments take about thirty per cent of the GNP, and the European Union states, who were much deeper involved in the fiscal social democratic movement, where the equivalent measure is between about sixty percent in the nearly bankrupt Sweden and forty percent in Britain, even after eighteen years of Tory rule. Some of these figures reflect different structures of states with federal tiers sometimes concealing quite substantial expenditures by more local authorities, although much of their revenue is often in fact collected by the central government. In South Australia, for example, the state government receives about sixty per cent of its revenue from the Federal government and carries a debt half as big again as its annual budget.

Perhaps even more significant are two other features: the budget priorities usually only change marginally when there is a change in administration, implying an underlying political consensus; and there is a certain commonality in expenditure patterns between the OECD states which suggests an emergent consensus among them on priorities. While it is true that newspapers will headline dramatic changes in taxation or expenditure patterns these are rarely more than at the margin unless the state has encountered a fundamental crisis that it must confront. This happened in Britain at the end of the 1970s when a trade union dominated government was not able to reinvigorate the British economy and the Thatcher led Tories introduced a painful readjustment towards commercial values. It also happened in New Zealand after the British joined the European Union in 1973 and started to close its most important market. At first the Nationalists (conservatives) under Piggy Muldoon refused to adjust and instead borrowed externally to meet the blossoming trade deficit. The Labour government led by David Lange after 1984 began a Thatcherite readjustment and eventually it and its reforming successors fixed the economic difficulty at great social cost. These were two governments which really did alter budget priorities.

Most governments fiddle at the margin with budgets. Even the Hawke government in Australia that faced similar problems to Britain and certainly New Zealand chose to go slowly after its election in 1983. This was no doubt partly because the country possessed a considerable buffer to its currency in the form of extensive natural resources. It did turn the country more slowly than its trans Tasman counterpart and indeed in its final years, after Paul Keating replaced Hawke as Prime Minister, there may be some doubt as to whether any further turning was done at all.[13] It was then left to the incoming Liberal-National Party coalition to try to alleviate the trade deficit by a tighter fiscal policy.

More commonly budget structures differ only marginally from one administration to another and the political consensus may be divined from the budget structure. The items that don't change much over time like infrastructure expenditure on roads, power generation, the justice system, the defence forces and other core business, represent the social consensus. Areas where change is rapid after an election changes a government or sends the surviving one a message about its behaviour, represent the party political, contentious or strengthened interests which have just won greater ascendancy. After Ronald Reagan's election in 1980 and his assuming office in 1981 for example, defence expenditure increased markedly and taxes on companies declined, to the cost of American solvency. Twelve years later Bill Clinton tried to direct resources away from the military, with some success, and towards welfare, with more caution since he was advised it would damage the economy.[14]

The annual budget is a good scorecard for revealing: the longer term objectives of the state; the priority it accords different interests, as opposed to their value in other states and compared with previous administrations; and the changing priorities over the recent past and immediate future. The budget papers always require close scrutiny, which of course they get in the media of all civilised states.

The Profession of Politics

'Politics is perhaps the only profession for which no preparation is thought necessary'.[15]

Democratic and representational theory rests ultimately on the role played by the representatives of interests and of the people. Much is said in the classical literature about the qualities that these people should and might possess. Little was said about their profession. This was understandable since for most of human history there were so few of them that their life form could be only the subject of speculation or idealist thought. True, many of the political philosophers who have been described so far have participated in the political process and some, including Mill and de Tocqueville, have been democratic politicians. Nonetheless they did not at that time represent a widespread occupation. There are now many democratic states and many politicians within them. Much more can be said about them.

In the late twentieth century politics has become a profession similar to the law, the stage, the screen or journalism. The major difference is the longevity of careers. In a mature democracy the life of a politician is precarious and the electorate fickle. Most states in fact try to offset this by making the rewards in terms of salaries and pensions substantial to attract people to an otherwise unrewarding life. The material rewards are never enough for the incumbent politicians, however, who spend much of their energies trying either to increase them for all by a pay rise or for themselves by promotion up the greasy pole of a political career. The decline of the idealist position - social democracy - has coincided with the instability of political life to produce a profession of non-ideological self interested careerists whose *leitmotiv* is best contained in the politician's greeting: 'Hello', he lied.

Most people become involved in the process of political life today because a particular issue or cause excites their passions and they wish to do something about it. They are in a word, idealistic. This leads them to join a protest group against a storm water drain, mobile telephone aerial or a war. From there one can proceed to protest the behaviour or lack of behaviour of the state, to approach politicians and be attracted by the possibility of wielding their power over the issue concerned, and others, on a regular basis. Other people again get involved in politics because it is the family business. While the traits of guile, conceit and deception may not be hereditary, the easy mastery of them is more apparent in the practitioner's family, the rewards more evident and the paths to power more accessible. These entrants are never idealist and have become prominently numerous. Joseph Kennedy bought the Presidency for one of his sons. Many Asian countries have powerful political families from which otherwise unpowerful women may acquire power, like Indira Gandhi or Corino Aquino. The continuing incidence of political families suggests that even in democracies blood remains thicker than both water and ideology.

To rise beyond the very first grip on the greasy pole - the nomination for election to office - the politician must abandon almost all principle and become the conduit of the political power which he/she seeks to both represent and acquire. There comes a moment in every political career, and the earlier it comes the better it serves, when the aspirant must choose between those values which he previously cherished and those he must represent. For the individual and his friends and family this appears as a crisis of conscience and a test of fealty. For the process of democracy it is, rather, an examination of the person's fitness to represent the people's as opposed to his own personal will. An excessive ego will impair the process of representation; insufficient determination will inhibit pursuit of the peoples' interest. The politician walks a fine path between self interest and greed. Greed often triumphs, particularly when it is clear that further progress up the greasy pole is no longer possible and it is time to seize all assets within grasp and flee.

In pursuit of the common desire and interest - which the politician must successfully fuse - and his own ambitions and career, which have now successfully transcended whatever issues of principle first launched him on the eventful trajectory, the politician joins others placed in a similar quandary in a political party. These entities usually have their origin in interests formed in civil society. These may be based on any number of interests shared by citizens, including social class, regional matters, environmental concerns, lifeform desires, ideological preoccupations, income enhancement or gender allegations. These are then fashioned into alliances of interests that are sufficiently broad to permit the creation of a political party large enough to acquire representation in the political process.

The coalition of interests required for this purpose will vary from place to place and time to time. One important determinant will be the constitution of the state itself. In a system of voluntary voting, first past the post, single member electorates, as is used in the British or US lower houses, a two party system is favoured and with it the broadest coalition is required. Although, even in Britain, it is often overlooked that as many as nine political parties may be represented in the Commons at one time. Where some method of proportional representation is used smaller coalitions of interest are necessary. For the politician the first system favours more anonymity since it is the political machine which is pre-eminent, the second flamboyant pursuit of interest based voters since smaller numbers are required. In general, the larger the constituency the greater the importance of the party machine.

It is within the political party that political platforms, or coalitions of interest based policies, for the distribution of state allocated resources are forged. During the industrial period these were created on the basis of social class and voting soon became a class based activity. The political spectrum mirrored the distribution of income within the civil society as parties claimed to represent the different income and wealth segments which more or less measured social class and occupation. Since for the most part these classes also existed within geographic areas or suburbs, voting patterns and distributions followed these physical and social patterns. These party political spectrums were created on a Left to Right continuum which ranged from communist to fascist, although as we have seen these extremes shared certain *modus operandi*.

The Left to Right terminology derived from the early sittings of the Estates General in the French Revolutionary period when the more conservative sat to the Right of the presiding officer (King) and the more radical to the Left. During the nineteenth century the terminology was extended to incorporate attitudes towards socialism as a mode of economic activity and the development of public ownership of economic capital. By the twentieth century the usages of these terms were pretty well established and accurately reflected class biased voting and political activities. The Right stood for lower taxes less progressively imposed, a smaller state sector and the preservation of a civil society that had been organically created at great cost and whose disturbance could well herald disaster. The Left wanted higher taxes progressively imposed to fund expanded state activities, a larger public sector and the refashioning of a civil society that oozed inequality through its very pores.

Some political philosophers sought to disprove this spectrum by emphasising another vertical axis representing attitudes towards social control.[16] On this other continuum political organisation were more - communists and Fascists - or less - anarchists and conservatives - authoritarian in a manner woven across the Left-Right differences. While this proposition is not without substance the principal divide remained Right to Left.

During the social democratic phase of civilised states the extremes of the political spectrum were effectively eliminated. Although communist parties continued to exist they became social democratic in all but name by the 1980s and the fascists of Europe are little more than a nuisance, except perhaps in the eastern zone of Germany where the communist regime stunted the growth of modern politics.[17] In their place centrist parties of differing hues came to dominate the political process and homogenise the career of politics and deprive it of any ideological form. The politician now came to live within a professional career structure formed by the party and the state. From this development springs the politician's grasp of the fact that while the other parties may constitute the opposition, his real enemies are within his own party. His dependence on the people was diminished and his entombment in the party almost complete. Since this occurred at the same time as the party structures themselves were becoming in turn more dependent on the state, the politician became more of a state functionary and less of a representative of civil society.

This can be seen in number of ways. The modern politician is paid well by the state and gets some form of superannuation entitlement in recognition that this is his career. He has the attachments of a state functionary including an office, staff, machinery and travel provided by the state. In most countries the state also pays some portion of the costs of running election campaigns which have risen considerably into the information age, particularly of television. And because the politician is part state functionary and only part representative of the people's will, he is generally as a species hated by the people. This springs in part from his function of having to defend all the activities of state when his party is in office, in part from the collection of taxes from the people, some of which are used to finance a lifestyle which seems extravagant to them, and in part from the fact that politicians (whether male or female) are habitual liars.

The profession of politics necessarily involves the skill of lying well but not necessarily credibly since most of the people are aware when the politician is lying. The logic of his position requires that he do so. The most profound and obvious instance of this situation is when the politician is on the losing side in the party room. His career then requires not only that he publicly support his new party position with great enthusiasm but that if possible he appear as if he supported it all along. Further, he must think of all the good reasons for the new position over the one that he originally held. Finally, and best of all, he should try and persuade him of the validity of the new cause, the better to persuade others. There are also numerous other situations in which it is better for the politician to lie, including: putting a bad gloss on emerging good information if in opposition, and a good gloss on bad trends if in government; in promising to pursue an issue when lacking the time or inclination to so do; or in recommending a person for preferment when their only talent is a political done deal.

Nonetheless a politician must strive to be popular. They go about this in various ways depending on their own characteristics and those of that section of the people to whom they must appeal. Clearly politicians cannot change all their traits but a surprising number are malleable and can be altered in such a way as to sustain popular support, otherwise all politicians would look like and sound like the most popular media stars of their time, as they increasingly try to do of course. An entire industry is engaged in forming the public persona of the politician, matching it to the public mood, as measured by another specialised industry of opinion polling, and marrying this to those policies which are a combination of what good government would require and what the mob want. The modern politician has turned Machiavelli on his head and declared 'it is better to be loved than feared' as he tries to take his state to fiscal hell on a broomstick.

The principal check on the politician's natural desire to destroy the Treasury by distributing largesse and reducing taxes in order to retain office, a system once sanctioned by Keynesian economics, is the state apparatus. The political party, a partial agency of the state, intersects with the state apparatus proper in the minister's office. Here the political demands of the people are negotiated against the requirements of the state for its successful continuation. Such an office may be physically dispersed but combines the authoritative information and real policy options presented by the state bureaucracy, with the political imperatives of personal and party advancement expressed by the political operatives, and the presentational requirements embodied in the public relations personnel therein employed. Campaigning in arguably Russia's first seriously democratic Presidential election in the history of the country in 1996, Boris Yeltsin faced a large gap in the opinion polls that seemed impossible to traverse. Enmeshed in the logic of his situation he did exactly what generations of representative politicians elsewhere have done - he handed out state money to gain support and votes. He won the election by this much tested method, interestingly with the tacit support of the International Monetary Fund which presumably saw the communist party alternative as an even greater fiscal menace.[18]

The minister of state is then immediately responsible for the policy thereby determined to three major forums: the Parliament or Congress; the Cabinet; and to the media, or the people, who he can only reach by this method. Periodically he will also have to answer directly to the people in elections. The Parliamentary system is the more demanding on ministers. Most Parliaments derive their procedures from Westminster where the distance between government and opposition was determined by the length of a sword. During most of their sitting time such chambers are in fact empty when the formalities of debate are pursued to conclusions predetermined in the party rooms and between the managers of government and opposition business. They are occasionally enlivened by noteworthy speeches by a Churchill on the backbench, by an Enoch Powell trying to turn the immigration policy, or when a sacked former Cabinet Minister in revenge brought down Margaret Thatcher. But in the day to day business of a Parliamentary system Question Time is the stand out.

Question Time procedures vary but their essence is the requirement that ministers answer questions on their portfolio without notice. The minister is briefed by his office, the opposition spokesman by his office and the battle commences, often in the early afternoon. The Prime Minister is usually the dominant performer in this testing ritual and a government will often only last as long as he can sustain this dominance, a period often similar in duration to a TV sit-com program's stay at the top of the ratings - two to five years - and for the same reason: familiarity breeds contempt. This ensures a usually frequent turn around of other ministers who are sacrificed for government mistakes. This is also a good device for preventing the overpoliticisation of the state bureaucracy which ministers try to stack with cronies.

The Cabinet is the meeting of all ministers under the chair of head of government - President or Prime Minister - to determine strategy and co-ordinate policy. Ministers invariably hate one another, since they are in constant conflict over resource allocation, and the head of government, whose job they cherish and know they could do better. At Cabinet the spending plans of those who seek modern love by largesse on education, health, sport and other bread and circuses, are challenged by those who represent modern fear in the form of the financial discipline of the Treasury. The head of government cultivates the leadership traits of wisdom and power to which he must periodically, like Borgia, sacrifice a hated lieutenant.

The media is of course a permanent menace to the career of the democratic politician and the daily political news a result of the conflict between competing interests in presentation. The politician seeks the best presentation of whatever news he can claim credit for or escape from. The journalist wants either the politician's scalp, usually, or a highly paid job in his office, sometimes. The management of the media want to create profits which usually increase with circulation and audience since these are sold to advertisers wanting to market other commodities. The mutual contempt expressed by these three camps helps ensure there are no secrets in the modern civilised state. For most of the people most of the time their information about the state comes through the media and confirms their hatred of most politicians. Some, however, meet politicians in person.

Most politicians try very hard to meet many people and yet hate to do so. Meeting people usually incurs some requests or demands on the state that the politician must do something to acknowledge but takes time away from the principal task of self promotion within the party and rising the greasy pole. The way to deal with this is to cultivate the politician's personality with its easily delivered and exaggerated bonhomie of hand shakes and backslaps with plenty of flattery all round. Enough of this disguises but never fully conceals the deceit and deception which form the politician's art. The politician's life is arduous and he is the site where the public interest of civil society and the state's pursuit of order intersect. It is the most important job in the civilised state and on his fashioning of statecraft its future depends. For the insecurity engendered, the personality traits deformed, and the deceptions practised, it is difficult to envision how he could be paid too much.

The democratic system of politics is an extremely messy way of dealing with the myriad of competing interests thrown up by modern civil society which is no longer comprised of three or four obvious social categories like classes. But it does recognise that conflicts of political interest are a permanent feature of human existence and that the state should try to resolve them in a civilised and non-violent way. These conflicts will be formed around ever shifting interest coalitions as new issues and social categories form and then dissemble. The democratic politician is the historical and logical product of this process. He embodies many of the characteristics which Plato and other idealist and elitist theorists so roundly criticise in the mob orator they imagined would conquer a popular democracy. And yet those who ascend the greasy pole also acquire some of the functions of the guardians, including the responsibility of stopping the mob from devouring the state by excessive demands. But there are many checks on such a politician's power, including the power of other politicians with whom he is constantly in conflict, the separation of state functions and powers, and the derision of the people. And behind the politician's mask of confidence lies a face of anguish anticipating the next opinion poll and the bad career move that could accompany it.

The mature modern democratic state is run by such people. They are rarely very accomplished in any other sphere, despite the claims of their publicity agents which are sometimes taken seriously by the media. They rarely know too much about any specific subject but will be well informed across a broad range. They are usually shorter on principle than the general population of a civilised society but must make much more of it publicly. They are the embodiment of the great advantage which the democratic and civilised state has over all others: the capacity to mobilise the energies and animal spirits of a broader range of the population into the process of government. Such states are managed by ordinary human beings given for a short time the opportunity to undertake extraordinary tasks. And they do it better than the Platonist guardians have ever achieved.

Directing the Beast

The state comprises activities undertaken by many of the people who comprise the civil society which it embraces. In the mature civilised state many, if not most of the adult community participate to varying degrees in the activities of the state: in its politics, employed in its administration, recipient of its programs, contributor to its revenues or merely become a voter at its periodic elections. The state deploys around a third of society's resources and controls more.

Many states sit astride society. The mature state is integrated with civil society and seeks to mobilise its energies and stimulate its functioning. To this end it has developed organs that in fact represent aspects of all previous types of state and it has retained those which may at times serve its present purpose. Its executive remains sovereign in character; its judiciary retains its aristocratic features; the military is little different to the fascist state; it has intelligence agencies which may transgress its own laws; it has a large bureaucratic apparatus which operates on the basis of administrative efficiency; and it has representative and democratic features centred on the Parliament or Congress. But how does the state determine which weapon to deploy from its armoury?

The state operates in the same way as the living organisms of which it its comprised. It has a large range of experiences which it stores in its memory banks which are as diverse themselves as the codification of administrative procedure, the case book of the customary laws, the constitution, the platforms of the various political parties and the scribblings of the intelligentsia. These memory banks contain options for political action which are developed both by practice and the theory of the state functionaries who tend them, be they judges, bureaucrats, politicians, archivists, Hansard stenographers or academic historians. When the time for decision arises these records are provided for politicians to decide the appropriate course of action.

Does that mean the timorous, faltering dolts previously described decide the fate of mass communities? Of course not. Most of the decisions required by the state are not made by political choice but by administrative fiat, judicial deliberation or executive action. The democratic facet of the state is a minor one. Even in the event of the annual budget the overwhelming proportion of resources are deployed without consideration as part of the ongoing process of the fiscal state. Exceptionally a single Cabinet may redeploy more than two per cent of the total. Most resource allocation decisions are made by the living state in continuing session. The creation and structure of the processes that ensure that these decisions are consistent with the wills of the civil society are the subject of the rest of this book. They are acquired over time and those that survive are those which have worked; those that do not are jettisoned.

This changes somewhat when the state is confronted with an emergency - war, insurrection, terrorism or natural disaster. During the life of most of the civilised states since 1945 these have been rare but not entirely unknown. The British and Americans have experienced frequent wars outside their territories, some very unpopular with the people and exciting social protest; the French have faced such wars, near civil war in the late 1950s and internal insurrection in 1968; the British have had an internal rebellion in Northern Ireland and resulting terror campaigns in the main islands; the Americans had to deal with a quasi insurrection by African Americans after the assassination of Martin Luther King in 1968; the Japanese and Americans have had severely destructive earthquakes in the 1990s and Australia a cyclone in Darwin, 1974; Italy has faced terror from Red Brigades and organised crime; and even New Zealand faced mass civil disobedience during the South African rugby tour of 1971. The civilised state then invokes emergency powers.

The history of the state contains records of threats to its security and the menace they pose. It maintains agencies and procedures designed to deal with them. Components of the state may indeed be viewed as almost permanently in emergency session, such as those police that deal with organised crime and terrorists, the military and secret security services, the natural disaster agencies, the emergency health system, the customs detection service and parts of the armed forces. When the state is faced with a new and intensified emergency that is beyond the scope of day-to-day emergency management, it expands the scope of its emergency functions and powers. There is ample provision in most constitutional arrangements for such emergency actions which typically have to be declared, as in the case of the US, when confronted with 'a clear and present danger'. The mature civilised state then functions for a time or in certain areas or with respect to some functions as a dictatorship. This comprises the practical resolution to the problem Weimar Germany failed to resolve, and over which Carl Schmitt disgraced himself for all time.

The mature civilised state has not been created by a theory, although some of it is the product of some theories. It has not been designed to fulfil particular ideals, although some of it does just that. That state has not been created by rational argument, although some parts of it have and function on the basis of continuing rational discourse. The state has also not been maintained for the purpose of ensuring the domination of some over others, although aspects of its functioning may have this effect. The mature civilised state has been created by historical processes to serve the needs of particular civil societies and continues to adapt as those needs change. To that extent the logic of Spinoza and Hegel convinces: what exists is what has survived and is therefore rational.

Notes

1. For a recent example see the collection of essays in David Trend, ed., *Radical Democracy: Identity, Citizenship and the State*, New York, Routledge, 1996.
2. Robert Michels, *Political Parties: A Sociological Study of the Oligargichal Tendencies of Modern Democracy*, [1915] trans. Eden and Cesar Paul, introduction by Seymour Martin Lipsett, New York, Collier, 1962.
3. Graham Freudenberg, *A Certain Grandeur: Gough Whitlam in Politics*, South Melbourne, Macmillan, 1977.

4. Michael Fowler and Julie Marie Bunck, *Law, Power and the Sovereign State: the Evolution and the Application of the Concept of Sovereignty*, University Park, Pa, Pennslyvania State University Press, 1996.
5. Noam Chomsky and Edward Herman, *Manufacturing Consent*, New York, Pantheon, 1988, is the most well known exponent of this viewpoint.
6. Cheryl Saunders, *Representing the People: The Role of the Parliament in Australian Democracy*, Carlton, Melbourne, 1993.
7. Dean Jaensch, *Parliament, Parties and People: Australian Politics Today*, Melbourne, Longman Cheshire, 1994.
8. David Horowitz, *The Fate of Midas and Other Essays*, San Francisco, Ramparts Press, 1973, for an early New Left theorist now reneged, and Michael Parenti, *Democracy for the Few*, 3rd ed., New York, St Martins, 1982, for a later one.
9. A. Gramsci, *The Modern Prince and Other Writings*, New York, International Publishers, 1967.
10. For example, Theresa Ranger, Yunas Samad, Ossie Short, eds., *Culture, Identity and Politics: Ethnic Minorities in Britain*, Aldershot, Avebury, 1996; and Stanley Aronwitz, *The Politics of Identity: Class, Culture, Social Movements*, New York, Routledge, 1992.
11. Raymond Aron, *The Opium of the Intellectuals*, trans T. Kilmartin, London, Secker and Warburg, 1957.
12. Irving Kristol, *Neoconservatism: The Autobiography of an Idea*, New York, Free Press, 1995.
13. Bob Catley, *Globalising Australian Capitalism*, Cambridge, Cambridge University Press, 1996.
14. Bob Woodward, *The Agenda: Inside the Clinton White House*, New York, Simon and Schuster, 1994.
15. Robert Louis Stevenson, *Familiar Studies of Men and Books*, 15th ed., London, Chatto and Windus, 1900.
16. Hans J. Eysenck, *Psychology of Politics*, London, Routledge, Paul & Kegan, 1957.
17. Mary Filbvote, *Anatomy of a Dictatorship: Inside the GDR, 1949-89*, New York, Oxford University Press, 1996; Michael Schmitt, *The New*

Reich: Violent Extremism in Unified Germany and Beyond, trans. Daniel Hirch, London, Hutchinson, 1993.
18. Daniel Treisman, 'How Yeltsin Won', *Foreign Affairs*, September - October 1996.

12 The Behaviour of States in the International Arena

> The beast with many heads butts me away
>
> *Coriolanus*, IV I, 1.

Modern political ideologies usually contain a component that seeks to create peace. Those that don't are rare and include notably fascism, with its emphasis on the martial virtues of courage and sacrifice, and militarism. Communism also proved to be a militaristic ideology in practice partly because it always used military analogies so casually, partly because of its use of Machiavelli's ruthless logic with respect to political tactics, and partly because the states which it created were dictatorships - of the working class. Communist states typically spent twice the amount of equivalent non-communist states on their military forces, a figure too high to explain by any variable other than their internal structure. They have also been regularly engaged in war, often with each other. Abolishing capitalism certainly did not abolish the impulses within a state which makes it create a strong military machine and which drive it to war.

    Liberalism and social democracy theory have both had within them a number of different strands in pursuing the cause of peace. Liberals have tended to the idea that as states develop economically and hence become more democratic, wars will be rarer between them.[1] The establishment of free trade between states they believe, will aid this process. These ideas were strong in nineteenth century liberal English thought, particularly in the works of Richard Cobden and John Hobson.[2] Social democrats were influenced by Marxism and tended to the view that the power of business needed to be constrained within states and that international organisations should replace the anarchy of the society of states. Kant was particularly strong on the latter project in *Perpetual Peace* where he proposed the formation of the League of constitutional republics, a somewhat different idea to the United Nations of course which incorporates all manner of states. Some people sought to revive the idea in the 1990s by suggesting a league of democratic states either operating within,[3] or in place of a United Nations dominated by primitive states.[4] These ideals melded together in twentieth century American liberal thought, partly because Presidents Woodrow Wilson and Franklin Roosevelt jointly tried to put them there in place of the traditional US pursuit of isolationism from the affairs of Europe.

The twentieth century has been the first for nearly a millennium which has been dominated by international organisations - in fact two in the form of the League of Nations and the United Nations. It has also seen the creation of more democratic states than at any time in human history. Yet it has also witnessed the two most destructive wars in history, over two hundred smaller wars during the Cold War period, and even since the end of the Cold War wars have been continuously fought. Coral Bell estimates that around eighty were fought in the five years which followed the dissolution of the Soviet Union.[5] And the states which have been involved in most wars since 1945 have been arguably the largest of the liberal states, the USA, Britain and France. How may we reconcile the general march of progress in the civilised states with the continuation of what von Clausewitz called politics by other means? And does this mean that no progress has been made towards eliminating war?

Realist International Relations Theory

The behaviour of states towards one another and the community which they create among themselves is, on one plane, determined by the very nature of a state itself. The state embodies the legitimate monopoly of the use of force within its territory and the requisite use of force for the protection of its vital interests, including its state territory, strategic locations and trade routes, externally. This has been the basis for traditional realist theories of state behaviour that describe the foreign policies of states as the remorseless pursuit of self interest and power defined in terms of the traditional territorial industrial and agricultural state. Some of these characteristics remain.

In his classic realist textbook, *Politics Among Nations*, first edition 1948 and last in 1985, the most intellectually influential for a long generation of Anglo-American scholars, Hans J. Morgenthau enunciated six principles of political realism from which derived the conclusion that states will pursue power in order to enforce their interests. This unending pursuit of interest is driven by the nature of the human beings that make up and direct the state,[6] for as Machiavelli warned, if the *Prince* does not protect the interests of those in his care he will be replaced by others who will. In his classic and also very influential realist attack on idealism, *Man, the State and War*, first published in 1959, Kenneth Waltz argues that the idealists who seek to end war by changing Man, usually through education, the State, by abolishing whatever they perceive to be its warmaking impulses, or the society of states by institutionalisation, have failed because they misperceive the essential and unchangeable nature of these things.[7] Waltz later defended realism against the interdependence theorists, who argued that increasing international trade and communication would reduce the impulses to conflict. They were extremely influential early in the administration of President Jimmy Carter, and in *Theory of International Politics*, published in 1979, Waltz maintained his earlier position and to the same effect. Henry Kissinger was to make much of his early reputation in claiming that the liberal idealists had got the US involved in the Vietnam War, and then extending this claim into a realist's history of the international system in *Diplomacy*.[8]

What has been particularly interesting about the American realist school is that they both insist that the state will by its very nature pursue power to enforce its interests *and* then criticise American foreign policy for often not doing that. Both Morgenthau and Kissinger criticised the US war in Vietnam for *not being in US interests*. Waltz criticised the Carter administration foreign policy intellectuals for advancing interdependence *instead of state interests*. Both positions, surely, could not be correct. In fact they were. The United States was in the process of developing a liberal foreign policy for a civilised state. This involved a civilised foreign policy towards civilised states, a realist foreign policy towards other kinds of state, and the establishment of a new liberal order between states where this was possible.[9] The emergence of this form of diplomacy by a superpower perplexed the realists who were able to deal with it only by creating the special theoretical category of 'American exceptionalism' which of course their own intellectual architecture could not permit were it to survive.

The realists begin their approach to inter-state behaviour, and indeed to politics in general, with Thucydides' *History of the Peloponnesian War*, wherein clashes of interest lead to violent struggle and the author invents often *ex post facto* the arguments used in debates over policy from the logic of the circumstances, because it was always thus. This tradition became well known again in Western Europe at about the time of the creation of a new regional system of states, like that found in ancient Greece, in renaissance Italy. As we have seen Machiavelli developed on this tradition in the belief that the *Prince* had to behave ruthlessly to protect the interests of those in his charge. And indeed Thucydides himself was translated by Hobbes. In classic realist tradition he describes the society of states in *Leviathan* as a state of nature and the war of all against all. After Westphalia, even the modest constraints of a universal church, under challenge since the papal investiture controversy polarised Christian loyalties, were removed. For the next three hundred years the realist analysis remained generally accurate. The essence of the state, whether derived from human nature, its own security dilemmas or the anarchic way in which the system of states was organised, led to the pursuit of interests, conflict and war.

Of course during these three hundred years the internal constitution of many of the states changed substantially and in the direction we have been describing in this book, that is, progressively. What impact has this had on the international behaviour of states, if any?

In the first instance all the states were agricultural and the long history of realist thought sprang from observing the behaviour of such agricultural states. Their wealth, and that of the class or elite that ruled them and made their foreign policies, was derived chiefly from the land. Agricultural production was the main industry and employed most of the work force. The state was often little more than a military force occupying settled and worked agricultural land.

Understandably, much of the foreign policy of such states was concerned with acquiring more land to increase wealth, by force of arms if necessary. Since the ruling elite in such societies tended towards a martial disposition, known in Europe as chivalry but also found elsewhere in similar societies like the Ottoman empire and Japan - but not Imperial China where the bureaucrat ruled - the capture of territory in war was regarded as doubly virtuous.

This was starting to change in the seventeenth century after the states of Western Europe began to extend their competitive quest for additional resources throughout the littoral territories of the Atlantic Ocean. Trade and with it commercial capital became more important sources of state power. Portugal went further east around the Cape to India and beyond, and Spain further west linking the Philippines to Europe through Mexico. But the limits of their power were established by the limits of their populations and technology. As agricultural states the impact of the Europeans on the Asian land mass with its vast populations and Africa with its difficult terrain was restrained. This changed with industrialisation.

For while, as the realists claim, some aspects of state behaviour are unchanging, on another plane, states do tend to adjust their behaviour according to the level of progress they have achieved.[10] Many of the objectives which in the past civilised states could only achieve by use of the traditional tools of statecraft are either no longer achievable by those methods, or such methods are no longer acceptable to their electorates, or those objectives can be more easily achieved by other means. The first such change in the quality of state policy took place during the transition from agricultural and realist to industrial and imperial states.

Imperial Europe

As states progress from agriculture to commerce and then to industry so their material requirements expand quicker than their ability to expand production. Not only does output of industry expand rapidly but the population also grows quickly as a result of the demographic transition produced by improved health and hygiene. This often produces an expansionist foreign policy designed to acquire resources by the quickest manner, that is seizure. An internal society of oligarchy or dictatorship, quite common during this phase, may facilitate this. This redistribution of world territory and resources was most readily accomplished when the newly industrialising states faced agricultural states which had much to offer and little to defend themselves with. The result was a few centuries of commercial and then industrial imperialism. If the commercial phase was dominated by Portugal and Spain they were to be overtaken by the northern European states.

The industrial revolution in Britain created a state whose behaviour, while recognisable as being similar to that which went before, so changed qualitatively in terms of its relative power and appetite as to present a new overall style of foreign policy. During the industrial revolution of the late eighteenth and early nineteenth centuries the material foundations of British power were fundamentally altered by a vast increase in population, in industrial production, and in technological innovation on a scale never before seen. One result was that London was able to effectively implement its balance of power statecraft and defeat Napoleon, even though he possessed most of Europe. Another was that, having largely lost much of its first empire during the American war of national liberation, it could build a second British empire in the mid-nineteenth century on the foundation of British industry and finance, the British fleet and *free trade*. The origins of the global order are to be found in this project, which was eventually to fail because of the ultimate weakness of the British state, comprising only forty million people on small islands off the coast of Europe possessing a temporary comparative advantage in industrial production. As other European states replicated its advantages the British hegemony evaporated after 1870.[11]

It is important to note here the ambition of the British liberal imperial project. Just as the British state reached the apogee of its external power in the mid nineteenth century so liberal ideas were in the ascendancy in its domestic political structure. The power of its industry and military machine opened vast tracts of territory containing a large proportion of humanity in South America, against both Spain and Portugal, in the Middle East against the declining Ottoman empire, in Africa and India in arrangements with local political authorities, and in the East Asian region against the closed systems of notably the Middle Kingdom. It did this, for the most part, with commerce, and sometimes force, yet not by the creation of new colonies.

But the liberal British free trade system could not survive the rise of new industrial states which began to use the tariff and colonial expansion to close off large parts of the world market to British trade. Most publicised here was the newly united German state in the 1870s. But it is often overlooked that the US expanded to the West and took its new territories behind the tariff. Similarly the Japanese took their new colonial possessions into their own orbit after they began imperial conquest, as did the French under the Third Republic. By the end of the century Britain too had thrown up the industrial political forces which demanded more state intervention in order to protect British industry from foreign competition and British labour from British capital. They combined to produce a new wave of British colonial expansion to replace a universal system based on liberal principles by just another colonial system. After 1870 Britain expanded its direct colonial rule in Africa, Asia and the Pacific and again became the world's leading imperial power. But the British had just made the first and unsuccessful attempt by an ordering state to create a universalist and liberal system.

The role of the British state in the creation of a progressive state system has been unique on three separate counts. In the first place it has for a number of reasons been one of the principal sites of the development of ideas and forces supporting the creation of a representative and civilised state from the *Magna Carta* to female enfranchisement. Secondly, because of its geopolitical strategy of the balance of power in Europe it has through the pursuit of its own interests been able to keep the European states free from imperial conquest and unification, by a number of decisive military interventions at critical times in European history. It has been large enough to swing the balance but too small to hold much ground in continental Europe. And thirdly, geography long gave it a natural defence which permitted it to create a maritime and commercial civilisation. This ensured that its empire did not consist of large armies of occupation stifling the enterprise of its colonial extensions. As Montesquieu noted, everywhere the British went they brought commercial civilisation. These fortuitous combinations gave England a unique role in the rise of civilisation and ensured that English became the world language.

The colonial scramble which followed the 1870s eventually produced the First World War. A series of confrontations between the European states over colonial territories, disputes over the spoils of the declining Turkish empire, and an arms race between the two great alliance systems of Britain, France and Russia, and Germany, Austria and Turkey led to war. Of course, to paraphrase Thucydides, in a geopolitical sense the rising power of Germany, and its fleet, alarmed the British (and everyone else) and led to war. Yet it was a war, nonetheless, to defend progress. The German regime was militaristic and illiberal, characteristics it had inherited from its origins in the Prussian dictatorship of Frederick the Great and which had been vindicated more recently in the manner of its unification. Its allies comprised two decadent imperial systems that had seen their best days three centuries earlier and offered little except repression, Islam and some good opera. The alliance of the more civilised states with the Tsarist autocracy was uncomfortable but geopolitically necessary, and in any case the Tsar looked quite benign when compared to his replacements. The civilised states were continuing to practise *realpolitik* in circumstances that left them little choice.[12]

With the onset of the War *realpolitik* became the order of the day. Although the US entry into the conflict and the defeat of Russia left a purer ideological conflict between representative and militarist governments London would still sup with the devil if it improved their hand against Berlin. The complicated and totally unprincipled diplomacy pursued by the liberal powers in the Middle East was designed to elicit the support of Jewish money, Arab nationalism and the region's oil. A longer term result was the ugly boundaries between states, the embattled Jewish homeland, and the vicious regimes for which the region has since been justly famous. Certainly the foundations for these conditions were firmly laid by over a millennium of Islamic idealism and centuries of Ottoman rule, but the mandate system did little to alter them.

Notwithstanding the recent depiction of the First World War, as fought on the Western Front in particular, as a purposeless conflict in which millions of soldiers were sent to their deaths by unthinking and uncaring generals - the *Oh What A Lovely War!* syndrome - the military strategy of the liberal powers achieved its desired result.[13] The Central Powers were defeated in the field by a Anglo-French-American combination which lacked the realist judgement to drive home their advantage in 1918. Instead of a prolonged and successful occupation and imposed social restructuring of the kind that liberalism enforced on Germany (and Japan) after 1945, the allies accepted that the weak state of the Weimar Republic dominated by the social democrats could contain the atavistic forces that recent German history had created. But instead of facing George Bernard Shaw and the Fabians, Weimar succumbed to the Nazis and the Carl Schmitts of this world and lacked the backbone to defend itself.[14]

The Tsarist autocracy was replaced in 1917 by a Marxist dictatorship which gave the world its first view of modern totalitarian government adopting the stringent methods of Machiavelli. Fascism was only to emulate its Leninist methods a decade or so later, in 1922 in Italy and then after 1933 in Germany. These two new forms of industrial states pursued the classical imperial foreign policies of resource hungry societies but in circumstances where the pickings could only be won by brutal conquest of heartland European territories. In fact they had to make these conquests against the forces of each other. The result was eventually the most destructive single battlefield in human history when perhaps forty million people perished in the Nazi-Soviet War.[15]

The liberal democracies, victorious in the First World War, attempted to deal with these industrial imperial regimes with the enlightenment tool of the League of Nations - Kant"s idea for a League of constitutional republics. Even this modest structure was unacceptable to the isolationist US Senate. The League was fashioned for civilised states to subscribe to a moral order and enforce it by international representative government on a Kantian scale. In fact it had to deal with Machiavellian dictatorships for whom politics was the principal purpose of existence and for the ends of which death was to be invited, if necessary on a large scale. They ignored the League, tore up treaties, attacked countries and murdered their own citizens on a scale that Ghengis Khan lacked the technology to achieve. The liberal powers were forced back to *realpolitik* to deal with this catastrophe. The French followed civil conflict and Maginot line fortress inactivity with military defeat and abject capitulation. The

British dragged themselves away from disarmament and pacifism in time to take some advantage of the struggle between the two great forces of darkness, communism and Nazism. The US only fully abandoned the isolationist delusion when attacked by Japan in 1941. But the point had been firmly made: in a world of barbaric states civilised states must behave in a realistic fashion. Liberalism is only possible on deck if Machiavelli is in the engine room.[16]

After the Second World War an intellectual and political revolution occurred in the major Western liberal powers of the US and Britain In the academy the realist tradition re-emerged as the dominant intellectual influence exemplified by the works of Hans J. Morgenthau in the US and E. H. Carr in Britain.[17] Their policy stance was characterised by a determination to explain the limited role that must be accorded to liberalism and idealism in political processes in general and in the field of geopolitics in particular. But, like Machiavelli and Hobbes before them, they have been too readily interpreted as believing that idealism has *no place* in the political process, which is far from the case. In fact the liberal powers, led by the United States, were to pursue a two pronged strategy combining both realist and idealist components.

In relation to the surviving industrial imperial power, the Soviet Union, Washington pursued a policy of containment after 1948, by which time it had become clear that the Soviet system did want to expand and would only be deterred from that policy by force of arms. In pursuit of this component of its global strategy the US used classic *realpolitik* and mobilised whatever forces were at hand to defeat the opposition and contain its power. The core of the defence against the Soviets was the alliance system of the Western powers centred on NATO. In this conflict the US also found its allies among the strangest bedfellows, including at various times military dictators, dissident communists, racist oligarchies and Islamic fundamentalists. It also used quite illiberal weapons in the form of covert action, assassination, torture and the threat of nuclear weapons. This combination was eventually, however, to prevail. The liberal and civilising component of US policy then became preponderant and it resumed almost exclusively the role of ordering the liberal trading states to which it had aspired in 1945, but from which it had been diverted by the onset of the Cold War.[18] In short, the US tried to recreate the British global order project of the mid-nineteenth century after the victory in 1945. At the end of the Cold War it started again.

Trading States

During the Cold War the civilised states undertook a transformation of their internal structure and external behaviour. These two developments were related. Their economies became more productive, the manufacturing sectors became correspondingly less important to employment levels, and international trade became a larger proportion of their production. The trading and service sector state replaced the industrial imperial state as the most civilised in the system. As societies move to a services orientation and a higher productivity economic base, it is generally easier for them to acquire resources by trade than by war. In a civilised state participating citizens become in any case less willing to undertake war - and certainly less willing to actually fight it themselves[19] - and this makes its use as an instrument of statecraft even more problematic. Acquisition by *force majeure* becomes a difficult option for such states to undertake. Trading states do not war on each other although they will need to protect their interests against the primitive, idealist or developmental states who will still exist in the system and continue to use war in the fashion of *realpolitik*.

This development towards a new and dual purpose strategic policy was somewhat masked during the Cold War because the leading civilised states, Britain, France and the USA, in fact fought more wars, indeed arguably more than those fought by other categories of state. These were in fact related to two other processes which were underway at the same time. The British and French were in the process of dismantling imperial systems which they had acquired as industrial and imperial states, chiefly during the late nineteenth century scramble for territorial possessions. In the new order they would no longer need them. The British quickly came to this realisation as they relinquished the Indian empire. Henceforth the colonial conflicts they fought were to try to ensure the emergence of democratic states and market economies in the post-colonial state.

The Soviet-backed communist parties, of course, sought to prevent this, and most of Britain's wars of colonial retreat were fought against them and in alliance with local democratic forces. The French were slower to see the advantages of relinquishing their colonial possessions and fought some bitter and anachronistic colonial wars - notably in Indo-China and Algeria - against the nationalist forces, who were often in alliance with the communists rather than the French, before the Gaullist revolution refashioned the French state and redirected its ambitions to development in Europe. This also helps explain the low rate of democracy prevailing among former French colonies.[20]

The USA was the first civilised state to realise that the transition to trading states and away from empire was occurring, and not only vacated the Philippines as quickly as possible but used its aid program, including the Marshall Plan, to Western Europe to lever the old imperial powers into decolonisation. They complied at different rates. After the electoral defeat of Churchill in 1945 the British quickly saw the writing on the wall under the social democrat Labour Party. But if the Belgians left the Congo with indecent haste, the Dutch had to be driven from their East Indies by internal insurrection and then US diplomatic pressure, while the Portuguese were impoverished by a series of colonial wars that ended only when disaffected military officers overthrew the fascist regime in 1974. The Americans' wars were, in fact, fought almost exclusively against the Soviet bloc in pursuit of progress.[21]

From 1948 when it supported the Greek government against communist attack and Berlin against the Soviet blockade, US forces were engaged in almost permanent war against political and military organisations supported by Moscow. This only ended with the dissolution of the Soviet empire in 1989 and the Soviet state in 1991. From 1948 until 1969 this was conducted on a global scale by the direct involvement of US personnel. At that time it became clear that the US would be defeated in Vietnam and the new President, Richard Nixon, began the retreat under the basis of establishing a 'decent interval' before the communists took over. By 1973 the US forces were gone and in 1975 the communist parties took over the three Indo-China states of Vietnam, Laos and Cambodia with what proved to be murderous results.[22]

The Soviets then began the process of consolidating the gains they had made as the 'correlation of forces' moved in their favour.

During the *détente* period of the 1970s they continued a substantial arms build up, encouraged the expansion of their clients and allies in Africa, Central America and Asia, and invaded and occupied Afghanistan. The Democrat administration of Jimmy Carter (1977-81), committed to interdependence theory, at first did little to resist this program and then stiffened its resolve in its final year before losing to the Republican Ronald Reagan in the 1980 election. Reagan confronted Soviet power with a renewed American arms build up, encouraging allies to be more determined against the Soviets and by pursuing the 'Reagan Doctrine' in the Third World of supporting whoever was opposing the aspiring hegemonic forces directed by the Soviets. This again took the US into many and diverse conflicts, often with unsavoury allies, although few of them produced the direct involvement of US forces. By the late 1980s this strategy had contributed to the dissolution of the Soviet system by adding an imperial overstretch problem to its existing difficulties of trying to reinvigorate an economy run by a communist dictatorship.[23]

These strategic matters had dominated considerations of US policy during the Cold War and tended to obscure the transformation in the civilised world that was taking place under US direction. America was recommencing the program first begun by Britain after its victory against Napoleon, of constructing a liberal global order. This US system, however, had a number of features which distinguished it from the earlier British model. Its most important building blocks were the United Nations, the financial institutions clustered around the Bretton Woods agreement and including the International Monetary Fund (IMF) and the World Bank, the General Agreement on Tariffs and Trade (GATT) later the World Trade Organisation (WTO), and the private trading institutions later known as multinational corporations. These bodies were under the control of the civilised states either on the basis of voting being proportionate to the financial contribution, as with the World Bank and similar bodies, or because they were owned within civilised states as with the private companies.

The United Nations system was intended to provide the multilateral political organisation to create order in the interstate system. It was Kant"s *Perpetual Peace* updated, the League of Nations with more commitment. It fell foul of two developments in the interstate system itself. The first was the Cold War. The UN Charter was designed to avoid the difficulties the League had faced in dealing with determined and aggressive great powers, then the Axis, by giving a veto on UN action to the great powers. The Security Council, which was to deal with issues leading to a breach of the peace by authorising multilateral action against any designated aggressor comprised five permanent members - the putative great powers of 1945, the US, Soviet Union, France, Britain and Republican China - each of whom could veto its activities. The result was that the UN only undertook one serious peacekeeping operation during the Cold War because the Soviet Union vetoed any attempt to take multilateral action against communist aggression. The major exception was the Korean War, a UN enterprise authorised when the Soviets were boycotting the Security Council because of the UN refusal to seat communist China. The UN's security function, its primary objective, was stymied until after the Cold War.[24]

Nonetheless, the other lesser functions of the UN could proceed through its functional organisations. Many of these had been initiated during the period of the League and inherited although sometimes renamed by the UN. They included the International Labour Organisation (ILO), the World Health Organisation (WHO), the International Telegraphic Union (ITU), the UN High Commission on Refugees (UHHCR), and the UN Education, Social and Cultural Organisation (UNESCO). These had the potential to lay the basis for an international civil society and their budget was funded by the wealthier states, particularly the United States. The UN headquarters was built in New York on land donated by one of America's richest families, the Rockefellers. This may have been unfortunate since as the UN was progressively taken over by the non-civilised states their behaviour was open to the closest scrutiny by the organisation's main sponsor and chief financial contributor.

By the 1970s and as the UN changed from a body dominated by the civilised states, and constrained by Soviet veto, to one where the newly independent and chiefly poor and primitive states had a majority, so its complexion altered. The so-called Third World caucus of at first seventy seven and then over one hundred states, still known as the Group of Seventy Seven, began to use the UN General Assembly and functional bodies where they had clear majorities, to make demands on the civilised world. These included branding Israel as racist and launching the campaign for a New International Economic Order (NIEO). The NIEO was wholly dependency theory derived and included the central plank of a large transfer of resources from the civilised to the primitive states for no reasons other than pseudo-Marxist theory and a numerical supremacy. It was greatly encouraged in this campaign by Moscow.[25]

In addition the supplicant states used this numerical advantage to ensure the majority of UN bureaucracy posts were staffed with their own nationals and paid by the civilised world. By the 1990s the United Nations system employed over fifty thousand bureaucrats who had extended their influence and interests to areas that many critics believed were within the proper domain of the state - like urban policy - and were holding end to end conferences which created the impression of a global elite let loose with first class airline vouchers. The budget for these activities, however, was mostly determined by a General Assembly dominated by the primitive states but raised from the civilised states notably the United States. This quickly produced a backlash particularly from Republicans who when they won the Congressional majority in 1994 slashed the US contribution.[26]

These two combined processes meant that the UN could not properly fulfil either of its major functions - peacekeeping and creating an international civil society - during the Cold War. One function was stopped by the leading idealist and dictatorial state, the Soviet, and the other by the primitive states. When the Cold War came to an end it also became clear that these functions would need to be further reconsidered since the United Nations would have trouble creating either peace or an international civil society while dominated by primitive states.

More successful was the US effort to create an international financial system which would play the same role as the pound sterling had for the British system in the nineteenth century. But unlike the British the US system had the capacity to survive the ending of American economic primacy. At first, and as agreed to at Bretton Woods in the US in 1945, all currencies, of the then forty five mostly civilised states agreeing to join the system, would be interchangeable with the US currency at fixed rates. Since the US dollar was fixed to the price of gold at thirty five dollars to the ounce theoretically redeemable, this marked the return to the gold standard and made trading across national boundaries again easier. At the same time the International Monetary Fund was set up to enable member states to survive temporary balance of payments problems by providing loan facilities and policy adjustment advice. The World Bank was intended to provide capital for development projects that might not readily attract private funding and developed into an advisory agency for policy development and capital raising.[27]

This financial structure expanded throughout the Cold War and helped create a period during which international trade, particularly between the civilised states, expanded quicker than production, which itself expanded at rates unparalleled historically. It created a wider system of regional development banks, like the Asia Development Bank, deeply involved in the process of economic growth by helping states raise capital and by improving policy regimes. It also helped develop an international private finance market built on fixed exchange rates and facilitating trade and investment flows. In the early 1970s this underwent its first serious crisis when the US faced a severe balance of payments deficit crisis and, instead of disciplining its fiscal policy, chose to print more dollars and spend them at the agreed price. In 1971 this policy was abandoned by President Nixon and fixed exchange rates ended among the most civilised states over the next few years.[28]

Currency exchange rates were mostly floating among developed states by the early 1980s. This development was accompanied by and related to the creation of real time international financial markets operated through electronic data processing and transmission systems, linked to the world's major stock exchanges. The financial system had by now become independent of the US, although its dollar remained the most important single trading currency despite its sharp devaluation in the 1980s and early 1990s as the US economy continued to run large trading deficits. For the first time the world had a global integrated capital market and states seeking development needed to access it, usually to be achieved most simply by the mechanism of making their currency freely convertible and global money markets thus available to their citizens.[29]

The GATT was signed at Geneva between 47 states in 1948 and played an equivalent role in the creation of a global market in goods and services. The GATT was designed to reduce barriers to trade and did so by negotiating a series of barrier reduction 'rounds' which concentrated on particular obstacles to liberal trade, and policy regimes were then agreed to in each case that would see their regulation reduced. The first of these concerned manufactured products which had been the principal commodities obstructed under the old colonial and *dirigiste* regimes. They then moved on to converting all barrier obstacles into tariffs, as the most transparent of such devices, and then in turn reducing them numerically. These agreements at first only included advanced Organisation for Economic Co-operation and Development (OECD) style states, but were then extended to include poorer states who got some preferential access to richer country markets. In the last 'Uruguay Round' of negotiations undertaken in the late 1980s agricultural products and services were added. At the conclusion of this round in 1995 the GATT became the World Trade Organisation (WTO). States wishing to access the world market on equal terms had to comply with WTO policy on related matters including copyright provisions, labour laws and subsidised exports. The effect was to enable a considerable growth of world trade and output and to make civilised state markets available to those development states who could produce appropriate product.[30]

This international system of liberalised trade in finance and commodities has been accessed by private commercial institutions which are now called multinational corporations. In the simple sense of a company trading across state borders, such companies have existed for some hundreds of years and were integral components of the European age of expansion. The British and the Dutch, for example, both used a private company to exploit their Asian possessions, the Dutch East India company and the East India company. With the creation in the mid-nineteenth century of the joint stock company, however, the quantity of capital that could be deployed by a single entity started to rise exponentially. At first such companies were often involved in commodity production like plantations or mining, but they spread to finance and manufacturing by the early twentieth century. Until 1945 they tended to be contained within the political boundaries of their parent state and its colonies but with the creation of a liberal international commercial system these confines were progressively broken. In the early post-war years they tended to be mostly American, reflecting its victory and relative lack of physical destruction, and to a lesser extent British who had consumed much of their foreign investment in paying for the war effort, often to the Americans. As the other civilised states recovered from the war so their companies began to assume multinational dimensions.

By the 1980s these multinational corporations were derived from all the civilised states and a few of the development states, and had created an international economy which was more truly cosmopolitan. It was mostly confined to the civilised states where individual purchasing powers were roughly comparable, and as commodity consumption followed similar paths from similar producing companies, so cultural forms started to assume similar dimensions. While it is true that Japanese autos, for example, assumed ascendancy in the 1980s this was quickly offset by a rising Yen and prices, the adoption of similar design and production techniques by competitors, and the entry of cheaper producers like South Korea into the market.

The interpenetration of the civilised states' economies appeared to be homogenising the materialist facets of their civil society. Most civilised states could boast such companies: Britain, BP Oil, Imperial Chemical Industries and finance firms like Lloyds; the French had Renault and Total; the Americans a large range that extended from oil through tobacco and food, to music, movies and Boeing aircraft; the Germans excelled in cars like Mercedes, BMW and VW; the Swedes for long had SAAB and Volvo; the Dutch, Philips and half Royal Dutch Shell; the Italians, Fiat; the Japanese entered with cameras and motorbikes, moved up to TVs and autos, and started the 1990s with banks, machine tools and entire factories; while Australia excelled in Fosters beer and the giant media News Corporation. By the 1990s the development states were also contributing to this process with Singapore Airlines, Taiwan's computer giants like ACER, and South Korea's conglomerates like Hyundai, Daiwa and Goldcorp.[31]

The lifeblood of this system was not provided by the state but by civil society. It is true that the states had consciously set out to create a liberal trade regime. It is also true that the state apparatuses created and defended the order within which the system flourished. It is further true that the states provided some of the inputs to this multinational economic system, including skilled labour, domestic energy and transport systems, although generally to a declining extent as the cause of privatisation gathered force throughout the civilised world in the last two decades of the twentieth century. The arteries of this system were maintained by the companies of civil society: oil and gas supplied privately fuelled the East Asia boom; the private companies ran the airlines and produced most of the aeroplanes; the banks kept the finance mobile and flowing; information ran hot on the privately owned electronic airwaves and cyberspace. The civilised states had successfully created the preconditions for the next wave of human progress.

The most successful trading state initially proved to be Japan. It utilised the free trade regime pursued and protected by the Americans to construct an efficient domestic economy capable of importing raw materials and transforming them into manufactures of ever increasing sophistication. It did this with no capacity to defend the far flung economic interests - energy sources, capital investments, markets - on which its prosperity depended. Rather, it developed the concept of 'comprehensive security' which saw it use non-military means to protect its interests and when this failed, the power of the ordering United States.[32]

Supplicant States and Post-Colonial Theory

Some of the primitive states have become supplicant states which have adopted some form or other of 'dependency theory' to excuse their own inability to develop. States which prove unable to create the preconditions for progress will often be also unable to escape a victimist ideology itself created within the intelligentsia of the civilised zone and deriving from that very condition of compassionate generosity the condition of civilisation fosters. This victimist and supplicant condition reached its apogee in the diplomatic campaign for a New International Economic Order but it has periodic outbreaks throughout the Western academy and deserves consideration.

The foundations of the supplicant tradition are laid by the historical school of blame and guilt in which the Europeans far from having created the idea of progress and having delivered on it for the last five hundred years are responsible for the impoverishment of much of the human race, a condition most of them have always enjoyed. The most exhaustive treatment of world history on this scale is offered by Stavrianos but lesser versions of the same tale abound.[33] Australian Aboriginals are alleged to have enjoyed a more decent living condition than the first Europeans who arrived - 'Aborigines were very kind to their children, although it is true they sometimes killed them at birth';[34] the Incas had a superior culture to the Spaniards;[35] the Africans lived in harmony with one another and nature;[36] the Chinese remained in advance of the Europeans until recently;[37] and everywhere cultures flourished and economies prospered before the arrival of European civilisation. From this claim, so at variance with the evident situation, is developed the notion that the unwanted and militaristic Europeans reduced the local people to penury and kept them there.

Now, until the creation of civilised states, a most recent development, the quite normal intercourse between different people encountering one another was war for conquest of the others' possessions and territory. This was common practice in circumstances as disparate as Aboriginal Australia, the Central American Aztec empire, between the different Polynesian islands, in the Central Eurasian steppes and among the different tribes of the southern African continent. When they had the capacity and the occasion, the peoples from outside Europe did the same to the Europeans, including Ghengis Khan, the Arabic Muslims and the Ottoman Turks. The Europeans did this to themselves, of course, for a thousand years in the name of *realpolitik* or religious orthodoxy. It is also the case that the diseases, which the Europeans are alleged to have uniquely transported to New Worlds, flowed both ways and that the Black Death came from Asia to decimate the population of the European continent. Certainly slavery was an abomination but one practised by Africans and Asians also. For many parts of the world the arrival of the Europeans brought the idea and the fact of progress to civilisations in which lives were often nasty, brutish and short. For the Marxist school of historiography, which can so readily accommodate an interpretation of Attilla the Hun as progressive because he contributed to the destruction of slave owning Rome, to embrace dependency theory for any reason other than the advantage of the Soviet state is breathtaking.

In the 1970s this was perfectly understandable of course. A fascinating alliance of interests coalesced around the NIEO. The Russians were on the rise and encouraged the primitives at the UN to blame the West for whatever crime they had placed on the international agenda that week. The radical OPEC states had just acquired considerable economic rent from sitting on oil and offered some of it to any one who would pursue their anti-Israel and anti-Western cause, and a few Western Trotskyite parties accepted. Many other Third World regimes could not get any progress started and were only too willing to blame some aspect of their contact with the West for that shortcoming. The Shah of Iran and the Chinese Communist Party joined this unlikely panoply in recognising the Palestine Liberation Organisation as the sole representative of the Palestinian people. They stopped short of officially according the terrorists in the Irish Republican Army, the German Baader-Meinhoff group, the Japanese Red Army Faction and Carlos the Jackal - all of whom received training, arms and money from primitive terrorist states - similar recognition. In such a context they began baying for US blood at the UN.[38]

The NIEO was claimed to represent the repayment of the historic debt owed by the developed countries to the primitives for reason of their earlier exploitation and impoverishment. Its components included four main planks. There should be an enormous increase in the percentage of the civilised states' output going in foreign aid. They should also agree to transfer capital to poorer countries so that they would be producing 25% of world industrial output by year 2000 A.D. The fluctuations in the primitives' commodity prices should be contained by a Common Fund, raised by taxes on the civilised states, which would buy surplus stocks in gluts and sell them during shortages. (A similar scheme for Australian wool had left $4 billion worth on the wharves by 1991.) And the poorer countries should have more representation on the IMF and World Bank with a view to controlling the civilised states' assets. It was a claim, of course, for taxation without representation, and should have been rejected out of hand.

The NIEO, the most extreme and formal codification of the dependency school theory, actually got an unduly fair hearing. Indeed, a group of eminent and mostly retired social democrat politicians, led by Willy Brandt, who had the extra and unusual qualification of being a German who had opposed Hitler at that time, took these proposals and turned them into a program for action which incorporated most of the demands.[39] It was justified with reference to the fact that the civilised countries were in a recession in the early 1980s while the poor countries lacked effective demand. Therefore in a classic piece of Keynesian logic the wealthy should redistribute to the poor thereby giving them the effective demand to buy more of their output. The Report was commissioned by the World Bank, which was at that time under the leadership of Robert MacNamara, President John Kennedy's former Secretary of State for Defence, who spent the last thirty years of his life apologising for his role in getting the US involved in the Vietnam War. He was later to do his best against Ronald Reagan's anti-Soviet strategy but with a similar lack of success.

At the time, and with Jimmy Carter still in the White House, that entire exercise in what might be termed moral geopolitics was taken quite seriously in the West. Even the English Tories had contributed to the farce by having Ted Heath, former British Tory Prime Minister, on the Brandt committee, which produced *The Common Crisis*, with its advocacy of a global redistribution of wealth system. The Australian conservatives led by farmer, Malcolm Fraser, also saw merit in the scheme. The election within two years of the Thatcher conservative government in the UK, 1979, and the Reagan Republicans in the US, 1981, saw the end of the campaign. Reagan vetoed the project at the Cancun summit called to discuss it and sent Jean Kirkpatrick, an International Politics Professor from the originally Jesuit Georgetown University, to be Ambassador at the UN and to tell them to be serious in their consideration of development issues. They did. Almost all civilised states started to wind down their commitment to aid programs subsequently.

The issue of dependency theory gradually abated in the political world from that point under a number of other influences. The radical states who continued to propound its doctrines of a separation from Western economic and political influences, like North Korea, Burma and Cambodia, were among the worst economic performers in the world. Those states who did best at emulating Western style development policies, like Singapore, South Korea and Taiwan, were among the best performers. And those regimes that pursued a course of virulent anti-Western diplomacy and terrorism like Libya, Cuba and Iraq, were dealt with by the Western powers with the same form of realpolitik they had used on the Soviet state and with the same kind of success. As a result, by the 1990s it was more common for aspiring developmental states to adopt the recommendations of the IMF or World Bank - what some academics were calling the 'Washington consensus' - than the *dirigiste* strictures about state planning and autarchy that had been more common when Moscow and Marxist idealist doctrines seemed to be doing quite well in the Cold War.

But dependency theory did not die in the academy. The theoretical and philosophical aspect of society is usually the last to grasp a change in reality. In the Western academy as Marxism was abandoned in its materialist form so it was replaced by other idealist thought forms in which new 'others' came to replace the proletariat. In this case it was an idealised Third World, misrepresented by the Western scholar. This deformation has already been alluded to. Two such instances may suffice here: Edward Said and Noam Chomsky.

Edward Said is a literature Professor at Colombia University from a Palestinian background. He has lived in New York for nearly three decades. During the Middle East War of 1973 he got quite excited, understandably, about the defeat of his previous people and started to write about their condition in the Palestinian *diaspora*. These people had been dispersed by the Israeli state after the 1948 War (started by the Arabs) from the territory now Israel but then mostly Palestine which had been promised to both by the British, for their own quite good and urgent reasons, during the First World War. They had then been treated as geopolitical pawns by the neighbouring Arab states who would not allow them to integrate into the larger Arab world, kept them in refugee camps on the Israeli borders, sponsored different factions in the Palestine Liberation Organisation, often in mortal and murderous combat with one another, and (except for in 1979 Egypt) refused to come to an agreement with Israel that might resolve the situation. Said, however, out of this particular and quite disastrous situation, has manufactured the theory of *Orientalism* wherein the entire non-Western world is misrepresented in a prejudiced and ignorant fashion by the civilised states and their media.⁴⁰

A basic appreciation of realist political science literature would reveal that all societies create images of themselves and of other societies in ways that conform to their current interests and that these change over time. The Israeli and American perceptions of the Palestinians and their Arab allies were certainly no more prejudiced than the Iranian mullahs' depiction of the USA and could be supplemented by the self image of their opponents at any time. The Western media has provided more information about other societies than its equivalent at any other time or any other place. Indeed, any policy towards the Third World adopted by civilised states is certain to be criticised, and those criticisms be widely publicised, by its internal opponents in a fashion that has brought some such policies undone, most famously the Vietnam War and the Contragate scandal. To think that incorrect stereotypes can be publicly sustained and propaganda caricatures manufactured in contemporary civilised states, as was common in primitive, Fascist or communist dictatorships, is to profoundly misunderstand their nature. In the information age the state can have no secrets.

And then when the PLO stood on the cusp of a resolution of its dispute with Israel and both prepared to trade long held positions for compromise and peace - a compromise that was to bring the assassination of Jewish leader Rabin by Jewish extremists - Said emerges from the depths of Manhattan to condemn Arafat for unprincipled compromise.

The American linguistics Professor, Noam Chomsky, made his mark as a critic of US foreign policy during the period of the Vietnam War in a series of impressive essays wherein he juxtaposed the values of American liberalism with the means it used to prosecute the war.⁴¹ When this was combined with his forensic capabilities and an intensive research effort, which often revealed quite new and damaging information, the impact on a generation of intellectuals was, and remains substantial. He then went on to be a major proponent of the view, not unrelated to Orientalism, that the odious Khmer Rouge regime in Cambodia had been misrepresented in the Western media. When it later became clear that this regime had in fact been guilty of the crime of genocide against its own people, as first claimed in the *Readers Digest*, Chomsky abandoned his support for that government but continued to argue that he had been wrong *for the correct reasons*. Since Washington had lied about the Vietnam War and deceived the media, he was correct to assume they were doing the same again.[42] As opposed to this, he claimed the West had ignored the Indonesian invasion of East Timor and the huge death toll that this had involved. In Australia it is difficult to take this claim seriously since the media hardly lets a week go by without an *exposé* and anti-Indonesian story on East Timor. Nonetheless, in view of the Professor's exalted status among idealists in the academy, some comment is deserved.

The Indonesian military-backed regime invaded East Timor in 1975 after the Left-governed Portuguese colonial power had done its best to put the communist-led Fretilin in control of the colony. Ten years earlier the New Order Indonesian regime had itself come to power in a violent conflict during which perhaps a million people were killed. Most of those killed were members of the Indonesian Communist Party (PKI) or its sympathisers who were trying to achieve state power, if necessary by force, in that country with the support of the Chinese Maoist regime. Shortly before, the same Chinese regime had killed about thirty million people *by economic miscalculation* during the Great Leap Forward. Six months before the invasion of East Timor the Khmer Rouge had come to power in Cambodia with a policy born from a combination of that Maoist Chinese practise and the anti-Western ideals of the Parisian communist *salons* of the 1950s and 1960s where its leadership had been educated. It killed about three million people from a total of eight million in three years, 1975-78, and was sponsored throughout by China. These were the geopolitical stakes then involved in East Timor. Chomsky, in an argument only possible from a Platonist idealist of the extreme school, reduces them to an exercise in moral philosophy and anti-Western media polemics of the kind deployed in the worst media studies courses in colleges of sociology.

Hegemons: the Habsburgs to Victorian England

One of the claims made by sovereign states is that, since they recognise no superior authority, they are all equal. This is among the least convincing of the political myths which keep the system functioning. In fact the modern international system has always had superior states which it has called great powers. The traditional definition of such a power has been one that could successfully wage war against any other two great powers, an almost tautological but effective working definition. A more revealing one would be a power that has interests throughout the system which it can effectively enforce. From time to time a great power has sought to extend this power even further and create the rules of the international system itself. Such a state would be a hegemon, exceeding the authority of a great power but falling short of that of an imperial power like ancient Rome or China. There have been a number of attempts by states to achieve such dominance in the system and become hegemonic. All have failed.

The Treaty of Westphalia of 1648 marked both the recognition of the creation of the modern sovereign state and the defeat of the first aspiring hegemon, the Habsburg Holy Roman Empire based on Spanish-Austrian power. Their extensive European lands were mostly united by the inheritance of Charles V but the Habsburgs added by conquest much of the Americas, save that reserved for Portugal by the Pope and what the north Europeans seized in the north, all of the Pacific and the Philippines. This was the first global power. It rested on the bullion of the Americas, the galleon, Spanish agriculture and the imperial Spanish infantry. It was defeated by a coalition of powers led by France, England and Sweden during the Thirty Years War, thus failing to resurrect the structure of Christendom united under a Habsburg imperial authority.

The French Bourbon monarchy then attempted a similar project. France was at that time the most populous state in Europe with a flourishing agriculture that generated the wealth to build the palace of Versailles and a large army. Louis XIV developed a formidable infantry augmented by an improved artillery and attempted to extend French power by force. It was defeated in the War of Spanish

Succession by a coalition led by England and the Dutch and settled for a negotiated peace at Utrecht in 1713.[43]

For the next fifty years the British state, augmented by Union with Scotland since 1707, pursued an imperial expansion, chiefly in the Americas, and fought global wars with European allies mostly against the French. British military power was chiefly naval but was now augmented by an army hugely improved following Cromwell's reforms. Since it was also in the first throws of the industrial revolution, that was eventually to change the world, it was also wealthy. This enabled it to subsidise continental allies in pursuit of balance of power diplomacy and to tie its rivals, like France, to deploying resources to land wars. After great successes in the War of Austrian Succession, 1740-48, and, following a complete reversal of the alliance system, the Seven Years War, 1756-63, the British were humbled in the War of American independence, 1776-83, when most of Europe supported the colonies. Power was once more dispersed throughout the system.

This changed with the French revolution in 1789. Already superior in numbers of population the French revolutionary state was able to mobilise a larger proportion of it by means of the *levee en masse*. It was very quickly putting an unprecedented million men in the field. As Machiavelli anticipated, this power was better used by a republic that threw up a greater share of genius, of whom Napoleon Bonaparte was the standout. The French Republic aimed at a transformation of the state system and when occupying much of Europe introduced a reform program, much of which, including the metric system and the legal code, remains today. But in the end Bonapartism was tyranny for the other states, as Beethoven knew when he renamed his dedicated symphony. These states combined under British and Russian leadership to overthrow Bonaparte and restore the state system in 1815.

The British emerged from the Napoleonic Wars as the greatest power in the world. Extended war had, as so often occurs, accelerated technological change and quickened the industrial revolution in Britain. Its fleet had not only been able to contain French power to the European continent and land expeditionary forces almost at will, particularly after the victory at Trafalgar in 1805, but also to extend British commercial influence. It seized many French colonies, initiated the liberation of many Spanish ones and took its own influences into Asia and the Pacific. With the old balance of power nicely re-established in Europe, and cared for by the wily Austrian Prince Metternich,[44] the British began the most ambitious hegemonic project thus far devised: a global empire of free trade.

In 1815 Britain was an oligarchic and aristocratic yet still representative state. The impulses of the French Revolution had been felt before the onset of Bonaparte's despotism and in the 1790s in particular it had its supporters. The fleet revolted and political repression of the lower classes helped populate the Australian penal settlements. But in the end it was Burke who won the great argument of the day despite the comment from the revolutionary sympathiser Fox, that Burke admired the plumage but forgot the dying bird. Nonetheless Britain could not defend the liberty of all Europe and maintain its own autocracy. The next century witnessed the extension of the franchise and liberties in Britain starting with the pathbreaking Great Reform Act of 1832 which enfranchised the growing middle class.

The period until the 1870s was the apogee of British liberal thought and action generating the Liberal Party of Gladstone, the works of Richard Cobden and John Stuart Mill, and the repeal of the Anti-Combination Acts, the Corn Laws and the Slave Trade. While retaining their existing colonies, many of whom acquired representative government, the British attempted to otherwise extend their influence through trade and not territorial acquisition. This commercial imperium rested on the power of the British fleet, which was maintained at a level designed to defeat all others combined, and British industry and commerce. The army was certainly used to open markets in Asia, as in the Opium War against China, in Africa against the Zulus, and in Australia and New Zealand against indigenous peoples, but it was an auxiliary force. The trading empire was based on commodities produced in British factories, the London finance market and clippers on the high sea trade routes.

This period of British hegemony ended when other powers challenged British supremacy in these spheres and the British were unable to sustain the system against colonising adversaries. The USA was reunited as a major market after 1865 and industrialised behind the tariff with a massive immigration program. The German state was united by 1870 and used the state apparatus to construct Europe's most efficient industrial structure. Shortly thereafter both countries began colonial expansion. The French also re-entered that business and conquered the second French empire in north Africa, east Asia and the Pacific. After the Meiji restoration the Japanese began the same policies in their region. The Russians continued their march to the east and even Belgium acquired a colonial appendage in the Congo (Zaire). Faced with the prospect of the world's markets being closed to its trade the British responded by becoming once more the leading imperial power and annexed the second British empire on which it was truly said, the sun never set.

From the onset of the New Imperialism, which Lenin with some justification but typically excessive monocausality attributed to the desire of capital markets to find profitable investment opportunities, until 1945, the great powers struggled for ascendancy. It is true that the US tried to create a new liberal system after the First World War but it lacked the determination and probably the power. By that time the British had lost the power and the inclination. The French will been destroyed in the trenches. The Russians were too weak and embroiled in a system which could only extend influence through military force. The Italians and Japanese were barely great powers. Only Germany had the potential capacity and a ruling class of sufficient determination to try to establish a new international order under its hegemony. Both World Wars were fought over that central issue and both the militarist monarchy and the Nazi state proved impressively violent but not up to the task.

The post-1945 Cold War was fought between a state, the USA, which was hegemonic in much of the world and a second, Soviet, state which established a smaller imperial system of opposition to that hegemony. The Americans were largely responsible for the refashioning of the post-war international order into a system of independent sovereign states engaged in increasingly liberal economic relations. They were also largely responsible for its overall defence against the predatory Soviet bloc.[45] With the defeat and dissolution of the Soviet challenge in 1991 a new opportunity arose for the first time in over a century for a hegemonic state to construct a world order in which the principles of progress may be given the chance to flourish and for civilised states to proliferate.

Ordering: American Primacy

In these circumstances the United States as the leader and defender of the civilised zone cannot afford to totally ignore the primitive and idealistic states because of the damage they may cause to the system as a whole by disease, refugees, environmental disaster or war. The civilised states must therefore pursue the new order by three methods.

The United Nations system has been a failure in the sphere of maintaining the peace because of the Cold War and some improvement in the function of the Security Council and its organs may be anticipated. There have already been some successes in the use of the Security Council to resolve conflicts in Cambodia, Namibia and in a more complex way the Gulf War. But many of these activities will still depend on the Great Powers, especially the United States, having their strategic interests involved. Where they are not, as in Burundi, Rwanda and Somalia - then the chaos is likely to continue. Where they are, as in Haiti, then a resolution is more likely.

Its functional bodies, however, have been a failure largely because they are dominated by primitive states and require extensive reform. The functional organisations are unlikely to rise above their present level of performance while they are recruiting personnel and having policy and administration determined on the democratic principle which gives the successful, civilised states the financial obligation, and the primitives the power. Putting a failed African politician in charge of UNESCO invited the farce it occasioned. Extending this principle to the more successful of the international organisations which operate in the finance field, like the World Bank and the IMF would be to extend incompetence to organisations of real significance.

The most successful conduits of progress have been those bodies that have pursued the replication of the conditions of progress through the GATT/WTO, global corporations, civil aid programs and globalisation. These institutions have had some success among those states able to take advantage of these processes, mostly the development states in the east Asian region. It is by this process, rather than one of imposing world government on states that the path of progress, will be most successful. Again, the replication of the form of civil society already found in the advanced states is the most substantial base that can be laid for progress and this can best be fashioned by the institutions of civil society.

But in order to maintain the zone of civilisation and progress which has been carefully nurtured and defended over centuries of hardship, a geopolitical strategy of the pursuit of self interest is required to prevent the primitive from overrunning the civilised. This involves the protection of the lines of commerce from assault, as for example undertaken by the US and its allies in the 1991 Gulf War.[46] It may also involve intervention against conditions of chaos which may spread, as occurred in Haiti, Cambodia and belatedly the former Yugoslavia.

This task will be for the most part easier for the United States than it was for the British or indeed for the Americans themselves during the Cold War if only for one reason. The American state is more powerful and more technologically advanced, than any other state or combination of states that exist in the system. Far from facing the decline which Left intellectuals periodically herald, the US is able to continually enforce its will against non-civilised states with relative ease. It stopped the North Korean nuclear program by use of a (for it) small bribe; it arrested the war waged by Serbia against Bosnia by some air strikes and a minor police action; it stopped the Chinese intimidation of Taiwan by cruising two of its thirteen aircraft carriers through the Taiwan Straits; it got the odious Saddam Hussein to desist from murdering more Kurds by dispatching less than thirty cruise missiles of which it has thousands; it assured the re-election of Boris Yeltsin in Russia by maintaining the supply of cash on which his pork barrelling depended; and it unilaterally extended the NATO umbrella to the Russian border. It has used this unprecedented power to create the conditions for globalisation.

Notes

1. Alex Inkeles, ed., *On Measuring Democracy: Its Consequences and Concomitants*, Transaction Publishers, New Jersey, 1991, explores these themes.

2. John A. Hobson, *The International Man: A Life of Richard Cobden*, London, T. F. Unwin, 1919.
3. Max Singer and Aaron Wildavsky,*The Real World Order*, Chatham, N. J., Chatham House Publishers, 1993.
4. Jesse Helms, 'How to Save the United Nations', *Foreign Affairs*, 1996.
5. Coral Bell, 'A Hard and Bitter Peace: The Cold War in Retrospect' *Quadrant*, March 1996.
6. Hans J. Morgenthau, *Politics Among Nations: the struggle for power and peace*, 4th ed., New York, Knopf, 1967.
7. Kenneth Waltz, *Man, The State and War, a theoretical analysis*, New York, Columbia University Press, 1959.
8. Henry Kissinger, *Diplomacy*, New York, Simon and Schuster, 1994.
9. Bob Catley, 'Hegemonic America: The Benign Superpower', *Contemporary Southeast Asia*, March 1997.
10. Robert D. Keohane, ed., *Neorealism and its Critics*, New York, Colombia University Press, 1986.
11. C. C. Eldridge, ed., *British Imperialism in the Nineteenth Century*, London, Macmillan, 1984; and Herman M. Schwartz, *States Versus Markets*, New York, St. Martins, 1994, particularly Chapter Eight.
12. C. H. Currey, *European History Since 1870 with special reference to the Causes of the War of 1914*, Sydney, Teachers College Press, 1918; and David G. Herrmann, *The Arming of Europe and the Making of the First World War*, Princeton, Princeton University Press, 1996.
13. Cyril Falls, *The Great War*, New York, Putnam, 1959.
14. Richard N. Hunt, ed., *The Creation of the Weimar Republic: Stillborn Democracy?*, Lexington, D.C. Heath, 1969; and Karl Dietrich Bracher, *The German Dictatorship: Its Origins, Structure, and Effects of National Socialism*, trans. Jean Steinberg, London, Weidenfeld and Nicolson, 1971.
15. John Erickson, *Stalin's War With Germany*, London, Weidenfeld and Nicolson, 1975; Alexander Dallin, *German Rule in Russia,1941-1945: A Study of Occupation Policies*, 2nd ed., London, Macmillan, 1981; Gerhard L. Weinberg, *A World at Arms: a global history of World War II*, Cambridge, Cambridge University Press, 1994.

16. Hans W. Gatzke, ed., *European Diplomacy Between Two Wars, 1919-1939*, Chicago, Quadrangle Books, 1972; and Thomas Knock, *To End All Wars: Woodrow Wilson and The Quest For A New World Order*, New York, Oxford University Press, 1992.
17. E. H. Carr, *The Twenty Years Crisis*, 2nd ed., London, Macmillan, 1951.
18. Tony Smith, *America's Mission: The United States and the Worldwide Struggle for Democracy in the Twentieth Century*, Princeton, Princeton University Press, 1994.
19. Edward Luttwak, 'Post-Heroic Armies', *Foreign Affairs*, July-August 1996.
20. Guy de Lusignan, *Frenchspeaking Africa Since Independence*, London, Pall Mall Press, 1969; and Robert Aldrich and John Connell, *France's Overseas Frontier: departments et territoires d'outre-mer*, Cambridge, Cambridge University Press, 1992.
21. Richard Crockatt, *The Fifty Years War: The United States and The Soviet Union in World Politics, 1941-1991*, London, Routledge, 1995.
22. Arnold R. Isaacs, *Without Honour: Defeat in Vietnam and Cambodia*, Baltimore, John Hopkins University Press, 1983.
23. Coral Bell, *The Reagan Paradox: American Foreign Policy in the 1980s*, Aldershot, Elgar, 1989.
24. Anjoli V. Patil, *The UN Veto in World Affairs, 1946-90*, Sarasota, UNIFO, 1992; and Gareth Evans, *Cooperating for Peace: The Global Agenda for the 1990s and Beyond*, Sydney, Allen and Unwin, 1993.
25. David B. H. Denuon, ed. *The New International Economic Order: A US Response*, London, Macmillan, 1980.
26. Jessie Helms, *op. cit.*
27. Paul Mosky, et al, *Aid and Power: The World Bank and Policy Based Lending*, London, Routledge, 1991; and Keith Horsefield, ed., *The International Monetary Fund: Twenty Years of International Monetary Cooperation*, Washington, International Monetary Fund, 1969.
28. Wilson E. Schmidt, *The US Balance of Payments and the Sinking Dollar*, New York, New York University Press, 1979.
29. A. G. Shetty, et al, *Finance: An Integrated Global Approach*, Burr Ridge, Irwin, 1995.

30. Bernard M. Hoekman and Michael M. Kostecki, *The Political Economy of the World Trading System: From GATT to WTO*, Oxford, Oxford University Press, 1995.
31. Michael R. Czinkota, et al, eds., *International Business*, Fort Worth, Dryden Press, 1994; UNCTAD, *Transnational Corporations and World Development*, New York Routledge, 1996; and Lorraine Ever and Evan H. Potter, eds., *Multinationals in the Global Poltical Economy*, New York, St Martins, 1993.
32. Craig Garby and Mary B. Bullock, eds., *Japan: A New Kind of Superpower?*, Washington, D. C., John Hopkins University Press, 1994.
33. L. S. Stavrianos, *Global Rift: the Third World comes of age*, New York, Morrow, 1981.
34. Aldo Massola, *The Aborigines of South-Eastern Australia as They Were*, Melbourne, Heinemann, 1971, page 78.
35. Keith Windshuttle, *The Killing of History: How A Discipline is Being Murdered by Literary Critics and Social Theorists*, Paddington, N. S. W., Macleay, 1994.
36. Walter Rodney, *How Europe Underdeveloped Africa*, London, Bogle-L'Ouverture, 1972.
37. Samuel Adshead, *China in World History*, Basingstoke, Macmillan, 1988.
38. Clare Sterling, *The Terror Network: The Secret War Of International Terrorism*, London, Weidenfeld and Nicolson, 1981.
39. *North-South: A Programme for Survival: A Report of the Independent Commission on International Development Issues*, Cambridge, Mass., MIT Press, 1980.
40. Edward Said, *Orientalism*, London, Penguin, 1995. For a balanced assessment of this doctrine which accords it more validity than required see Fred Halliday, *Rethinking International Relations*, Houndmills, Macmillan, 1994.
41. Noam Chomsky, *For Reasons of State*, New York, Pantheon, 1973, a trenchant but warranted attack on US Vietnam policy. Later the theme is extended beyond justification to *Deterring Democracy*, London, Verso, 1991.

42. Noam Chomsky and Edward S. Herman, *Manufacturing Consent: The Political Economy of the Mass Media*, New York, Pantheon, 1988.
43. James B. Collins, *The State In Early Modern France*, Cambridge, Cambridge University Press, 1995. Andrew Wheatcroft, *The Habsburgs: Embodying Empire*, Penguin, 1996.
44. H. Kissinger, *A World Restored*, London, Weidenfeld & Nicolson, 1957.
45. For a critical appreciation of this project see Gabriel Kolko, *The Politics of War; The World and United States Foreign Policy, 1943-45*, New York, Random House, 1968; and Robert Keohane, *After Hegemony: Cooperation and Discord in the World Political Economy*, Princeton, Princeton University Press, 1984.
46. Lawrence Freedman and Efraim Kersh, *The Gulf Coflict 1990-91*, Princeton, Princeton University Press, 1993.

13 Globalisation and the State

> So if you meet me have some courtesy,
> Have some sympathy and some taste;
> Use all your well learned politesse or I'll lay your soul to waste.
>
> Mick Jagger & Keith Richards, 'Sympathy for the Devil'

In the civilised states the industries that have been described as the information sector have become ascendant. As the societies of the civilised zone create this information order so the functions of these states change and some of the functions of earlier orders, notably labour intensive secondary industry, may be devolved to the other development states where they have progressed sufficiently to undertake them. In particular much of the secondary industry which characterised the industrial/imperial state will be either made capital intensive or relocated to low wage states where regulations on industry concerning environmental degradation, safety standards or other add-on costs are less stringent. For example, one of the first things the Japanese conglomerates did as the yen rose in value in the 1970s and 1980s and anti-pollution legislation was enacted based on the Muskie model from the US, was to move plant offshore. They moved labour intensive factories to low wage East Asian countries as export platforms,[1] and more capital intensive plants to the markets in the US and the European Union.

In part, the result is an internationalisation or globalisation of production and of society, particularly among the civilised states. This is caused in some measure by the common social features they exhibit at a similar stage of development. The American fast food chains like Kentucky Fried Chicken and McDonalds hamburgers, for example, have become a world wide phenomenon as other societies have entered a similar consumption rate and the value of the time spent in food preparation exceeds the price of a hamburger for a mass market. Australian media companies like Rupert Murdoch's News Limited, beer, especially Fosters, and express delivery companies led by Sir Peter Ables have acquired the skills to go global in their reach. Italian men's tailors set the standard for many in their field. Japanese video equipment is the market leader almost everywhere. French couturiers like Yves Saint Laurent have made their brand names the standard in mass mid-market fashion even though production may well take place in Asian sweat shops. The manufacturers of highly labour intensive fashion sports shoes like Nike require tenders to get the cheapest production costs in poor countries while they handle complex design and sports hero oriented marketing from their headquarters in the civilised states, which is why a sport shoe costing $10 to make retails for $150. Taiwan can replicate the $2,000 Rolex for $10 but the WTO regime stops them from being sold in civilised states where the regulated markets support high income French and Swiss watch makers.

This process is accelerated by 'regulated free trade' and the interpenetration of a growing number of activities across national boundaries, including economic production, culture, education, the media, tourism and sport. Motor cars are now rarely produced wholly in one country but assemblers will source where the quality and price of, say, rear view mirrors or steering columns are best. Even the Japanese who have historically favoured closely allied component makers are now buying some parts from lower cost states. The highest grossing movies in most civilised states and some of the developmental states are made by an international industry that is concentrated in the US/Hollywood but has smaller branches in Europe and elsewhere. Increasingly Hollywood casting is designed to cater for other markets than the US and lesser parts will be given to stars from targeted market countries. The number of students, particularly those at University level, who study abroad is growing every year, mostly between civilised states but also from poorer countries to the wealthy. Rarely is the flow the other way, despite post-modernist thought, unless research of an anthropological nature is being pursued in more primitive societies.

The media has been international for well over a century and with technological innovation this has intensified: the telegraph gave rapid newspaper stories from far afield; the radio then permitted instant verbal coverage; satellite Television starting in the 1960s provided global reporting hookups; and by the 1990s whole global networks were competing as 24 hour news stations led by Ted Turner's CNN and the British BBC.[2] International tourism became one of the world's fastest growing industries in the 1970s with the introduction of wide bodied jetliners which reduced the unit cost of travel. Sport increasingly became a commercial industry at the top level sold to Television especially Foxtel to produce a market to promote other products. At the same time it became increasingly internationalised among the civilised states, most spectacularly represented by the professionalisation of the Olympic Games. Workers from poor states were recruited into the industry in sectors as diverse as soccer, athletics and sumo wrestling, but this usually involved them living in the civilised states where the activities and markets were concentrated.

This internationalised civilised world has formed enclaves in the development states and their policies will essentially be to try to expand their size and influence. In the early development state of East Asia, Japan, this was deliberate state policy after the Meiji Restoration of 1868 and undertaken in order to strengthen Japan and therefore to defend it against the obviously stronger but barbarian states who were then dominating East Asia. Delegations were sent to other countries with a view to implementing what we would now call world best practice in all spheres. At the time this involved the British Parliament, the American assembly line, the German army, and so on. The South Koreans and Taiwanese were to undertake a similar policy but since it was capital and technology that they sought, they set up Free Trade Zones to attract foreign investors into tax free and cheap labour havens which could be used as re-export platforms. They also of course sent their best students to Western and particularly

American Universities and by the 1990s most of the Taiwanese Cabinet were Ph.Ds and most of those from the US.[3]

These policies worked so well that the Chinese communists used the same devices when they determined to accelerate economic growth in the 1980s. Indeed the role of the Taiwanese model was very important in the evolution of more liberal economic policies by the Chinese communists in the 1980s. At that stage they hoped to evolve a similar economic structure alongside an authoritarian regime, although that model did not in fact survive in Taiwan. The Chinese communists established a series of such special economic zones where the rules of socialism were abandoned and the market allowed to determine economic activity. They also set out to attract foreign investment into them. The most successful of these zones have been in the southern and coastal parts of the country. For historical reasons the old socialist industrial heart is in the north. In the south large capitalist cities like Zhenzen have sprung up fuelled by foreign capital, perhaps 75% of which is from overseas Chinese. To drive this growth of up to 25% annually locally and 13% nationally the peasantry is on the move - perhaps 100 million attracted by the low wage jobs of Chinese capitalism and liberated by the privatisation of the communes.[4]

To a much more limited extent, these enclaves will also extend into those primitive states that have not seriously begun the process of progress. But there they play a more complex role. Burma was taken over by the military led by Ne Win in 1962 and underwent what was called the Burmese Road To Socialism under the Burmese Socialist Program Party. The country was isolated from the world, nationalised all its industry, heavily regulated its farming, particularly of rice, and plunged into an extended civil war involving ethnic secessionists, drug producing armies and communist revolutionaries. The economy stagnated and living standards fell. In 1988 a new round of demonstrations against the Government led to a new military leadership coming to power calling itself the State Law and Order Restoration Council.[5] It undertook a new wave of repression killing over 20,000 in Rangoon alone in late 1988. But SLORC did then start to open the economy to the international market in the hope of generating the kind of development model which was being achieved elsewhere in Southeast Asia. It was backed in this endeavour by the supply of $1.5 billion worth of arms from China, a trickle of capital from the West and the political support of the ASEAN countries.

Economy

But just as the poor states of all political hues attempt to achieve the first steps of industrial progress, so in the advanced zone the new information sector is becoming the dominant activity led by an expanded education sector. This has been made necessary by the demand for a highly skilled and motivated labour force in constant need of retraining. In this process Universities have been transformed from elite, hierarchical, theory based institutions to mass education centres to cater for the continuing education needs of an information society. This process was led by the United States where tertiary education became a mass activity by the 1950s. This was often scorned by the less advanced British who viewed many of the American Universities as not up to British Oxbridge intellectual standards. While this may have been true it was no longer the valid yardstick.[6]

As civil society sought to generate self motivated workers prepared to undertake unsupervised work at their own initiative in the new information industry sectors, so Universities had to reach further down the IQ cohorts to achieve outcomes which were previously restricted to a small elite formed by a combination of privilege and merit. In this process the University staff IQ level also had to fall and the subject matter taught be made simpler. The result was, of course, a lower level of intellectual achievement, the stratification of institutions by quality, the strengthening of managerial and state control and the intensification of simplistic idealist thought in the weaker Universities as an easy option to serious research. World best Universities opened themselves to the same doggerel when trying to protect themselves against the charge of elitism. Easy ideologies based on collective pathologies and personal advancement - feminism, post-modernism, queer theory, multiculturalism - competed to displace traditional curricula.[7]

The cutting edge for this new information industry sector was the revolution in electronic communication systems and especially the computer. The computer revolutionised the finance markets of the

1980s by enabling instant global market deals to be made and so provided the basis for the Lockean counterrevolution against state regulation. It then spread rapidly through the manufacturing, distribution, and services sectors. By the mid-1990s the personal computer was spreading through a work force increasingly able to access work from home and a myriad of other locations through the use of modem technology. In order to ensure that their societies could access these systems states got out of the provision of communications infrastructure and privatised and de-monopolised telecommunications as a means for ensuring rapid technological innovation through the proven method of competition.

The invention of the powerful personal computer is usually attributed to the Apple company in the 1980s but within a decade the IBM-based system had overtaken it because the copyright was less restrictive and cloning by rivals both reduced the price and improved the product. Indeed by the 1990s the Taiwanese computer firms were competing with IBM for market share and quality reputation. The production of computers continued to be sufficiently labour intensive for much of it to be undertaken by cheap female labour in poor countries. But the innovation of design and hard ware was concentrated in civilised states where the greater mass of University trained workers threw up more entrepreneurs like the owner of Microsoft, Bill Gates. Since computers increasingly provided entertainment for the young in civilised states so it is there that such innovations particularly in software design will continue to be made.[8]

The effects of these innovations are continuing to be felt in the old sectors by increasing their productivity and reducing their labour content. In agriculture for example the production of grapes and other fruit has been made hugely more productive by the use of weed controlling plastics and computerised irrigation systems. Most crops can now be increased by the use of high yield seed, pesticides and fertilisers, the result of laboratory research by multinational companies. These products are then increasingly harvested and transported by capital intensive machinery and processed in such a way that their distribution through the wholesale and retailing sector is controlled by computer. The labour power required to accomplish these tasks that used to dominate the economies of what have become civilised states reduces every year. As a result the price of unprocessed food has generally fallen and the famines which occur in the primitive states are not from the absence of production but due to the failure of their distribution systems - often caused by civil strife or, as in Stalin's Ukraine, Mao's Great Leap Forward and Mengistu's Ethiopia, deliberate policy by ruthless idealist politicians.

The secondary industries which produced the initial industrial revolution in Britain are also in sharp decline as employers of labour and therefore in social and political significance. Textiles are now most efficiently produced in automated plants, which are themselves produced in the civilised states, which require workers only to supervise and service them. It is more difficult to automate fashion clothing so the top end of the clothing market often stays in the rich countries with highly specialized and well paid designers. Mass produced product has left for development states. Steel works are similarly automated and have shed labour on a large scale during the 1980s in all civilised states. The automated and robotised assembly line is producing standard commodities like refrigerators, cars, washing machines and television sets all over the world.

At first the labour shedding in the traditional sectors was compensated by the application of mass production techniques first used in secondary industry to the service sector. Retail outlets, large offices with typing pools and housing estates with mass undifferentiated labour dominated the work force. This too has come to an end. Shopping complexes now incorporate boutique outlets. With the middle managerial strata each issued with a computer their own need for secretarial assistance has declined since most people can type on a Personal Computer as quickly as they can formulate. As population growth has ceased the construction worker is more like a specialist extender, renovator or architect than a bricklayer.

The common theme in all these developments in the work force is the destruction of mass production as the most common form of industrial organisation. If it can be done in mass it can be automated and done with little labour and low cost. The new commodities in demand require specialised labour or services for their production. Some commentators have called these industries post-Fordist to reflect the fact that the assembly line system of production associated with Henry Ford's car factories and the industrial design systems of Taylorism are now ever more redundant. They might be better termed the new information sector in which workers sell their knowledge or information into a market that demands it. And if it does not they have to aquire new knowledge.

Government

In such high productivity economies output now depends on more highly skilled labour devoted to more specialised tasks. People come together in more diversified and shorter term arrangements to complete an assignment or contract and then move on to the next one. In such circumstances the government presides over a market economy producing abundance but can guarantee it for no individual who has increasingly to cater for himself. The old system of aggregate demand management that may have been appropriate for a regime dominated by the mass production of physical commodities, is now unusable not only because of the constraints of the international finance markets but also because there is no longer such an obvious economic lever as aggregate demand. Full employment will no longer reappear with strong economic growth because some of the workers no longer have the skills to match demand in a highly skilled differentiated and segmented work force. If a textile factory hand in Bradford has been laid off because the sector has closed and he/she has no other skills he/she will find it hard to gain reemployment if the new growth sector is set design in the British cinema. For such circumstances, which are increasingly evident, the role of government is to provide a basic services and income safety net and to urge retraining on the individual.[9]

But for the employed worker, who is now more likely to be in a smaller enterprise or even self employed, the role of the state in his life is more likely to recede. Because a more significant proportion but still small minority of the population are going to be in a supplicant situation even during growth phases than was the case during the industrial period government will target its services to them and expect the prosperous of whom there are also many more to provide for themselves. This will involve the restructuring of what were universal government provided services towards the provision of them only to the needy and indigent. Thus in most civilised countries welfare programs that were previously provided to all are being reduced and heavily means tested, while most people have to find their own employment income on the market. Such programs include health systems which are experiencing extensive privatisation; pension systems that are provided by the worker in a portable form and managed privately; and education at all levels from primary to University. In addition the old utilities are being privatised all over the world and market pricing mechanisms introduced to drive efficiencies in transport, electricity, gas and water provision. The state is withdrawing to its core business of making and enforcing the law, defending the realm, providing the currency and looking after the people not able to look after themselves. Otherwise in many respects the Thatcher revolution marked a return to the determination of Henry VIII to restore initiative to the British population.

This process represents a counter revolution in political life to correspond to the advance of free market doctrines in the economic sphere. It is a Lockean vision of a benign civil society to contrast with that Hobbesian version which had recently prevailed, of it being, a zone in which life was nasty brutish and short unless alleviated by state intervention. After a generation or two of steadily expanding states as measured by the proportion of national income they consumed or by the number of functions undertaken, the state is now everywhere in retreat. The most successful of the civilised states are now trimming state expenditure to achieve a figure of around thirty per cent of GDP and a budget deficit of close to zero and the European Union-states are chasing similar targets set by the 1991 Maastricht Treaty.

This is not to say that the state will disappear - quite the contrary, it will acquire new functions. These will include a greatly expanded role in the establishment of a system of labour retraining which will run for the duration of a person's life. It will also include a much more active role of protecting the physical environment, both natural and constructed, against the assaults of a very productive and therefore potentially destructive capitalist economy. And it will also involve ensuring that the front line information industries are rapidly accessed by its citizens since to miss a generation at the present pace of technological change could be fatal.[10]

What kind of person will run the state into this new era? As has already been described they will be professional politicians. In the industrial era the great forces of undifferentiated labour and industrial capital were well represented in the civilised world's legislatures and executives. In the new order it will be workers from the new information sector that will come to dominate. It is they who will have the informational and presentation skills, it is they who will have the initiative and it is they who will best understand the new social functions. As a result there will be more teachers, consultants, academics, lawyers, media workers and women, who are proportionately stronger in the new industries, involved in the running of the state. And since they will be closer to the intellectual world of the day it becomes even more critical that it not lag behind reality and fall into a miasma of idealism.

Culture and Globalisation

As we have seen the civilised state was the result of the convergence of a number of religious, political, social, economic, technological, and intellectual forces. Since the Second World War civilised states have been militarily stronger than their enemies, and since the end of the Cold War considerably stronger. But such strength rests upon contingencies which may not always be favourable. In addition to preserving strong military capabilities the survival of the civilised states requires a healthy economy to fund the technological advancements which provide military advantages. But a strong economy and a strong military advantage are not sufficient conditions for ensuring the continuity of the civilised state. The more civilised states that exist, the less likely the chances of warfare within the civilised zone.

Civilised states, however, can only be sustained if an array of cultural values dominate the society: especially the values of liberty and tolerance. Economic prosperity is a common way in which these values may emerge in societies which otherwise were not 'naturally' disposed to them. As a people become more economically prosperous the opportunities for them to consume a greater range of cultural goods increases. Cultural artifacts, in their turn, provide increased economic opportunities, and the general prosperity within the civilised society means that more people have access to more cultural information and have more choice about what they want to believe, eat, be entertained by, play, wear, learn, build, join, in sum - do, than in any other form of society. Yet, the dominant perspective of those writing in the field of cultural studies is that the overall effect of the global spread of cultural artifacts and technologies is negative, that mass communications are shrinking the world, that differences of taste and identity which once seemed vast are now being minimised, and that there is an increasing homogenisation of life experiences, as well as the artistic expression of those experiences, being created by our common technologies and communication systems.[11]

Certainly, global cross-fertilisations are evolving. And although this is not happening everywhere, and where it is happening it is happening to different degrees and at different levels, there is occuring a process of cultural global fusion on an unprecedented scale — simply because more cultures are involved. It is also true that the terms of the fusion are not egalitarian, and that not all cultural practices are equally assimilated and valued by the members of civilised states, or by primitive states. To appreciate a Hindu temple is not the same as appreciating the Hindu caste system, and to appreciate Indian cuisine, music and art does not mean that one should appreciate the practice of widows throwing themselves onto fires. Likewise, the rulers of Islamic states want Western technologies but not Western freedoms.

For an increasing number of intellectuals in the academy such discriminations when exercised by Westerners are indicative of a major problem. For them, instead of celebrating the fact so much of the world can be accessed in one form or another, they deplore that the world is being Americanized.

A recent book which puts the case for the increasing cultural barbarisation of the world due to the spread of tastes and technologies from America is Benjamin Barber's *Jihad vs. McWorld: How the Planet is Both Falling Apart and Coming Together and What This Means for Democracy*.[12] If Barber's tirade is stripped of its doomsday rhetoric it amounts to a few curious gripes. One is that too many people are spending time shopping and amusing themselves rather than sitting in libraries or churches or political backrooms, and that Hollywood and shopping malls encourage this.[13] He also laments the fact that common shopping malls and football stadiums in different parts of the world look more alike than churches, and that as more people have access to types of experience that they were previously unable to have there is a homogenisation of architectural styles. Barber also sees it as a matter of grave importance that the number one restaurant chain in terms of volume of food sold in Japan is McDonald's, and number two is Kentucky Fried Chicken. Further of McDonald's nearly 15,000 restaurants, nearly 4,500, or one third are outside the United States; there are over one thousand in Japan alone. He also points out that McDonald's serves 20 million customers a day. The $2.4 billion worth of pizza sold in 1991 by the privately owned Domino's earned enough revenues to fund the combined government expenditures of Senegal, Uganda, Bolivia and Iceland.

It is difficult to see, however, what conclusion one should draw from these facts. First, why is it a problem that the two most popular franchises of fast food restaurants in Japan are owned by Americans? Is it that the Japanese economy is being bled by America? Hardly since the Japanese run huge trade surpluses with the United States. Is it that Japanese cuisine is somehow being eliminated by the presence of McDonald's and Kentucky Fried Chicken? Surely not. Barber does not mention the fact that there has been a general explosion of service industries and of food outlets generally in the developed world in the last thirty years, that more people are eating in restaurants as well as take away food than ever in history. Likewise, there are now also more Japanese restaurants in more countries in the world than previously in history. But it is not only Japanese food that is finding more outlets. Consider the rapid expansion in the market for Asian food in America, Britain, Europe and Australia in the last fifteen years, a market which extends not only to restaurants, but to grocery shops and supermarkets. Why anyone should be getting upset about the introduction of new culinary habits is a mystery.

Another major sphere of popular culture which is frequently cited by critics is in the general area of entertainment. Barber also sees Western entertainment as pernicious. The importance of entertainment for the American economy cannot be underestimated. As of 1994, the top 17 American companies in entertainment, telecommunications or information have $140 billion in sales. The audio-visual industry is the second largest after aerospace. Focusing first upon movies, Barber draws attention to the fact that America controls over 80% of the European movie market, while Europe has less than 2% of the

American market. Although if we turn to India or China the dominance of Hollywood is hardly as imposing. But all this simply suggests that Hollywood knows how to produce better popular films. It is a matter of taste whether one thinks that popular films are good. The attack that Barber mounts against Hollywood is the Platonist's attack upon the simpler pleasures of the mass market. People like Barber focus upon what they see as the infantilisation of the popular mind. But the spread of popular culture arises from more people having more leisure and more money. In any case one could argue on the same premise that the popular culture which Barber sees as being displaced is equally infantile. The irony of Barber's contempt for the global patterns of consumer preference is that Barber presents himself as a radical democrat, but only as long as everyone shares the 'sophisticated' aesthetic sensibilities (which include quaint traditions) he does.

Rock Music: An Example of the Potency of Global Civil Society

One area of popular culture which has aroused the ire of cultural guardians, communists and conservatives alike (and Barber), and which perhaps more than any single art form has transformed the life style of people throughout the world is rock music. Rocks stars, said Viktor Chebrikov, the head of the KGB, in 1987, 'nudged the population into the position of criticism, demagogy and nihilism.'[14] Similar sentiments were expressed by the vice-president of the Soviet Academy of Pedagogical Sciences who condemned rock bands for spreading a plague which was 'the moral equivalent of AIDS.' Certainly, the spread of rock music in the Soviet block was the spread of a subversive style, attitude, and message. Western rock bands promised freedom, not in the Marxist-Leninist sense of the realisation of a utopia, but in the sense of the free exploration of human intensities. It was precisely because it was a vehicle for expressing emotions of loss, love, hate, longing, that rock music was so subversive in the communist world. Vaclav Havel, the Czech playwright, dissident and eventual President of the Czech Republic, even argued that the most significant dissident organization in communist Czechoslovakia, Charter 77, 'may not have taken place were it not for a campaign he and others launched against the trial and imprisonment of the underground rock group, the Plastic People of the Universe.'[15] The Plastic People of the Universe had been arrested for disturbing the peace and singing indecent songs. The lyrics of one song in particular was cited in the charge:

> What do you resemble in your greatness?
> Are you the truth?
> Are you God?
> What do you resemble in your greatness?
> A piece of shit, a piece of shit, a piece of shit...[16]

The imprisonment of the Plastic People of the Universe was seen by Havel and other Czech dissidents as an attack 'on the very notion of living within the truth'. The freedom to play rock music was understood as a human freedom and thus as essentially the same as the freedom to write, the freedom to express, and defend the various social and political interests of society.[17]

The reaction of the apparachiks in the Soviet bloc to rock was no different to the reaction of many American adults when initially confronted with the growing spread of rock music in the fifties. As John Street points out in *Rebel Rock*: 'In the USA in the 1950s, Elvis Presley records were burnt in public. Church leaders spoke out against the new music, arguing that it came from the devil to subvert the youth of America'. In 1955 'the Juvenile Delinquency and Crime Commission of Houston, Texas banned more than fifty songs in one week.' The subversive appeal of rock, then, was not something only experienced by the youth and apparachiks of communist states, but just as intensely in the United States and Great Britain throughout the fifties, sixties and, then with punk, into the seventies.

Like the Russian and East European communists and the church leaders of the fifties, Barber sees rock music as culturally damaging. He seems very upset that MTV's global audience is over a quarter of a billion households in 71 countries. Barber's silly tirade against MTV proceeds in ignorance of what the real cultural significance of rock music is for the spread of civilisation, something that should be appreciated irrespective of whether one actually likes rock music; that is to say the virtue of global cultural artifacts extend beyond merely aesthetic horizons. In the first instance, to see rock music as simply a

Western phenomenon is simplistic. It was from its inception a creative synthesis of global styles and technologies. At its heart was the blues, and blues was built upon a combination of the voice and guitar. Blues had evolved out of gospel and Negro spirituals, a music that would have been impossible without the fusion of black man's and woman's lament for being torn from Africa and thrown into slavery and the hymns they learnt in church. The guitar, however, evolved in Spain. But it was in America that the first electric guitars began being made in 1924. It was from jazz that rock inherited the drum kit. Jazz itself originated in New Orleans, but the confluence of social fusions which made it possible were West Indian, African, Cuban and European (British, French and Spanish).

But such facts are ignored by the Barbers of academe: instead there is the sounding of deathknells and the preaching of impending doom. Underpinning the great cultural fear they peddle is that old favourite enemy of twentieth century Marxists, the multi-national company. It may, on first impression, sound sinister or unfair that six global corporations dominate the popular music industry, not only in the United States but across the world. But while such a fact is frequently trotted out to indicate that there is little opportunities for popular musicians, the opposite is the case. New labels continually spring up to fill market niches the lumbering multi-nationals cannot completely dominate. Nowadays many rock bands are able to finance their own recordings from gig money and sell their CDs at gigs, and many artists do not want to be corporately controlled because they will be squeezed into the formulae of the larger corporations who have to spread their product as far as possible to get profits or even returns from the massive advertising campaigns needed to get rewards. There are more people able to earn an income by being entertainers today than at any other time in history. As multi-nationals bring different styles of music into different homes and different recording technologies, local musicians receive hitherto unimaginable opportunities. In places where recording was not possible, it suddenly becomes possible for musicians to record and get air-play. Kids that had little interest in music develop an interest. This may create less interest in the indigenous music, but often just the opposite tends to happen, the development of musical ability sends musicians in search of their traditions as well as others. Recording studios pop up like mushrooms in cities and towns all over the world. The equivalent to recording facilities that once were impossibly expensive become affordable, as musicians buy eight and sixteen track recording equipment.

The greatest value to civilised states in the spread of popular culture lies precisely in the spread of the potency of civil society itself. The significance of rock music for civilisation is that it is the expression of independence, creativity, industry, history, personality, the intensities (both dark and bright) of the soul, and above all it appeals to people to live passionately by paying attention to one's own energies. The Mullahs in Iran are smart to forbid it, for while rock music is politically neutral in the short term, in the long term the practices which generate around it are most compatible with a secular society which values the dangerous freedoms of creative expression, voluntary associations, lack of censorship, youthful rebelliousness, and self-exploration.

Rock music is only one strand of the globalisation of culture that is also manifest in cuisine and the cinema. It is also occurring more widely in architecture, clothing, design, language and, of course, commerce. This is not a new phenomenon although the pace of change has accelerated. It is creating an international civil society which broadly radiates from the civilised zone and then is accommodated and modified elsewhere. As it spreads it also serves to create some of the conditions for the creation of a liberal social and political order and to that extent is a harbinger of progress. But it is also secular and this produces other nuances. To suggest that popular music which is often created by drug addicts, manic-depressives, alcoholics, and the occasional talented paedophile may be advancing and spreading the cause of Western civilisation (and not as post-modernists think, subverting it) is to suggest that tolerance and joy and commercial prosperity go hand in hand.

The globalisation of culture - represented in part and illustrated here by rock music - also coincides with the destruction of traditional religion. In the West, the German philosopher, Ludwig Feuerbach, had grasped in the 1840s that religious beliefs would dissipate as the empirical sciences came to play an increasingly large part in society.[18] By the end of the second millennium, institutional religion in the civilised world is in decline everywhere. Traditional institutional religions tend to paint the spirit more and more in social worker colours, while primordial irrational longings which are still widely prevalent in civilised society, as is evident when one walks into any books store, find outlets through more private spiritual quests. It remains to be seen what will happen as the social capital of traditional religion dries up. The martyr to National Socialism, Dietrich Bonhoeffer,[19] and Eugen Rosenstock-Huessy, both Christians, had seen in the middle of this century that a post-religious age had commenced, that those truths about existence which were previously disseminated through religion would have to find very different outlets.

Civilisation was built on soil cultivated by Christendom. As those religious roots disappear, therefore, the biggest danger facing civilisation may become the declining number of groups willing to sacrifice themselves for protecting it, and the absence of generations willing to show fiscal restraint, and not live beyond their means so that the next generation picks up the bill. A civilised state will only survive if each generation believes that it has something worth protecting and something worth building. Secular societies are always in danger of sacrificing the future to immediacy, and the pessimism of the intelligentsia gives little cause to behave otherwise. We are entering into unknown territory. For godless societies are historical anomalies. Is this a cause for pessimism or optimism? That, as Nietzsche so sharply put it, depends upon whether we are willing to face up to being the murderers of God. It is up to us to create an abundant culture. It is certainly not something for a group of politicians or bureaucrats to plan.

Notes

1. Walter Hatch and Kozo Yamamura, *Asia in Japan's Embrace*, Cambridge, Cambridge University Press, 1996.
2. John Sinclair, Elizabeth Jacka and Stuart Cunningham, eds., *New Patterns in Global Television: Periperal Vision*, New York, Oxford University Press, 1995; Hank Whittemore, *CNN: The Inside Story*, Boston, Little Brown, 1990.

3. Derek Healey, *Taiwan's Economic Future: some thoughts from a 1990 vantage point*, Adelaide, University of Adelaide, Dept. of Economics, 1990.
4. Greg O'Leary, 'China: The Long Road', *Current Affairs Bulletin*, June/July, 1996.
5. Bob Catley,' Burma: The Next Frontier?' *Quadrant*, July 1996.
6. Tom Schuller, ed., *The Changing University?*, Bristol, Open University Press, 1995.
7. Mary M. Day et al, *Discursively Knowing the Modern With/in Postmodern Pedagogy: Reflexivity in Teaching Acounting Theory*, Campbelltown, University of Western Sydney, 1995; and Richard Parker and John Gagnon, eds., *Conceiving Sexuality: Approaches to Sex Research in a PostModern World*, New York, Routledge, 1995.
8. George Anderla and Anthony Dunning, *Computer Strategies, 1990-99: Technologies, Costs, Markets*, Chichester, Wiley, 1987.
9. G. W. Ford, *Technology Transfer, Technocultures and Skill Formation*, South Melbourne, CIRCIT, 1990; and Roger Penn, Michael Rose and Jill Rubery, eds., *Skill and Occupational Change*, Oxford, Oxford University Press, 1994.
10. Michael Welourne, *et al*, *The Pace of Change: Technology Uptake and Enterprise Improvement*, Canberra, AGPS, 1994; and John Magedoorn, ed., *Technical Change and the World Economy*, Aldershot, Edward Elgar, 1995.
11. William J. Martin, *The Global Information Society*, Aldershot, Gower, 1995.
12. New York, Times Books, 1995.
13. *Ibid.*, page 97.
14. Pedro Ramet and Sergei Zamasvikov,'The Soviet Rock Scene', *Journal of Popular Culture*, Summer 1990, vol. 24:1, page 151.
15. Tony Mitchell, 'Rock Music in Czechoslovakia', in *Popular Music*, 1992 vol. 11/2, page 189.
16. John Street, *Rebel Rock: The Politics of Popular Music*, Oxford, Blackwell, 1986, page 14.
17. Vacláv Havel, 'The Power of the Powerless', in *The Power of the Powerless: citizens against the state in central-eastern Europe*, J.

Keane, ed., New York, M. E. Sharpe, 1985, pages 46-7, cited in *Rebel Rock*, page 189.
18. Ludwig Feuerbach, *The Essence of Christianity*, trans. George Eliot, New York, Harper, 1957.
19. Dietrich Bonhoeffer, *Letters and Papers from Prison*, trans. R. H. Fuller, London, SCM Press, 1971.

14 The Future of the State

> And what rough beast, its hour come round at last
> Slouches towards Bethlehem to be born?
>
> W. B. Yeats, *The Second Coming*

The sovereign state system has been the most enduring political institution of the modern era. Since the creation of sovereign states out of the hierarchical structure of political power and spiritual legitimacy that was Medieval Christendom, the civil society of these states and many of their other characteristics have changed substantially. The civilised ones are urban in population, industrial or post-industrial in economy, internationalised in trade, bureaucratised in structure and mostly use ideological/rational discourse rather than physically repressive methods as their control mechanisms. As a result, and hardly surprisingly, there is a considerable literature devoted to the issue as to whether these changes have changed the nature of the state itself.[1] This issue has taken a number of forms.

The Erosion of National Sovereignty?

It has been argued that the processes of globalisation have eroded the very quality of sovereignty which makes the state distinctive.[2] This is an argument advanced principally by Left wing authors and mostly by Europeans. It is claimed that many of the functions of the state that were integral to its sovereignty have been eliminated by the internationalisation of the global economy. The state can no longer control fiscal policy, regulate its currency in isolation and plan economic output. The reasons for this are said to include the growth of large companies which operate across national boundaries, plan their production and markets on a global basis and whose favours are sought by states in such a way that they cannot sustain their autonomy. In addition many state owned enterprises have been sold off to private ownership in pursuit of efficiency gains for the national economy as a whole, particularly where they involve infrastructure provision like energy, communications and transportation. The Left of course as part of its historical ideology wants to build up the power of the state and regulate or abolish private property, to combat these companies.

Some of these claims are valid. The modern, post-Cold War civilised state has tended to reduce obstacles to trade such as tariffs and quotas on imports as part of the World Trade Organisation regime in such a way as the old system of nurturing infant industries through state protection is now no longer viable. But it is still practised and accepted for developmental and primitive states to so behave just as some of the presently advanced ones did at that stage of their development. More persuasive is the point that with the internationalisation of world finance markets states must frame their fiscal and monetary polices in conformity with them if they are not to risk a run on their currency. If this occurs they become a more risky location for investment capital and indeed may face a capital flight. While this is true, it is also the case that it has been true for over a hundred years, although it was temporarily disguised by the Bretton Woods system of fixed exchange rates that effectively came to an end in the early 1970s. In any case to the extent that states have reduced their control over these economic management functions, it is because they have chosen to do so usually believing, on the advice of economists, that it will improve their rate of economic growth.

In point of fact, many of the other functions of the state, even among the advanced states, have actually been strengthened including its police forces with computerised records, taxation collecting agencies, its labour retraining programs, its environmental protection bodies and leading edge technology subsidisation programs. In many of the development states, in addition, more effective control of the national population and territory has also coincided with internationalisation. In Burma for example state control of its territory was only achieved in 1996 after two generations of secessionist and communist rebellions. Throughout the ASEAN states there has been a substantial increase in the armed forces and a substantial military procurement build up. One of the problems associated with the difficulties of development in some primitive states is precisely the overdeveloped state apparatus in comparison with a fragile civil society. In Africa this has contributed to the overmilitarisation of the state and paradoxically regime instability because they rest on narrow social bases and no broad civil society.

The reason for the insistence that the state is experiencing an erosion of its sovereignty is to be found in part among those who propound the view. In Europe there has been a consensual state policy of reducing the areas of control that the state retains and handing them to the European Union. How far this process will proceed is a matter for legitimate and important conjecture among the scholars of these states who tend to see this as a universal phenomenon, which it isn't. Only the European states are undertaking such a project. In the other major centres of economic power regional economic organisations have come into being like the Asia Pacific Economic Cooperation, the proposed East Asian Economic Caucus and the North American Free Trade Agreement. But these are not envisaged to develop as successors to the existing sovereign state members.[3]

Further, Left wing intellectuals are understandably concerned that the functions of the state to which they attached such importance, particularly aggregate demand management, are being abandoned. They see this, correctly, as signalling the end of the state's commitment to maintain what they call full employment. But this was never more than a political program for some political parties during a particular and short historical period of the post-1945 economic boom. Its abandonment has no necessary consequence for the quality of sovereignty.

It should also be noted that in the part of the world in which Left intellectuals pinned so many of their hopes - the old Soviet bloc - the reassertion of national state apparatuses has created a new generation of jealously sovereign communities. This development has produced a new round of wars in Eastern Europe as the territorial and national divisions and boundaries are more precisely determined. The international wars between the successor states of the old Yugoslavia could have been fought at any time over the last thousand years on the same issues and with the same ruthless methods. Each of the combatants pursued the same cause, the maximisation of its state territory, argued its moral right to the world in terms of national self determination, used realpolitik in search of its objectives and slaughtered the opposition when it was expedient. Machiavelli would have recognised the type.[4]

War

It has also been alleged that the globalisation process has reduced the capacity of the state to fight war.[5] This is caused by the state losing authority over its citizens, who become reluctant to die on its behalf, over its territory (to multi-national companies), for which it will no longer fight, and over resources which can now be more easily traded than fought over. As a result the military functions of the state and the resources devoted to them are being greatly reduced. Many of these arguments predate the globalisation proposition and were advanced by the interdependence school in the 1970s. Kenneth Waltz sought to refute them in his seminal book, *Theory of International Politics*.[6] Even earlier, in *Man, The State and War*, he had confronted the liberal and other idealist schools on the issue of the prevention of war and divided them into three broad categories and refuted them in detail. The first category attributed war to human nature which it believed to be malleable and, therefore, subject to a re-education program, war could be eliminated. The Communist Manifesto and UNESCO Charter were classic examples of this thinking. Waltz argued that since humans are not infinitely malleable some will always be prepared to use force in pursuit of their interests and thus cause war. This point was made at length previously.

The second school of idealists attributed war to the kind of state which existed and believed that a transformation of the state to a democratic, socialist, republican or feminist form, depending on the precise orientation of this idealist argument, a generalised peace might be attained. Waltz showed that the form of state made little difference to their preparedness to use force to pursue their ends. He argued that democratic states, despite the desire of their electorates for peace would in fact go to war if their other more important objectives, like access to Kuwait's oil output, were threatened. He could show with little effort that socialist states would use force and against each other if necessary. It is also clearly the case that republics will fight, if necessary, as quickly as monarchies, something that Alexander Hamilton and before him Machiavelli well knew. Waltz was writing before the high water mark of feminist idealism with its desire to change the parameters of thinking about the state by arguing that women are intrinsically more peaceful, so he did not have to make the point that three of the most expansionist states in the history of the system had female leaders: Elizabeth I and Queen Victoria of Britain and Catherine the Great of Russia.

The third believed that the anarchic society of states permitted wars to occur and that they could be prevented by the strengthening of international civil society, international law and international organisations. Waltz argued that these institutions had not stopped states from using force to pursue interest in the past, like the Axis powers in the 1930s, and would not in future. This amounts to a refutation of Kant's proposal for a *Perpetual Peace* and is a commonly held interpretation of certainly the League of Nations and also the United Nations among international relations scholars.

Waltz later confronted the interdependency theorists, associated with the journal influential during the Carter administration, *International Organisation*, from a similar intellectual perspective. He said that while it might be true that states were becoming more interdependent economically, culturally and financially, they were still independent political units and would pursue independent political interests, if necessary by force. He pointed out that in the decade before World War One the states of Europe had become increasingly interdependent but had been prepared to fight a long and bloody war over clashes of interests nonetheless. His corollary was of course that the United States should be prepared to defend and advance its state interests by force if required.

The realist school had the better of most of these arguments. But in fact the end of the Cold War has presented two different systems of interstate behaviour. On the one hand among the civilised states many of the features of international society that the liberal idealist schools advocated and pursued have actually been achieved. Educated people are not as ready to use war as an instrument of policy and are even less keen to do the fighting themselves. Democratic states do not fight wars with one another and obey international law and the dictates of the United Nations to an extraordinary degree. For example, although the United Nations Convention on the Law of the Sea (UNCLOS) was drawn up by underdeveloped states seeking to extend their territorial possessions and increase the economic rent they could charge the civilised states for using them, the developed countries, who had generally opposed it, complied with UNCLOS after the agreed number of sixty states ratified it in 1994. Among themselves civilised states behave in a civilised fashion and do not fight wars for pursuit of interest.

But in relations with the other types of state it is often necessary to use force, since those states will use force in relation to one another and the civilised states. Since the end of the Cold War there have been about eighty wars almost exclusively fought among non-civilised states. A small number of conflicts have been fought between civilised and non-civilised states including the Gulf War of 1991. And civilised states have also used force to protect their interests against disturbances generated in the other zones, including Haiti, Cambodia, Somalia and the former Yugoslavia. The civilised state most exposed to this problem is, of course, Israel that has faced extinction since its inception if it were to lose the preponderance of military power it has so far possessed and been prepared to use.

Since the preponderance of power is clearly with the civilised states, even after they have undertaken the large reduction in arms expenditure which they did after the Cold War, for the most part this two sided strategic behaviour does not involve any great difficulties. When Iraq unilaterally threatened the disruption of world energy distribution, remedial military action was relatively swift and decisive (although the Iraqi dictator was unwisely left *in situ*). The Haiti dictatorship was also dismantled when it threatened to present the

US with an intolerable refugee burden. The brutal realpolitik of Belgrade was belatedly stopped after it threatened to destroy totally both Bosnia and the already low credibility of United Nations peacekeeping operations. But when it comes to the question of China, as with the Soviet Union previously, the very size of the state changes the character of the problem.

China As A Great Power

China cannot be treated like a civilised state because it is undemocratic, lacks a developed civil society, is economically undeveloped and is quite prepared to use extreme force in pursuit of state interests, as for example with Taiwan or the Spratly Islands.[7] It is also unwilling to comply with international agreements from which it will generally benefit when it sees clauses as being contrary to its interests. Thus it uses prison labour, breaks copyright agreements and subsidises exports, contrary to WTO, the ILO and US imports policy, if it can get away with it. Nonetheless geopolitics dictates that a policy which is appropriate for Libya - such as aerial bombardment in 1986 - may not be and may not work for the world's largest population armed with nuclear weapons. In this instance a combination of armed *realpolitik* together with a diplomacy of inclusion and confidence building measures that encourages China to conform to civilised state behaviour norms, may be the required mix.

China is on the brink of being a serious and possibly global great power.[8] Whether it will in fact achieve this status is of course open to all manner of questions. It has a large economy and population and a nuclear weapons program and arsenal. The economy is only large, however, when measured by Purchasing Power Parity (PPP) which means in effect internal purchasing power. This gives less indication about its status as an internationally competitive production system or its level of technological development. Since it has not fought a major war since the attack it launched on Vietnam in 1979, when it was badly beaten, it is not possible to estimate its military capability. In any case it has had nearly two decades of military and other modernisation to make up for earlier deficiencies. At present it seems unlikely that it can project conventional military power far outside

Chinese territory as the 1996 Taiwan Straits crisis appeared to show when it backed off in the face of a two carrier US task force.

The Chinese nuclear arsenal is another matter altogether. It is usually estimated that the Chinese have about twenty nuclear war heads that have been developed in a nuclear program that has been immune since its inception in the 1950s to the various political gyrations which have characterised the communist party. A few of these may be capable of hitting the US if Chinese technology is sufficiently reliable for that feat. In 1996 a Chinese satellite launcher was officially claimed to be lost only to be discovered by a European tourist with video camera as having crashed on nearby town with considerable loss of life. The development of an arsenal sufficiently large and reliable to permit deterring the US against enforcing the international order in East Asia against what may soon be Chinese local conventional supremacy may be some time off. It should be recognised, however, that such a strategic development may produce a problem at a different order of magnitude.

But among the civilised states themselves the condition of perpetual peace has been achieved by a league of democratic republics who have common values and have eschewed war as a means of pursuing state interests. To achieve the global elimination of war will involve the expansion of such states throughout the system in ways that have been previously discussed. There is no assurance that such a process will occur. Until and unless it does those states need to maintain the military apparatuses of state in good order.

Economic Management

The economic management functions of the advanced states were progressively augmented after the decline of the liberal and minimalist state in England from the late nineteenth century onwards, until the revival of liberal economic thought in the 1980s. The onset of the interventionist state came from a number of impulses including the desire of late developers like Germany and in different forms the US and Australia to nurture domestic industries, and the rise of the social democratic political program.

After 1945, and despite Keynes' unsuccessful opposition to the Bretton Woods agreement as leader of the British delegation, Keynes' ideas were widely accepted in advanced countries and enthusiastically by social democratic parties. In essence the application of the doctrines involved the state utilising its budgetary powers to stimulate economic demand and make economic growth faster and employment levels higher. This could be achieved by budget deficits. This ran two major risks. One was that the printing of currency to pay for the deficits would eventually devalue the currency against the value of other currencies whose state managers did not undertake this exercise. At first, governments were able to offset this by controls on trade, like tariffs, and on currency exchange, like licenses and controls on the capital and money markets. The other problem was that the growth of the supply of money at a quicker rate than that of real goods and services would bid up prices and lead to generalised inflation. This started to happen almost immediately.

Nonetheless for three decades after 1945 the Keynesian system of demand stimulation by deficit budgets and associated devices was adopted throughout the civilised world. It coincided with a period of prolonged economic growth, low unemployment and weak business cycles. It was pronounced a huge success. In 1975 it started to fail and came under sustained attack from the so called monetarist school of Milton Friedman and from other variants of liberal economists.[9] The occasion for this assault was the recession of 1974-5 which was accompanied by rampant inflation and worsened by the 400 per cent increase in the price of oil which the OPEC countries were able to impose on the world market. The liberal economists argued that the post-war boom had been as much to do with a fortuitous bout of post-war reconstruction as Keynesian policies and that if financial disciplines were not restored permanent inflation would wreck the market economies. These prescriptions were progressively taken on board by the governments of the civilised states.

This counter-revolution in economic doctrines and policy, closely associated with Mrs Thatcher but spreading much wider than Britain, led to closer attention being paid to monetary policy and to states being unwilling to run regular budget deficits. But an even more powerful factor was also at work. The excess production of US dollars had led to their export to cover the country's continuing trade deficit in the 1960s and early 1970s. A market developed trading these dollars outside American government jurisdiction. This money market soon began to trade other currencies, and as the Bretton Woods fixed rates were abandoned and currencies floated through the 1970s, so aggregate national demand management by states as dictated by preferred growth or employment levels was abandoned. The protection of the currency in a global money market became more important. With an integrated global finance and capital market in place by the late 1980s, Keynes' system lay in ruins. It could no longer be used.

In its place emerged what some have called the 'Washington Consensus' formulated and encouraged by the US government, the IMF and the World Bank. In this conception the economic role of the state is to apply market discipline to economic issues and to integrate as far as a possible with the world economy. It claims the success of the East Asian development states results from that and not from state intervention.[10] In any case the counter-revolution in economics has destroyed the political dominance of the Keynesian intellectual system and with it the pursuit of full employment which had been for a social democratic generation a primary goal of state policy. But, momentous as this change might appear to a socialist theorist it was not a change in the character of the state, merely of its policy regime. And in any case levels of total employment actually rose during the abandoning of the Keynesian regimes as more workers, particularly women, entered the work force during the global boom of the 1980s.

Because of the obsession of social democrats with the issue of full employment its abandonment by the civilised states as a primary objective of policy has been taken to signify a diminution of sovereignty. It was in fact a subordinate national goal of some European countries for two or so decades. It has now passed.[11] As we have argued, the age of the efficiency of mass production is increasingly being replaced by the age of the opportunity of market segmentation. And this has led to the erosion of the solidarity basis of the political formations of social democracy. In a workforce where most occupations are characterised by the performance of individual tasks with a high degree of initiative and individual skill, and in a consumption society differentiated by individual tastes which can be separately catered, the political appeal of class based solidarity doctrines and the organisations which they created are greatly diminished. The dominant sector of the union movement has ceased to be that which represents labour against private capital and become that which represents the claim of the public sector worker on the tax payer. The social democratic phase of the evolution of the civilised states has come to an end.

Political Theory

Political theory about the state during the last generation has in fact been fractured into a number of different arguments about different kinds of state. The civilised states have been the subject of a number of major debates: the Left arguments about how precisely the capitalist class exploited the workers and the role which the state played in this activity, debates which ranged the English empiricists[12] against the French philosophers[13] but which the collapse of their Soviet patron terminated; arguments about identity and emancipation for groups such as feminist women or ethnic minorities; liberal and communitarian discussions about how and in what direction justice and democratic rights might be best extended; and debates between economists about how the state sector could be reformed to create a more efficient economy, a battle won by the 'Washington Consensus'.[14] The direction of state policy has been towards a more liberal and democratic state as civil society has been consolidated against the state apparatus and it in turn has been subjected to ever more transparent popular controls.

In the study of development states, the most important of which are in East Asia, the primary focus has been on whether the state apparatus has managed the high rates of economic growth,[15] or, as the World Bank argues, fiscal prudence has enabled the civil society to prosper.[16] This debate started about Japan but has been replicated in analyses of other East Asian economies. In general it appears that the state assumes a more directing economic and repressive political role at lower levels of development and tends to liberalise as economic progress precedes. This was also the case in most of Europe except Britain.

A lesser debate has also pursued the issue of whether the rapid rate of economic growth will produce a democratisation of the region's states apparatuses. The conclusions here are more contentious but a move to representative or more responsive government does appear to accompany economic progress.[17] Japan of course was democratised only after total military defeat and a six year occupation during which its political structure was totally transformed by the Americans and British, for whom the Australians acted. Taiwan and South Korea were thereby liberated and became democracies after four decades of very rapid economic growth. Thailand and the Philippines were also to become democratic following peoples power movements in 1992 and 1986 respectively. There are signs of growing liberalisation in many of the other states of the region but whether these will lead to democratisation will depend on the balance of political forces.

The remaining authoritarian regimes of the region offer degrees of liberalisation but seek to justify their resistance to democracy on a variety of ideological grounds. The Chinese communists still refer to socialist values but base their rule on strident calls to Chinese nationalism which has an increasingly anti-American orientation and seems well received. The Vietnamese communists periodically backslide on even their economic liberalisation program in recognition of the threat it poses to their dictatorship. The Burmese generals have pursued open repression in pursuit of their maintenance of state power.

The other former British colonies of Singapore and Malaysia have developed a more sophisticated justification of their one party rule. In essence both states took over the emergency powers which the British used to repress the communist insurgents during the period of home rule and used them to control Parliamentary opposition after independent states were created. These include censorship, arrests without trial, political use of the courts and government contracts, openly racist discrimination against ethnic Chinese, gerrymandering and so on. They also achieved quite impressive growth rates which took Singapore to nearly $US20,000 per capita per annum, or

European levels, by the mid 1990s and Malaysia to $US3,000 or Newly Industrialising Country standard. From this they derived the idea of "Asian Values" to justify their abuses of human rights and refusal to reform towards democracy.[18]

In 1996 the Deputy Premier of Malaysia, the engaging Anwar Ibrahim, took this attack on supposed Western values of democracy, by which the Malaysian political elite excises its dictatorial rule, a stage further by utilising the post-modernist critique of the modern civilised state: 'The malaise of modernity is well known and is continually being lamented by searching minds in the West. The Enlightenment has exhausted its possibilities. Not only has it failed to solve the manifold problems of the West, it is now being regarded as the root cause of its current predicament.'[19]

In an extreme twist of irony the authoritarian regimes of the East Asian development states have started to use the ideas of disillusioned Western communists in their post-modernist form to excuse repressive political practices taken in the interests of capitalistic growth. It is little different to the late Shah of Iran quoting dependency theory while celebrating the mock 2,500 year anniversary of his Peacock throne. In fact his father had been placed on that throne by the British in 1923, and his wealth depended on the production of oil for Western technology - the internal combustion engine and chemical industry.

During the Cold War the communist states were the subject of one of the central Left arguments of the period: how was socialism to be achieved? Proponents of Marxism debated the merits of the apparently different approaches taken by the bureaucratic Soviet Union, workers control Yugoslavia, Maoist China and revolutionary Cuba. Critics of course regarded each of these states as alternative forms of dictatorship with little to recommend them. The critics won the argument and the former Soviet bloc states are now usually seen as transitional states trying to create market economies and democratic states. In those countries where a strong civil society and market economy flourished before communist power and it did not last long, the transition appears more easily achieved.

The states of South America were the first to spawn the ideas of dependency theory, probably because their intelligentsia tried to explain their lack of development and progress despite a century of political independence without reference to the obvious but politically unacceptable reason: their own incompetence and a militarist tradition. They are now being examined principally in the context of how they can shed their strong militarist tradition and create more liberal and democratic regimes, a process now generally occurring in the region. This has involved, of course, shedding the bizarre notion that their underdevelopment could be blamed on the British and the Americans. It might also deserve mention that a similar trajectory took place in Spain and Portugal, the creators of the states of modern South America, and also ended there only when the military/fascist regimes had been overthrown in the mid-1970s. They were able then to join the generalised prosperity of Europe which geography kindly assisted.

In South Asia the continuation of mass poverty in a region, that has been able to maintain some reasonable democratic states inherited from the British, dominates the agenda. The Indian Union has retained its democratic form almost continuously but has been unable to advance from mass poverty on an appalling scale which make its cities in particular caricatures of modern living. Whatever debates it imports from the West and however sophisticated their local proponents the fact that they are conducted in a civil society primitive in its material and stratified forms makes them little short of irrelevant to the rest of the world. India was poor before, during and after the British.

In Africa the failure of states to achieve any economic progress under any government form in the face of continuing tribal based conflict and disproportionate military power continue to be the major intellectual challenge. Living conditions in all the states of sub-Saharan Africa have been in steady decline for a generation. Wars within and between these states have been common. And periodically there occur natural disasters on a scale that their primitive state apparatuses cannot resolve. Recently these have included famine in the Sahel, genocide tribal warfare in Rwanda and Burundi, the collapse of the state in Somalia, Liberia and parts of Zaire, and the accession to power in many states of an army with a capacity for power exertion that far outweighs that of civil society. Even in the most developed state, South Africa, the achievement of democracy/independence has been accompanied by a rising tide of violence so rapid that the prospects for its progress are now in question. Some leading African intellectuals have been so appalled by the record of post-independence Africa they have actually suggested the re-colonisation of the continent.[20]

In the arc of states that swings from the Middle East up into the former Soviet Republics of central Asia the unfortunate combination of revived Islam with military dictators, who usually call themselves some brand of socialist, continues to perplex theorists. Some are wealthy from oil alone; others poor from sustained civil conflict; others again groan under the yoke of vicious dictators deploying modern means of administrative terror to ancient societies. In none has the building of a civil society been even begun to lay the basis for the process of progress, except Israel which has for the last twenty years been the major object of Left idealist criticism in the region.

In this context the structure of the civilised states deserve the greatest attention precisely because they are the most advanced political form yet devised. Although they account for only about fifteen per cent of the world population they offer the richest examples for the creation of a mass civil society of free people enjoying representative government, assured liberties and freedom from want. It is because of these freedoms that these societies have such vigorous debates about themselves and other societies in the course of which many then lose the essential truth that these are states without parallel in history or in the contemporary world. This is well known by ordinary people who display what may be an insatiable desire to migrate from the primitive, idealist, and even successful development states to the civilised.

When the idealist intellectuals criticise the civilised states for their racism, sexism, environmental policies or international behaviour it is against an ideal and unattainable condition which they, like Plato and Marx, imagine. The racist policies of African tribalism are illegal in all civilised states. The subservience of women so widespread in the Islamic republics was abandoned in the civilised states generations ago. The environmental assaults being launched throughout the primitive zone would be stopped by police in civilised countries. And the *force majeure* used to periodically subjugate its neighbours by India, would have Washington once more in flames. The relativism of the post-colonial or post-modernist theorist is best practised in a civilised state where its absurdities are further distant than the view from the window. The history of political thought offers many examples of idealist philosophers who have imagined the advanced states and tried to replicate them in the backward states. Post-modernists are one of the few schools who imagine the primitive and would permit their replication in the advanced.

In 1942 there were seven civilised states in the world - Britain, the US, Canada, Australia, New Zealand, Sweden and Switzerland. The last two had in fact become dependencies of Nazi Germany and had their policies for dealing with that monster been universalised they too would have become fascist in time. Many of the democratic states which subsequently revived did so because of the use of Anglo-Saxon power as was well known at the time but since too readily ignored. Norway, France, Belgium, Denmark, the Netherlands, Luxembourg and Austria and much of Asia were all liberated by the Anglo-Americans. The Soviets would have succumbed to Hitler without their support. Democracy was only planted securely on German soil by two consecutive and extremely costly defeats of German militarism in two separate guises. The Italian state had to be entirely remade after 1943 and then continually patrolled against its own extremists. Since the defeat of the Soviets it is again the Anglo-Americans that have had to try to construct some form of civilisation on the rubble which Stalin made.

The point is not that the Anglo-Americans have created the modern world, but that at critical moments they have prevented it from succumbing to the forces of barbarism. The interstate system, because of its divided sovereignty, allows different communities to establish different forms of political processes. A small number of these have chosen to adopt a system of representative government in which people are free to pursue the activities of civil society unhindered by state control. In an even smaller number these civil societies have been sufficiently cohesive and productive to have created wealthy communities and civilised states. Since 1942 their number has increased from seven to twenty seven or so. Their survival is now better assured, but still not a certainty. Without them progress would be even less certain.

Nationalism

Nationalism has been one of the bedrocks on which the civil societies of advanced states have been built. It has emerged organically with such states although as the ideological capacities of these states have been extended so the state has tried, sometimes with effect to manipulate its structures. The sense of shared community, however, is difficult to create by public policy alone. Even in the oldest continuous democracy, Britain, it has not been possible to unite two distinct communities in one of its own provinces, Northern Ireland, after three centuries.

Western idealist academics have criticised nationalism on three counts: that it is a fraudulent deception practised by ruling elites on the working classes to divert them away from the real class-based divisions in societies; that it contains within it a racist component that, unlike class analysis, has no rational basis; and that it is in any case a dying force being destroyed by the same processes of globalisation they imagine are destroying the state itself. Nationalism is a vital system of ideas, as most political philosophers have recognised, and has at critical moments like 1914 intervened to prevent projects based on other imagined social categories, like socialism, coming to fruition. The real objections of contemporary idealists, however, derive from their alienation from national culture which often flows from their own participation in other imagined ideals from which their fellow citizens are in fact excluded. This is often compounded by the occupational geographic mobility of university academics and their participation in one of the leading edge information industries with a most atypically globalist character.

Nationalism is the most natural sociological association system that a human being can devise, based as it so often is on a shared language, religion or belief system and the proximity of sharing the same economy.[21] Some form of such association has been widely found in areas as far from Europe as the Pacific islands, Japan and the Southeast Asian kingdoms. The size of the community concerned has been determined by a combination of the level of technological development and the density of the population. As the modern states of Europe came into existence they experienced the first, rapid growth phase of the demographic transition and the greatly augmented population bases grew with the state. In some areas outside Europe the creation of modern national states has not been particularly problematic, especially where there is a coincidence between political and linguistic boundaries as in Thailand, Vietnam and to a lesser extent Burma. The real problem arises when these boundaries diverge sharply as is the case in much of Africa and the Middle East and entire nationalities like the Kurds are alienated. But even then some states have been able to successfully generate a sense of nationalism among a wide diversity of organically created communities. Switzerland is a long standing case in point.

The most striking thing about the policy of states outside the civilised zone is their determination to try to *create nations* within their states. Indeed the most successful of the post-colonial states have been precisely those who have been most successful in this respect. Large, poorer but oil endowed states like Indonesia and Nigeria have both had military government for a generation but Indonesia's has been able to maintain economic growth and a growing sense of nationalism which contrasts it from its African counterpart. This attempt to create nationality even where it has not previously existed is in recognition of the positive role it has played in state political, social and economic cohesion. Such policies have of course been pursued in Marxist states even while they have instructed the communist parties which they controlled to condemn such allegiances in civilised states. Are these policies designed to win oppressed classes away from liberation struggles? Only in the mind of Platonist idealists who have imagined categories for conditions they do not and have not experienced and are surprised when the human beings concerned pursue their own social objectives, including nations of their own.

Is nationalism racist? Of course it has this potential since most of the organically developed communities in the civilised states were historically developed around a linguistic base which, in view of restricted transport, often coincided with racial characteristics. Since the Nazi regime it has been extremely impolite to discuss or even acknowledge race as a social category in the civilised states so it gets little attention. Nonetheless it has been associated with national formation for historical reasons and still plays a considerable role in newer states and older non-politically correct cultures - which means all of them. The former Yugoslavia broke into wars of national secession as soon as it became clear the federal communist controlled army could be defeated. The Chinese are settling the central Asian provinces including Tibet with Han Chinese as a better guarantee of their borders than the ethnic minorities. Australia had a Whites only immigration policy until national cohesion was assured. The extremely small Polynesian state of Tuvulu seceded from the merely small Micronesian state of Kiribas rather than be ruled by aliens. The consequence of the long exclusion of African Americans from the civil society of the American nation is still to be seen in almost every set of sociological measurements available.

Is globalisation eroding the very concept of nationalism? While it is true that concept is being modified in the advanced information industry sectors of the civilised states where people tend to become more mobile and cosmopolitan, and is thus making war, the final expression of national allegiance, more difficult to fight, this is by no means a universal phenomenon.[22] Because some Left intellectuals resist recruitment to national tribes does not mean others will behave in the same way. In parts of Europe ideas of nationalism may diminish somewhat in the face of integrative political tendencies, but so far there is at least as much movement in the direction of breaking up previously multinational states. In much of Asia, also, the process may be running in exactly the opposite direction as states get stronger, people get wealthier and more self-confident in their combined achievements, and the memory of colonialism is becoming no more than that.

But in the end it is the national community that commands primary allegiance, exceeded only by that of the biological unit, the family. It should be no surprise that in a period when the civil societies of the civilised states, built on the family and nation, are experiencing their greatest triumphs and being most widely emulated, that intellectuals nourished by them should hold them up for abuse and ridicule. The alienated post-modern and feminist residents of those protected workshops for the intellectually advantaged, the universities, have denounced the nation as a bourgeois plot to entrap workers and the family as a male plot to subjugate women. Nonetheless, the family and nation are the cores of the civilised state.

Given the persistence of nationalism it should not be surprising that the so-called 'multicultural societies', like the USA and Australia, are generally only cohesive when held together at their core by a single community united around a single value system, legal system and language. For that reason many of the genuinely multicultural states of Europe, like Yugoslavia, the Soviet Union and Czechoslovakia, did not survive the Cold War. The problem of cultural, racial, ethnic composition, however, takes on particular importance in settler states, most clearly in those regions - including South Africa most famously - where the mixture of cultures has presented problems of divergent civil societies.

We may take Canada as an example of a mature civilised settler state which has to deal with cultural disparity. Canada was settled by two civil societies, the British and the French, which makes its continuing existence problematic.[23] The French speaking settlers dominated the band of territory that ran down the St Lawrence river through Quebec into the Mississippi River to New Orleans, until the British won the wars for North America which culminated in the Seven Years War 1756-63. Although they then lost the thirteen colonies to the new American state they retained the Canadian provinces. As they demanded and got independence they progressively joined in the Canadian federation which was established under the British North America Act of 1867. In 1948 the last province, Newfoundland, also joined.

This history left Canada with three distinct sociological problems. The most important is its bilingual national character. The French speakers were not treated well during the first century of Anglophone domination and the resentment has remained. They behaved much like the South African Afrikaners and Catholic Irish during the two world wars and were very reluctant participants. They also staged a revolt at much the same time as the Boer War as the doctrines of European linguistic nationalism spread through the

British empire. And since the 1960s the Francophones have been regrouping around the demand for an independent Quebec where they form the majority and over eighty per cent of the population speak French as their first language. In the referendum of 1995 they came within one per cent of achieving this outcome prevented only, they claimed, by the votes of recent immigrants to Canada. Quebec would in fact be a viable state with a population of seven million and an economy larger than most in the world.[24]

The second characteristic makes the first much worse. Unlike Australia, Canada is a confederation, a term used by political scientists to denote a non-unitary state in which the provinces have those residual powers which are not clearly specified in the constitution that amalgamates them.[25] When the constituent states to a federation wish to secede they are usually prevented from legally so doing by the constitution. When Western Australia voted in a referendum to leave the Australian Commonwealth in the 1930s this was deemed inoperable. In a confederation, however, the right to secede remains with the constituent states. In many former British colonies this has in fact already occurred on a number of occasions, particularly when a confederation which has been put together for London's convenience has not been sustained by interest coalitions on the ground. The West Indian Federation hardly survived its proposal and broke up into a number of small island states, except for international cricket where interests coincided. The Central African Federation did not survive the Southern Rhodesian/Zimbabwe declaration of independence in 1965. The Malaysian federation lasted only two years before Singapore left to become independent. In a somewhat different context the Irish Catholic state demanded and got independence from the United Kingdom of Great Britain and Northern Ireland. The Indian Raj could not be held together and was divided into Burma, Ceylon/Sri Lanka, Pakistan for the Muslims and the secular Republic of India. In turn Pakistan was divided in 1971 with Bangla Desh seceding and Sri Lanka may also be partitioned.

The Quebec independent state may be only a matter of time in coming since it is based on the real civil society of the Francophone population who with the North American Free Trade Agreement could now enjoy the advantages of national existence together with access to the larger economic activities nearby. In the case of Quebec, however, there might be some case for a negotiated provision for special conditions for the resulting new minorities in the Francophone state, including 75,000 indigenous people.

The third issue is the indigenous Indian population. They are divided into different national groups and may number over a million in total. The Eskimos comprise the second largest and have acquired rights to the vast northern areas of the country which they used to roam before the Europeans arrived. The Canadians have tried to resolve the problems of cohabiting with indigenous cultures by granting what amounts to statehood in parts of the country to indigenous nationalities. Concern that the Quebecois might not do the same has led indigenees to support the preservation of Canada.

The diversity of ethnic and cultural loyalties in Canada thus leaves its very existence under a question mark, but the secession of the Quebecois would only compound the problems of the indigenes. There looks to be no happy solution to this state of affairs. The policy of multi-culturalism simply wallpapers over the entrenched diverse interests of different ethnic groups. After generations, one of the richest and most civilised states in the world finds it had to survive and foster civil society.

Conclusion

What we face as we move into the next millennium are different options of social reproduction. We enter into the millennium with four forms of the state — primitive, idealist, developmental, and mature states. The classifiers, primitive, developmental, and mature suggests that there is a single highway which states will all travel. But this is not the case. Different states face different futures, and a shift in the culture or conquest may drag a developmentalist or even a state on the verge of maturity into a primitivist or idealist nightmare. We have defended a progressivist model as a means for understanding social and political forms of organisation. But there is nothing inevitable about progress.

We have argued that the modes of political organisation have arisen in conjunction with the pressures of social organisation. We have suggested that the societies with the most abundant material fruits are ones with vibrant civil societies. The association between a political form which enables the broadest possible spectrum of talents, energies and options and a civil society which generates material abundance has been a long time in the making. It has been the result of the unforeseen convergence of contingencies, a long series of lucky accidents, which when viewed in retrospect give the appearance of history having a meaning. But it is always us who imbue history with meaning. In surveying the canon of political philosophy we have selected those narratives which we believe have contributed most to the civilised state form. We have also entered into areas where the canon has not gone. There is no classical work to show us where we are, precisely because our present is in the making and a classic is a testament to what has proven its worth after the swirl of reality is sufficiently settled for some kind of pattern to be discerned.

We see that there are signs of social and political progress, that the struggles and efforts of those who sought first spiritual unity (the European legacy of the Christian tradition), and then freedom, equality and prosperity (the 'modern' defenders of social stability, liberal democracy and rights) have not been in vain. We have suggested that the current academic fashions are too enmeshed in idealisations to appreciate the bounties of social and political evolution.

Politics has always involved power. Where political conflict is most savage and where there is little room for compromise, the state reveals itself to be grounded in the more bestial energies of human beings. In the mature civilised state the beast has not vanished, and were the civilised state to lose its bestial energies, civilisation would quickly perish. Against criminals and enemies the savagery of the beast reveals itself. But the bestial energies of the mature civilised state are not randomly activated. Generally, for such energies to be unleashed processes of legitimation must be traversed. The bestial energies are frequently sublimated, so that politics itself may seem to be simply the expression of the law. This was what the idealist philosophers always hoped to attain. We have argued that this can never completely be the case. And we have argued that the realist approach to politics is correct not to ignore the centrality of violence in politics. But the mature civilised state manages to fuse realism and Kantian based idealism to good effect. The great beast is thus often well behaved, benign even to the point of people loving it. For a while the beneficiaries of social democracies thought that the beast was a kind of Santa Claus, a delusion which has been largely cured by the grim necessities of economics reminding us that the public benefit of material abundance requires the pursuit of private market interests.

If we cast our eyes at the primitive and idealist states with their politically enforced famines, their everyday resort to torture, and persistent abuse of any legal standards, their civil wars, and genocidal impulses, we see the bestial energies of the species in their full horror when they are not channelled to good effect. The same energies have also been unleashed in the formation of civilisation, and, indeed, for its continued preservation. They are an intrinsic part of the human story. What distinguishes the mature civilised states is that something that supersedes the infinite repetition and wastage of life has been discovered, something has been re-membered so that evolution can take place, a combination of noble ideals and a search for rules, principles, and legality, on the one hand, and, on the other, an appreciation of the dark processes that must be marshalled both to preserve and create the conditions of peace, prosperity, and freedom.

But among the idealist intelligentsia such talk of evolution is anathema. The restricted life style and experience of the cloistered ones allow the forces of history and personal anxiety to rest heavily on shoulders little fitted for the task of seeing actual life processes at work. And even as evidence of progress mounts high in the scene through the window, the intellectual sees regression: the owl of Minerva only flies at dusk.

Notes

1. Mathew Horsman and Andrew Marshall, *After the Nation-State: Citizens, Tribalism and the New World Disorder*, Harper Collins, London, 1994, contains a good summary of these arguments.
2. See Peter Dicken, *Global Shift*, London, Guildford, 1992; and Catley,

Globalising Australian Capitalism, chapters one and two.
3. Alvin Y So and Stephen Chiu, *East Asia and the World Economy,* Thousand Dales, Sage, 1995; Alan Milward, *The Frontier of National Sovereignty,* London, Routledge, 1993.
4. Mark Almond, *Europe's Backyard War,* rev. ed., London, Mandarin, 1994; Ian Bremner and Ray Taras, eds., *Nation and Politics in the Soviet Successor States,* Cambridge, Cambridge University Press, 1993.
5. Jane E. Nolan, ed., *Global Engagement: Cooperation and Security in the 21st Century,* Washington, Brookings Institute, 1994; cf Michael Brown, *et al,* eds., *The Perils of Anarchy: Contemporary Realism and International Security,* Cambridge, Mass., MIT, 1995.
6. Waltz, *op cit.*
7. Bob Catley and Makmur Keliat, *Spratlys! The Conflict in the South China Sea,* Dartmouth, UK, 1997.
8. Stuart Harries and Gary Klintworth, eds., *China As A Great Power: myths, realities and challenges in the Asia-Pacific region,* Melbourne, Longman, 1995.
9. Richard T. Selden, ed., *Capitalism and Freedom: Problems and Prospects; Proceedings of a conference in honour of Milton Friedman,* Charlottesville, University of Virginia, 1975.
10. The World Bank, *The East Asian Miracle, Economic Growth and Public Policy,* New York, Oxford University Press, 1993.
11. Robert Leeson, *How Chicago Overcame Cambridge,* Perth, Murdoch University, Working Paper, 151, 1996.
12. Ralph Miliband, *The State in Capitalist Society,* London, Weidenfeld and Nicolson, 1969 remains the classic.
13. Nicos Poulantsas, *Political Power and Social Classes,* trans. T. O' Hagan, London, Verso, 1978 is the best known.
14. John Williamson, ed., *The Political Economy of Policy Reform,* Institute for International Economics, Washington DC, 1994.
15. Medhi Krongkapw, ed., *Thailand's Industrialisation and Its Consequences,* Houndmils, Macmillan, 1995; Rajah Rasiah, ed., *Foreign Capital and Industrialisation in Malaysia,* Basingstoke, Macmillan, 1995
16. *The East Asian Miracle, op. cit.*

17. As Harold Crouch has recently argued in the case of Malaysia, *Contemporary Malaysian Government and Politics*. Sydney, Allen and Unwin, 1996.
18. Christopher Lingle, *Singapore's Authoritarian Capitalism: Asian Values, Free Market Illusions and Political Dependency*, Barcelona, Edicions Sirocco, S. L., 1996.
19. *The Australian*, 21 August 1996, page 13.
20. See Ali A. Mazrui, *The African Condition: a political diagnosis*, London, Heinemann Educational, 1980.
21. John Hutchison and Anthony D. Smith, eds., *Nationalism*, Oxford, Oxford University Press, 1994.
22. Peter Waterman, *Globalisation, Civil Society, Solidarity: The Politics and Ethics of a World Bot Real and Universal*, The Hague, Institute of Social Studies, 1993; Daniele Archibugr and David Held, eds. *Cosmopolitan Democracy*, Cambridge, Polity, 1995; cf Robert Boyer and Daniel Drache, eds., *States Against Markets: The Limits of Globalisation*, New York, Routledge, 1996.
23. Philip Lawson, *The Imperial Challenge: Quebec and Britain in the Age of the American Revolution*, Montreal, McGill-Queens University Press, 1990.
24. Stephen McBride and John Shields, *Dismantling a Nation: Canada and the New World Order*, Halifax, Fernwood, 1993.
25. Campbell Sharman, ed., *Parties and Federalism in Australia and Canada*, Canberra, Australian National University, 1994.

Index

Ables, P. 377
Aboriginals, 16, 29, 360
Acheson, D. 113
Adair, D. 281
Afghanistan, 36, 353
Africa, 5, 14, 19, 21, 39, 40, 41, 45, 48, 50-52, 60, 66, 92, 102, 109, 110, 113, 170, 337, 345-47, 353, 368, 369, 390, 397, 408, 412, 414
Afrikaans Nationalist Party, 110
Alcibiades, 224
Algeria, 93, 352
Algerian War, 27, 93
Allende, S. 43
Althusser, L. 250
America, 11, 13, 18, 19, 20, 21, 23, 37, 39, 42, 43, 46, 48, 76, 78, 94, 181, 236, 237, 257, 258, 262, 265-68, 270-73, 275-81, 283, 284, 294, 302, 304, 307, 321, 322, 324, 326, 346, 353, 354, 386, 387, 389, 390, 407, 414
Angola, 51, 52, 53, 71
Aquinas, St. T. 189, 195
Aquino, C. 329
Arabs, 6, 363
Arafat, Y. 364
Argentina, 31, 43, 49, 68, 70, 306
armed forces, 12, 13, 27, 33, 40, 47, 49, 51, 82, 111, 338, 397
Arnold, E. 54
Aron, R. 258
ASEAN, 34, 113, 380, 397
Ashton, T.E. 85
Asia Minor, 91
Asia, 7, 12, 15, 19, 21, 23, 31-34, 37, 39, 41, 42, 45, 47, 50, 51, 53, 60, 69, 71, 76, 78, 85, 91, 112,

Index

114, 170, 307, 347, 353, 356, 359, 360, 368, 369, 378, 392, 397, 402, 405, 408, 409, 410, 413, see East Asia
Assyria, 2
Aung, S.S. K. 70
Austin, J. 211
Australasia, 11, 20
Australia, 15, 19, 23, 24, 26, 27, 32, 33, 44, 47, 48, 52, 84, 91, 94, 106, 283, 287, 304-7, 311, 316, 319, 326, 327, 337, 358, 360, 365, 368, 387, 402, 410, 413-15
Australian Labor Party, 79
Austria, 23, 61, 67, 348, 410
Aztecs, 267

Bach, J.S. 6
Bacon, F. 227, 276
Bakunin, M. 167
Barber, B. 386-89
Barker, E. 216
beast, 8, 10, 59, 88, 95, 159, 186, 194, 215, 220, 245, 260, 270, 310, 341, 395, 417
Belgium, 14, 23, 369, 410
Bell, C. 342
Bell, D. 77,
Bergson, H. 175
Berlin, 39, 51, 348, 352
Berlin, I. 183
Berman, H. 216
Bernstein, E. 29, 303, 304

Bill of Rights, 24, 235, 240
birth rate, 12
Bismarck, O. von 67, 70
blues, 390
Bolivar, 49
Bolivia, 387
Bonald, L. 207
Bonhoeffer, D. 392
Bonney, R. 54
Brandt, W. 362
Brazil, 31, 39, 43, 45
Britain see England
British Labour Party, 79
British, 13, 16, 17, 19, 24-30, 32, 34, 38, 41, 45-50, 66, 67, 70, 73, 79, 97, 113, 114, 260, 261, 264, 287, 306, 307, 326, 330, 337, 346-48, 350-53, 355, 357, 362, 363, 367-69, 371, 378, 380, 383, 384, 390, 403, 406-8, 414, 415
Brodie, F. 281
Brown, Sir Thomas 220
Brunei, 35
Brüning, H. 201
Buddhism, 60
budget, 24, 78, 107, 325-27, 337, 354, 355, 384, 403
Bukharin, N. 171
bureaucracy, 25, 27, 61, 90, 115, 116, 167, 300, 333, 334, 355
Burke, E. 163, 236, 245, 256, 368
Burma, 18, 19, 35, 50, 60, 64, 70, 72, 85, 379, 397, 412, 415

Index

Burns, R. 155
Burundi, 52, 267, 370, 408

Callaghan, K.A. 54
Cambodia, 35, 51, 71, 73, 156, 352, 364, 365, 370, 371, 400
Canada, 19, 23, 48, 319, 410, 414-16
capitalism, 3, 33, 99, 101, 163, 165, 166, 172, 177, 341, 379
Caribbean, 39, 42, 64
Carr, E.H. 350
Castro, F. 72, 113, 170, 324
Catherine the Great, 304, 399
Catley, R., 85, 86
Céline, F. 183
Chamberlain, J. 297
Charles I, 238
Charter 77, 388
Chazan, 54
Chile, 31, 324
China, 7, 10-12, 14, 31, 32, 34-36, 41, 45, 51, 53, 60-62, 64, 65, 67, 69-71, 74, 85, 91, 105, 112, 172, 345, 352, 354, 365, 366, 368, 380, 388, 401, 407
Choi, J. M. 54
Chomsky, N. 363-65
Christendom, 7, 10, 62, 106, 162, 187-89, 190, 192, 226, 236, 366, 392, 395
Church, 7, 16, 61, 62, 188, 227, 248, 389

CIA, 324
civil society, 4, 8, 9, 14, 18, 21, 23, 26-34, 37, 42, 46, 49, 51-53, 61, 64, 66, 68, 73, 74, 77-82, 91, 92, 108-11, 166, 173, 181, 186, 197, 198, 225, 237, 239, 240, 305, 307, 310, 318, 324, 325, 329-31, 335-37, 354, 355, 358, 371, 380, 384, 391, 395, 397, 399, 401, 405, 407-10, 413, 415-17
civil war, 1, 23, 27, 40, 50, 52, 63, 65, 92, 93, 96, 187, 191-94, 199, 215, 234-36, 238, 241, 275, 306, 337, 379, 418
civilised zone, 31, 45, 80, 107, 359, 370, 376, 385, 391, 412
Clark, M. 85, 304
class, 18, 20, 72, 76, 78, 81, 84, 89-91, 96, 97, 99, 100, 163, 164, 166, 168-70, 172, 173, 175-77, 180, 181, 207, 209, 222, 247, 249, 286-89, 291, 294, 295, 297, 300-3, 322, 323, 329, 330, 341, 344, 355, 368, 369, 405, 411
Clausewitz, C. von 342
CNN, 82, 378
Cobden, R. 341, 368
Code of Hamurabi, 221
Cold War, 20, 21, 43, 70, 77, 304, 307, 324, 342, 351, 353-56, 363, 369, 370, 371, 385, 396, 400, 407, 414

Index

Colombia, 43, 62, 85, 363
communism, 21, 36, 49, 53, 59, 61, 94, 99, 163, 165, 167-69, 172, 173, 177, 180, 210, 215, 216, 280, 288, 300, 301, 305, 307, 310, 350
computers, 81, 113, 381
Condorçet, M.J.A. Marquis de 290, 301
Congo, 51, 71, 352, 369
Congress, 24-26, 51, 333, 336
conquest, 19, 39, 45, 64, 97, 159, 347, 349, 360, 366, 416
Constant, B. 245
constitution, 4, 9, 24, 26, 33, 41, 44, 104, 112, 193, 204, 205, 210, 212, 223, 224, 247, 250, 252, 253, 261, 264, 268, 269, 278, 281, 283, 284, 315, 316, 320, 330, 344, 415
Contract, 293, 295
Contragate, 324, 364
Cook Islands, 44, 52
corporatist state, 76, 181
Cortés, D. 207, 208
Creon, 96
criminals, 2, 232, 239, 417
critical legal theory, 105
Cromwell, O. 64, 70, 367
Cropsey, J. 242, 258
Cuba, 42, 53, 71, 72, 85, 113, 363, 407
cuisine, 13, 15, 386, 387, 391

culture, 11, 13, 15, 16, 18, 20, 28, 48, 80, 81, 83, 89, 90, 92, 94, 96, 97, 102, 104, 162, 182, 198, 212, 216, 278, 314, 319, 323, 360, 377, 387, 388, 391, 392, 411, 416
Cyprus, 23
Czech Republic, 388

De Gaulle, C. 93, 117
de Grazia, S. 183
de Klerk, F.W. 110
de Man, P. 324
death rate, 11
decolonisation, 50, 52, 113, 307, 352
defence, 4, 5, 12, 91, 92, 99, 111, 172, 186, 198, 200, 211, 227, 230, 232, 234, 236, 257, 260, 284, 295, 298, 300, 327, 347, 350, 369
Defoe, D. 291
Deng, X. 35, 74, 93
Denmark, 23, 46, 67, 410
Dethloff, H. 281
developmental state, 4, 22, 31, 35, 75, 351, 363, 377
dictatorship, 21, 22, 35, 37, 43, 63, 65, 69, 73, 94, 109, 110, 165, 208, 210, 258, 269, 338, 346, 348, 349, 353, 400, 406, 407
Diderot, D. 256, 300
dirigisme, 33, 76, 113
Dole, B. 314

Dominican Republic, 42
Downing, D. 54
Dutch, 14, 16, 46, 51, 205, 352, 357, 358, 367

East Asia, 20, 23, 31-33, 39, 45, 69, 71, 76, 77, 112, 359, 376, 378, 397, 402, 404, 405, 407
Ecuador, 43
Egypt, 106, 363
Eichmann, A. 163
Eisenhower, D. 306
Elizabeth I, 62, 399
enemies, 13, 27, 38, 43, 63, 90, 92, 104, 159, 160, 169, 171, 192, 200-4, 206, 210, 215, 270, 272, 324, 331, 385, 417
energy, 17, 50, 65, 116, 176, 215, 247, 269, 278, 284, 285, 287, 310, 312, 321, 359, 396, 400
Engels, F. 60, 164, 165, 166, 294, 301
England, 1, 14, 19, 46, 61-64, 85, 165, 166, 181, 187, 199, 209, 211, 236, 248, 249, 260, 278, 280, 291, 294, 298, 299, 302, 303, 320, 322, 366, 367, 402
Enlightenment, 5, 63, 31, 32, 34, 103, 112, 281, 300, 407
entertainment, 13, 17, 80, 81, 84, 381, 387
equality, 7, 15, 32, 61, 80, 195, 207, 222, 249, 262, 264, 265, 271, 272, 274, 276, 278, 280, 283, 284, 292-94, 300, 302, 311, 417
Ethiopia, 40, 52, 53, 71, 382
ethnicity, 20, 90
Euphrates, 91
Europe, 10, 11, 13, 16, 20, 22, 23, 25, 31, 33, 34, 36, 37, 42, 45-47, 49, 53, 54, 60-67, 70, 77-79, 92, 93, 97, 100, 111, 112, 114, 166, 170, 187, 227, 260, 270, 271, 283, 304-6, 331, 342, 344-47, 352, 360, 366-69, 377, 387, 397-99, 406, 408, 411, 413, 414
evil, 39, 105, 155, 156, 159, 162, 192, 195, 203, 207, 228, 268, 273, 297

faction, 2, 94, 73, 214, 265
faith, 61, 62, 102, 172, 179, 211, 237, 238, 241, 258, 262, 263, 265, 288, 301, 316, 325
Fanon, F. 176
fascism, 18, 32, 46, 49, 54, 59, 71, 163, 174, 176-78, 180-82, 280, 305, 306, 341
fear, 74, 97, 106, 159, 160, 186, 191, 193-99, 213, 215, 227, 229, 230, 234, 260, 292, 334, 390
federal, 20, 26, 41, 48, 266, 275, 280, 319, 320, 326, 413

Index

Federalists, 24, 112, 245, 261, 262, 264-66, 268, 270, 271, 278, 286
feminism, 3, 8, 19, 90, 380, 399, 406, 445
Ferguson, A. 250
Feuerbach, L . 391
Fichte, J.G. 302
Fiji, 44
Filmer, R. 238
Finland, 23
First World, 13, 20, 22, 38, 49, 177, 182, 204, 307, 348, 349, 363, 369
force, 2, 3, 9, 12, 19, 42, 43, 47, 60, 67, 76, 80, 93, 96, 107, 115, 166, 170, 175-77, 179, 192-94, 196, 202, 220, 228, 232, 234, 235, 237, 238, 241, 250, 255, 263-65, 267, 270, 277, 279, 283, 302, 313, 342, 344, 347, 350, 351, 359, 365, 366, 368, 369, 380-83, 398-402, 404, 410, 411
Ford, H. 76, 382
Fourier, C. 301
Fourierist, 288
France, 18, 23, 25, 27, 46, 52, 61, 63-67, 70, 79, 92, 93, 112, 166, 177, 247-49, 252, 257, 258, 260, 261, 270, 271, 280, 298, 301, 302, 306, 317, 342, 348, 351, 354, 366, 367, 410

franchise, 1, 5, 24, 64, 66, 240, 241, 258, 266, 268, 277, 289, 319, 368
Fraser, M. 362
Frederick the Great, 19, 348
freedom, 3, 6, 17, 22, 29, 49, 112, 181, 198, 204, 207, 213, 216, 227, 229, 230, 233, 234, 239, 246, 253, 254, 262, 269, 271, 272, 276, 280, 285, 292-94, 296-98, 302, 303, 321, 388, 389, 409, 417, 418
French Polynesia, 53
Fritsch, General W. von 201
Fuller, L. 97, 117

Gaddafi, Colonel M. A. 137
Galileo, G. 227
Ganges, 91
GATT, 353, 356, 370
Gellner, E. 54
gender, 20, 29, 63, 90, 99, 101, 277, 291, 329
General Chun, 69
General Park, 69
general will, 107, 108, 253-55, 260, 317, 323
Gentile, G. 155, 178, 179, 182
Georgia, 53, 277
Germany, 3, 13, 19, 23, 25, 26, 30, 46, 47, 52, 67, 70, 78, 93, 97, 166, 177, 202, 203, 205, 209,

210, 215, 298, 302, 305, 331, 338, 348, 349, 369, 402, 410
Ghana, 51
Ghandi, I. 41
Gierke, O. 216, 242
Gingrich, N. 314
globalisation, 80, 84, 370, 377, 391, 395, 398, 411, 413
glory, 93, 158, 161, 162, 194, 200, 221
Gobineau, A. de 272
GOLKAR, 69
Gorbachev, M. 72, 73, 109, 113
Gramsci, A. 89, 174, 175, 177, 323
Great Britain, 166, 389, 415
Great Leap Forward, 74, 172, 365, 382
Greece, 16, 23, 106, 242, 344
Greek, 7, 197, 221, 352
Green, T. H. 3, 293-97, 303
Greengrass, M. 54
Gregor, A.J. 178
Grenada, 42
guardians, 22, 335, 336, 388
Guinea, 44, 51
Gulf War, 6, 370, 371, 400
gunpowder, 61, 92

Haiti, 42, 370, 371, 400,
Hamsun, K. 183
Hare, T. 286
Hatch, W. 392

Hauptmann, G. 183
Havel, V. 388, 389
Hawke, B. 327
Hélvetius, C.A. 252
Hemings, S. 262
Henry III, 187
Henry VIII, 62, 248, 249, 384
Heydrich, R. 202
Hill, H. 85, 293
Hindu, 386
Hobsbawm, E. 74
Holy Roman Emperor, 187
Honecker, E. 170
Hong Kong, 34, 53
Horsman, M. 418
House of Representatives, 319
Humboldt, W. von 284, 303
Hume, D. 54, 245, 256
Hungary, 23, 37

Ibrahim, A. 407
Iceland, 23, 387
idealism, 5, 36, 74, 155, 163, 170, 172-74, 182, 187, 190, 223, 224, 253, 289, 343, 348, 350, 385, 399, 418
idealist state, 3, 22, 36-38, 71, 418
Idris, King 37
Incas, 267, 360
India, 6, 11, 24, 41, 42, 45, 47, 50, 53, 71, 91, 345, 346, 357, 388, 408, 410, 415

Index

indigenous people, 15, 28, 48, 257, 267, 268, 322, 368
Indonesia, 12, 14, 19, 34, 51, 69, 166, 412
inequality, 63, 105, 274, 277, 290, 297, 302, 331
Inkeles, A. 371
intellectuals, 18, 36, 95, 172, 173, 182, 209, 288, 304, 323-25, 343, 364, 371, 386, 397, 409, 413
intelligentsia, 3, 63, 117, 166-68, 172, 176, 182, 201, 256, 288, 323, 324, 337, 359, 392, 407, 418
interests, 2, 8, 9, 32-34, 36, 50, 51, 63, 72, 88, 89, 95, 99, 108-10, 113, 114, 116, 160, 161, 163-65, 177, 186, 188, 191, 207, 226, 231-33, 238, 239, 241, 246, 251, 252, 254, 257, 261, 262, 265, 266, 268, 269, 276, 277, 285-88, 299, 302, 303, 307, 314, 315, 317, 321, 322-25, 327-30, 334, 335, 342-44, 347, 351, 355, 359, 361, 364, 366, 370, 389, 398, 399-402, 407, 415, 416, 418
Iran, 3, 6, 36, 38, 94, 176, 361, 391, 407
Iraq, 6, 36, 94, 363, 400
Ireland, 23, 27, 29, 73, 337, 411, 415
Irvin, G. 85

Israel, 14, 37, 66, 355, 361, 363, 364, 400, 409
Italy, 3, 11, 23, 25, 40, 61, 67, 79, 181, 182, 190, 251, 305, 337, 344, 349

Jacka, E. 392
Jagger, M. 376
James II, 238
Japan, 7, 12, 20, 23, 32, 33, 45, 47, 69, 79, 113, 326, 345, 349, 350, 359, 378, 387, 392, 405, 406, 411
jazz, 390
Judaism, 213
judiciary, 14, 24, 25, 115, 251, 269, 320, 336
Jung, C. 183
Junger, E. 183
justice, 8, 9, 95-106, 158, 168, 189, 199, 220, 221, 223, 224, 250, 265, 292, 293, 297, 298, 327, 405

Kant, I. 4, 9, 54, 162, 179, 196, 245, 284, 290, 295, 296, 342, 349, 353, 399
Kautsky, K. 167
Kazakhstan, 53
Keating, P. 29, 79, 319, 327
Kelsen, H. 205, 211
Kennedy, J. 329, 362
Kentucky Fried Chicken, 377, 387
Kenya, 52

Keynes, J.M. 78, 305, 403, 404
Keynesianism, 76, 98
KGB, 388
Khan, 38, 349, 360
Khmer Rouge, 61, 364, 365
Kim Il Sung, 71, 85, 170
Kirchheimer, O. 202
Kirkpatrick, J. 362
Kitto, H.D.F. 117
Koch, A. 281
Kohl, H. 78
Krabbe, 205
Kuo Ming Tan (KMT), 68
Kuromiya, H. 85

Lange, D. 326
language, 7, 13, 14, 18, 28, 46, 229, 234, 272, 294, 323, 348, 391, 411, 414, 415
Laos, 352
Laothamatas, E. 85
Laski, H. 304
Lassalle, F. 302
law, 2, 5, 7, 14, 15, 20, 24-26, 29, 38, 95, 96-98, 101, 104, 105, 116, 159, 168, 169, 170, 179, 188-90, 195-99, 205, 206, 208, 211, 214, 215, 221, 222, 229, 235, 246, 249-51, 253, 256, 263, 270, 275, 277, 297-99, 312, 324, 328, 384, 399, 400, 417 *see* legal
LDP, 27, 79

League of Nations, 24, 49, 342, 349, 399
Lee, L.K. 26
legal positivism, 190, 211, 215
legal, 6, 14, 26, 28, 44, 96-98, 105, 169, 170, 188, 190, 191, 200, 204, 205, 208, 209, 211, 215, 234, 246, 253, 275, 280, 302, 311, 367, 414, 418
Lenin, V. 106, 156, 163, 165-71, 174-76, 369
Lerner, M. 183, 242
Lewis, W. 183
liberal democracy, 174, 179, 182, 206, 209, 234, 236, 289, 316, 417
liberalism, 182, 186, 201, 203, 204, 206-11, 213-15, 245, 253, 283, 289, 292-95, 297, 298, 303, 305, 349, 350, 364
Liberia, 408
Libya, 36, 37, 363, 401
Lincoln, A. 6
life expectancy, 22, 39
living standards, 19, 38, 42, 64, 274, 294, 313, 314, 322, 379
Louis XIV, 366
love, 6, 103, 158, 159, 162, 192, 197, 223, 236, 247, 262, 275, 288, 334, 388
Lowenthal, D. 258
Luxembourg, 23, 410
lying, 332

Index

Machiavelli, N. 4, 61, 63, 156-62, 170, 171, 173, 182, 183, 186, 190, 192, 194, 197, 200, 204, 224, 237, 265, 332, 341, 343, 344, 349, 350, 367, 398, 399
Mackenny, R. 85
MacKinnon, C. 90, 117
MacNamara, R. 362
Magna Carta, 24, 236, 2249, 347
Maistre, J. de 207
Malaysia, 14, 26, 34, 50, 406, 407
Mandela, N. 40
Mao, 7, 43, 74, 93
Maoists, 7, 61, 74, 75
Mao Zedong, 74
Marco Polo, 62
Marcos, F. 71
Marx, 4, 15, 18, 21, 60, 98, 99, 106, 155, 156, 163-68, 170, 171, 174-77, 180, 271, 277, 294, 299, 300, 302, 409
marxist, 3, 8, 11, 12, 27, 74, 89, 90, 105, 164, 167, 174-76, 181, 183, 202, 212, 250, 322-24, 350, 356, 362, 365
mature civilised state, 1, 2, 4, 6-9, 22, 23, 90, 114, 311, 336, 338, 417, 418
Mayans, 267
McShea, R. 242

media, 9, 29, 66, 75, 80-83, 117, 320, 323, 327, 332-34, 336, 358, 364, 365, 377, 378, 385
Melanesian, 43
men, 3, 6, 49, 70, 90, 91, 157, 159, 160, 162, 165, 175, 188, 189, 191-94, 196, 197, 199, 214, 220, 221, 223, 224, 227, 230-33, 238, 250, 255, 257, 265, 266, 285, 291-93, 295, 297, 300, 301, 311, 367, 377
Menzies, R. 306
Mesopotamia, 2, 221
Mexico, 21, 31, 48, 345
Michels, R. 182, 312
Micronesian, 413
Middle East, 6, 36, 38, 50, 53, 307, 346, 348, 363, 409, 412
migration, 19, 30, 94, 108
Mises, L. von 98, 298
Mitterand, F. 78
monarchy, 32, 63, 70, 93, 112, 116, 161, 221, 222, 238, 247, 249, 256, 264, 270, 271, 284, 366, 369
Morelly, 298, 299, 300
Morgenthau, H. 343, 350
Mozambique, 51, 52, 53
Mozambique, 71
MTV, 389
Muir, E. 310
Muldoon, R. 326
Murdoch, R. 75, 377

Murphy, J. W. 54

Namibia, 51, 370
Napoleon Bonaparte, 367
Napoleonic Code, 25
nation, 11, 13, 17-20, 24, 61, 62, 69, 94, 98, 102, 113, 115, 169, 174, 177-80, 201, 236, 238, 246-49, 251, 261, 285, 287, 302, 316, 317, 413
natural law, 7, 95, 96, 188-90, 195-97, 199, 211, 235
natural law, 95, 96
Nauru, 11
Nazism, 202, 210, 211, 213, 214, 216, 350
Neher, C.D. 85
Netherlands, 23, 51, 61, 65, 410
Neumann, F. 202, 214, 215, 250
New Caledonia, 52
New Deal, 284, 305
New International Economic Order (NIEO) 355
New Zealand, 23, 26, 44, 52, 84, 114, 305, 307, 326, 327, 337, 368, 410
Nicaragua, 71
Nigeria, 412
Nile, 91
Nixon, R. 77, 352, 356
noble savage, 6, 256

North Korea, 21, 71, 72, 85, 362, 371
Norway, 23, 410
Nozick, R. 298
OECD, 20, 84, 326, 357
Okin, S.M. 99
oligarchy, 116, 192, 222, 346
OPEC, 20, 37, 361, 403
order, 6, 12, 16, 18, 22, 28, 29, 41, 42, 46, 49, 53, 59, 60, 61, 70, 80, 82, 88, 92, 96, 99, 100, 110-12, 114, 155, 159, 161, 168, 186, 187, 199, 201-3, 206, 207, 214, 216, 220, 222, 228-30, 233, 236, 237, 252, 270, 292, 294, 296, 298, 300, 316, 325, 333, 335, 343, 344, 346-49, 351, 353, 369-71, 376, 378, 381, 385, 391, 402,
Orff, C. 183
Orientalism, 18, 91, 364
Owenist, 288

Pakistan, 41, 50, 415
Papua New Guinea, 44
Paraguay, 43
parliament, 25-27, 30, 36, 76, 78, 79, 88, 89, 177, 204, 201, 210, 211, 238-40, 266, 275, 286, 306, 311, 312, 314, 315, 317, 319, 322, 323, 330, 331, 337, 351, 352, 361, 397, 403, 412
Party, 67, 313
Payne, S.G. 85

Index

peace, 3, 7, 22, 39, 50, 63, 160, 161, 171, 182, 183, 186, 190, 198-200, 202, 203, 226, 236, 238, 250, 251, 262, 301, 341, 354, 355, 364, 367, 370, 389, 398, 401, 402, 418
Peden, W. 281
per capita income, 20, 22, 23, 31, 34, 39, 109
Perón, Colonel J.D. 43, 287
Peru, 43, 237
Philippines, 34, 45, 71, 345, 352, 366, 406
philosopher king, 182, 231
philosophers, 5, 7, 18, 49, 62, 116, 157, 162, 182, 192, 207, 227, 231, 240, 289, 298, 328, 331, 405, 410, 411,417
philosophy, 1, 4, 32, 37, 61, 63, 157, 159, 174, 175, 177, 183, 187, 188, 193, 198, 208, 227, 228, 230, 292, 297, 299, 324, 365, 417
Pinochet, A. 324
Plastic People of the Universe, 389
play, 14, 16, 17, 70, 104, 111, 156, 165, 190, 194, 212, 223, 293, 301, 323, 355, 379, 386, 389, 390, 391
PLO, 37, 364
Presley, E. 389
Pockock, J. 183

Pol Pot, 35, 51, 156, 170
Poland, 37, 174
politicians, 28, 52, 68, 69, 83, 84, 101, 104, 265, 322, 323, 328, 332-35, 337, 362, 382, 392
Polynesian, 43, 44, 360, 413
Polynices, 96
Pope Gregory VII, 187
population, 1, 10, 11, 14-16, 22, 23, 35, 36, 37, 39, 41, 42, 44, 52, 60, 65-67, 70, 75, 77, 81, 97, 110, 116, 209, 226, 251, 261, 275, 277, 297, 316, 317, 321, 336, 345, 346, 360, 367, 382, 383, 388, 395, 396, 401, 409, 412, 415, 416
Portugal, 23, 53, 61, 79, 93, 306, 345, 346, 366, 408
positive law, 211
Powell, E. 333
power, 1, 3, 4, 9, 14-23, 25-27, 29, 31-33, 36, 37, 39, 40, 43, 45-48, 50-53, 59, 60, 62-67, 69-7173, 74-76, 79, 82, 83, 88, 89, 92, 93, 96, 97, 103, 106, 110, 112-14, 116, 155-58, 160, 161, 163-71, 173, 175, 176, 179, 181, 183, 186, 188-93, 195-99, 201-6, 208-11, 213-16, 220-22, 224-26, 228-32, 234, 235, 237, 238, 240, 249-52, 254, 257, 258, 261, 262, 264, 267-70, 275, 276, 278-80, 283-87, 289-91, 294, 296-99,

303, 305, 306, 310, 311, 313,
  315, 316, 319, 320, 325, 327-29,
  334, 335, 341, 343, 345-48, 350,
  353, 359, 365-70, 379, 381, 395-
  97, 400, 401, 406-8, 410, 417
primitive state, 22, 42, 43, 45,
  61, 64, 65, 76, 80, 82, 342, 354,
  355, 359, 370, 379, 382, 386,
  396, 397, 408, 409
progress, 4-6, 19, 31-33, 36, 39-
  42, 47, 51, 52, 54, 91, 92, 94,
  112, 113, 196, 233, 241, 272,
  288, 292, 294, 301,307, 314,
  329, 342, 345, 348, 352, 359-61,
  369-71, 379, 380, 391, 406, 408,
  409, 411, 416-18
Protagoras, 231
Proudhon, P.J. 301-2
Quebec, 414-14
Quebec, 46
Queen Victoria, 399
queer theory, 3, 380

radical democracy, 3, 167
Rawls, J. 99-101, 103, 298
realism, 68, 194, 343, 418
Redman, C. 242
Reformation, 112, 225
refugees, 10, 30, 41, 370
religion, 13, 15, 28, 29, 50, 84,
  95, 98, 99, 107, 108, 114, 159,
  162, 247, 253, 272, 276, 313,
  391, 411

representation, 2, 3, 7, 14, 25, 37,
  167, 193, 204, 221, 224, 240,
  256, 261, 264, 266, 268, 269,
  271, 275, 284, 286, 287, 292,
  311, 319, 321, 325, 329, 330, 361
revolution, 9, 16, 32, 35, 46, 64-
  66, 70, 72, 81, 83, 112, 163, 165,
  167, 168, 170, 176, 177, 179,
  188, 190, 236, 247, 256-58, 300,
  316, 346, 350, 352, 367, 380,
  382, 384, 403, 404
Richards, K. 376
Richelieu, Cardinal 62, 92
Riefenstahl, L. 183
rights, 2, 4, 5, 7, 22, 27, 63, 75,
  99, 195, 196, 199, 207, 209, 228,
  229, 231, 234-42, 245, 246, 255,
  257, 260, 261, 265-67, 269, 270,
  273, 291, 292, 295, 296, 298,
  300, 311, 314, 317, 320, 324,
  405, 407, 416, 417
rock music, 388, 389, 391
Roman, 7, 62, 92, 109, 187, 188,
  366
Russia, 13, 61, 165-67, 170, 333,
  348, 371, 399
Rwanda, 52, 370, 408
Sade, Marquis de 228
Saggs, H.W.F. 242
Sartre, J.P. 176
Saudi Arabia, 36
Schmitt, C. 186, 200-16, 324, 338
Scots, 19

Index

Second World War 21, 76, 304, 306, 350, 385
security, 8, 13, 50, 72, 88, 159, 161, 194, 196, 199, 200, 229, 232, 294, 297, 338, 344, 354, 359
Selth, A. 85
Senate, 24, 26, 319, 349
Senegal, 387
service industries, 6, 387
Shah of Iran, 361, 407
Shaw, G.B. 304, 349
Sherover, C. 281
Sinclair, J. 392
Singapore, 23, 24, 26, 34, 47, 50, 85, 358, 363, 406, 415
slavery, 5, 24, 48, 106, 112, 195, 221, 238, 267, 268, 272, 274, 275, 296, 300, 301, 360, 390
SLORC, 19, 35, 65, 70, 379
Slovakia, 14,
Slovenia, 23, 37
social democracy, 4, 9, 78-80, 284, 303, 305-7, 310, 328, 341, 404
social justice, 9, 99-103, 106, 293, 297, 298
socialism, 42, 105, 113, 163, 165, 170, 172, 175, 177, 207, 288, 292, 303, 305, 323, 330, 379, 407, 411
societies, 1, 2, 3, 9, 11, 12, 15, 17, 18, 22, 31, 32, 39, 42, 43, 45, 47, 49, 50, 54, 60-64, 66, 76, 80, 84, 90, 91, 92, 98, 107, 111, 112, 116, 157, 181, 213, 222, 253, 268, 274, 278, 304, 305, 316, 323, 324, 338, 345, 349, 351, 364, 376-78, 381, 385, 392, 409-11, 413, 414, 417
Socrates, 189, 222, 231
Solomon Islands, 44
Somalia, 370, 400, 408
Sophocles, 6, 117
Sorel, G. 175, 176, 177
South Africa, 14, 19, 27, 39, 40, 52, 92, 109, 110, 337, 409, 414
South America, 13, 31, 37, 42, 43, 76, 267, 307, 346, 407
South Asia, 41, 60, 408
South Korea, 69, 71, 113, 358, 363, 378, 406
South Pacific, 11, 16, 43, 44, 52
sovereign, 10, 26, 30, 45, 48, 49, 54, 60, 62, 63, 188, 190, 191, 194, 195, 198, 199, 205, 206, 209, 211, 215, 220, 225, 226, 228-30, 232-34, 238, 239, 261, 268, 284, 316, 336, 366, 369, 395, 397
Soviet Union, 11, 36, 41, 53, 68, 71, 73, 74, 95, 97, 105, 108, 109, 110, 172, 173, 181, 215, 304-7, 342, 350, 354, 401, 407, 414
Spain, 14, 23, 42, 17, 61, 79, 85, 93, 306, 345, 346, 390, 408

Index

Spanish, 13, 39, 42, 43, 45, 48, 49, 93, 117, 307, 366, 368, 390
sport, 17, 80, 81, 83, 334, 377
Spratly Islands, 401
Sri Lanka, 42, 50, 415
Stavrianos, L. 360
Strauss,L. 242, 258
Stubbs, J. 85
Sudan, 39
Suh, D. 85
Sweden, 23, 63, 326, 366, 410,
Switzerland, 23, 410, 412
Syngman Rhee, 69
Syria, 53

Taiwan, 23, 34, 35, 69, 73, 113, 358, 363, 371, 377, 379, 401, 402, 406
Tanzania, 52
tariff protection, 40, 67
tax, 40, 42, 61, 92, 107, 314, 378, 405
technology, 7, 8, 10, 35, 40, 45, 66, 73, 80, 82, 91, 111, 112, 164, 273, 301, 345, 349, 378, 381, 396, 402, 407
television, 63, 81, 106, 331, 382
Tennyson, A. 88
tension, 188, 205
tension, 280, 311, 314, 319-21
territory, 10-13, 16, 19, 32, 40, 69, 88, 94, 261, 265-67, 342,
345, 346, 360, 363, 392, 397, 398, 402, 414
Thailand, 19, 34, 70, 109, 406, 412
Thatcher, M. 28, 78, 326, 333, 362, 384, 403
The Bahamas, 23
Third World, 20, 21, 22, 353, 354, 361, 363, 364
Thompson, E.P. 85
Tito, M. 170
tolerance, 30, 213, 223, 234, 250, 318, 319, 385, 391
Tonga, 44
trade, 28, 33, 39, 46, 48, 49, 62, 73, 75, 76, 81, 84, 166, 167, 182, 196, 211, 248, 249, 278, 294, 322, 326, 327, 341-43, 346, 347, 351, 356-59, 364, 368, 369, 377, 387, 395, 396, 403, 404
trading states, 350, 352
Trebilcock, C. 85
Truman, H. 306
Turgot, A.R.J. 301
Turkey, 348
Turner, T. 82, 378
Tuvalu, 44

Uganda, 387
Ukraine, 382
United Kingdom, 64, 66, 415

435